THE BOOK ®

Austin/MG Metro
Service and Repair Manual

A K Legg LAE MIMI and Finn Deacon

Models covered

All Austin and MG Metro models including Turbo, Vanden Plas, automatic (inc. 1991 model), Van and special/limited edition models; 998 cc and 1275 cc

Does not cover revised Rover Metro range introduced May 1990

(718-224-11AC16)

D1585072

© Haynes Publishing 1999

ABCDE
FGHIJ
KL

4

A book in the **Haynes Service and Repair Manual Series**

Printed in the USA

ISBN **1 85960 145 6**

Haynes Publishing
Sparkford, Nr Yeovil, Somerset BA22 7JJ, England

Haynes North America, Inc
861 Lawrence Drive, Newbury Park, California 91320, USA

Editions Haynes S.A.
Tour Aurore - IBC, 18 Place des Reflets,
          Défense 2, Cedex, France
              ska AB
          , Sverige

British Library Cataloguing in Publication
A catalogue record for this book is available

Contents

Contents

REPAIRS & OVERHAUL

The Austin Metro was first introduced in October 1980 and was initially only on sale to the UK market, export sales to the European market following in early 1981.

The 998 cc and 1275 cc engines are fitted, with low compression and economy versions available.

The body is of computer-based design and is assembled and welded by computer-controlled robots. The "A-Plus" engine and gearbox assembly is similar to that fitted to the Mini range, although it is much improved, with durability and economy prime considerations. Drive is through the front wheels and the engine/gearbox unit is fitted transversely across the front of the car.

The most significant design characteristics are bolt-on front wings, self-cleaning distributor contact points, fully closed crankcase ventilation system, front-mounted aluminium radiator, dual circuit braking system, and Hydragas suspension. Instrumentation is comprehensive and includes a seat belt warning lamp, brake pad wear warning lamp, and handbrake warning lamp.

Later additions to the range include a luxurious Vanden Plas version, sporty MG and MG Turbo versions, and 1.0 and 1.3 Vans. The range from 1985 includes 5-door as well as 3-door versions.

Metro 1.3 HLS

Your Metro Manual

The aim of this manual is to help you get the best from your car. It can do so in several ways. It can help you decide what work must be done (even should you choose to get it done by a garage), provide information on routine maintenance and servicing and give a logical course of action and diagnosis when random faults occur. However, it is hoped that you will use the manual by tackling the work yourself. On simpler jobs it may even be quicker than booking the car into a garage and going there twice to leave and collect it. Perhaps most important, a lot of money can be saved by avoiding the costs the garage must charge to cover its labour and overheads.

The manual has drawings and descriptions to show the function of the various components so that their layout can be understood. Then the tasks are described and photographed in a step-by-step sequence so that even a novice can do the work.

Its arrangement

The manual is divided into Chapters, each covering a logical sub-division of the vehicle. The Chapters are each divided into Sections, numbered with single figures, e.g. 5; and the Sections are divided into numbered paragraphs.

It is freely illustrated, especially in those parts where there is a detailed sequence of operations to be carried out. The reference numbers used in illustration captions pinpoint the pertinent Section and the paragraph within that Section. That is, illustration 3.2 means that the illustration refers to Section 3, and paragraph 2 within that Section.

There is an alphabetical index at the back of the manual, as well as a contents list at the front. Each Chapter is also preceded by its individual contents list.

References to the "left" or "right" of the vehicle are in the sense of a person in the driver's seat, facing forwards.

Unless otherwise stated, nuts and bolts are removed by turning anti-clockwise, and tightened by turning clockwise.

Vehicle manufacturers continually make changes to specifications and recommendations, and these, when notified, are incorporated into our manuals at the earliest opportunity.

Metro Vanden Plas

MG Metro Turbo

Acknowledgements

Thanks are due to Champion Spark Plug, who supplied the illustrations showing spark plug conditions. Thanks are also due to Rover for the supply of technical information. Draper Tools Limited provided some of the workshop tools. Special thanks are due to all those people at Sparkford who helped in the production of this manual.

Working on your car can be dangerous. This page shows just some of the potential risks and hazards, with the aim of creating a safety-conscious attitude.

General hazards

Scalding

• Don't remove the radiator or expansion tank cap while the engine is hot.
• Engine oil, automatic transmission fluid or power steering fluid may also be dangerously hot if the engine has recently been running.

Burning

• Beware of burns from the exhaust system and from any part of the engine. Brake discs and drums can also be extremely hot immediately after use.

Crushing

• When working under or near a raised vehicle, always supplement the jack with axle stands, or use drive-on ramps.

Never venture under a car which is only supported by a jack.
• Take care if loosening or tightening high-torque nuts when the vehicle is on stands. Initial loosening and final tightening should be done with the wheels on the ground.

Fire

• Fuel is highly flammable; fuel vapour is explosive.
• Don't let fuel spill onto a hot engine.
• Do not smoke or allow naked lights (including pilot lights) anywhere near a vehicle being worked on. Also beware of creating sparks (electrically or by use of tools).
• Fuel vapour is heavier than air, so don't work on the fuel system with the vehicle over an inspection pit.
• Another cause of fire is an electrical overload or short-circuit. Take care when repairing or modifying the vehicle wiring.
• Keep a fire extinguisher handy, of a type suitable for use on fuel and electrical fires.

Electric shock

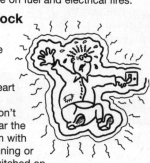
• Ignition HT voltage can be dangerous, especially to people with heart problems or a pacemaker. Don't work on or near the ignition system with the engine running or the ignition switched on.

• Mains voltage is also dangerous. Make sure that any mains-operated equipment is correctly earthed. Mains power points should be protected by a residual current device (RCD) circuit breaker.

Fume or gas intoxication

• Exhaust fumes are poisonous; they often contain carbon monoxide, which is rapidly fatal if inhaled. Never run the engine in a confined space such as a garage with the doors shut.
• Fuel vapour is also poisonous, as are the vapours from some cleaning solvents and paint thinners.

Poisonous or irritant substances

• Avoid skin contact with battery acid and with any fuel, fluid or lubricant, especially antifreeze, brake hydraulic fluid and Diesel fuel. Don't syphon them by mouth. If such a substance is swallowed or gets into the eyes, seek medical advice.
• Prolonged contact with used engine oil can cause skin cancer. Wear gloves or use a barrier cream if necessary. Change out of oil-soaked clothes and do not keep oily rags in your pocket.
• Air conditioning refrigerant forms a poisonous gas if exposed to a naked flame (including a cigarette). It can also cause skin burns on contact.

Asbestos

• Asbestos dust can cause cancer if inhaled or swallowed. Asbestos may be found in gaskets and in brake and clutch linings. When dealing with such components it is safest to assume that they contain asbestos.

Special hazards

Hydrofluoric acid

• This extremely corrosive acid is formed when certain types of synthetic rubber, found in some O-rings, oil seals, fuel hoses etc, are exposed to temperatures above 400°C. The rubber changes into a charred or sticky substance containing the acid. *Once formed, the acid remains dangerous for years. If it gets onto the skin, it may be necessary to amputate the limb concerned.*
• When dealing with a vehicle which has suffered a fire, or with components salvaged from such a vehicle, wear protective gloves and discard them after use.

The battery

• Batteries contain sulphuric acid, which attacks clothing, eyes and skin. Take care when topping-up or carrying the battery.
• The hydrogen gas given off by the battery is highly explosive. Never cause a spark or allow a naked light nearby. Be careful when connecting and disconnecting battery chargers or jump leads.

Air bags

• Air bags can cause injury if they go off accidentally. Take care when removing the steering wheel and/or facia. Special storage instructions may apply.

Diesel injection equipment

• Diesel injection pumps supply fuel at very high pressure. Take care when working on the fuel injectors and fuel pipes.

⚠️ *Warning: Never expose the hands, face or any other part of the body to injector spray; the fuel can penetrate the skin with potentially fatal results.*

Remember...

DO

• Do use eye protection when using power tools, and when working under the vehicle.

• Do wear gloves or use barrier cream to protect your hands when necessary.

• Do get someone to check periodically that all is well when working alone on the vehicle.

• Do keep loose clothing and long hair well out of the way of moving mechanical parts.

• Do remove rings, wristwatch etc, before working on the vehicle – especially the electrical system.

• Do ensure that any lifting or jacking equipment has a safe working load rating adequate for the job.

DON'T

• Don't attempt to lift a heavy component which may be beyond your capability – get assistance.

• Don't rush to finish a job, or take unverified short cuts.

• Don't use ill-fitting tools which may slip and cause injury.

• Don't leave tools or parts lying around where someone can trip over them. Mop up oil and fuel spills at once.

• Don't allow children or pets to play in or near a vehicle being worked on.

Roadside repairs

Jacking and vehicle support

The jack provided with the vehicle is designed primarily for emergency wheel changing, and its use for servicing and overhaul work on the vehicle is best avoided. Instead, a more substantial workshop jack (trolley jack or similar) should be used. Whichever type is employed, it is essential that additional safety support is provided by means of axle stands designed for this purpose. Never use makeshift means such as wooden blocks or piles of house bricks, as these can easily topple or, in the case of bricks, disintegrate under the weight of the vehicle. When jacking up the car with a trolley jack, lift under the widest points of the subframe **(see illustration)**. To raise both wheels at the same time use a 36 in (914 mm) length of square steel tubing placed beneath the subframes with a central spigot to fit the jack. *Never* jack up the car beneath the suspension arms. To support the car, place axle stands under the jacking points beneath the sills or under the widest points of the subframe.

If removal of the wheels is not required, the use of drive-on ramps is recommended. Caution should be exercised to ensure that they are correctly aligned with the wheels, and that the vehicle is not driven too far along them so that it promptly falls off the other ends, or tips the ramps.

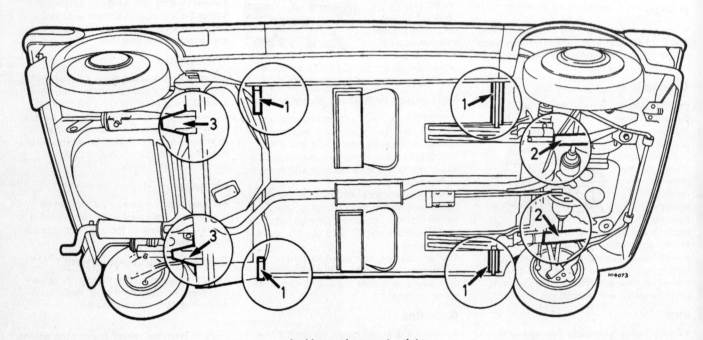

Jacking and support points

1 Jacking brackets   *2 Front jacking points (servicing)*   *3 Rear jacking points (servicing)*

Towing

Provided a fault has not developed in the gearbox or final drive, the car may be towed on its four wheels using either lashing eye located on the front subframe. The lashing eye located beneath the left-hand rear underbody is intended for use on a transporter only, and should not be used for towing another vehicle **(see illustration)**.

On automatic transmission models always check that the engine oil level is correct before towing the car. Do not tow the car at speeds greater than 30 mph (50 km/h) or for a distance of more than 30 miles (50 km). If these conditions cannot be met, or if transmission damage is suspected, the car must be towed with the front wheels clear of the ground.

Rear lashing eye - not to be used for towing

Wheel changing

To change a roadwheel, remove the spare wheel and tool kit from the well in the rear compartment **(see illustration)**. Apply the handbrake and chock the wheel diagonally opposite the one to be changed. Make sure that the car is located on firm level ground. Lever off the hub cover **(see illustration)** and slightly loosen the wheel nuts with the spanner provided. Raise the jack and insert the peg in the nearest jacking point to the wheel being removed **(see illustration)**. Using the handle provided, raise the jack until the wheel is free of the ground **(see illustration)**. Unscrew the wheel nuts and remove the wheel, then remove the wheel finisher if fitted.

Fit the finisher to the spare wheel and fit the wheel on the studs. Fit and tighten the wheel nuts with their tapered ends towards the wheel. Lower the jack, then finally tighten the wheel nuts and refit the hub cover. Remove the chock, and refit the wheel and tool kit to the rear compartment.

Spare wheel compartment

Levering off the hub cover

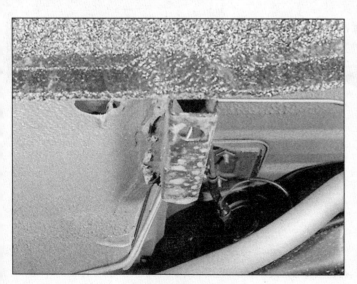

Body jacking point

Jacking the car

Identifying leaks

Puddles on the garage floor or drive, or obvious wetness under the bonnet or underneath the car, suggest a leak that needs investigating. It can sometimes be difficult to decide where the leak is coming from, especially if the engine bay is very dirty already. Leaking oil or fluid can also be blown rearwards by the passage of air under the car, giving a false impression of where the problem lies.

 Warning: Most automotive oils and fluids are poisonous. Wash them off skin, and change out of contaminated clothing, without delay.

 The smell of a fluid leaking from the car may provide a clue to what's leaking. Some fluids are distinctively coloured. It may help to clean the car carefully and to park it over some clean paper overnight as an aid to locating the source of the leak.
Remember that some leaks may only occur while the engine is running.

Sump oil

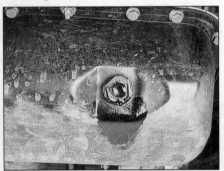

Engine oil may leak from the drain plug...

Oil from filter

...or from the base of the oil filter.

Gearbox oil

Gearbox oil can leak from the seals at the inboard ends of the driveshafts.

Antifreeze

Leaking antifreeze often leaves a crystalline deposit like this.

Brake fluid

A leak occurring at a wheel is almost certainly brake fluid.

Power steering fluid

Power steering fluid may leak from the pipe connectors on the steering rack.

Jump starting

HAYNES HiNT

Jump starting will get you out of trouble, but you must correct whatever made the battery go flat in the first place. There are three possibilities:

1 *The battery has been drained by repeated attempts to start, or by leaving the lights on.*

2 *The charging system is not working properly (alternator drivebelt slack or broken, alternator wiring fault or alternator itself faulty).*

3 *The battery itself is at fault (electrolyte low, or battery worn out).*

When jump-starting a car using a booster battery, observe the following precautions:

✔ Before connecting the booster battery, make sure that the ignition is switched off.

✔ Ensure that all electrical equipment (lights, heater, wipers, etc) is switched off.

✔ Take note of any special precautions printed on the battery case.

✔ Make sure that the booster battery is the same voltage as the discharged one in the vehicle.

✔ If the battery is being jump-started from the battery in another vehicle, the two vehicles MUST NOT TOUCH each other.

✔ Make sure that the transmission is in neutral (or PARK, in the case of automatic transmission).

1 Connect one end of the red jump lead to the positive (+) terminal of the flat battery

2 Connect the other end of the red lead to the positive (+) terminal of the booster battery.

3 Connect one end of the black jump lead to the negative (-) terminal of the booster battery

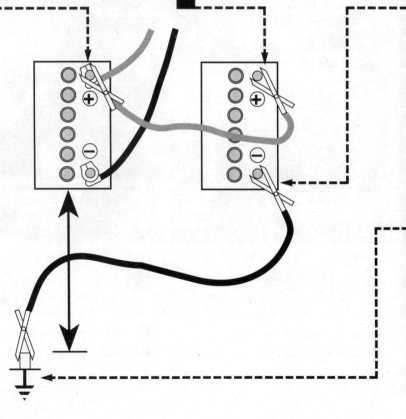

4 Connect the other end of the black jump lead to a bolt or bracket on the engine block, well away from the battery, on the vehicle to be started.

5 Make sure that the jump leads will not come into contact with the fan, drive-belts or other moving parts of the engine.

6 Start the engine using the booster battery and run it at idle speed. Switch on the lights, rear window demister and heater blower motor, then disconnect the jump leads in the reverse order of connection. Turn off the lights etc.

Introduction

There are some very simple checks which need only take a few minutes to carry out, but which could save you a lot of inconvenience and expense.

These "Weekly checks" require no great skill or special tools, and the small amount of time they take to perform could prove to be very well spent, for example;

☐ Keeping an eye on tyre condition and pressures, will not only help to stop them wearing out prematurely, but could also save your life.

☐ Many breakdowns are caused by electrical problems. Battery-related faults are particularly common, and a quick check on a regular basis will often prevent the majority of these.

☐ If your car develops a brake fluid leak, the first time you might know about it is when your brakes don't work properly. Checking the level regularly will give advance warning of this kind of problem.

☐ If the oil or coolant levels run low, the cost of repairing any engine damage will be far greater than fixing the leak, for example.

Underbonnet check points

A Oil level dipstick

B Engine oil filler cap

C Coolant expansion tank cap

D Brake fluid reservoir

E Windscreen washer reservoir

F Battery

Engine oil level

Before you start

✔ Make sure that your car is on level ground.
✔ Check the oil level before the car is driven, or at least 5 minutes after the engine has been switched off.

 HAYNES HiNT *If the oil is checked immediately after driving the vehicle, some of the oil will remain in the upper engine components, resulting in an inaccurate reading on the dipstick!*

The correct oil

Modern engines place great demands on their oil. It is very important that the correct oil for your car is used (See "Lubricants and Fluids").

Car Care

● If you have to add oil frequently, you should check whether you have any oil leaks. Place some clean paper under the car overnight, and check for stains in the morning. If there are no leaks, the engine may be burning oil *(see "Fault Finding").*

● Always maintain the level between the upper and lower dipstick marks (see photo 3). If the level is too low severe engine damage may occur. Oil seal failure may result if the engine is overfilled by adding too much oil.

1 The engine oil level is checked with a dipstick that extends through the dipstick tube on the side of the cylinder block and into the sump at the bottom of the engine.

3 Note the oil level on the end of the dipstick, which should be between the upper ("MAX") mark and lower ("MIN") mark. Approximately 0.5 litre of oil will raise the level from the lower mark to the upper mark.

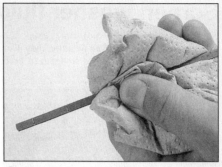

2 Using a clean rag or paper towel remove all oil from the dipstick. Insert the clean dipstick into the tube as far as it will go, then withdraw it again.

4 Oil is added through the filler cap. Unscrew the cap and top-up the level; a funnel may help to reduce spillage . Add the oil slowly, checking the level on the dipstick frequently. Avoid overfilling (see *"Car Care"*).

Coolant level

 Warning: DO NOT attempt to remove the expansion tank pressure cap when the engine is hot, as there is a very great risk of scalding. Do not leave open containers of coolant about, as it is poisonous.

Car Care

● With a sealed-type cooling system, adding coolant should not be necessary on a regular basis. If frequent topping-up is required, it is likely there is a leak. Check the radiator, all hoses and joint faces for signs of staining or wetness, and rectify as necessary.

● It is important that antifreeze is used in the cooling system all year round, not just during the winter months. Don't top-up with water alone, as the antifreeze will become too diluted.

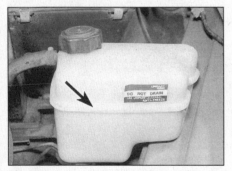

1 The coolant level varies with the temperature of the engine. When the engine is cold, the coolant level should be as shown. When the engine is hot, the level may rise slightly above the "MAX" mark.

2 If topping-up is necessary, **wait until the engine is cold**. Slowly turn the expansion tank cap anti-clockwise to relieve the system pressure. Once any pressure is released, turn the cap anti-clockwise until it can be lifted off.

3 Add a mixture of water and antifreeze through the expansion tank filler neck until the coolant reaches the "MAX" level mark. Refit the cap, turning it clockwise as far as it will go until it is secure.

Screen washer fluid level

Screenwash additives not only keep the winscreen clean during foul weather, they also prevent the washer system freezing in cold weather - which is when you are likely to need it most. Don't top up using plain water as the screenwash will become too diluted, and will freeze during cold weather. On no account use engine antifreeze in the washer system - this could discolour or damage paintwork.

1 On all MG Turbo models, a combined reservoir is mounted in the left-hand rear of the luggage compartment

2 Early models have separate reservoirs for the windscreen and tailgate, being located on the left-hand front of the engine compartment and the left-hand rear of the luggage compartment

3 Later models with front and rear washers have a combined reservoir in the left-hand front of the engine compartment. Models with windscreen washers only, have a single reservoir.

Brake fluid level

⚠️ *Warning: Brake hydraulic fluid can harm your eyes and damage painted surfaces, so use extreme caution when handling and pouring it.*

● *Do not use fluid that has been standing open for some time, as it absorbs moisture from the air which can cause a dangerous loss of braking effectiveness.*

HAYNES HiNT
● *Make sure that your car is on level ground.*
● *The fluid level in the master cylinder reservoir will drop slightly as the brake pads wear down, but the fluid level must never be allowed to drop below the 'MIN' mark.*

Safety first

● If the reservoir requires repeated topping-up this is an indication of a fluid leak somewhere in the system, which should be investigated immediately.

● If a leak is suspected, the car should not be driven until the braking system has been checked. Never take any risks where brakes are concerned.

1 The brake reservoir is mounted on the right-hand side next to the air filter. The "MAX" and "MIN" marks are indicated on the side of the reservoir. The fluid level must be kept between the marks.

2 If topping-up is necessary, first wipe the area around the filler cap with a clean rag before removing the cap.

3 When adding fluid, it's a good idea to inspect the reservoir. The system should be drained and refilled if dirt is seen in the fluid (see Chapter 9 for details).

4 Carefully add fluid avoiding spilling it on surrounding paintwork. Use only the specified hydraulic fluid; mixing different types of fluid can cause damage to the system. After filling to the correct level, refit the cap securely, to prevent leaks and the entry of foreign matter. Wipe off any spilt fluid.

Clutch fluid level (if applicable)

Warning: Brake and clutch hydraulic fluid can harm your eyes and damage painted surfaces, so use extreme caution when handling and pouring it.

● *Do not use fluid that has been standing open for some time, as it absorbs moisture from the air which can cause a dangerous loss of braking effectiveness.*

Before you start:

✔ Park the vehicle on level ground.

✔ The engine should be turned off.

 For improved access, remove the air cleaner as described in Chapter 4

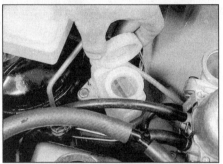

1 The clutch master cylinder (if fitted) is located next to the brake master cylinder. Unscrew the filler cap and top-up the clutch master cylinder to the bottom of the filler neck with hydraulic fluid.

Safety First:

● The need for frequent topping-up indicates a leak, which should be investigated immediately.

Electrical system

✔ Check all external lights and the horn. Refer to the appropriate Sections of Chapter 12 for details if any of the circuits are found to be inoperative.

✔ Visually check all wiring connectors, harnesses and retaining clips for security, and for signs of chafing or damage.

 If you need to check your brake lights and indicators unaided, back up to a wall or garage door and operate the lights. The reflected light should show if they are working properly.

1 If a single indicator light, brake light or headlight has failed it is likely that a bulb has blown and will need to be replaced. Refer to Chapter 12 for details.
If both brake lights have failed, it is possible that the brake light switch above the brake pedal needs adjusting. This simple operation is described in Chapter 9.

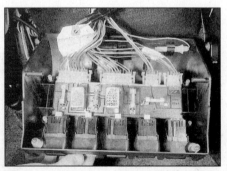

2 If more than one indicator light or headlight has failed it is likely that either a fuse has blown or that there is a fault in the circuit (refer to *"Electrical fault-finding"* in Chapter 12).
On early models, the fuses are located behind the switch panel on the right-hand side of the facia. Access is gained by removing the two screws from the switch panel, and pivoting the panel downwards.

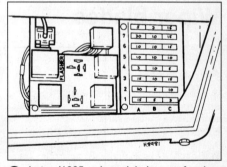

3 Later (1985-on) models have a fusebox located below the right-hand side of the facia. Remove the cover by twisting the retainers using a coin.
To replace a blown fuse, simply prise it out. Fit a new fuse of the same rating, available from car accessory shops.
It is important that you find the reason that the fuse blew - a checking procedure is given in Chapter 12.

Battery

Caution: *Before carrying out any work on the vehicle battery, read the precautions given in "Safety first" at the start of this manual.*

✔ Make sure that the battery tray is in good condition, and that the clamp is tight. Corrosion on the tray, retaining clamp and the battery itself can be removed with a solution of water and baking soda. Thoroughly rinse all cleaned areas with water. Any metal parts damaged by corrosion should be covered with a zinc-based primer, then painted. The exterior of the battery should be inspected periodically for damage such as a cracked case or cover.

✔ Periodically (approximately every three months), check the charge condition of the battery as described in Chapter 5.

✔ If the battery is flat, and you need to jump start your vehicle, see *"Roadside Repairs"*.

✔ If the battery is of maintenance-free type, it is not possible to check the electrolyte level.

1 The battery is located on the left-hand side of the engine compartment. The electrolyte level may be checked and if necessary topped up. If the battery is of standard or low-maintenance type, check that the level of electrolyte is approximately 15 mm above the tops of the cell plates. If necessary top-up the level, using only distilled or demineralised water.

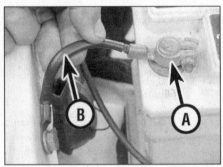

2 Check the tightness of battery clamps (A) to ensure good electrical connections. You should not be able to move them. Also check each cable (B) for cracks and frayed conductors.

HAYNES HiNT

Battery corrosion can be kept to a minimum by applying a layer of petroleum jelly to the clamps and terminals after they are reconnected.

3 If corrosion (white, fluffy deposits) is evident, remove the cables from the battery terminals, clean them with a small wire brush, then refit them. Accessory stores sell a useful tool for cleaning the battery post ...

4 ... as well as the battery cable clamps

Wiper blades

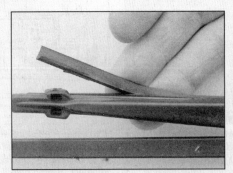

1 Check the condition of the wiper blades; if they are cracked or show any signs of deterioration, or if the glass swept area is smeared, renew them. For maximum clarity of vision, wiper blades should be renewed annually, as a matter of course.

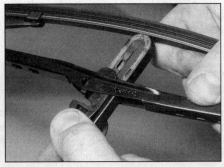

2 To remove a wiper blade, pull the arm fully away from the glass until it locks. Swivel the blade through 90°, press the locking tab(s) with your fingers, and slide the blade out of the arm's hooked end. On refitting, ensure that the blade locks securely into the arm.

Tyre condition and pressure

It is very important that tyres are in good condition, and at the correct pressure - having a tyre failure at any speed is highly dangerous. Tyre wear is influenced by driving style - harsh braking and acceleration, or fast cornering, will all produce more rapid tyre wear. As a general rule, the front tyres wear out faster than the rears. Interchanging the tyres from front to rear ("rotating" the tyres) may result in more even wear. However, if this is completely effective, you may have the expense of replacing all four tyres at once! Remove any nails or stones embedded in the tread before they penetrate the tyre to cause deflation. If removal of a nail does reveal that the tyre has been punctured, refit the nail so that its point of penetration is marked. Then immediately change the wheel, and have the tyre repaired by a tyre dealer.

Regularly check the tyres for damage in the form of cuts or bulges, especially in the sidewalls. Periodically remove the wheels, and clean any dirt or mud from the inside and outside surfaces. Examine the wheel rims for signs of rusting, corrosion or other damage. Light alloy wheels are easily damaged by "kerbing" whilst parking; steel wheels may also become dented or buckled. A new wheel is very often the only way to overcome severe damage.

New tyres should be balanced when they are fitted, but it may become necessary to re-balance them as they wear, or if the balance weights fitted to the wheel rim should fall off. Unbalanced tyres will wear more quickly, as will the steering and suspension components. Wheel imbalance is normally signified by vibration, particularly at a certain speed (typically around 50 mph). If this vibration is felt only through the steering, then it is likely that just the front wheels need balancing. If, however, the vibration is felt through the whole car, the rear wheels could be out of balance. Wheel balancing should be carried out by a tyre dealer or garage.

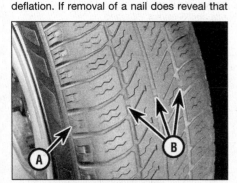

Tread Depth - visual check

1 The original tyres have tread wear safety bands (B), which will appear when the tread depth reaches approximately 1.6 mm. The band positions are indicated by a triangular mark on the tyre sidewall (A).

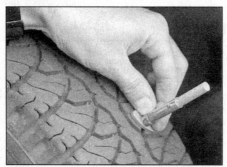

Tread Depth - manual check

2 Alternatively tread wear can be monitored with a simple, inexpensive device known as a tread depth indicator gauge.

Tyre Pressure Check

3 Check the tyre pressures regularly with the tyres cold. Do not adjust the tyre pressures immediately after the vehicle has been used, or an inaccurate setting will result. Tyre pressures are shown on the next page.

4 *Tyre tread wear patterns*

Shoulder Wear

Underinflation (wear on both sides)
Under-inflation will cause overheating of the tyre, because the tyre will flex too much, and the tread will not sit correctly on the road surface. This will cause a loss of grip and excessive wear, not to mention the danger of sudden tyre failure due to heat build-up.
Check and adjust pressures
Incorrect wheel camber (wear on one side)
Repair or renew suspension parts
Hard cornering
Reduce speed!

Centre Wear

Overinflation
Over-inflation will cause rapid wear of the centre part of the tyre tread, coupled with reduced grip, harsher ride, and the danger of shock damage occurring in the tyre casing.
Check and adjust pressures

If you sometimes have to inflate your car's tyres to the higher pressures specified for maximum load or sustained high speed, don't forget to reduce the pressures to normal afterwards.

Uneven Wear

Front tyres may wear unevenly as a result of wheel misalignment. Most tyre dealers and garages can check and adjust the wheel alignment (or "tracking") for a modest charge.
Incorrect camber or castor
Repair or renew suspension parts
Malfunctioning suspension
Repair or renew suspension parts
Unbalanced wheel
Balance tyres
Incorrect toe setting
Adjust front wheel alignment
Note: *The feathered edge of the tread which typifies toe wear is best checked by feel.*

Lubricants and fluids

Engine/gearbox (transmission)	Multigrade engine oil, viscosity SAE 15W/50 (pre August 1983) or 10W/40 (August 1983 on) *(Duckhams QXR Premium Petrol Engine Oil, or Duckhams Hypergrade Petrol Engine Oil)*
Suspension grease points	General-purpose lithium-based grease *(Duckhams LB 10)*
Distributor	Multigrade engine oil, viscosity SAE 15W/50 or 10W/40 *(Duckhams QXR Premium Petrol Engine Oil, or Duckhams Hypergrade Petrol Engine Oil)*
Carburettor piston damper	Multigrade engine oil, viscosity SAE 15W/50 or 10W/40 *(Duckhams QXR Premium Petrol Engine Oil, or Duckhams Hypergrade Petrol Engine Oil)*
Brake and clutch fluid reservoirs	Brake and clutch fluid to DOT 4+ or DOT 4 *(Duckhams Universal Brake and Clutch Fluid)*
Cooling system	Ethylene glycol-based antifreeze *(Duckhams Antifreeze and Summer Coolant)*

Choosing your engine oil

Engines need oil, not only to lubricate moving parts and minimise wear, but also to maximise power output and to improve fuel economy. By introducing a simplified and improved range of engine oils, Duckhams has taken away the confusion and made it easier for you to choose the right oil for your engine.

HOW ENGINE OIL WORKS

• Beating friction

Without oil, the moving surfaces inside your engine will rub together, heat up and melt, quickly causing the engine to seize. Engine oil creates a film which separates these moving parts, preventing wear and heat build-up.

• Cooling hot-spots

Temperatures inside the engine can exceed 1000° C. The engine oil circulates and acts as a coolant, transferring heat from the hot-spots to the sump.

• Cleaning the engine internally

Good quality engine oils clean the inside of your engine, collecting and dispersing combustion deposits and controlling them until they are trapped by the oil filter or flushed out at oil change.

OIL CARE - FOLLOW THE CODE

To handle and dispose of used engine oil safely, always:

OIL BANK LINE
0800 66 33 66

- **Avoid skin contact with used engine oil. Repeated or prolonged contact can be harmful.**
- **Dispose of used oil and empty packs in a responsible manner in an authorised disposal site. Call 0800 663366 to find the one nearest to you. Never tip oil down drains or onto the ground.**

DUCKHAMS ENGINE OILS

For the driver who demands a premium quality oil for complete reassurance, we recommend synthetic formula **Duckhams QXR Premium Engine Oils**.

For the driver who requires a straight-forward quality engine oil, we recommend **Duckhams Hypergrade Engine Oils**.

For further information and advice, call the Duckhams UK Helpline on 0800 212988.

Capacities (approx.)

Engine/manual gearbox oil (without filter)	8.5 pints (4.8 litres)
Oil filter (manual gearbox)	0.6 pint (0.3 litres)
Engine/automatic transmission oil (without filter)	8.8 pints (5.0 litres)
Oil filter (automatic transmission)	1.0 pint (0.6 litre)
Cooling system (including heater)	8.5 pints (4.8 litres)
Fuel tank:	
(early models)	6.6 Imp gals (30 litres)
1986-on models	7.8 Imp gals (35 litres)

Tyre pressures

Pressures (cold) - psi (bar)	Front	Rear
135 SR 12	32 (2.2)	28 (2.0)
165/70R 12	32 (2.2)	26 (1.8)
165/60 HR 13	28 (2.0)	28 (2.0)
150/65 R315	30 (2.1)	28 (2.0)
155/70 SR 12	28 (2.0)	32 (2.2)
165/65 HR 13	28 (2.0)	28 (2.0)
160/65 R315	28 (2.0)	26 (1.8)
185/55 13	29 (2.0)	29 (2.0)

Note: *Pressures apply only to original-equipment tyres, and may vary if any other make or type is fitted; check with the tyre manufacturer or supplier for correct pressures if necessary.*

Chapter 1
Routine maintenance and servicing

Contents

Degrees of difficulty

Easy, suitable for novice with little experience	Fairly easy, suitable for beginner with some experience 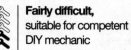	Fairly difficult, suitable for competent DIY mechanic	Difficult, suitable for experienced DIY mechanic	Very difficult, suitable for expert DIY or professional

1 Maintenance schedule

The maintenance intervals in this manual are provided with the assumption that you will be carrying out the work yourself. These are the minimum maintenance intervals recommended by the manufacturer for vehicles driven daily. If you wish to keep your vehicle in peak condition at all times, you may wish to perform some of these procedures more often. We encourage frequent maintenance, because it enhances the efficiency, performance and resale value of your vehicle.

If the vehicle is driven in dusty areas, used to tow a trailer, or driven frequently at slow speeds (idling in traffic) or on short journeys, more frequent maintenance intervals are recommended.

Always road test your car after servicing.

Every 250 miles (400 km) or weekly - whichever comes first

☐ Refer to "Weekly Checks"

Every 6000 miles (10 000 km) or 6 months - whichever comes first

In addition to the previous Section, carry out the following:

☐ Renew the engine oil and filter (Section 3).
☐ Clean the magnetic drain plug (Section 3).
☐ Check the carburettor piston damper and top-up if necessary (Section 15, paragraph 2).
☐ Check the operation of the transmission selector (automatic models only) (Section 4).

Every 12 000 miles (20 000 km) or 12 months - whichever comes first

In addition to the previous Section, carry out the following:

☐ Renew the air cleaner element (Section 5).
☐ Renew the spark plugs (Section 6).
☐ Renew the fuel line filter (Turbo only) (Section 7).
☐ Renew the carburettor vent filter (where fitted) (Section 8).
☐ Check the crankcase ventilation system (Section 9).
☐ Check the condition of the battery and clean the terminals (Section 10).
☐ Check the antifreeze concentration (Section 11).
☐ Check the cooling system and hoses for leaks (Section 12).
☐ Check and adjust the contact breaker points (Section 13).
☐ Check the alternator and water pump drivebelt; renew and retension if necessary (Section 14).
☐ Check and adjust the valve clearances (Chapter 2A).
☐ Check and adjust the engine idle speed and carburettor mixture (Section 15).
☐ Check, and if necessary adjust, the ignition timing (Section 16).
☐ Check the fuel supply system for damage, deterioration and leaks (Section 12).
☐ Check the clutch hydraulic pipes for leaks (Section 12).
☐ Check the driveshaft gaiters for splits and leakage (Section 17).
☐ Check, and adjust if necessary, the clutch return stop clearance (Section 18).
☐ Check the exhaust system for leaks and security (Section 19).
☐ Check the door and bonnet locks for operation (Section 20).
☐ Check the seat belts for operation and damage (Section 21).
☐ Check the headlight beam alignment (Section 22).
☐ Check the brake line and flexible hose (Section 23).
☐ Check the front brake pads and discs for wear (Section 24).

Every 12 000 miles (20 000 km) or 12 months (continued)

☐ Check the brake pad warning indicators (Section 24).
☐ Check the rear brake linings and drums for wear (Section 24).
☐ Check the steering rack unit for security and damage (Section 25).
☐ Check the steering joints and arms for wear and damage (Section 25).
☐ Check the steering gaiters for splits and leakage (Section 25).
☐ Check the suspension joints and mountings for wear and damage (Section 25).
☐ Grease the front and rear suspension pivots (Section 25).
☐ Check the Hydragas units and lines for leaks (Section 26).
☐ Check the handbrake operation and adjust if necessary (Section 27).
☐ Lubricate the handbrake linkages and cables (Section 27).
☐ Check, and if necessary adjust, the front wheel alignment (Section 28).
☐ Road test (Section 29).

Every 18 000 miles (30 000 km) or 18 months - whichever comes first

In addition to the 6000 miles (10 000 km) Section, carry out the following:

☐ Renew the brake fluid (Section 30).
☐ Renew the clutch fluid (Section 31).

Every 24 000 miles (40 000 km) or 2 years - whichever comes first

In addition to the 12 000 miles (20 000 km) Section, carry out the following:

☐ Drain the cooling system and flush it, then refill with new antifreeze solution (Section 32).
☐ Renew the oil filler cap (Section 33).
☐ Renew the distributor contact points (Section 34).
☐ Renew the alternator drivebelt (Section 14).

Every 36 000 miles (60 000 km) or 3 years - whichever comes first

In addition to the 18 000 miles (30 000 km) Section, carry out the following:

☐ Renew the brake fluid and all the fluid seals and flexible hoses in the brake hydraulic circuit (Section 30).

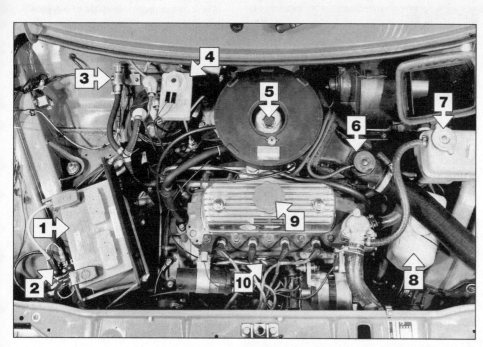

Under bonnet view of MG Metro 1300

1 Battery
2 Starter motor solenoid
3 Anti run-on valve
4 Brake hydraulic reservoir
5 Carburettor damper cap
6 Air cleaner vacuum motor
7 Expansion tank filler cap
8 Windscreen washer reservoir
9 Oil filler cap
10 Engine oil dipstick

View of the front underside of a typical vehicle

1 Steering gear
2 Tie-rod end
3 Front suspension lower arm
4 Brake pad wear sensor wiring
5 Disc/caliper
6 Engine/transmission oil drain plug
7 Front subframe mounting
8 Oil filter
9 Front lashing eye
10 Anti-roll bar
11 Brake flexible hydraulic hoses
12 Driveshaft
13 Front subframe
14 Front exhaust system
15 Gearchange rods
16 Gearchange remote control housing

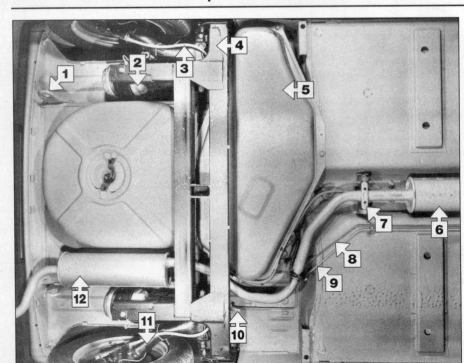

View of the rear underside of a typical vehicle

1 Rear lashing eye
2 Rear Hydragas unit
3 Handbrake cable
4 Rear subframe
5 Fuel tank
6 Intermediate silencer
7 Exhaust mounting
8 Brake rigid hydraulic line
9 Fuel supply pipe
10 Charging valve for Hydragas units
11 Rear suspension radius arm
12 Rear exhaust system and silencer

Maintenance procedures

1 Introduction

1 This Chapter is designed to help the home mechanic maintain his/her vehicle for safety, economy, long life and peak performance.
2 The Chapter contains a master maintenance schedule, followed by Sections dealing specifically with each task in the schedule. Visual checks, adjustments, component renewal and other helpful items are included. Refer to the accompanying illustrations of the engine compartment and the underside of the vehicle for the locations of the various components.
3 Servicing your vehicle in accordance with the mileage/time maintenance schedule and the following Sections will provide a planned maintenance programme, which should result in a long and reliable service life. This is a comprehensive plan, so maintaining some items but not others at the specified service intervals, will not produce the same results.
4 As you service your vehicle, you will discover that many of the procedures can - and should - be grouped together, because of the particular procedure being performed, or because of the close proximity of two otherwise-unrelated components to one another. For example, if the vehicle is raised for any reason, the exhaust can be inspected at the same time as the suspension and steering components.
5 The first step in this maintenance programme is to prepare yourself before the actual work begins. Read through all the

Sections relevant to the work to be carried out, then make a list and gather all the parts and tools required. If a problem is encountered, seek advice from a parts specialist, or a dealer service department.

2 Intensive maintenance

1 If, from the time the vehicle is new, the routine maintenance schedule is followed closely, and frequent checks are made of fluid levels and high-wear items, as suggested throughout this manual, the engine will be kept in relatively good running condition, and the need for additional work will be minimised.
2 It is possible that there will be times when the engine is running poorly due to the lack of regular maintenance. This is even more likely if a used vehicle, which has not received regular and frequent maintenance checks, is purchased. In such cases, additional work may need to be carried out, outside of the regular maintenance intervals.
3 If engine wear is suspected, a compression test (refer to Chapter 2A, Section 1) will provide valuable information regarding the overall performance of the main internal components. Such a test can be used as a basis to decide the extent of the work to be carried out. If, for example, a compression test indicates serious internal engine wear, conventional maintenance as described in this Chapter will not greatly improve the performance of the engine, and may prove a waste of time and money, unless extensive

overhaul work (Chapter 2B) is carried out first.
4 The following series of operations are those most often required to improve the performance of a generally poor-running engine:

Primary operations

a) Clean, inspect and test the battery (Section 10).
b) Check all the engine-related fluids (See "Weekly Checks").
c) Check the condition and tension of the auxiliary drivebelt (Section 14).
d) Renew the spark plugs (Section 6).
e) Inspect the distributor components and HT leads - as applicable (Chapter 5).
f) Check the condition of the air cleaner filter element, and renew if necessary (Section 5).
g) Renew the fuel filter, if fitted (Section 7).
h) Check the condition of all hoses, and check for fluid leaks (Section 12).
i) Check the engine idle speed and mixture settings - as applicable (Section 15).
5 If the above operations do not prove fully effective, carry out the following secondary operations:

Secondary operations

a) Check the charging system (Chapter 5).
b) Check the ignition system (Chapter 5).
c) Check the fuel system (Chapter 4).
d) Renew the distributor cap, points, condenser and rotor arm - as applicable (Chapter 5).
e) Renew the ignition HT leads - as applicable (Chapter 5).

6000 Miles (10 000 Km) / 6 Months

3 Engine oil and filter renewal

1 Frequent oil and filter changes are the most important preventative maintenance procedures that can be undertaken by the DIY owner. As engine oil ages, it becomes diluted and contaminated, which leads to premature engine wear.

2 Before starting this procedure, gather all the necessary tools and materials. It is a good idea to renew the drain plug washer each time you replace the engine oil. Also make sure that you have plenty of clean rags and newspapers handy, to mop up any spills. Ideally, the engine oil should be warm, as it will drain better, and more built-up sludge will be removed with it. Take care, however, not to touch the exhaust or any other hot parts of the engine when working under the vehicle. To avoid any possibility of scalding, and to protect yourself from possible skin irritants and other harmful contaminants in used engine oils, it is advisable to wear gloves when carrying out this work. Access to the underside of the vehicle will be greatly improved if it can be raised on a lift, driven onto ramps, or jacked up and supported on axle stands (see "Jacking and vehicle support"). Whichever method is chosen, make sure that the vehicle remains level, or if it is at an angle, that the drain plug is at the lowest point.

3 Slacken the drain plug about half a turn. Position the draining container under the drain plug, then remove the plug completely. If possible, try to keep the plug pressed into the sump while unscrewing it by hand the last couple of turns. Recover the sealing washer from the drain plug (see illustrations).

HAYNES HINT *As the plug releases from the threads, move it away sharply so the stream of oil issuing from the sump runs into the container, not up your sleeve!*

4 Allow some time for the old oil to drain, noting that it may be necessary to reposition the container as the oil flow slows to a trickle.

5 After all the oil has drained, wipe off the drain plug with a clean rag. Check the sealing washer for condition and renew it if necessary. Clean the area around the drain plug opening, and refit the plug. Tighten the plug to the specified torque.

6 Move the container into position under the oil filter. It is located at the front of the engine at the side of the block.

Manual gearbox models

7 On these models the filter is a cartridge type. Using an oil filter removal tool if necessary, slacken the filter initially, then unscrew it by hand the rest of the way (see illustrations). Discard the old filter. Clean the oil filter head.

8 Apply a light coating of clean engine oil to the sealing ring on the new filter, then screw it into position on the engine. Tighten the filter firmly by hand only - do not use any tools.

Automatic transmission models

9 Automatic models use a canister with an internal disposable element (see illustration). With these models unscrew the centre bolt on the canister. Empty the oil from the canister into the container and discard the filter. Clean the area around the filter mounting.

10 Insert the new element in the bowl. Using a new sealing ring, locate the bowl centrally and tighten the centre bolt, to the specified torque.

All models

11 Remove the old oil and all tools from under the car, then lower the car to the ground (if applicable).

12 Remove the oil filler cap. Fill the engine, using the correct grade and type of oil (see

1

3.3a Location of engine/gearbox oil drain plug - manual gearbox

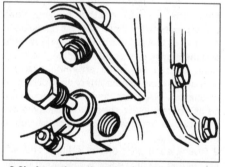

3.3b Location of engine/transmission oil drain plug - automatic transmission

3.7a The oil filter cartridge

3.7b Removing the oil filter cartridge

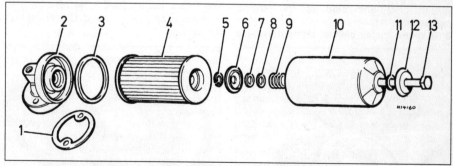

3.9 Oil filter components on automatic transmission models

1 Gasket	5 Circlip	8 Washer	11 Seal
2 Head	6 Pressure plate	9 Spring	12 Collar
3 Sealing ring	7 Seal	10 Bowl	13 Centre bolt
4 Element			

"Lubricants, fluids and capacities"). An oil can spout or funnel may help to reduce spillage. Pour in half the specified quantity of oil first, then wait a few minutes for the oil to fall to the sump. Continue adding oil a small quantity at a time until the level is up to the lower mark on the dipstick. Adding 0.5 litre at a time, bring the level up to the upper mark on the dipstick. Insert the dipstick and refit the filler cap.

13 Start the engine and run it for a few minutes; check for leaks around the oil filter seal and the sump drain plug. Note that there may be a delay of a few seconds before the oil pressure warning light goes out when the engine is first started, as the oil circulates through the engine oil galleries and the new oil filter before the pressure builds up.

14 Switch off the engine, and wait a few minutes for the oil to settle in the sump once more. With the new oil circulated and the filter completely full, recheck the level on the dipstick, and add more oil as necessary.

15 Dispose of the used engine oil safely, with reference to "General repair procedures" in the reference Sections of this manual.

4 Automatic transmission selector check

1 To check, select "N" and start the engine. Move the lever to "R" and check that the reverse is engaged, then slowly move the lever back to "N" - the gear should disengage when the lever reaches the "N" position, or slightly before. Repeat the check but this time select "1".

2 When carrying out the adjustment check, it may be found that either first or reverse gear does not disengage when the selector lever reaches the "N" position.

3 If "R" remains engaged in position "N", reduce the gap at the end of the selector lever travel by 0.01 in (0.25 mm). Refer to Chapter 7B, for further details.

4 If "1" remains engaged in position "N" increase the gap at the end of the selector lever travel by 0.01 in (0.25 mm).

5 Recheck the adjustment and repeat paragraph 3 or 4 as necessary.

6 Check that the starter motor can be operated only in positions "P" and "N". Adjust the starter inhibitor switch if necessary as described in Chapter 7B.

12 000 Miles (20 000 Km) / 12 Months

5 Air filter element renewal

Non-Turbo models

1 Unscrew and remove the two wing nuts on the top of the air cleaner (see illustration).

2 Withdraw the air cleaner, at the same time disconnecting it from the hot air shroud tube.

3 To remove the element, use a wide-bladed screwdriver to separate the lid from the body, then lift out the element and discard it (see illustration).

4 Clean the interior of the air cleaner with a fuel-moistened cloth, and wipe dry.

5 Install the new element and snap the cover onto the body.

6 Check that the seal is in good condition, then refit the air cleaner and connect it to the hot air shroud tube. Insert and tighten the two wing nuts.

MG Turbo models

7 The air cleaner on MG Turbo models is remote from the carburettor, being mounted on the left-hand side of the engine compartment.

8 To renew the air cleaner element, release the spring clips and take off the cover. Extract the element, wipe clean the inside of the housing and fit a new element. Refit the cover and secure with the spring clips.

6 Spark plug renewal

1 The correct functioning of the spark plugs is vital for the correct running and efficiency of the engine. It is essential that the plugs fitted are appropriate for the engine (as specified at the end of this Chapter). If this type is used and the engine is in good condition, the spark plugs should not need attention between scheduled replacement intervals. Spark plug cleaning is rarely necessary, and should not be attempted unless specialised equipment is available, as damage can easily be caused to the firing ends.

2 Check each plug one at a time. This will ensure that the plug leads are replaced in their correct location (see illustration).

3 Pull the lead from each plug by gripping the end fitting, not the lead, otherwise the lead connection may be fractured. Check the lead for damage.

4 Unscrew the plugs using a spark plug spanner, a box spanner or a deep socket and extension bar. Keep the socket aligned with the spark plug - if it is forcibly moved to one side, the ceramic insulator may be broken off. As each plug is removed, examine it as follows.

5 Examination of the spark plugs will give a good indication of the condition of the engine. If the insulator nose of the spark plug is clean and white, with no deposits, this is indicative of a weak mixture or too hot a plug (a hot plug transfers heat away from the electrode slowly, a cold plug transfers heat away quickly).

6 If the tip and insulator nose are covered with hard black-looking deposits, then this is indicative that the mixture is too rich. Should the plug be black and oily, then it is likely that the engine is fairly worn, as well as the mixture being too rich.

7 If the insulator nose is covered with light tan to greyish-brown deposits, then the mixture is correct and it is likely that the engine is in good condition.

8 The spark plug electrode gap is of considerable importance as, if it is too large or too small, the size of the spark and its efficiency will be seriously impaired. The gap should be set to the value given in the Specifications at the end of this Chapter.

5.1 Removing the air cleaner lid

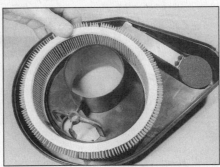

5.3 Lifting out the air cleaner element

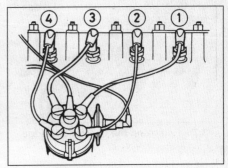

6.2 HT lead connections and distributor orientation

6.9a Measuring the spark plug gap with a feeler blade

6.9b Measuring the spark plug gap with a wire gauge . . .

6.9c . . . and adjusting the gap using a special tool

9 To set the gap, measure it with a feeler blade or wire gauge and then bend open, or close, the outer plug electrode until the correct gap is achieved **(see illustrations)**. The centre electrode should never be bent, as this will crack the insulator and cause plug failure, if nothing worse. If using feeler blades, the gap is correct when the appropriate-size blade is a firm sliding fit.

10 Special spark plug electrode gap adjusting tools are available from most motor accessory shops, or from some spark plug manufacturers.

11 Before fitting the spark plugs, check that the threaded connector sleeves are tight, and that the plug exterior surfaces and threads are clean.

HAYNES HINT

It is very often difficult to insert spark plugs into their holes without cross-threading them. To avoid this possibility, fit a short length of 5/16 inch internal diameter rubber hose over the end of the spark plug. The flexible hose acts as a universal joint to help align the plug with the plug hole. Should the plug begin to cross-thread, the hose will slip on the spark plug, which prevents damage to the cylinder head.

12 Remove the rubber hose, and tighten the plug to the specified torque using the spark plug socket and a torque wrench.

13 Repeat the process with the remaining spark plugs.

7 Fuel filter renewal (Turbo only)

⚠ *Warning: Before carrying out the following operation, refer to the precautions given in 'Safety first!' at the beginning of this manual, and follow them implicitly. Petrol is a highly dangerous and volatile liquid, and the precautions necessary when handling it cannot be overstressed.*

Removal

1 The fuel filter is located in the fuel line between the pressure regulator and the carburettor. It should be renewed if filter blockage is suspected.

2 Take precautions against fire when removing the filter, and do not smoke. Residual pressure in the fuel lines may lead to significant fuel spillage when the filter is removed.

3 Release the hose clamps on each side of the filter and carefully pull off the hoses. Inspect the hoses and clips; renew these too, if necessary. Mop up any fuel spilt.

Refitting

4 Fit the new filter. A directional arrow or an "OUT" marking should point towards the carburettor; an "IN" marking should face the pressure regulator. Without any markings the filter may be fitted either way round.

5 Secure the new filter with the hose clamps. When all spilt fuel has been removed from the engine bay, start the engine and check for leaks.

8 Carburettor vent filter renewal

The SU HIF carburettor requires an unrestricted flow of air to the float chamber through the vent pipe. If the pipe is allowed to become blocked, kinked or even incorrectly routed the mixture will be weakened, causing poor performance and difficult starting. On 1.0 litre models fitted with "economy" engines, a small air filter is fitted to the vent to improve

carburettor calibration. This filter must be renewed at the specified interval, or the mixture will become excessively weak during part-load running. The filter must never be omitted or the fuel consumption will increase.

9 Crankcase ventilation system check

Check all crankcase ventilation and vacuum hoses for damage and leakage (refer to Chapter 2A). Where necessary remove the hoses and clear them of any blockage.

10 Battery terminal check

Caution: Before carrying out any work on the vehicle battery, read through the precautions given in 'Safety first!' at the beginning of this manual.

1 The battery is located on the left-hand side of the engine compartment. The exterior of the battery should be inspected periodically for damage such as a cracked case or cover.

2 Check the tightness of the battery cable clamps to ensure good electrical connections, and check the entire length of each cable for cracks and frayed conductors. Check the positive cable between the battery and the starter motor.

3 If corrosion (visible as white, fluffy deposits) is evident, remove the cables from the battery terminals, clean them with a small wire brush, then refit them.

HAYNES HINT *Corrosion can be kept to a minimum by applying a layer of petroleum jelly to the clamps and terminals after they are reconnected.*

4 Make sure that the battery retaining clamp is secure.

5 Corrosion on the retaining clamp and the battery terminals can be removed with a solution of water and baking soda. Thoroughly rinse all cleaned areas with plain water.

1

6 Any metal parts of the vehicle damaged by corrosion should be covered with a zinc-based primer, then painted.

7 Periodically (approximately every three months), check the charge condition of the battery as described in Chapter 5.

8 Further information on the battery, charging and jump starting can be found in Chapter 5 and in the preliminary sections of this manual.

11 Antifreeze (coolant) concentration check

1 The antifreeze should always be maintained at the specified concentration. This is necessary not only to maintain the antifreeze and coolant properties, but also to prevent corrosion that would otherwise occur as the corrosion inhibitors become progressively less effective.

2 The check should be made with the engine cold, and it will be necessary to obtain an antifreeze tester from a car accessory shop.

3 Slowly unscrew the cap from the top of the coolant expansion tank, then draw coolant into the tester. Check the concentration of the antifreeze according to the manufacturer's instructions. The most common tester consists of three coloured balls of varying density - a high concentration will cause all three balls to float whereas a low concentration may only cause one ball to float.

4 If the concentration is incorrect, slight adjustments may be made by drawing some of the coolant out of the expansion tank and replacing it with undiluted antifreeze. If the concentration is excessively out, it will be necessary to completely drain the system and renew the solution with reference to Section 32.

5 Tighten the cap onto the expansion tank on completion.

12 Hose and fluid leak check

1 Visually inspect the engine joint faces, gaskets and seals for any signs of water or oil leaks. Pay particular attention to the areas around the camshaft cover, cylinder head, oil filter and sump joint faces. Bear in mind that, over a period of time, some very slight seepage from these areas is to be expected - what you are really looking for is any indication of a serious leak. Should a leak be found, renew the offending gasket or oil seal by referring to the appropriate Chapters in this manual.

2 Also check the security and condition of all the engine-related pipes and hoses. Ensure that all cable-ties or securing clips are in place and in good condition. Clips that are broken or missing can lead to chafing of the hoses, pipes or wiring, which could cause more serious problems in the future.

3 Carefully check the radiator hoses and heater hoses along their entire length. Renew any hose that is cracked, swollen or deteriorated. Cracks will show up better if the hose is squeezed. Pay close attention to the hose clips that secure the hoses to the cooling system components. Hose clips can pinch and puncture hoses, resulting in cooling system leaks.

4 Inspect all the cooling system components (hoses, joint faces etc.) for leaks. A leak in the cooling system will usually show up as white or rust-coloured deposits on the area adjoining the leak. Where any problems of this nature are found on system components, renew the component or gasket with reference to Chapter 3.

5 Check that the pressure cap on the expansion tank is fully tightened and shows no sign of coolant leakage.

6 With the car raised, inspect the petrol tank and filler neck for punctures, cracks and other damage. The connection between the filler neck and tank is especially critical. Sometimes a rubber filler neck or connecting hose will leak due to loose retaining clamps or deteriorated rubber.

7 Carefully check all rubber hoses and metal fuel lines leading away from the petrol tank. Check for loose connections, deteriorated hoses, crimped lines, and other damage. Pay particular attention to the vent pipes and hoses, which often loop up around the filler neck and can become blocked or crimped. Follow the lines to the front of the vehicle, carefully inspecting them all the way. Renew damaged sections as necessary.

8 From within the engine compartment, check the security of all fuel hose attachments and pipe unions, and inspect the fuel hoses and vacuum hoses for kinks, chafing and deterioration.

9 If applicable, check the clutch hydraulic circuit for leaks or damage.

13 Ignition check and adjustment

Note: *Some models are fitted with breakerless, electronic distributors, which require minimal maintenance.*

1 It will be easier to work on the distributor if it is removed (as described in Chapter 5), but this is not essential.

2 Release the clips and lift off the distributor cap, leaving the HT leads connected. Take off the rotor arm.

Mechanical distributor

3 Open the points and examine the condition of their faces. If they are blackened or pitted, remove them as described in Section 34 and clean them using emery tape or a grindstone. On the Ducellier distributor, take care to maintain the contour of the points. If the points are worn excessively, renew them. Refer to Section 34 for further details.

4 If the contact points do not show any excessive pitting, turn the drive dog until the heel of the movable contact is on the high point of one of the cam lobes.

5 Using a feeler blade, check that the gap between the two points is as given in the Specifications. If not, loosen the fixed contact screw and reposition the fixed contact until

13.5 Adjusting the contact breaker points gap (Lucas)

the feeler blade is a firm sliding fit between the two points. When the gap is correct, tighten the fixed contact screw **(see illustration)**.

6 Apply one drop of engine oil to the felt pad in the cam recess, then refit the rotor arm.

7 Wipe clean the ignition coil tower and the distributor cap, and make sure that the carbon brush moves freely against the tension of the spring. Clean the metal segments in the distributor cap, but do not scrape away any metal otherwise the HT spark at the spark plugs will be reduced.

8 If removed, refit the distributor as described in Chapter 5. Use a dwell meter to check the dwell angle of the points. This angle should be within the parameters given in the Specifications. Reduce the contacts points gap to increase the dwell angle, or increase the gap to reduce it. Refer to Section 16 to adjust the timing.

Electronic distributor

9 Thoroughly clean the distributor cap inside and out with a dry lint-free rag. Examine the four HT lead segments inside the cap. If the segments appear badly burned or pitted, renew the cap. Make sure that the carbon brush in the centre of the cap is free to move and that it protrudes by approximately 0.1 in (3 mm) from its holder.

10 Lift off the rotor arm. On pre-1985 models, remove the plastic anti-flash shield and carefully apply two drops of engine oil to the felt pad in the centre of the cam spindle. Also lubricate the centrifugal advance mechanism by applying two drops of oil through the square hole in the baseplate. On 1985 and later models, lubricate the bearing in the upper housing with a little engine oil, and

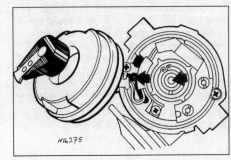

13.10 Breakerless distributor lubrication points (arrowed)

14.4 Checking the drivebelt tension

lubricate the centrifugal advance mechanism by prising the plastic plug from the lower housing **(see illustration)**. Wipe away any excess oil and refit the anti-flash shield (where fitted), rotor arm and distributor cap.

11 If removed, refit the distributor as described in Chapter 5. Adjust the ignition timing as described in Section 16.

14 Drivebelt check (and renewal)

1 The drivebelt is used to drive the water pump and alternator from the crankshaft pulley.

2 Examine the drivebelt for cracks, splitting, fraying, glazing (shiny patches) or any other damage. Renew the belt at service interval or if any damage is found.

3 To renew, loosen the alternator pivot bolts and adjustment nut. Swivel the alternator towards the cylinder block. Remove the belt.

4 Fit new belt over the pulleys and lever the alternator away from the block until the specified tension is achieved **(see illustration)**. Lever the alternator at the drive end to avoid damage to end cover.

5 Tighten the adjustment and pivot bolt nuts.

6 Run the engine at 1000 rpm for five minutes, then recheck and adjust as necessary.

15 Engine idle and fast idle adjustment

Note: *Accurate adjustment of the carburettor is only possible after adjustment of the ignition timing, contact breaker gap, and spark plug gaps. Incorrect valve clearances can also affect carburettor adjustment.*

Note: *Depending on operating territory and production date, the idle mixture adjustment screw may be "tamperproofed" by means of a plastic cap or seal, which must be destroyed in order to make an adjustment. The object of fitting the seal is to discourage (and to detect) adjustment by unqualified or unskilled operators. If you wish to remove a tamperproof seal, satisfy yourself that you are not breaking any local or national anti-pollution laws by so doing. Fit a new seal on completion where this is required by law.*

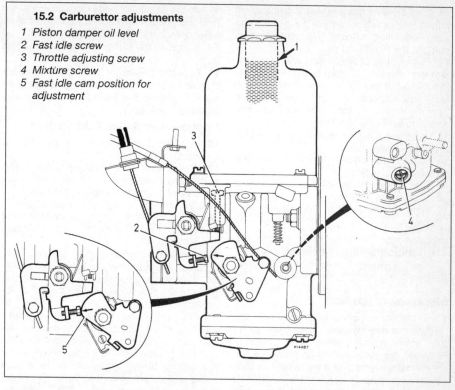

15.2 Carburettor adjustments

1 *Piston damper oil level*
2 *Fast idle screw*
3 *Throttle adjusting screw*
4 *Mixture screw*
5 *Fast idle cam position for adjustment*

1 Connect a tachometer to the engine in accordance with the manufacturer's instructions. Remove the air cleaner.

2 Unscrew the piston damper and check that the oil level is level with the top of the hollow piston rod **(see illustration)**. If not, top-up with clean engine oil. Refit the piston damper. On MG Turbo models there is a securing clamp that must be released first and secured afterwards. *Failure to secure the damper cap may result in dangerous fuel leakage.*

3 Check that the choke control cable has 0.08 in (2 mm) free play.

4 If available, connect an exhaust gas analyser to the engine in accordance with the manufacturer's instructions.

5 Run the engine at a fast idling speed until it reaches its normal operating temperature, indicated by the electric cooling fan operating. Continue to run the engine for a further five minutes.

6 Increase the engine speed to 2500 rpm for 30 seconds and repeat this at three-minute intervals during the adjustment procedure. This will ensure that any excess fuel is cleared from the inlet manifold.

7 Allow the engine to idle and check the idling speed against that given in the Specifications. If necessary, turn the throttle adjustment screw on top of the carburettor clockwise to increase the speed or anti-clockwise to decrease the speed **(see illustration)**.

8 To adjust the idling mixture, slowly turn the mixture screw, located on the right-hand side of the carburettor, clockwise (to enrich) or anti-clockwise (to weaken), until a point is reached where the engine speed is fastest **(see illustration)**.

9 Slowly turn the mixture screw anti-clockwise until the engine speed just starts to drop.

10 Turn the throttle adjustment screw to regain the specified idling speed.

15.7 Adjusting the idling speed

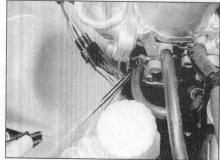

15.8 Adjusting the mixture

11 If an exhaust gas analyser is being used, adjust the mixture screw to obtain the specified idling exhaust gas content, then readjust the throttle screw.

12 Pull out the choke control knob until the arrow on the fast idle cam is aligned with the fast idle adjusting screw, then check that the fast idle speed is as given in the Specifications. If not, turn the fast idle adjusting screw as necessary.

13 Lubricate the throttle and choke controls and check connections.

14 Return the choke control knob, and switch off the engine.

15 Disconnect the tachometer and exhaust gas analyser as necessary.

16 Refit the air cleaner with reference to Chapter 4.

16 Ignition timing check and adjustment

Mechanical ignition

1 For the home mechanic, there is only one method that may be used to time the ignition - the stroboscopic timing light method. However, for initial setting-up purposes (i.e. after a major overhaul, or if the timing has been otherwise completely lost), a basic static timing method should be used to get the engine started. This involves the use of a test bulb. Once the engine is running, the timing should then be correctly set using the stroboscopic timing light method. A further method, employing the light emitting diode (LED) sensor bracket and timing disc located on the bottom of the timing cover, may be used, but the equipment for use with this system will not normally be available to the home mechanic.

Test bulb method

2 Remove the No 1 spark plug (crankshaft pulley end) and place the thumb over the aperture.

3 Turn the engine in the normal running direction (clockwise from crankshaft pulley end) until pressure is felt in No 1 cylinder, indicating that the piston is beginning its compression stroke. Use a spanner on the crankshaft pulley bolt, or engage top gear and pull the car forwards on manual gearbox models.

4 Continue turning the engine until the V-notch in the crankshaft pulley is exactly in line with the timing cover pointer representing 4° BTDC . Note that the large pointer indicates top dead centre (TDC) and the remaining pointer peaks are in increments of 4° BTDC.

5 Remove the distributor cap and check that the rotor arm is pointing in the direction of the No 1 terminal of the cap.

6 Connect a 12 volt test bulb between the end of the moving contact spring and an earthing point on the engine.

7 Loosen the distributor clamp plate bolt.

8 Switch on the ignition. If the bulb is already lit, turn the distributor body slightly anti-clockwise until the bulb goes out.

9 Turn the distributor body clockwise until the bulb *just* lights up, indicating that the points have just opened. Tighten the clamp bolt.

10 Switch off the ignition and remove the test bulb.

11 Refit the distributor cap and No 1 spark plug and HT lead. Once the engine has been started, check the timing as follows and adjust as necessary.

Stroboscopic timing light method

12 Disconnect and plug the vacuum pipe at the distributor.

13 Wipe clean the crankshaft pulley notch and timing cover pointers. If necessary, use white paint or chalk to highlight the marks.

14 Connect the timing light to the engine in accordance with the manufacturer's instructions (usually between No 1 spark plug and HT lead).

15 Connect a tachometer to the engine in accordance with the manufacturer's instructions.

16 Start the engine and run it at the speed given in the Specifications, in Chapter 5, for stroboscopic timing.

17 Point the timing light at the timing marks and they should appear to be stationary with the crank pulley notch in alignment with the appropriate mark: refer to the Specifications for the ignition timing applicable to the engine being worked on. Note that the large pointer indicates top dead centre (TDC) and the remaining pointer peaks are in increments of 4° BTDC **(see illustration)**.

18 If adjustment is necessary (i.e. the pulley notch does not line up with the appropriate mark), loosen the distributor clamp plate bolt and turn the body clockwise to advance and anti-clockwise to retard the ignition timing. Tighten the bolt when the setting is correct.

19 Gradually increase the engine speed while still pointing the timing light at the timing marks. The pulley notch should appear to move anti-clockwise proving that the centrifugal weights are operating correctly. If the ignition advance is not in accordance with the information given in the Specifications, Chapter 5, the distributor should be replaced as described in the same Chapter.

20 Switch off the engine and remove the timing light and tachometer.

21 Reconnect the vacuum pipe to the distributor. Disconnect the pipe from the carburettor and remove the distributor cap. Suck on the end of the pipe and check that the baseplate (Lucas) or pivot link (Ducellier) move to advance the points. If not, the vacuum unit may be faulty.

22 Refit the distributor cap and vacuum pipe.

Electronic ignition system

Static timing

23 The only method of electronic ignition timing for road use, is using a stroboscopic lamp. However, for initial setting-up purposes (e.g. after engine overhaul, or if the timing has been completely lost) the following procedure will enable the engine to be run in order to undertake dynamic timing.

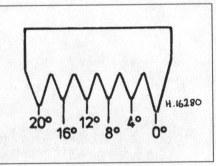

16.17 Typical timing scale. Moving mark is on the crankshaft pulley

24 Pull off the HT lead and remove No 1 spark plug (nearest the crankshaft pulley).

25 Place a finger over the plug hole and turn the engine in the normal direction of rotation (clockwise from the crankshaft pulley end) until pressure is felt in No 1 cylinder. This indicates that the piston is beginning its compression stroke. The engine can be turned with a socket and bar on the crankshaft pulley bolt.

26 Continue turning the engine until the notch in the crankshaft pulley is aligned with the TDC pointer on the timing scale.

27 Remove the distributor cap and check that the rotor arm is pointing towards the No 1 spark plug HT lead segment in the cap.

28 On pre-1985 models, lift off the rotor arm and anti-flash shield and observe the position of the reluctor in relation to the pick-up coil. One of the teeth on the reluctor should be aligned with, or very near to the small limb, of the pick-up coil. Slacken the distributor clamp retaining bolt and turn the distributor body until the reluctor tooth and pick-up limb are directly in line. Using feeler blades, preferably of plastic or brass, measure the air gap between the reluctor tooth and pick-up assembly **(see illustration)**. If the measured dimension is outside the tolerance given in the Specifications, slacken the adjusting nuts on the pick-up assembly and reposition the unit as necessary. Tighten the distributor clamp and refit the anti-flash shield and the rotor arm.

29 On 1985-on models, if the rotor arm is not pointing towards the No 1 spark plug HT lead

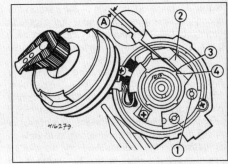

16.28 Reluctor air gap adjustment

1 Adjusting nuts
2 Pick-up coil
3 Pick-up limb
4 Reluctor tooth
A Specified gap

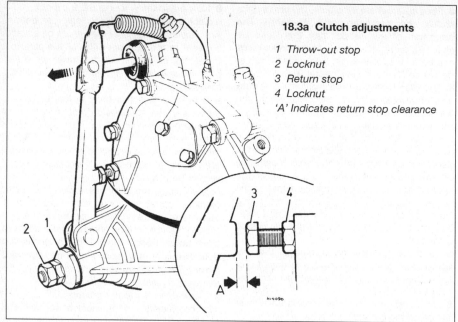

18.3a Clutch adjustments

1 Throw-out stop
2 Locknut
3 Return stop
4 Locknut
'A' Indicates return stop clearance

18.3b Checking the clutch return stop clearance

segment in the cap, slacken the distributor clamp bolt and turn the distributor body as necessary, then tighten the bolt. It is not possible to align the reluctor arms as they are totally enclosed within the distributor.

30 Refit the distributor cap, No 1 spark plug and the HT lead.

31 It should now be possible to start and run the engine, enabling the ignition timing to be checked accurately using a stroboscopic timing light, as described earlier in this section.

17 Driveshaft rubber gaiter check

1 With the vehicle raised and securely supported on stands, turn the steering onto full lock, then slowly rotate the roadwheel. Inspect the condition of the outer constant velocity (CV) joint rubber gaiters, squeezing the gaiters to open out the folds. Check for signs of cracking, splits or deterioration of the rubber, which may allow the grease to escape, and lead to water and grit entry into the joint. Also check the security and condition of the retaining clips. Repeat these checks on the inner CV joints. If any damage or deterioration is found, the gaiters should be renewed as described in Chapter 8.

2 At the same time, check the general condition of the CV joints themselves by first holding the driveshaft and attempting to rotate the wheel. Repeat this check by holding the inner joint and attempting to rotate the driveshaft. Any appreciable movement indicates wear in the joints, wear in the driveshaft splines, or possibly a loose driveshaft retaining nut.

18 Clutch - adjustment and maintenance

1 To improve access, remove the battery as described in Chapter 5.

2 To adjust the return stop, pull the release lever out against the tension of the slave cylinder return spring until all the free movement is taken up.

3 Using a feeler blade, check that the clearance between the return stop and the release lever is as given in the Specifications **(see illustrations)**. If not, loosen the locknut and reposition the return stop screw as necessary, then tighten the locknut. Make sure that the lever is held against the spring tension during the adjustment.

4 To adjust the throw-out stop, unscrew the locknut on the end of the release plunger to the limit of the thread, then unscrew the throw-out stop to the locknut.

5 Have an assistant fully depress the clutch pedal and keep it depressed. Screw in the throw out stop until it contacts the housing.

6 With the clutch pedal released, screw in the stop one further flat (60°), and tighten the locknut while holding the stop stationary.

19 Exhaust system check

Warning: If the engine has been running take care not to touch the exhaust system, especially the front section, as it may still be hot.

1 Position the car over an inspection pit or on car ramps. Alternatively raise the front and rear of the car and support on axle stands (see "Jacking and vehicle support").

2 Examine the exhaust system over its entire length checking for any damaged, broken or missing insulators or mountings, the security of the pipe retaining clamps, and the condition of the system with regard to rust and corrosion.

3 Lower the vehicle to the ground on completion.

20 Hinge and lock lubrication

1 Work around the vehicle, clean and then lubricate the hinges of the doors, bonnet and tailgate with a light machine oil.

2 Lubricate the bonnet release mechanism, hinges and safety locks with a smear of petroleum jelly.

3 Check carefully the security and operation of all hinges, latches and locks, adjusting them where required. Check the operation of the central locking system (if fitted).

4 Check the condition and operation of the tailgate struts, renewing them if either is leaking or no longer able to support the tailgate securely when raised.

5 On completion check the operation of all door locks, tailgate/boot locks and the fuel filler flap. Check that the child safety catches on the rear doors operate correctly.

21 Seat belt check

1 Working on each seat belt in turn, carefully examine the seat belt webbing for cuts or any signs of serious fraying or deterioration. Pull the belt all the way out, and examine the full extent of the webbing.

2 Fasten and unfasten the belt, ensuring that the locking mechanism holds securely and releases properly when intended. Check also that the retracting mechanism operates correctly when the belt is released.

3 Check the security of all seat belt mountings and attachments that are accessible, without removing any trim or other components, from inside the vehicle.

1

22 Headlight beam alignment check
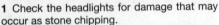

1 Check the headlights for damage that may occur as stone chipping.
2 The headlamp alignment should be checked every 12 000 miles (20 000 km) or 12 months, whichever occurs first.
3 It is recommended that the alignment is carried out by a Rover dealer or specialist, using modern beam setting equipment. However, in an emergency, the following procedure will provide an acceptable light pattern.
4 Position the car on a level surface with the ride heights correct, the car normally laden and the tyres correctly inflated, approximately 10 metres (33 feet) in front of, and at right-angles to, a wall or garage door.
5 Draw a horizontal line on the wall or door at headlamp centre height. Draw a vertical line corresponding to the centre line of the car, then measure off a point either side of this, on the horizontal line, corresponding with the headlamp centres.
6 Switch on the main beam and check that the areas of maximum illumination coincide with the headlamp centre marks on the wall. If not, turn the plastic knobs located on the rear of the headlamps turn both knobs to raise or lower the beam, and one knob (either will do) to move the beam horizontally.

23 Brake line and flexible hose check

1 Raise the front and rear of the car and securely support on axle stands (see "*Jacking and vehicle support*"). Remove all wheels.
2 Thoroughly examine all brake lines and brake flexible hoses, including the servo hose, for security and damage. To check the flexible hoses, bend them slightly in order to show up any cracking of the rubber.
3 Check the complete braking system for any signs of brake fluid leakage.
4 Where necessary carry out repairs to the braking system with reference to Chapter 9.

24 Front brake pad and rear brake lining check

 Warning: Read the 'Safety First' section, in the Preliminary Chapter, before proceeding.

1 Firmly apply the handbrake, then jack up the front of the car and support it securely on axle stands (see "*Jacking and vehicle support*"). Remove the front roadwheels.
2 For a quick check, the thickness of friction material remaining on each brake pad can be measured through the aperture in the caliper body. If any pad's friction material is worn to the specified thickness or less, all four pads on that axle must be renewed as a set.

3 For a comprehensive check, the brake pads should be removed and cleaned. The operation of the caliper can then also be checked, and the condition of the brake discs can be fully examined on both sides. Further details can be found in Chapter 9.
4 The disc pad warning indicators should also be checked. To do this, first locate the twin terminal black plastic sockets located on the wiring harness over each wheel arch. Switch on the ignition and connect a bridging wire between the terminals of one socket; the pad wear warning light should be illuminated on the instrument panel. If not, either the warning bulb is blown or there is a fault in the circuit. Repeat the check on the remaining front brake. On some models the pad wear system is only fitted to the right-hand side inner pad.
5 To check the rear brake linings, the rear wheels and drums need to be removed. For full details including adjustment procedures, refer to Chapter 9.
6 On completion refit the wheels and lower the car to the ground.

25 Steering, suspension and shock absorber check
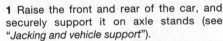

1 Raise the front and rear of the car, and securely support it on axle stands (see "*Jacking and vehicle support*").
2 The front and rear suspension should be lubricated with a grease gun. The front grease nipple is located on the upper suspension arm at the pivot end. The rear nipple is located on the outer end of the radius arm pivot. Always clean the nipple before using the grease gun.
3 Check all the suspension joints and mountings for security and damage.
4 Check the steering gaiters for splitting, and examine the steering balljoints for wear. Check the steering gear for security.
5 Visually inspect all balljoint dust covers and the steering rack gaiters for splits, chafing or deterioration. Any wear of these components will cause loss of lubricant, together with dirt and water entry, resulting in rapid deterioration of the balljoints or steering gear.
6 The front and rear suspension should be lubricated with a grease gun. The front grease nipple is located on the upper suspension arm at the pivot end. The rear nipple is located on the outer end of the radius arm pivot. Always clean the nipple before using the grease gun.
7 Grasp each front roadwheel in turn at the 12 o'clock and 6 o'clock positions, and try to rock it. Very slight free play may be felt, but if the movement is appreciable, further investigation is necessary to determine the source. Continue rocking the wheel while an assistant depresses the footbrake. If the movement is now eliminated or significantly reduced, it is likely that the hub bearings are at fault. If the free play is still evident with the footbrake depressed, then there is wear in the suspension joints or mountings.

8 Now grasp the wheel at the 9 o'clock and 3 o'clock positions, and try to rock it as before. Any movement felt now may again be caused by wear in the hub bearings or the steering track-rod balljoints. If the inner or outer balljoint is worn, the visual movement will be obvious.
9 Using a large screwdriver or flat bar, check for wear in the suspension mounting bushes by levering between the relevant suspension component and its attachment point. Some movement is to be expected as the mountings are made of rubber, but excessive wear should be obvious. Also check the condition of any visible rubber bushes, looking for splits, cracks or contamination of the rubber.
10 Check for any signs of fluid leakage around the front shock absorbers. Should any fluid be noticed, the shock absorber is defective internally, and should be renewed.
Note: *Shock absorbers should always be renewed in pairs on the same axle.*
11 Lower the car to the ground.
12 The efficiency of the shock absorbers may be checked by depressing each corner of the car in turn. If the shock absorbers are in good condition, the body will rise and then settle in its normal position. If it continues to rise and fall, the shock absorber is probably suspect. Examine also the shock absorber upper and lower mountings for any signs of wear.
13 With the car standing on its wheels, have an assistant turn the steering wheel back and forth about an eighth of a turn each way. There should be very little, if any, lost movement between the steering wheel and roadwheels. If this is not the case, closely observe the joints and mountings previously described, but in addition, check the steering column universal joints for wear, and the rack-and-pinion steering gear itself.

26 Hydragas units check

Note: *Checking the pressure of this units, along with repressurising and depressurising must be done by either a Rover dealer or specialist with the necessary equipment needed.*

1 A fault in a Hydragas unit can be determined by checking the car ride height as shown. If the measurements are less than those specified (refer to Chapter 10), first check the units and rear interconnecting pipe for signs of leakage, which will appear as a slight residue left after the fluid has evaporated.
2 If the cause is a union, tighten the nut and have the system repressurised.
3 Where a leak in a Hydragas unit is suspected, clean the area around the charging valve threads to determine whether the valve is the source of the leak (Talcum powder dusted around the clean valve may be helpful in tracing a leak).

4 If it is established that the leak is occurring round the valve threads, have the system depressurised, then unscrew the valve.

5 Screw in a new valve, using a sealant on the threads. Tighten the valve to the specified torque (see Chapter 10). Have the system repressurised on completion, and check for leaks.

6 If it is determined that a Hydragas unit is leaking fluid, renew the unit and again have it repressurised.

7 If no fluid leak can be found, it is possible that nitrogen has leaked from the unit. To check this, have the unit checked with the pressure pump. The fluid pressure should increase rapidly to the pressure of the nitrogen, and thereafter increase at a noticeably slower rate. If nitrogen has been leaking, the pressure will have dropped and the fluid pressure will increase rapidly above the normal nitrogen pressure.

8 If it is determined that a Hydragas unit has leaked nitrogen, renew it and have the suspension repressurised.

27 Handbrake adjustment

1 Chock the front wheels, then jack up the rear of the car and support it on axle stands (see "Jacking and vehicle support").

2 Apply the handbrake four times to settle the compensator and cable positions.

3 Adjust the rear brakes as described in Chapter 9.

4 Apply the handbrake six notches on an old cable, or four notches on a new cable, then check that both rear wheels are locked.

5 To adjust the handbrake, loosen the cable locknut using a spanner through the access slot in the carpet behind the handbrake. Turn the adjusting nut until the correct tension is achieved, then tighten the locknut.

6 Lubricate the linkages and cables.

7 Release the handbrake and check that the wheels rotate freely, then lower the car to the ground.

28 Front wheel alignment check

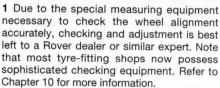

1 Due to the special measuring equipment necessary to check the wheel alignment accurately, checking and adjustment is best left to a Rover dealer or similar expert. Note that most tyre-fitting shops now possess sophisticated checking equipment. Refer to Chapter 10 for more information.

2 Before having the front wheel alignment checked, all tyre pressures should be checked and if necessary adjusted (see "Weekly Checks").

29 Road test (after every service)

Instruments and electrical equipment

1 Check the operation of all instruments and electrical equipment.

2 Make sure that all instruments read correctly, and switch on all electrical equipment in turn to check that it functions properly. Check the function of the heating control systems.

Steering and suspension

3 Check for any abnormalities in the steering, suspension, handling or road 'feel'.

4 Drive the vehicle, and check that there are no unusual vibrations or noises.

5 Check that the steering feels positive, with no excessive 'sloppiness', or roughness, and check for any suspension noises when cornering, or when driving over bumps.

Drivetrain

6 Check the performance of the engine, clutch (if applicable), gearbox/transmission and driveshafts. On Turbo models, check that the boost pressure needle moves up to the red zone during brief acceleration.

7 Listen for any unusual noises from the engine, clutch (if applicable) and gearbox/transmission.

8 Make sure that the engine runs smoothly when idling, and that there is no hesitation when accelerating.

9 On manual gearbox models, check that the clutch action is smooth and progressive, that the drive is taken up smoothly, and that the pedal travel is correct. Also listen for any noises when the clutch pedal is depressed. Check that all gears can be engaged smoothly, without noise, and that the gear lever action is not abnormally vague or 'notchy'.

10 On automatic transmission models, make sure that all gearchanges occur smoothly without snatching, and without an increase in engine speed between changes. Check that all the gear positions can be selected with the vehicle at rest. If any problems are found, they should be referred to a Rover dealer.

11 Listen for a metallic clicking sound from the front of the vehicle, as the vehicle is driven slowly in a circle with the steering on full lock. Carry out this check in both directions. If a clicking noise is heard, this indicates wear in a driveshaft joint, in which case, refer to Chapter 8.

Check the operation and performance of the braking system

12 Make sure that the vehicle does not pull to one side when braking, and that the wheels do not lock prematurely when braking hard.

13 Check that there is no vibration through the steering when braking.

14 Check that the handbrake operates correctly, without excessive movement of the lever, and that it holds the vehicle stationary on a slope.

15 Test the operation of the brake servo unit (where applicable) as follows. With the engine off, depress the footbrake four or five times to exhaust the vacuum. Start the engine, holding the brake pedal depressed. As the engine starts, there should be a noticeable 'give' in the brake pedal as vacuum builds up. Allow the engine to run for at least two minutes, and then switch it off. If the brake pedal is depressed now, it should be possible to detect a hiss from the servo as the pedal is depressed. After about four or five applications, no further hissing should be heard.

18 000 Miles (30 000 Km) /18 Months

30 Brake fluid renewal

Warning: Brake hydraulic fluid can harm your eyes and damage painted surfaces, so use extreme caution when handling and pouring it. Do not use fluid that has been standing open for some time, as it absorbs moisture from the air. Excess moisture can cause a dangerous loss of braking effectiveness.

1 The procedure is similar to that for the bleeding of the hydraulic system as described in Chapter 9, except that the brake fluid reservoir should be emptied by syphoning. Use a clean poultry baster or similar before starting, and allowance should be made for the old fluid to be expelled when bleeding a section of the circuit.

2 Working as described in Chapter 9, open the first bleed screw in the sequence, and pump the brake pedal gently until nearly all the old fluid has been emptied from the fluid reservoir. Top-up to the "MAX" level with new fluid, and continue pumping until only the new fluid remains in the reservoir, and new fluid can be seen emerging from the bleed screw. Tighten the screw, and top the reservoir level up to the "MAX" level line.

3 Old hydraulic fluid is invariably much darker in colour than the new, making it easy to distinguish the two.

4 Work through all the remaining bleed screws in the sequence, until new fluid can be seen at all of them. Be careful to keep the master cylinder reservoir topped-up to above the "MIN" level at all times, or air may enter the system and greatly increase the length of the task.

5 When the operation is complete, check that all bleed screws are securely tightened, and that their dust caps are refitted. Wash off all traces of spilt fluid, and recheck the reservoir fluid level.

6 Check the operation of the brakes before taking the car on the road.

31 Clutch fluid renewal (if applicable)

1 Remove the air cleaner (Chapter 4).

2 Unscrew the filler cap. Top-up the clutch master cylinder to the bottom of the filler neck with hydraulic fluid.

3 Connect a bleed tube to the bleed screw on the slave cylinder and place the free end in a jar.

4 Open the bleed screw three-quarters of a turn and have an assistant fully depress the clutch pedal slowly.

5 Tighten the bleed screw, then allow the clutch pedal to return to its stop. Pause for a moment, then repeat the procedure twice more. Top-up the master cylinder reservoir, and continue bleeding the system until the fluid entering the jar is free of air bubbles. The fluid must never drop more than half way down the reservoir.

6 Check the tightness of the bleed screw, and fit the filler cap after topping up the reservoir to the bottom of the filler neck.

7 Refit the air cleaner with reference to Chapter 4.

24 000 Miles (40 000 Km) / 2 Years

32 Antifreeze (coolant) renewal

⚠️ *Warning: Wait until the engine is cold before starting this procedure. Do not allow antifreeze to come in contact with your skin, or with the painted surfaces of the vehicle. Rinse off spills immediately with plenty of water. Never leave antifreeze lying around in an open container - antifreeze can be fatal if ingested.*

Draining

1 It is preferable to drain the cooling system when the engine has cooled. If this is not possible, place a cloth over the expansion tank filler cap. Turn it slowly in an anti-clockwise direction until the first stop is reached, then wait until all the pressure has been released.

2 Remove the filler cap.

3 Place a container beneath the left-hand side of the radiator.

4 Loosen the clip and ease the bottom hose away from the radiator outlet. Drain the coolant into the container.

5 Place a second container beneath the cylinder block drain plug located on the rear right-hand side next to the clutch slave cylinder. If necessary, remove the hot air stove from the exhaust manifold (Chapter 4), to improve access to the drain plug. Unscrew the plug and drain the coolant.

Flushing

6 After some time the radiator and engine waterways may become restricted or even blocked with scale or sediment, which reduces the efficiency of the cooling system. When this occurs, the coolant will appear rusty and dark in colour and the system should then be flushed. In severe cases, reverse flushing may be required as described later.

7 Disconnect the top hose from the cylinder head outlet elbow, and the bottom hose from the radiator outlet.

8 Insert a hose in the top hose, and allow water to circulate through the radiator until it runs clear from the outlet.

9 Insert the hose in the expansion tank filler neck and allow water to run out of the cylinder head outlet elbow and bottom hose until clear.

10 Disconnect the heater inlet hose from the front of the cylinder head, insert the hose, and allow water to circulate through the heater and out through the bottom hose until clear.

11 In severe cases of contamination, the system should be reverse flushed. To do this, remove the radiator, invert it, and insert a hose in the outlet. Continue flushing until clear water runs from the inlet.

12 If the engine is to be reverse flushed, remove the thermostat, and insert a hose into the cylinder head. Continue flushing until clear water runs from the cylinder block drain plug and bottom hose.

13 The use of any good proprietary cleaning agent may be necessary if the system is severely contaminated (always read manufacturer's instructions). Reverse flushing is also recommended to cleanse the cooling system and restore maximum efficiency. To prevent contamination occurring in future, regular renewal of the antifreeze is necessary.

Filling

14 Reconnect the radiator bottom hose and heater hose.

15 Refit the thermostat if removed, and reconnect the top hose to the outlet elbow.

16 Insert and tighten the cylinder block drain plug.

17 Pour coolant into the expansion tank filler until it reaches the level mark. Refit the cap.

18 Run the engine at a fast idling speed for three minutes, then stop the engine and check the level in the expansion tank. Top-up the level as necessary, being careful to release pressure from the system before removing the filler cap if necessary.

Antifreeze mixture

Caution: Do not use engine antifreeze in the windscreen/tailgate washer system, as it will cause damage to the vehicle paintwork.

19 The antifreeze should always be renewed at the specified intervals. This is necessary not only to maintain the antifreeze properties, but also to prevent corrosion that would otherwise occur as the corrosion inhibitors become progressively less effective.

20 Always use an ethylene-glycol based antifreeze that is suitable for use in mixed-metal cooling systems. The quantity of antifreeze and levels of protection are indicated in the Specifications.

21 Before adding antifreeze, the cooling system should be completely drained, preferably flushed, and all hoses checked for condition and security.

22 After filling with antifreeze, a label should be attached to the expansion tank filler neck, stating the type and concentration of antifreeze used, and the date installed. Any subsequent topping-up should be made with the same type and concentration of antifreeze.

33 Oil filler cap renewal

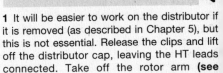

To maintain efficiency of the crankcase ventilation system, renew the oil filler cap.

34 Contact breaker points renewal (if applicable)

1 It will be easier to work on the distributor if it is removed (as described in Chapter 5), but this is not essential. Release the clips and lift off the distributor cap, leaving the HT leads connected. Take off the rotor arm **(see illustration)**.

Continued on page 1•16

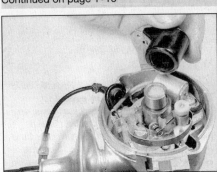

34.1 Removing the rotor arm (Lucas)

Engine

Oil filter:

Manual gearbox models (except MG Turbo) . . . . Cartridge type (Champion C103)
Manual gearbox models (MG Turbo only) . . . . Cartridge type (Champion C106)
Automatic transmission models . . . . Paper element type (Champion X113)

Cooling system

Note: *Refer to antifreeze manufacturer for latest recommendations.*
Antifreeze mixture:

28% antifreeze . . . . Protection down to -15°C (5°F)
50% antifreeze . . . . Protection down to -30°C (-22°F)

Fuel system

Refer to Chapter 4, for further details.
Air cleaner element:

All models (except MG Turbo) . . . . Champion W250
MG Turbo models . . . . Champion W114
Fuel filter:
MG Turbo models . . . . In-line type
Idling speed (all models) . . . . 765 ± 165 rpm
Fast idle speed (all models) . . . . 1200 ± 150 rpm
Exhaust gas CO content:
Except MG Turbo models . . . . 1.5 to 3.5%
MG Turbo . . . . 0.5 to 2.5%

Ignition system

Spark plug type:

998 cc:
Up to September 1986 . . . . Champion RN9YCC
October 1986 onwards . . . . Champion RN11YCC
1275 cc:
All models except MG Turbo . . . . Champion RN9YCC
MG Turbo . . . . Champion RN7YCC
Electrode gap* . . . . 0.8 mm (0.032 in)
* The spark plug gap quoted is that recommended by Champion for their specified plugs previously. If spark plugs of any other type are to be
fitted, refer to their manufacturer's recommendations.
Contact breaker gap (where applicable):
Lucas . . . . 0.014 to 0.016 in (0.35 to 0.40 mm)
Ducellier (initial) . . . . 0.015 in (0.38 mm)
Dwell angle:
Lucas . . . . 54°± 5°
Ducellier . . . . 57°± 2.5°
Air gap . . . . 0.006 to 0.010 in (0.15 to 0.25 mm)

Brakes

Brake pad minimum thickness (all models) . . . . 0.125 in (3 mm)
Brake shoe lining minimum thickness (all models) . . . . 0.063 in (1.6 mm)
Disc minimum thickness:

Plain disc . . . . 0.34 in (8.6 mm)
Ventilated disc . . . . 0.74 in (18.7 mm)

Tyres

Sizes . . . . 135 SR 12, 165/70R 12, 165/60 HR 13, 150/65 R315, 155/70 SR 12,
155/70 SR 12, 165/65 HR 13, 160/65 R315, 160/65 R315, or
185/55 13 (depending on model).
Pressures . . . . see *"Weekly Checks"*

Wiper blades

Windscreen and tailgate . . . . Champion X-41

Torque wrench settings

	lbf ft	Nm
Automatic transmission drain plug	28	39
Manual gearbox drain plug	30	41
Oil drain plug	28	39
Oil filter centre bolt (automatics only)	16	22
Roadwheel bolts	42	58
Rocker cover	3.5	5
Spark plugs	18	25

1

Lucas distributors

2 Press the moving contact spring from the insulator post and slide out the low tension connector **(see illustration)**.

3 Unscrew the fixed contact retaining screw and remove the contact breaker set from the baseplate and pin **(see illustration)**.

Ducellier distributors

4 Remove the spring clip from the two pivot posts.

5 Remove the fibre washer and lift the moving contact from the pivot post. Slide the LT wire retaining block from the distributor body and disconnect the condenser lead.

6 Remove the screw and washer and withdraw the fixed contact from the baseplate.

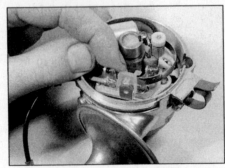

34.2 Disconnecting the contact spring from the insulator (Lucas)

All distributors

7 Refitting is a reversal of removal. Adjust the points gap as described in Section 13. On the

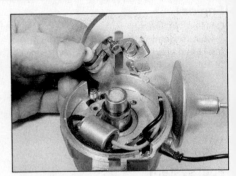

34.3 Removing the contact breaker set (Lucas)

Lucas version, make sure that the nylon plate engages the pin.

Chapter 2 Part A:
Engine in-car repair procedures

Contents

Degrees of difficulty

Easy, suitable for novice with little experience	Fairly easy, suitable for beginner with some experience	Fairly difficult, suitable for competent DIY mechanic 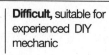	Difficult, suitable for experienced DIY mechanic 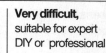	Very difficult, suitable for expert DIY or professional

Specifications

998 cc engine

Type	Four in-line, overhead valve
Bore	2.543 in (64.59 mm)
Stroke	3.0 in (76.2 mm)
Capacity	998 cc (60.96 cu in)
Firing order	1 - 3 - 4 - 2

Compression ratio (typical)

Early models:
Low compression models, (inc. 1.0, L and Van)	8.3 : 1
Standard compression (inc. 1.0, L and Gala)	9.6 : 1
High compression (inc. L, HLE and City X)	10.3 : 1

1984:
Engine 99H907P	9.6 : 1
Engine 99HA06P and 99HA08P	10.3 : 1

1985 to 1986 (all models):

Note: *Replace dashes (`- -`) with listed code.*

99HA - - P:
64, 68, 69	8.3 : 1 (Low compression)
67, 71	9.6 : 1 (Standard compression)
65, 66, 70, 75	10.3 : 1 (High compression)

99HB - - P:
39, 96, 97, 98, 99	8.3 : 1 (Low compression)
38, 87, 88, 89, 94, 95	9.6 : 1 (Standard compression)
90, 91, 92, 93	10.3 : 1 (High compression)

1987 to 1988:

99HD - - P:
32, 33, 34, 35	8.3 : 1 (Low compression)
30, 31	9.6 : 1 (Standard compression)
27, 28, 29	10.3 : 1 (High compression)

1989-on:

99 HD - -:
32, 33	8.3 : 1 (Low compression)
27, 29, 30, 31	10.3 : 1 (High compression)

1989-on (95 RON unleaded fuel specification):
99H E38 and 99H E39	8.3 : 1 (Low compression)

99H E- -:
35, 67, 68, 69, 70, 76, 94	9.6 : 1 (Standard compression)

Rocker gear

Rocker shaft diameter	0.5615 to 0.5625 in (14.26 to 14.29 mm)
Clearance in rockers	0.0005 to 0.0025 in (0.01 to 0.07 mm)

Lubrication system

System pressure:

Idling	15 lbf/in² (1.05 kgf/cm²)
Running	60 lbf/in² (4.2 kgf/cm²)
Warning light switch operating pressure	6 to 10 lbf/in² (0.4 to 0.7 kgf/cm²)
Pressure relief valve operating pressure	60 lbf/in² (4.2 kgf/cm²)
Pressure relief valve spring free length	2.86 in (72.63 mm)

1275 cc engine (except MG Turbo)

Note: *Specifications as 998 cc engine except for the following differences:*

Bore	2.78 in (70.61 mm)
Stroke	3.2 in (81.28 mm)
Capacity	1275 cc (77.8 cu in)

Compression ratio

Early models	9.4 : 1
1982:	
Low compression models	8.0 : 1
1.3, L, Vanden Plas manual and Van	9.4 : 1
MG	10.5 : 1
1983 (otherwise as 1982):	
Gala, Moritz and Automatic	9.4 : 1
HLE	9.75 : 1
1984	as 1983

1985 to 1986 (all models):

Note: *Replace dashes ('- -') with listed code.*

Engine codes:	
12HA73AA, 12HA84AA, 12HB37AA, 12HC17AA, 12HC18AA, 12HC19AA	8.0 : 1 (Low compression)
12HA - - AA:	
60, 61, 62, 71, 72, 80, 86, 87	9.75 : 1 (Standard compression)
12HB - - AA:	
09, 22, 36	9.75 : 1 (Standard compression)
12HC - - AA:	
01, 02, 03, 04, 05, 06, 07, 08, 09, 10, 11	9.75 : 1 (Standard compression)
12HA83AA, 12HA42AA, 12HC14AA, 12HC15AA	10.5 : 1 (High compression)
1987 to 1988:	
12HD18AA, 12HD19AA, 12HD20AA	8.0 : 1 (Low compression)
12HD - - AA:	
09, 10, 11, 12, 13, 14, 15, 21, 22, 23	9.75 : 1 (Standard compression)
1989-on:	
12HD18, 19, 20	8.01 : 1 (Low compression)
12HD - -:	
09, 10, 11, 12, 13, 14, 15, 21, 22, 23	9.75 : 1 (Standard compression)
17, 24, 25	10.5 : 1 (High compression)
1989-on (95 RON unleaded fuel specification):	
12HE - -:	
41, 42	8.0 : 1 (Low compression)
24, 25, 48, 71, 72, 73	9.4 : 1 (Standard compression)
12HF	10.0 : 1 (High compression)

1275 cc engine (MG Turbo)

Compression ratio	9.4 : 1

Torque wrench settings

	lbf ft	Nm
Brake servo pipe banjo	37	51
Camshaft locating plate	8	11
Camshaft nut	65	89
Connecting rod big-end - bolts	37	51
Connecting rod big-end - nuts	33	46
Crankshaft pulley bolt (except MG Turbo)	75	103
MG Turbo	105	145
Cylinder head nuts (except MG Turbo)	50	69
Cylinder head nuts (oiled) (MG Turbo)	55	76
Cylinder head bypass plug	12	17
Cylinder head outlet elbow nuts	16	22
Cylinder block side cover (998 cc only)	3.5	5
Engine mountings:		
⅜ in UNC	30	41
M8	22	30
M10	33	46
M12	53	73
Right-hand, from late 1986	21 to 26	29 to 36
Front plate to bearing cap	5	7
Front plate to crankcase	16	22
Main bearing bolts	63	87
Manifold to cylinder head	16	22
Oil filter head nuts	16	22
Oil pipe banjo	57	78
Oil pressure switch	18	25
Oil pump bolts	8	11
Oil separator to flywheel housing	15	20
Pressure relief valve nut	45	62
Rocker cover	3.5	5
Rocker shaft pedestal	24	32
Sump drain plug	28	39
Sump screws	8	11
Timing cover to front plate:		
¼ in diameter	5	7
⁵⁄₁₆ in diameter	12	17
Valve clearance adjusting nut	16	22
Water jacket drain plug	27	37

1 General description

How to use this Chapter

1 This part of Chapter 2, describes those repair procedures that can reasonably be carried out on the engine while it remains in the car. If the engine has been removed from the car, and is being dismantled as described in Part B, any preliminary dismantling procedures can be ignored.

2 Note that, while it may be possible physically to overhaul items such as the piston/connecting rod assemblies while the engine is in the car, such tasks are not normally carried out as separate operations. Usually, several additional procedures (not to mention the cleaning of components and of oilways) have to be carried out. For this reason, all such tasks are classed as major overhaul procedures, and are described in Part B of this Chapter.

3 Part B describes the removal of the engine/transmission from the vehicle, and the full overhaul procedures that can then be carried out.

Engine description

4 The engine is of four cylinder, in-line, overhead valve type mounted transversely at the front of the car and fitted over the gearbox. A low compression version is available for fleet use.

5 The crankshaft is of three bearing type, and the centre main bearing incorporates thrustwashers to control crankshaft endfloat. A torsional damper is fitted.

6 The camshaft is chain driven from the crankshaft and is supported in three bearings. The timing chain tensioner is of spring plate and bonded rubber type. The valves are operated from the camshaft by pushrod and rocker arm.

7 The oil pump is driven from the rear (flywheel) end of the camshaft, and a skew gear on the camshaft drives the distributor by way of a driveshaft.

8 The main design differences between the 998 cc and 1275 cc engines are as follows:

a) The 998 cc engine has side covers which can be removed to remove the tappets whereas the 1275 cc engine has no side covers; the tappets can only be removed from the crankcase (see illustrations).

b) The 998 cc engine has diagonally split big-end bearings and fully floating gudgeon pins. Whereas the 1275 cc engine has cross split big-end bearings and gudgeon pins which are an interference fit in the connecting rods.

9 The engine has been designated the "A Plus" since it is an improved version of the "A-Series" engine fitted to Mini models. The improvements include a toughened crankshaft, a crankshaft torsional damper, and hard wearing exhaust valves and seatings. A fully closed crankcase ventilation system is employed, and piston blow-by gases are drawn into the inlet manifold through oil separators and a port on the carburettor.

Compression Test

10 When engine performance is down, or if misfiring occurs which cannot be attributed to the ignition or fuel systems, a compression test can provide diagnostic clues as to the engine's condition. If the test is performed regularly, it can give warning of trouble before any other symptoms become apparent.

11 The engine must be fully warmed-up to normal operating temperature, the battery

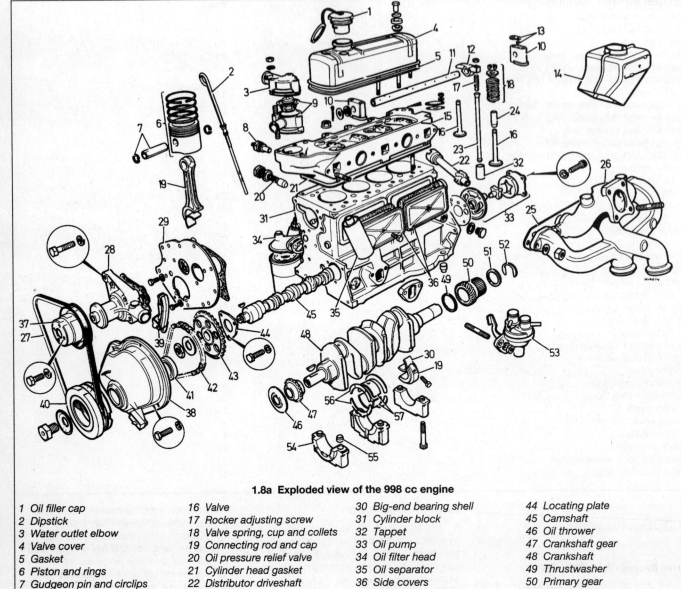

1.8a Exploded view of the 998 cc engine

1 Oil filler cap	16 Valve	30 Big-end bearing shell	44 Locating plate
2 Dipstick	17 Rocker adjusting screw	31 Cylinder block	45 Camshaft
3 Water outlet elbow	18 Valve spring, cup and collets	32 Tappet	46 Oil thrower
4 Valve cover	19 Connecting rod and cap	33 Oil pump	47 Crankshaft gear
5 Gasket	20 Oil pressure relief valve	34 Oil filter head	48 Crankshaft
6 Piston and rings	21 Cylinder head gasket	35 Oil separator	49 Thrustwasher
7 Gudgeon pin and circlips	22 Distributor driveshaft	36 Side covers	50 Primary gear
8 Temperature sender unit	23 Pushrod	37 Water pump pulley	51 Backing ring
9 Thermostat and housing	24 Valve guide	38 Timing cover	52 Thrustwasher
10 Rocker shaft pedestal	25 Manifold gasket	39 Chain tensioner	53 Fuel pump
11 Rocker shaft	26 Inlet and exhaust manifold	40 Crankshaft pulley	54 Main bearing cap
12 Rocker arm	27 Drivebelt	41 Oil seal	55 Dowel
13 Lockplate and screw	28 Water pump	42 Timing chain	56 Crankshaft thrustwashers
14 Hot air stove	29 Front mounting plate	43 Camshaft gear	57 Main bearing shells
15 Cylinder head			

must be fully charged, and all the spark plugs must be removed (see Chapter 1). The aid of an assistant will also be required.

12 Disable the ignition system by disconnecting the ignition HT coil lead from the distributor cap, and earthing it on the cylinder block. Use a jumper lead or similar wire, to make a good connection. Alternatively, disconnect the low-tension wiring plug from the distributor.

13 Fit a compression tester to the No 1 cylinder spark plug hole - the type of tester which screws into the plug thread is to be preferred.

14 Have the assistant hold the throttle wide open, and crank the engine on the starter motor; after one or two revolutions, the compression pressure should build up to a maximum figure, and then stabilise. Record the highest reading obtained.

15 Repeat the test on the remaining cylinders, recording the pressure in each.

16 All cylinders should produce very similar pressures; a difference of more than 2 bars between any two cylinders indicates a fault. Note that the compression should build up quickly in a healthy engine; low compression on the first stroke, followed by gradually-increasing pressure on successive strokes, indicates worn piston rings. A low

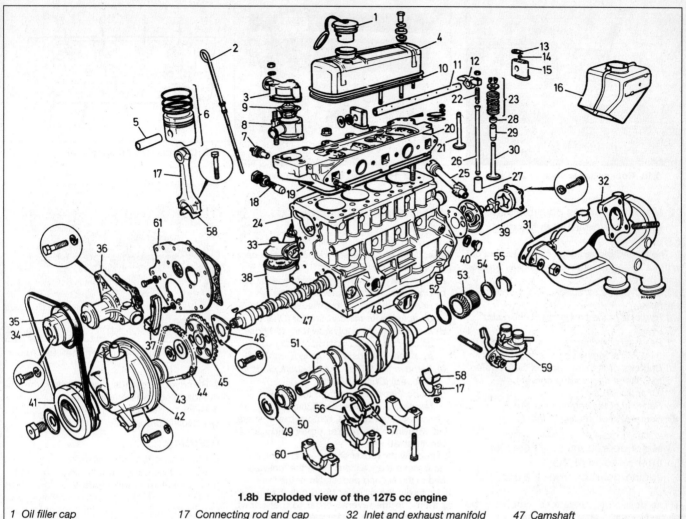

1.8b Exploded view of the 1275 cc engine

1 Oil filler cap	17 Connecting rod and cap	32 Inlet and exhaust manifold	47 Camshaft
2 Dipstick	18 Oil pressure relief valve	33 Oil filter head	48 Fuel pump insulator block
3 Water outlet elbow	19 Cylinder head gasket	34 Drivebelt	49 Oil thrower
4 Valve cover	20 Cylinder head	35 Water pump pulley	50 Crankshaft gear
5 Gudgeon pin	21 Exhaust valve	36 Water pump	51 Crankshaft
6 Piston and rings	22 Adjusting screw	37 Chain tensioner	52 Thrustwasher
7 Temperature transmitter	23 Valve spring, cup and collets	38 Oil filter	53 Primary gear
8 Housing	24 Cylinder block	39 Oil pump	54 Backing ring
9 Thermostat	25 Distributor driveshaft	40 Drain plug	55 Thrustwasher
10 Gasket	26 Pushrod	41 Crankshaft pulley	56 Crankshaft thrustwashers
11 Rocker shaft	27 Tappet	42 Timing cover and oil separator	57 Main bearing shell
12 Rocker arm	28 Inlet valve seal	43 Oil seal	58 Big-end shell
13 Lockplate	29 Valve guide	44 Timing chain	59 Fuel pump
14 Locating screw	30 Inlet valve	45 Camshaft gear	60 Main bearing cap
15 Pedestal	31 Manifold gasket	46 Locating plate	61 Front mounting plate
16 Hot air stove			

compression reading on the first stroke, which does not build up during successive strokes, indicates leaking valves or a blown head gasket (a cracked head could also be the cause). Deposits on the undersides of the valve heads can also cause low compression.

17 If the pressure in any cylinder is low, carry out the following test to isolate the cause. Introduce a teaspoonful of clean oil into that cylinder through its spark plug hole, and

repeat the test.

18 If the addition of oil temporarily improves the compression pressure, this indicates that bore or piston wear is responsible for the pressure loss. No improvement suggests that leaking or burnt valves, or a blown head gasket, may be to blame.

19 A low reading only from two adjacent cylinders is almost certainly due to the head gasket having blown between them; the

presence of coolant in the engine oil will confirm this.

20 If one cylinder is about 20 percent lower than the others and the engine has a slightly rough idle, a worn camshaft lobe could be the cause.

21 On completion of the test, refit the spark plugs and reconnect the ignition system and fuel pump as necessary.

2A

4.1a Rocker cover washer and seal

4.1b Removing the rocker cover

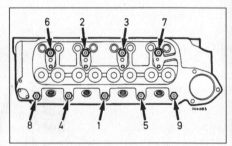

4.3 Cylinder head nut tightening sequence

2 Major operations possible with the engine/gearbox in the car

1 The following operations can be carried out without having to remove the engine/gearbox from the car:
   a) Removal and servicing of the cylinder head.
   b) Removal of the timing cover chain and gears.
   c) Removal of the tappets (cam followers) on the 998 cc engine only.
   d) Removal of the flywheel and clutch (refer to Chapter 6) or torque converter (Chapter 7B).
   e) Renewal of the engine mountings.
   f) Renewal of oil coolers (if fitted).

3 Major operations only possible after removal of the engine/gearbox from the car

1 The following operations can only be carried out after removal of the engine/gearbox from the car:
   a) Removal of the camshaft.
   b) Removal of the oil pump.
   c) Removal of the piston/connecting rod assemblies.
   d) Renewal of the crankshaft main bearings and big-end bearings.
   e) Removal of the tappets (cam followers) on the 1275 cc engine only.
2 Refer to Chapter 2B, for further details on these procedures.

4 Cylinder head - removal and refitting

Note: *If the engine is still in the car, first carry out the following operations:*
   a) *Disconnect the battery negative lead.*
   b) *Drain the cooling system (Chapter 3).*
   c) *Remove the inlet and exhaust manifold complete with the carburettor (Chapter 4).*
   d) *Disconnect the cooling system top hose, heater hose, and expansion tank hose from the thermostat housing (Chapter 3).*
   e) *Remove the HT leads (and spark plugs if required) (Chapter 5).*
   f) *Disconnect the lead from the water temperature sender unit (Chapter 3).*

1 Unscrew the two nuts, remove the washers, and withdraw the rocker cover and gasket **(see illustrations)**.
2 Unscrew the rocker shaft pedestal small nuts and remove the washers. Note the lockwasher fitted to the second pedestal from the front.
3 Unscrew the cylinder head nuts half a turn at a time in the reverse order to that shown **(see illustration)**. Remove the coil and bracket.
4 Lift the rocker shaft and pedestals from the studs **(see illustration)**.
5 Shake the pushrods free from the tappets (cam followers), then withdraw them from the cylinder head keeping them in strict order to ensure correct refitting **(see illustration)**.
6 Lift the cylinder head from the block **(see illustration)**. If it is stuck, tap it free with a wooden mallet. *Do not insert a lever into the gasket joint - you may damage the mating surfaces.*

4.4 Removing the rocker shaft assembly

7 Remove the cylinder head gasket from the cylinder block **(see illustration)**.
8 Refer to Section 6, in Chapter 2B, for the overhauling procedures.

Refitting

9 Make sure that the faces of the cylinder head and block are perfectly clean, then fit the new gasket over the studs with the words "TOP" and "FRONT" correctly positioned **(see illustration)**. Do not use jointing compound on the cylinder head gasket.
10 Lower the cylinder head over the studs and onto the gasket.
11 Insert the pushrods in their original locations, then lower the rocker shaft and pedestals over the studs, at the same time guiding the adjusting screws into the pushrods.
12 Locate the coil and bracket on the stud furthest from the thermostat, and fit the rocker shaft lockwasher to the second pedestal from the front.

4.5 Removing a pushrod

4.6 Removing the cylinder head (1275 cc engine)

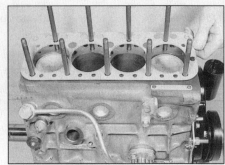

4.7 Removing the cylinder head gasket (1275 cc engine)

4.9 Cylinder head gasket "FRONT" marking

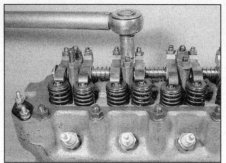

4.13 Tightening the cylinder head nuts

4.14 Tightening the rocker shaft pedestal nuts

13 Fit the cylinder head nuts and tighten them to half the specified torque in the order shown **(see illustration 4.3)**. After several minutes, tighten the nuts to the final torque, again in the order recommended **(see illustration)**.

14 Fit the rocker shaft pedestal washers and nuts, and tighten them evenly to the specified torque **(see illustration)**.

15 Adjust the valve clearances as described in Section 5.

16 Fit the valve cover with a new gasket and tighten the two nuts.

17 If the engine is in the car, reverse the removal procedure given in paragraphs 1 to 6, and refill the cooling system with reference to Chapter 3.

18 Drive the car for five to ten miles, then allow the engine to cool and remove the valve cover. Working in the order shown **(see illustration 4.3)**, loosen half a turn, then immediately tighten, each cylinder head nut to the specified torque. Readjust the valve clearances, then refit the valve cover.

5 Valve clearances - adjustment

Adjustment

1 The valve clearances must be adjusted with the engine cold.

2 Remove the valve cover and gasket.

3 Turn the engine with a spanner on the crankshaft pulley bolt until No 8 valve (No 4 cylinder exhaust) is fully open. Alternatively, the engine can be turned by engaging 4th gear,

releasing the handbrake, and rocking the car backwards and forwards.

4 Insert a feeler blade of the correct thickness between the rocker arm and valve stem of No 1 valve (No 1 cylinder exhaust). If the blade is not a firm sliding fit, loosen the locknut on the rocker arm with a ring spanner and turn the adjusting screw with a screwdriver **(see illustration)**. Tighten the locknut whilst holding the adjusting screw stationary, then recheck the adjustment.

5 Repeat the procedure given in paragraphs 3 and 4 on the remaining valves using the "rule of nine" method as given below:

Valve open	Adjust valve
8 exhaust	1 exhaust
6 inlet	3 inlet
4 exhaust	5 exhaust
7 inlet	2 inlet
1 exhaust	8 exhaust
3 inlet	6 inlet
5 exhaust	4 exhaust
2 inlet	7 inlet

6 Check the valve cover gasket for damage and renew it if necessary. Refit the valve cover and gasket with the filler cap towards the timing chain end of the engine. Tighten the nuts to the specified torque.

6 Timing cover, chain, and gears - removal, overhaul and refitting

Note: If the engine is still in the car, first carry out the following operations:
a) Disconnect the battery negative lead.
b) Remove the drivebelt and the water pump pulley (Chapter 3).

Removal

1 On models with the three-point engine mounting system the following additional operations are required when removing the timing cover with the engine in situ. Disconnect the windscreen washer pump plug and move the reservoir to one side.

2 Using a spanner on the crankshaft pulley bolt, rotate the engine until No 4 piston is at top dead centre on the compression stroke. This will align the timing gear marks.

3 On the 1275 cc engine, disconnect the crankcase ventilation hose from the oil separator on the timing cover.

4 Unlock and unscrew the crankshaft pulley bolt. When removing the crankshaft pulley bolt with the engine still in the car, there is insufficient room to use a normal socket due to the location of the right-hand engine mounting. A ring spanner may be used instead, but if the bolt is particularly tight, tool 18G 98A **(see illustration)**, should be obtained from a tool hire agent. The tool has a strengthened tip for hitting with a heavy hammer.

5 If the engine is removed, a block of wood placed between a crankshaft web and the crankcase will keep the crankshaft stationary. If the engine is in the car, select top gear and apply the handbrake.

6 Lever the pulley and damper off the front of the crankshaft **(see illustration)**.

7 After removing the crankshaft pulley, lift the alternator so that its adjusting link is clear of the timing cover. Wedge or clamp the alternator in this position while the cover is removed.

2A

5.4 Checking the valve clearances

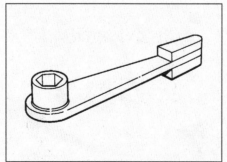

6.4 Tool 18G 98A for unscrewing the crankshaft pulley bolts

6.6 Removing the crankshaft pulley and damper (1275 cc engine)

6.8 Removing the timing cover (1275 cc engine)

6.9 Correct location for the crankshaft oil thrower

6.10 Removing the camshaft gear retaining nut

8 Unbolt and remove the timing cover, and remove the gasket **(see illustration)**.
9 Remove the oil thrower, noting which way round it is fitted **(see illustration)**. Recover any shims (used for gear wheel alignment), noting their fitted positions.
10 Flatten the lockwasher, then unscrew the camshaft gear retaining nut **(see illustration)**. Use a screwdriver through one of the gear holes to restrain the gear. Remove the lockwasher.
11 Check that the alignment marks on the timing gears are facing each other, then unbolt and remove the chain tensioner.
12 Using two levers, ease the two gears and chain from the camshaft and crankshaft.
13 Remove the gears from the chain, but identify the outer face of the chain so that it can be refitted in its original position if necessary.

Overhaul

14 Examine all the teeth on the camshaft and crankshaft sprockets. If these are "hooked" in appearance, renew the sprockets.
15 Examine the chain tensioner for wear and renew it if necessary.
16 Examine the timing chain for wear. If it has been in operation for a considerable time, or if when held horizontally (rollers vertical) it takes on a deeply bowed appearance, renew it.
17 Check the timing cover for damage and renew it if necessary. It is good practice to renew the timing cover oil seal whenever the timing cover is removed. To do this, drive out the old seal with a drift, and install the new seal using a block of wood to make sure that it enters squarely **(see illustration)**.
18 Early crankshaft pulley bolts may be found to have a shoulder that can foul the end of the crankshaft and cause the pulley to

become loose. Where this has occurred, renew the pulley and fit the later modified bolt together with a lockwasher. The later bolt does not have a shoulder.

Refitting

19 Locate the timing gears on the crankshaft and camshaft without the chain, and check their alignment using a straight edge and feeler blade as shown **(see illustrations)**.
20 Remove the gears, and if necessary extract the Woodruff key and fit shims to the crankshaft to obtain the alignment. Refit the key **(see illustration)**.
21 Turn the crankshaft so that the Woodruff key is at top dead centre, and turn the camshaft so that the key is at 2 o'clock. In this position No 4 cylinder is at TDC compression.
22 Loop the timing chain over the two gears so that the timing marks are facing each other on the centre line **(see illustration)**.
23 Locate the two gears on the crankshaft and camshaft and press them firmly home. Using a straight edge check that the timing marks are still on the centre line.
24 Fit the camshaft gear retaining nut and lockwasher, and tighten the nut while using a screwdriver through one of the gear holes to restrain the gear. Bend the lockwasher to lock the nut **(see illustrations)**.

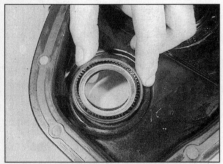

6.17 Fitting the timing cover oil seal

6.19a Checking the timing gear alignment by comparing the camshaft gear teeth-to-rule dimension . . .

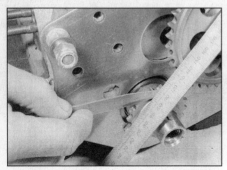

6.19b . . . with the crankshaft gear teeth-to-rule dimension

6.20 Crankshaft gear shim location

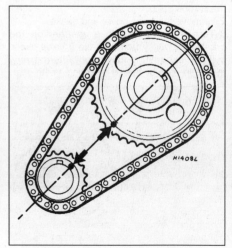

6.22 Timing gear alignment marks (arrowed) and centre line

6.24a Tightening the camshaft gear retaining nut

6.24b Camshaft gear retaining nut locked, and timing marks aligned

6.25 Fitting the timing chain tensioner

25 Fit the chain tensioner and tighten the bolts, while keeping firm thumb pressure against the top of the bracket to provide the preload **(see illustration)**.

26 Locate the oil thrower on the crankshaft with the side marked "F" facing outwards.

27 Stick the timing cover gasket to the front plate, then fit the timing cover and retain it with two upper bolts inserted loosely.

28 Oil the timing cover oil seal, then temporarily fit the crankshaft pulley to centralise the timing cover. Insert and tighten evenly the upper retaining bolts, then remove the pulley and fit the lower bolts.

29 Fit the crankshaft pulley and damper on the crankshaft followed by the lockwasher and bolt. Tighten the bolt to the specified torque **(see illustration)**. If the engine is removed, place a block of wood between a crankshaft web and the crankcase, if the engine is in the car, select top gear and apply the handbrake.

30 Bend the lockwasher to lock the bolt. Remove the block of wood as applicable.

31 On the 1275 cc engine, connect the crankcase ventilation hose to the oil separator on the timing cover.

32 If the engine is in the car, refitting is a reversal of the removal procedure.

7 Tappets (998 cc engine only) - removal and refitting

Note: *For information on tappets for the 1275cc engine, refer to Chapter 2B, Section 7. If the engine is still in the car first carry out the following operations:*
a) Disconnect the battery negative lead.
b) Remove the inlet and exhaust manifold complete with carburettor.
c) Remove the rocker cover.
d) Remove the rocker shaft and pushrods.

Removal

1 Disconnect the crankcase ventilation hose from the oil separator on the side cover nearest the timing chain.

2 Unbolt the side covers from the cylinder block and remove the gaskets. Remove the bolts, cup washers, and seals from the side covers.

3 Lift the tappets from their bores, keeping

them in strict order so that they can be refitted in their original positions. Identify them if necessary. Replace as necessary.

Refitting

4 Lubricate the tappets with engine oil and insert them in their original locations.

5 Refit the side covers together with new gaskets, and insert the bolts with the seals and cup washers. Tighten the bolts to the specified torque.

6 Reconnect the crankcase ventilation hose to the oil separator.

7 If the engine is in the car, refitting is a reversal of the removal procedure, but adjust the valve clearances as described in Section 5. Retighten the cylinder head nuts referring to Section 4.

8 Crankcase ventilation system - description

1 The crankcase ventilation system comprises hoses from the crankcase area linked and connected to a port on the carburettor **(see illustration)**. One hose is attached to an oil separator bolted to the flywheel housing (manual gearbox models only), and the other is attached to an oil separator on the cylinder block side cover (998 cc) or timing cover (1275 cc).

2 Periodically the hoses should be examined for security and condition. Cleaning them will not normally be necessary except when the engine is well worn and sludge has accumulated.

8.1 Showing the location of the crankcase ventilation hoses (1275 cc engine)

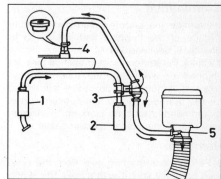

6.29 Tightening the crankshaft pulley bolt

3 The crankcase ventilation system on MG Turbo models is modified slightly from the standard design in order to prevent the turbocharger pressurising the crankcase **(see illustration)**.

4 At low engine speeds and on the overrun, fumes are drawn into the inlet manifold through the one-way restrictor valve.

5 As the engine speed rises and the inlet manifold becomes pressurised, the one-way restrictor valve closes. Fumes are then inducted by way of the regulator valve into the air cleaner.

6 The valves should be cleaned periodically and renewed if their operation is suspect.

8.3 Crankcase ventilation system fitted to MG Turbo models

1 Oil separator (flywheel housing)
2 Oil separator (timing cover)
3 Regulator valve
4 One-way restrictor valve
5 Air cleaner nozzle

2A

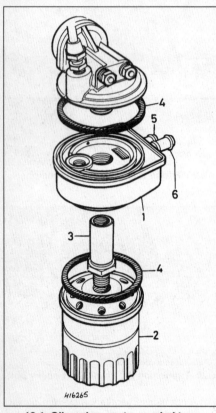

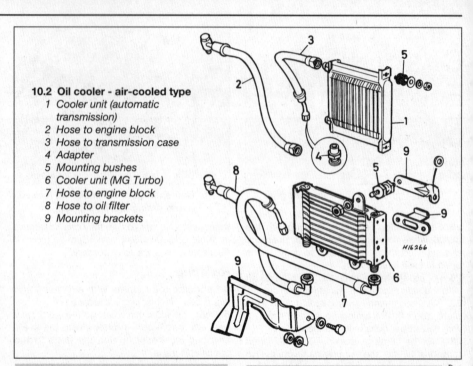

10.2 Oil cooler - air-cooled type
1 Cooler unit (automatic transmission)
2 Hose to engine block
3 Hose to transmission case
4 Adapter
5 Mounting bushes
6 Cooler unit (MG Turbo)
7 Hose to engine block
8 Hose to oil filter
9 Mounting brackets

10.1 Oil cooler - water-cooled type
1 Oil cooler
2 Oil filter
3 Fixing bolt
4 Sealing rings
5 Coolant inlet
6 Coolant outlet

9 Flywheel/torque converter ring gear - examination, removal and refitting

Examination

1 Examine the clutch driven plate mating surface of the flywheel with reference to Chapter 6, Sections 6 or 7.
2 Check the starter ring gear teeth; if they are chipped or worn the ring gear must be renewed. Although the procedure is identical for the flywheel and torque converter, it is recommended that the work on the torque converter is entrusted to a Rover dealer.

Removal

3 Partially drill the ring gear from the side, then carefully split it with a cold chisel and remove it, taking precautions to prevent injury from flying fragments.

Refitting

4 Heat the new ring to 392°F (250°C) in an electric oven, then quickly fit it to the flywheel/torque converter. Allow the ring to cool naturally without quenching.

10 Oil coolers - description

Description

1 Two types of oil cooler may be encountered. The first type, fitted to MG 1300 and Vanden Plas models, uses engine coolant as the heat exchange medium **(see illustration)**.
2 This type of cooler fits in between the oil filter head and the oil filter itself. The second type of cooler, fitted to Automatic and MG Turbo models, uses air as the heat exchange medium and is similar in appearance to a coolant radiator **(see illustration)**.
3 Depending on operating territory and production date, oil coolers may be encountered on models other than those mentioned above.

11 Oil cooler (water-cooled) - removal and refitting

Removal

1 Drain the cooling system (Chapter 3).
2 Disconnect the coolant hoses from the oil cooler.
3 Remove the oil filter cartridge as described in Chapter 1.
4 Unscrew the centre fixing bolt and remove the oil cooler. Recover the sealing ring if this did not come away with the cooler.

Refitting

5 Refitting is a reversal of the removal procedure. Use a new sealing ring and a new oil filter cartridge. Refill the cooling system and check the engine oil level after running the engine.

12 Oil cooler (air-cooled) - removal and refitting

Removal

1 Remove the air cleaner assembly to improve access.
2 Disconnect and plug the hoses at the cooler. Be prepared for oil spillage from the cooler itself.
3 Release the cooler from its mounting brackets and bushes. (In the case of the MG Turbo, release the top bracket from the body and remove the bracket and bush with the cooler).
4 With the cooler removed, flush it through with petrol or cellulose thinners if internal blockage or contamination was the reason for removal. Blow through with compressed air to dry out the cleaning solvent. Clean the fins with paraffin or detergent. Do not forget to flush the hoses too if necessary.

Refitting

5 Refitting is a reversal of the removal procedure. Use new mounting bushes if the old ones were in poor condition. On MG Turbo models, fit the outlet hose in line with the oil cooler, and the inlet hose offset at an angle of 10°.
6 Top-up the engine oil level (by approximately the amount lost). Start the engine and check for leaks. On MG Turbo models, do not rev the engine for at least 10 seconds after this start-up, otherwise there is a danger of damaging the turbocharger bearings. Recheck the oil level after stopping the engine.

Chapter 2 Part B:
Engine removal and general overhaul procedures

Contents

Degrees of difficulty

Easy, suitable for novice with little experience	Fairly easy, suitable for beginner with some experience	Fairly difficult, suitable for competent DIY mechanic	Difficult, suitable for experienced DIY mechanic	Very difficult, suitable for expert DIY or professional

Specifications

998 cc engine

Oil pump:
Type	Bi-rotor
Outer rotor endfloat	0.005 in (0.127 mm)
Inner rotor endfloat	0.005 in (0.127 mm)
Outer rotor-to-body clearance	0.010 in (0.254 mm)
Rotor lobe clearance	0.006 in (0.152 mm)

Crankshaft
Main journal diameter	1.7505 to 1.7512 in (44.46 to 44.48 mm)
Main bearing running clearance:	
Early models	0.0007 to 0.0029 in (0.018 to 0.074 mm)
1982-on	0.001 to 0.003 in (0.025 to 0.068 mm)
Main journal minimum regrind diameter	1.7305 in (43.96 mm)
Crankpin journal diameter:	
Early models	1.6252 to 1.6259 in (41.28 to 41.298 mm)
1982-on	0.001 to 0.0025 in (0.025 to 0.064 mm)
Crankpin running clearance	0.001 to 0.0027 in (0.025 to 0.069 mm)
Crankpin minimum regrind diameter	1.6052 in (40.77 mm)
Endfloat	0.002 to 0.003 in (0.051 to 0.076 mm)

Connecting rods
Length between centres	5.75 in (146.05 mm)

Pistons
Skirt clearance in cylinder:	
Top	0.0021 to 0.0033 in (0.053 to 0.084 mm)
Bottom	0.0004 to 0.0014 in (0.010 to 0.036 mm)
Oversizes available	0.010, 0.020, 0.030, and 0.040 in (0.254, 0.508, 0.762, and 1.016 mm)

Piston rings
Clearance in groove:	
Top compression	0.002 to 0.0035 in (0.051 to 0.089 mm)
2nd and 3rd compression	0.002 to 0.004 in (0.051 to 0.102 mm)
End gap:	
Compression	0.007 to 0.012 in (O.178 to 0.305 mm)
Oil control rails	0.014 to 0.041 in (0.38 to 1.04 mm)

2B

Gudgeon pins

Fit in piston . . . . Hand push at 20°C (68°F)
Running clearance in connecting rod . . . . 0.0007 to 0.001 in (0.02 to 0.03 mm)

Camshaft

Journal diameter:
    Front . . . . 1.6655 to 1.6660 in (42.304 to 42.316 mm)
    Centre . . . . 1.62275 to 1.62325 in (41.218 to 41.231 mm)
    Rear . . . . 1.37275 to 1.3735 in (34.868 to 34.887 mm)
Running clearance in bearings . . . . 0.001 to 0.00225 in (0.025 to 0.057 mm)
Endfloat . . . . 0.003 to 0.007 in (0.076 to 0.178 mm)
Valve lift:
    Inlet . . . . 0.318 in (8.08 mm)
    Exhaust . . . . 0.300 in (7.62 mm)
Tappet outside diameter . . . . 0.812 in (20.62 mm)

Rocker gear

Rocker shaft diameter . . . . 0.5615 to 0.5625 in (14.26 to 14.29 mm)
Clearance in rockers . . . . 0.0005 to 0.0025 in (0.01 to 0.07 mm)

Valves

Seat angle . . . . 45°
Head diameter:
    Inlet . . . . 1.093 to 1.098 in (27.76 to 27.89 mm)
    Exhaust . . . . 1.000 to 1.005 in (25.40 to 25.53 mm)
Stem diameter:
    Inlet . . . . 0.2793 to 0.2798 in (7.094 to 7.107 mm)
    Exhaust . . . . 0.2788 to 0.2793 in (7.082 to 7.094 mm)
Clearance in guide:
    Inlet . . . . 0.0015 to 0.0025 in (0.038 to 0.064 mm)
    Exhaust . . . . 0.002 to 0.003 in (0.051 to 0.076 mm)
Valve guides:
    Length . . . . 1.687 in (42.85 mm)
    Outside diameter . . . . 0.470 to 0.471 in (11.94 to 11.96 mm)
    Inside diameter . . . . 0.2813 to 0.2818 in (7.145 to 7.158 mm)
    Fitted height above head:
        Early model . . . . 0.594 in (15.09 mm)
        1982-on (valves modified for inlet valve oil seals) . . . . 0.540 in (13.72 mm)
Valve springs:
    Free length . . . . 1.95 in (49.53 mm)
Valve timing (at valve clearance of 0.021 in/0.53 mm):
    Inlet opens . . . . 9° BTDC
    Inlet closes . . . . 41° ABDC
    Exhaust opens . . . . 49° BBDC
    Exhaust closes . . . . 11° ATDC

Valve clearance, inlet and exhaust (cold):

Early models . . . . 0.012 in (0.30 mm)
All models 1983 to 1986 (except 1983 1.0, L, HLE and City) . . . . 0.012 to 0.014 in (0.30 to 0.36 mm)
1983 1.0, L, HLE and City . . . . 0.012 in (0.30 mm)
All models - 1986 on . . . . 0.011 to 0.013 in (0.27 to 0.33 mm)

1275 cc engine (except MG Turbo)

Note: *Specifications as 998 cc engine except for the following differences:*

Crankshaft

Main journal diameter:
    Early models . . . . 2.0011 to 2.0017 in (50.83 to 50.84 mm)
    1986-on:
        Red colour code . . . . 2.0005 to 2.0009 in (50.81 to 50.82 mm)
        Green colour code . . . . 2.0009 to 2.0013 in (50.82 to 50.83 mm)
        Yellow colour code or no colour code . . . . 2.0012 to 2.0017 in (50.83 to 50.84 mm)
Main bearing running clearance:
    Early models . . . . 0.0003 to 0.0024 in (0.008 to 0.076 mm)
    1986-on . . . . 0.0007 to 0.0023 in (0.017 to 0.058 mm)
Main bearing shell thickness:
    Yellow colour code . . . . 0.0713 to 0.0717 in (1.811 to 1.821 mm)
    Green colour code . . . . 0.0717 to 0.0721 in (1.821 to 1.831 mm)
    Red colour code . . . . 0.0721 to 0.0725 in (1.831 to 1.841 mm)

Crankshaft (continued)

Main journal minimum regrind diameter .... 1.9811 in (50.32 mm)
Crankpin journal diameter .... 1.7497 to 1.7504 in (44.44 to 44.46 mm)
Crankpin running clearance .... 0.0015 to 0.0032 in (0.0381 to 0.0813 mm)
Crankpin minimum regrind diameter .... 1.7297 in (43.93 mm)

Pistons

Skirt clearance in cylinder:
  Top .... 0.0029 to 0.0045 in (0.074 to 0.114 mm)
  Bottom .... 0.0009 to 0.0025 in (0.023 to 0.064 mm)
Oversizes available .... 0.010 and 0.020 in (0.254 and 0.508 mm)

Piston rings

Clearance in groove:
  Top compression .... 0.0015 to 0.0035 in (0.038 to 0.089 mm)
  2nd compression .... 0.0015 to 0.0035 in (0.038 to 0.089 mm)
End gap:
  Top compression .... 0.010 to 0.017 in (0.25 to 0.45 mm)
  2nd compression .... 0.008 to 0.013 in (0.20 to 0.33 mm)
  Oil control rails .... 0.015 to 0.041 in (0.38 to 1.04 mm)

Gudgeon pins

Fit in piston .... Drop through to hand push at 20°C (68°F)
Interference fit in connecting rod .... 0.0008 to 0.0015 in (0.02 to 0.04 mm)

Camshaft

Valve lift:
  Inlet and exhaust .... 0.318 (8.08 mm)
Tappet outside diameter .... 0.812 in (20.62 mm)

Valves

Head diameter:
  Inlet (except 1275 Sport, MG and Vanden Plas) .... 1.307 to 1.312 in (33.20 to 33.32 mm)
  Inlet (1275 Sport, MG and Vanden Plas) .... 1.401 to 1.406 in (35.58 to 35.71 mm)
  Exhaust .... 1.1515 to 1.1565 in (29.25 to 29.38 mm)
Valve guides (fitted height above head) .... 0.540 in (13.72 mm)
Valve timing, at valve clearance of 0.021 in (0.53 mm):
  Early models:
  HLE:
    Inlet opens .... 9° BTDC
    Inlet closes .... 41° ABDC
    Exhaust opens .... 49° BBDC
    Exhaust closes .... 11° ATDC
  MG 1300:
    Inlet opens .... 16° BTDC
    Inlet closes .... 56° ABDC
    Exhaust opens .... 59° BBDC
    Exhaust closes .... 29° ATDC
  1986-on:
  All models except 1275 Sport, MG and Vanden Plas:
    Inlet opens .... 9° BTDC
    Inlet closes .... 41° ABDC
    Exhaust opens .... 55° BBDC
    Exhaust closes .... 17° ATDC
  1275 Sport, MG and Vanden Plas:
    Inlet opens .... 16° BTDC
    Inlet closes .... 56° ABDC
    Exhaust opens .... 59° BBDC
    Exhaust closes .... 29° ATDC

Valve clearances (cold):

1982 and 1983 MG:
  Inlet .... 0.012 to 0.014 in (0.30 to 0.36 mm)
  Exhaust .... 0.015 to 0.017 in (0.38 to 0.43 mm)
1982 Vanden Plas (inlet and exhaust) .... 0.012 in (0.30 mm)
1983 L, HLE and 1.3 automatic (inlet and exhaust) .... 0.012 in (0.30 mm)
1985 to 1986 MG and Vanden Plas manual (inlet and exhaust) .... 0.013 to 0.015 in (0.33 to 0.38 mm)
All other models (inlet and exhaust) .... 0.012 to 0.014 in (0.30 to 0.36 mm)
1986-on (inlet and exhaust):
  All models except those shown below .... 0.011 to 0.013 in (0.027 to 0.33 mm)
  MG, Vanden Plas with manual gearbox and 1275 Sport .... 0.013 to 0.015 in (0.33 to 0.38 mm)

2B

1275 cc engine (MG Turbo)

Valve clearances (cold):

1982 and 1983:
Inlet . . . . 0.014 in (0.35 mm)
Exhaust . . . . 0.016 in (0.40 mm)
1984-on:
Inlet . . . . 0.012 to 0.014 in (0.30 to 0.35 mm)
Exhaust . . . . 0.014 to 0.016 in (0.35 to 0.40 mm)

Valves

Stem diameter:
Exhaust . . . . 0.3131 to 0.3137 in (7.955 to 7.970 mm)
Clearance in guide:
Exhaust . . . . 0.0031 to 0.0032 in (0.079 to 0.081 mm)
Valve guides:
Inside diameter (reamed) - exhaust . . . . 0.3164 to 0.3169 in (8.036 to 8.049 mm)
Valve springs free length:
Inner . . . . 1.703 in (43.256 mm)
Outer . . . . 1.740 in (44196 mm)

1 Engine overhaul - general information

Note: *An engine which has had regular and frequent oil and filter changes, as well as other required maintenance, should give many thousands of miles of reliable service. Before beginning the engine overhaul, read through the entire procedure, to familiarise yourself with the scope and requirements of the job.*

General

It is not always easy to determine when, or if, an engine should be completely overhauled, as a number of factors must be considered.

High mileage is not necessarily an indication that an overhaul is needed, while low mileage does not preclude the need for an overhaul. Frequency of servicing is probably the most important consideration. An engine which has had regular and frequent oil and filter changes, as well as other required maintenance, should give many thousands of miles of reliable service. Conversely, a neglected engine may require an overhaul very early in its life.

Excessive oil consumption is an indication that piston rings, valve seals and/or valve guides are in need of attention. Make sure that oil leaks are not responsible before deciding that the rings and/or guides are worn.

Check the oil pressure with a gauge fitted in place of the oil pressure switch, and compare it with that specified. If it is extremely low, the main and big-end bearings, and/or the oil pump, are probably worn out.

Loss of power, rough running, knocking or metallic engine noises, excessive valve gear noise, and high fuel consumption may also point to the need for an overhaul, especially if they are all present at the same time. If a complete service does not remedy the situation, major mechanical work is the only solution.

An engine overhaul involves restoring all internal parts to the specification of a new engine. During an overhaul, the cylinders are rebored (where necessary) and the pistons and the piston rings are renewed. New main and big-end bearings are generally fitted; if necessary, the crankshaft may be renewed or reground, to restore the journals. The valves are also serviced as well, since they are usually in less-than-perfect condition at this point. While the engine is being overhauled, other components, such as the distributor (where applicable), starter and alternator, can be overhauled as well. The end result should be an as-new engine that will give many trouble-free miles.

Critical cooling system components such as the hoses, thermostat and water pump should be renewed when an engine is overhauled. The radiator should be checked carefully, to ensure that it is not clogged or leaking. Also, it is a good idea to renew the oil pump whenever the engine is overhauled.

Before beginning the engine overhaul, read through the entire procedure, to familiarise yourself with the scope and requirements of the job. Overhauling an engine is not difficult if you follow carefully all of the instructions, have the necessary tools and equipment, and pay close attention to all specifications. It can, however, be time-consuming. Plan on the car being off the road for a minimum of two weeks, especially if parts must be taken to an engineering works for repair or reconditioning. Check on the availability of parts, and make sure that any necessary special tools and equipment are obtained in advance. Most work can be done with typical hand tools, although a number of precision measuring tools are required for inspecting parts to determine if they must be renewed. Often the engineering works will handle the inspection of parts, and will offer advice concerning reconditioning and renewal.

Always wait until the engine has been completely dismantled, and until all components (especially the cylinder block/crankcase and the crankshaft) have been inspected, before deciding what service and repair operations must be performed by an engineering works. The condition of these components will be the major factor to consider when determining whether to overhaul the original engine, or to buy a reconditioned unit. Do not, therefore, purchase parts or have overhaul work done on other components until they have been thoroughly inspected. As a general rule, time is the primary cost of an overhaul, so it does not pay to fit worn or sub-standard parts.

As a final note, to ensure maximum life and minimum trouble from a reconditioned engine, everything must be assembled with care, in a spotlessly-clean environment.

2 Major operations only possible after removal of the engine/gearbox from the car

Note: *The engine and gearbox assembly must be lifted from the car as a complete unit, then the engine separated from the gearbox on the bench.*

The following operations can only be carried out after removal of the engine and gearbox from the car:

a) *Removal of the camshaft.*
b) *Removal of the oil pump.*
c) *Removal of the piston/connecting rod assemblies.*
d) *Renewal of the crankshaft main bearings and big-end bearings.*
e) *Removal of the tappets (cam followers) on the 1275 cc engine only.*

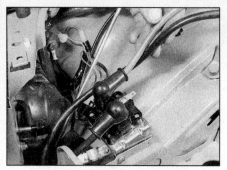

3.3 Removing the solenoid

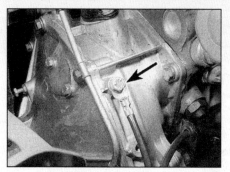

3.10 Engine earth lead location

3.27 Suitable engine lifting bracket

3 Engine/gearbox assembly - removal, examination and refitting

Removal

1 Remove the bonnet (refer to Chapter 11, if necessary) and place it securely to one side.
2 Disconnect the battery negative then positive leads, and remove the battery as described in Chapter 5.
3 Remove the solenoid and place it to one side, then unbolt and remove the battery carrier **(see illustration)**.
4 Drain the cooling system (Chapter 3).
5 Unscrew the drain plug and drain the engine/gearbox oil into a container. Refit the drain plug.
6 Remove the radiator (Chapter 3).
7 Unbolt and remove the crossmember stay. Disconnect the bonnet lock cable and remove the crossmember.
8 Remove the air cleaner (Chapter 4).
9 Disconnect the exhaust system from the manifold with reference to Chapter 4.
10 Unbolt the engine earth lead from the flywheel housing **(see illustration)**. Disconnect and remove the starter supply lead.
11 Disconnect and remove the hose from the water pump, expansion tank, and heater.
12 Disconnect the expansion tank vent pipe and heater hose from the thermostat housing.
13 Disconnect and plug the fuel supply hose from the fuel pump.
14 Where fitted, disconnect the brake servo vacuum hose from the inlet manifold.
15 Remove the clutch slave cylinder (if applicable), as described in Chapter 6, but leave it attached to the hydraulic hose.
16 Identify then disconnect the wiring from the coil low tension terminals, alternator, water temperature sender unit, and oil pressure switch.
17 Remove the cross-head screws and withdraw the air cleaner elbow from the carburettor. Remove the gasket.
18 Unscrew the speedometer cable from the gearbox and place it to one side.
19 Disconnect the choke and throttle cables from the carburettor (Chapter 4).
20 Turn the steering as necessary to allow

access from the front, and remove the rebound buffers from the subframe on both sides. The buffers are located beneath the suspension upper arms and are secured by two cross-head screws.
21 Insert distance pieces such as suitably sized nuts in place of the buffers to retain the suspension in the normal running position.
22 Apply the handbrake, jack up the front of the car, and support it on axle stands (see "*Jacking and vehicle support*").
23 On manual gearbox models, drive out the roll pin and disconnect the gear selector rod from the selector shaft. Unbolt the steady rod from the gearbox.
24 On automatic transmission models, unbolt the bellcrank cover plate from the right-hand side of the gearbox and disconnect the selector cable (refer to Chapter 7B if necessary). Disconnect the pipes from the oil cooler.
25 On all models where fitted, unbolt the exhaust downpipe bracket from the gearbox.

26 The driveshaft inner joints must now be released from the spring rings on the differential side gears. To do this use two levers but take care not to damage the differential side covers. If difficulty is experienced, rotate the front wheel slightly to a different position. Once released, the inner joints can be prevented from engaging the spring rings again by wrapping a length of thick wire or plastic tubing around the driveshaft.
27 Attach a hoist to the engine/gearbox unit; two brackets fitted to the valve cover nuts may be used for lifting **(see illustration)**. Take the weight of the unit.
28 Unscrew and remove the engine front mounting bolts, and remove the spacers, noting their location. Note that during 1982, the four point engine mounting system was replaced with a three point system, as shown **(see illustrations)**.
29 Unscrew and remove the engine rear mounting nuts, right-hand side from the top

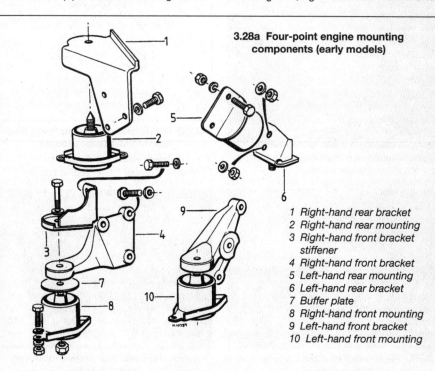

3.28a Four-point engine mounting components (early models)

1 Right-hand rear bracket
2 Right-hand rear mounting
3 Right-hand front bracket stiffener
4 Right-hand front bracket
5 Left-hand rear mounting
6 Left-hand rear bracket
7 Buffer plate
8 Right-hand front mounting
9 Left-hand front bracket
10 Left-hand front mounting

2B

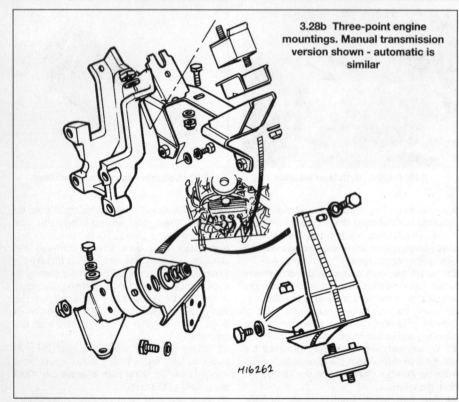

3.28b Three-point engine mountings. Manual transmission version shown - automatic is similar

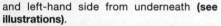

3.28c Left-hand engine mounting (from above)

3.28d Left-hand front engine mounting (from below)

and left-hand side from underneath (see illustrations).

30 Raise the engine/gearbox unit from the engine compartment and at the same time lever the driveshaft inner joints from the

differential side gears. Make sure that all wires, cables, and hoses have been disconnected, and take care not to damage any component mounted on the bulkhead or engine compartment panels (see illustrations).

31 Lower the units onto a workbench or a large piece of wood placed on the floor.

32 Refer to Chapters 7A and 7B for separation of the gearbox/transmission.

3.28e Right-hand front engine mounting (from below)

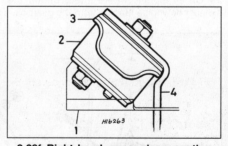

3.28f Right-hand rear engine mounting fitted to MG Turbo models

1 Subframe bracket   3 Snubber
2 Mounting rubber   4 Engine bracket

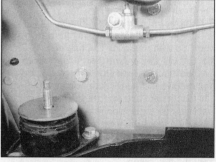

3.29a Right-hand rear engine mounting (from above) - engine removed

3.29b Right-hand rear engine mounting (from below)

3.29c Left-hand rear engine mounting (from below)

3.30a Removing the engine/gearbox

3.30b Engine compartment with engine/gearbox removed

5.1a Left-hand rear engine mounting

5.1b Oil pressure switch

Examination

33 With the engine completely stripped, clean all the components and examine them for wear. Each part should be checked, and where necessary renewed or renovated as described in the following Sections. Renew main and big-end shell bearings as a matter of course, unless you know that they have had little wear and are in perfect condition.

Refitting

34 Refitting is a reversal of the removal procedure, but note the following additional points:

a) *Insert the left-hand side driveshaft into the differential unit first, then twist the engine and insert the right-hand side driveshaft.*

b) *Adjust the choke and throttle cables (Chapter 4).*

c) *Refill the engine/gearbox with oil.*

d) *Refill the cooling system (Chapter 3).*

e) *On automatic transmission models adjust the selector cable (Chapter 7B).*

4 Engine - dismantling and reassembly

Dismantling

1 If possible, mount the engine on a stand for the dismantling procedure, but failing this, support it in an upright position with blocks of wood placed under each side of the crankcase.

2 Cleanliness is most important, and if the engine is dirty, it should be cleaned with paraffin while keeping it in an upright position.

3 Avoid working with the engine directly on a concrete floor, as grit presents a real source of trouble.

4 As parts are removed, clean them in a paraffin bath. However, do not immerse parts with internal oilways in paraffin as it is difficult to remove, usually requiring a high pressure hose. Clean oilways with nylon pipe cleaners.

5 It is advisable to have containers to hold small items according to their use, as this will help when reassembling the engine and also prevent possible losses.

6 Always obtain complete sets of gaskets when the engine is being dismantled, but retain the old gaskets with a view to using them as a pattern to make a replacement if a new one is not available.

7 When possible, refit nuts, bolts, and washers in their location after being removed, as this helps to protect the threads and will also be helpful when reassembling the engine.

8 Retain unserviceable components in order to compare them with the new parts supplied.

Reassembly

9 The following sections deal with examining and replacing the various components, however note the following.

10 To ensure maximum life with minimum trouble from a rebuilt engine, not only must everything be correctly assembled, but it must also be spotlessly clean. All oilways must be clear, and locking washers and spring washers must be fitted where indicated. Oil all bearings and other working surfaces thoroughly with engine oil during assembly.

11 Before assembly begins, renew any bolts or studs with damaged threads.

12 Gather together a torque wrench, oil can, clean rag, and a set of engine gaskets and oil seals, together with a new oil filter cartridge.

5 Ancillary components - general

General

1 With the engine separated from the gearbox, the externally mounted ancillary components can be removed. For further details on these items refer to the appropriate Chapter.

a) *Inlet and exhaust manifold and carburettor (Chapter 4).*

b) *Fuel pump (Chapter 4).*

c) *Alternator (Chapter 5).*

d) *HT leads and spark plugs (Chapter 5).*

e) *Oil filter (Chapter 1).*

f) *Rear engine mountings and brackets* **(see illustration).**

g) *Distributor (Chapter 5).*

h) *Dipstick.*

i) *Oil pressure switch* **(see illustration)** *and water temperature switch.*

j) *Water pump (Chapter 3).*

k) *Thermostat (Chapter 3).*

6 Cylinder head - dismantling, overhaul and reassembly

Note: *For details on the cylinder head removal and refitting, refer to Chapter 2A.*

Dismantling

1 Using a valve spring compressor, compress each valve spring in turn until the split collets can be removed **(see illustration)**. Release the compressor and remove the cup and spring. If the cups are difficult to release, do not continue to tighten the compressor, but gently tap the top of the tool with a hammer. Always make sure that the compressor is held firmly over the cup.

2 On the 1275 cc engine remove the oil seals from the inlet valve guides **(see illustration)**. A small seal may also be fitted at the bottom of the collet groove on the valve stems.

6.1 Removing the valve split collets

6.2 Removing an inlet valve guide oil seal (1275 cc engine)

2B

6.3a Removing an inlet valve

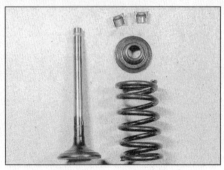

6.3b Valve components

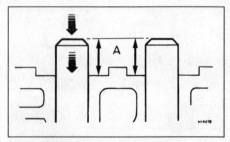

6.13 Valve guide fitted height dimension "A"

Arrow indicates direction of removal and refitting

3 Remove each valve from the combustion chambers keeping them in their order of removal, together with the respective valve springs and cups **(see illustrations)**. Identify each valve according to the cylinder, remembering that No 1 cylinder is at the thermostat end of the cylinder head.

Overhaul

4 The operation will normally only be required at comparatively high mileage. However, if persistent pinking occurs and performance has deteriorated even though the engine adjustments are correct, decarbonising and valve grinding may be required.

5 With the cylinder head removed, use a scraper to remove the carbon from the combustion chambers and ports. Remove all traces of gasket from the cylinder head surface, then wash it thoroughly with paraffin.

6 Use a straight edge and feeler blade to check that the cylinder head surface is not distorted. If it is, it must be resurfaced by a suitably equipped engineering works.

7 If the engine is still in the car, clean the piston crowns and cylinder bore upper edges, but make sure that no carbon drops between the pistons and bores. To do this, locate two of the pistons at the top of their bores and seal off the remaining bores with paper and masking tape. Press a little grease between the two pistons and their bores to collect any carbon dust; this can be wiped away when the piston is lowered. To prevent carbon build-up, polish the piston crown with metal polish, but remove all traces of the polish afterwards.

8 Examine the heads of the valves for pitting and burning, especially the exhaust valve heads. Renew any valve which is badly burnt. Examine the valve seats at the same time. If the pitting is very slight, it can be removed by grinding the valve heads and seats together with coarse, then fine, grinding paste.

9 Where excessive pitting has occurred, the valve seats must be recut or renewed by a suitably equipped engineering works.

10 Valve grinding is carried out as follows. Place the cylinder head upside down on a bench with a block of wood at each end to give clearance for the valve stems.

11 Smear a trace of coarse carborundum paste on the seat face and press a suction grinding tool onto the valve head. With a semi-rotary action, grind the valve head to its seat, lifting the valve occasionally to redistribute the grinding paste. When a dull matt even surface is produced on both the valve seat and the valve, wipe off the paste and repeat the process with fine carborundum paste as before. A light spring placed under the valve head will greatly ease this operation. When a smooth unbroken ring of light grey matt finish is produced on both the valve and seat, the grinding operation is complete.

12 Scrape away all carbon from the valve head and stem, and clean away all traces of grinding compound. Clean the valves and seats with a paraffin soaked rag, then wipe with a clean rag.

13 If the valve guides are worn, indicated by a side-to-side motion of the valve, new guides must be fitted. To do this, use a mandrel to press the worn guides downwards and out through the combustion chamber. Press the new guides into the cylinder head in the same direction until they are at the specified fitted height **(see illustration)**.

14 If the original valve springs have been in use for 20 000 miles (32 000 km) or more, renew them. Where fitted, the inlet valve oil seals should also be renewed whenever the cylinder head is dismantled.

15 Examine the pushrods and rocker shaft assembly for wear and renew them as necessary. Dismantling and reassembly of the rocker components is straightforward **(see illustration)**.

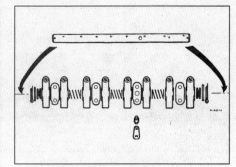

6.15 Rocker shaft components

Reassembly

16 The valve stem oil seals fitted to the larger engine, are now fitted to the smaller engine as well. This has the effect of reducing oil consumption.

17 The fitting of the seals has also required the fitting of modified valves (with cotter grooves nearer the end of the stem). The valve spring seat has also been raised by 0.05 in (1.2 mm).

18 New type valves and seals can be fitted to old type cylinder heads, in complete sets only, with the addition of a shim 0.05 in (1.2 mm) thick underneath each spring. These shims may also be found already fitted to engines which left the factory with new type valves and seals in unmodified heads.

19 Fit the valves in their original sequence or, if new valves have been obtained, to the seat to which they have been ground.

20 Oil the valve stems liberally and, on the 1275 cc engine, fit the oil seals to the inlet valve guides and collet grooves where applicable.

21 Working on one valve, fit the spring and cup, then compress the spring with the compressor and insert the split collets. Release the compressor and remove it.

22 Repeat the procedure on the remaining valves. Tap the end of each valve stem with a non-metallic mallet to settle the collets.

7 Camshaft - removal, examination and refitting

Removal

1 Remove the engine and gearbox as described in Section 3. It is not necessary to separate the engine from the gearbox, unless the tappets are to be removed on the 1275 cc engine.

2 Remove the rocker cover, rocker shaft, and pushrods.

3 On the 998 cc engine, remove the tappets as described in Chapter 2A.

4 On both the 998 cc and 1275 cc engines, remove the distributor (Chapter 5) and the fuel pump (Chapter 4).

5 Using a ⁵⁄₁₆ in bolt, remove the distributor

7.5 Removing the distributor driveshaft

7.8 Removing the camshaft locating plate

7.9 Removing the camshaft on the 1275 cc engine (crankshaft removed for clarity)

driveshaft from the cylinder block **(see illustration)**.

6 Remove the timing cover, chain, and gears as described in Chapter 2A.

7 On the 1275cc engine, invert the engine so that the tappets are clear of the camshaft.

8 Unbolt the camshaft locating plate from the engine front plate **(see illustration)**.

9 Withdraw the camshaft from the timing chain end of the cylinder block, taking care not to damage the three camshaft bearings as the lobes of the cams pass through them **(see illustration)**.

10 If the 1275 cc engine is separated from the gearbox, remove the tappets keeping them identified for location **(see illustration)**. If the 1275 cc engine is not separated from the gearbox, do not place it upright otherwise the tappets will fall into the gearbox.

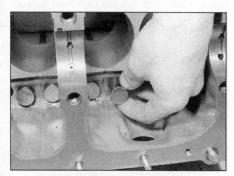

7.10 Removing the tappets (1275 cc engine)

Examination

11 Examine the camshaft bearing surfaces, cam lobes, and skew gear for wear. If excessive, renew the shaft.

12 Check the locating plate for wear and renew it if necessary.

13 Check the camshaft bearings for wear and if necessary remove them with a length of tubing. Fit the new prefinished bearings with their oil holes aligned with the oilways in the cylinder block.

14 Examine the tappets for wear and renew them if necessary.

Refitting

15 If the 1275 cc engine is separated from the gearbox, lubricate the tappets with engine oil and insert them in their original locations with the engine inverted.

16 Oil the camshaft bearings and carefully insert the camshaft from the timing chain end of the cylinder block. Make sure that the oil pump spindle engages the slot in the camshaft.

17 Fit the locating plate to the front plate and tighten the bolts evenly.

18 Temporarily refit the camshaft sprocket then, using a dial gauge, vernier calipers, or feeler blade and bridging piece, check that the camshaft endfloat is within the specified limits. If not, renew the locating plate.

19 With the engine upright, refit the timing cover, chain, and gears as described in Chapter 2A.

20 Turn the engine until No 1 piston is at top

dead centre (TDC) on the compression stroke. If the cylinder head is not yet fitted, use two pushrods to determine the point when No 4 cylinder valves are rocking - in this position No 1 piston is at TDC compression.

21 Using the ⁵⁄₁₆ in bolt, insert the distributor driveshaft into the cylinder block with the larger segment uppermost, and the slot in the 4 o'clock position. As the driveshaft engages the skew gear on the camshaft, it will turn anti-clockwise to the 2 o'clock position. Remove the bolt **(see illustrations)**.

22 Refit the distributor (Chapter 5) and the fuel pump (Chapter 4).

23 On the 998 cc engine refit the tappets as described in Chapter 2A.

24 Refit the pushrods and rocker shaft and adjust the tappets as described in Chapter 2A. Refit the rocker cover.

25 Refit the engine and gearbox as described in Section 3.

2B

8 Oil pump - removal, overhaul and refitting

Removal

1 Remove the engine and gearbox as described in Section 3.

2 Remove the flywheel/torque converter housing with reference to Chapters 7A and 7B.

3 On automatic transmission models only, remove the oil feed pipe from the oil pump.

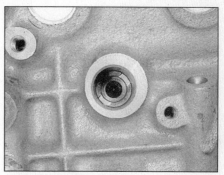

7.21a Distributor driveshaft fitting procedure

1 Initial fitting position 2 Fitted position

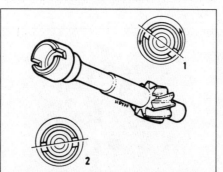

7.21b Distributor driveshaft fitting procedure for 1985-on 1.3 models

1 Initial fitting position 2 Fitted position (TDC)

7.21c Installed position of the distributor driveshaft

8.4a Removing the oil pump . . .

8.5 Removing the oil pump cover

8.4b . . . and gasket

4 On all models, flatten the lockwashers, then unbolt the oil pump from the cylinder block and remove the gasket **(see illustrations)**.

Overhaul

5 Remove the retaining screw and withdraw the cover from the locating dowels **(see illustration)**.
6 Lift the two rotors from the pump body.
7 Clean the components with paraffin and wipe dry.
8 Refit the rotors to the pump body, making sure that the chamfer on the outer rotor enters the body first.
9 Using a feeler blade, and where necessary a straight edge, check that the rotor clearances are as given in the Specifications **(see illustrations)**. If any clearance is outside that specified, or if damage is evident on any component, renew the complete oil pump.
10 If the oil pump is serviceable, refit the

cover and tighten the retaining screw. Operate the pump in clean engine oil to prime it.

Refitting

Note: *Prime the pump with clean engine oil before fitting.*
11 Make sure that the mating faces of the oil pump and cylinder block are clean, then fit the oil pump together with a new gasket, and tighten the retaining bolts evenly to the specified torque (see *"Specifications"* in Chapter 2A). Make sure that the cut-outs in the gasket are correctly aligned with the pump, and, if the camshaft is already in position, make sure that the pump spindle engages the slot in the camshaft.
12 Bend the lockwashers to lock the bolts.
13 On automatic transmission models only, fit the oil feed pipe together with new O-rings if necessary.

14 If the engine and gearbox were removed purposely to remove the oil pump, refit the flywheel/torque converter housing with reference to Chapter 7A and 7B, and refit the engine and gearbox as described in Section 3.

9 Pistons and connecting rods - removal, overhaul and refitting

Removal

1 Remove the engine and gearbox as described in Section 3.
2 Separate the engine from the gearbox as described in Chapters 7A and 7B.
3 Remove the cylinder head (Chapter 2A).
4 Check the big-end caps for identification marks. If necessary, use a centre punch on the caps and connecting rods to identify them; mark them on the camshaft side to ensure correct refitting.

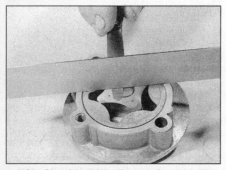

8.9a Checking the oil pump inner rotor endfloat . . .

8.9b . . . outer rotor endfloat . . .

8.9c . . . outer rotor clearance . . .

8.9d . . . rotor lobe clearance (central) . . .

8.9e . . . and rotor lobe clearance (off centre)

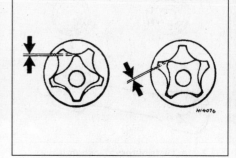

8.9f Oil pump rotor lobe clearance checking points

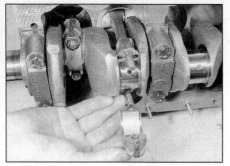

9.6 Removing a big-end bearing cap

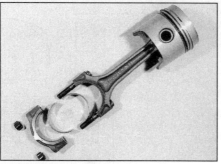

9.10 Piston and connecting rod components (1275 cc engine)

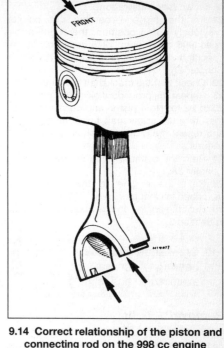

9.14 Correct relationship of the piston and connecting rod on the 998 cc engine

5 Turn the crankshaft so that No 1 crankpin is at its lowest point. Using a ½ in AF socket, unscrew the big-end bearing bolts (998 cc) or nuts (1275 cc).

6 Withdraw the cap complete with the bearing shell **(see illustration)**.

7 Using the handle of a hammer, tap the piston and connecting rod from the bore and withdraw it from the top of the cylinder block.

8 Loosely refit the cap to the connecting rod.

9 Repeat the procedure given in paragraphs, 5 to 8 on No 4 piston and connecting rod, then turn the crankshaft through half a turn and repeat the procedure on No 2 and No 3 pistons.

Overhaul

10 Examine the pistons for ovality, scoring, and scratches. Check the connecting rods for wear and damage **(see illustration)**.

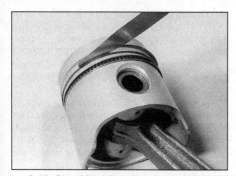

9.17 Checking the compression ring groove clearance (1275 cc engine)

11 If the pistons or connecting rods are to be renewed on the 1275 cc engine and 1987-on 998 cc engines, it is recommended that this work is carried out by a Rover dealer, who will have the necessary tooling to extract the gudgeon pins from the connecting rods.

12 To remove the pistons from the connecting rods on the 998 cc engine, extract the circlips and push out the gudgeon pin. If the ambient temperature is below 20°C (68°F), heat the piston in hot water first.

13 Check the small-end bushes for wear, and if necessary have a Rover dealer fit and ream new bushes.

14 Lubricate the gudgeon pin and bores with graphite oil, then locate the connecting rod in the piston as shown **(see illustration)**, and press in the gudgeon pin. Note that the diagonal split on the connecting rod must face the camshaft side of the piston. Fit the circlips.

15 If new rings are to be fitted to the original pistons, expand the old rings over the top of the pistons. The use of two or three old feeler blades will be helpful in preventing the rings dropping into empty grooves. Note that the oil control ring is in three sections.

16 Before fitting the new rings to the piston, insert them into the cylinder bore and use a feeler blade to check that the end gaps are within the specified limits.

17 After fitting the rings, check the compression rings for groove clearances using a feeler blade **(see illustration)**. Make sure that the word "Top", where marked on the compression rings, is towards the top of

the piston. Arrange the compression ring gaps at 90 degrees to each other on the camshaft side of the piston.

Refitting

18 Clean the backs of the bearing shells and the recesses in the connecting rods and big-end caps.

19 Press the big-end bearing shells into the connecting rods and caps in their correct positions and oil them liberally **(see illustrations)**.

20 Fit a ring compressor to No 1 piston, then insert the piston and connecting rod into No 1 cylinder. With No 1 crankpin at its lowest point, drive the piston carefully into the cylinder with the wooden handle of a hammer, and at the same time guide the connecting rod onto the crankpin **(see illustration)**. Make sure that the "Front" mark on the piston

2B

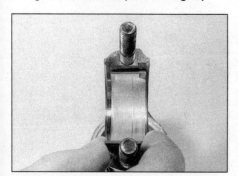

9.19a Installing a big-end bearing shell

9.19b Lubricating a crankpin

9.20a Installing a piston and connecting rod

crown is facing the timing chain end of the engine, and that the connecting rod offset is as shown **(see illustration)**.

21 Fit the big-end bearing cap in its previously noted position, then tighten the bolts (998 cc) or nuts (1275 cc) evenly to the specified torque (see "*Specifications*" in Chapter 2A).

22 Check that the crankshaft turns freely.

23 Repeat the procedure given in paragraphs 20 to 22 for No 4 piston and connecting rod, then turn the crankshaft through half a turn and repeat the procedure on No 2 and No 3 pistons.

24 Refit the cylinder head as described in Chapter 2A.

25 Refit the engine to the gearbox as described in Chapters 7A and 7B.

26 Refit the engine and gearbox as described in Section 3.

---

10 Crankshaft and main bearings - removal, examination and refitting

Removal

1 Follow the procedure for removing the pistons and connecting rods described in Section 9, but it is not necessary to completely remove them from the cylinder block.

2 Remove the timing cover, chain, and gears as described in Chapter 2A.

3 Unbolt the front plate from the engine, and remove the gasket **(see illustration)**. Invert the engine.

10.3 Removing the engine front plate

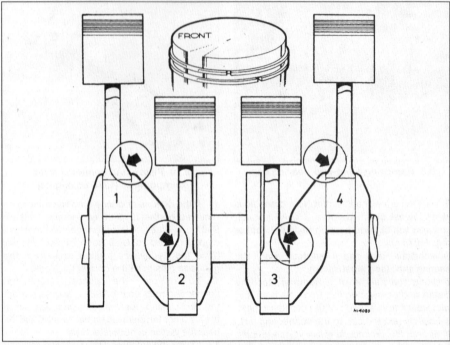

9.20b Diagram showing connecting rod offset - arrowed

4 Check the main bearing caps for identification marks, and if necessary use a centre punch to identify them.

5 Before removing the crankshaft, check that the endfloat is within the specified limits by inserting a feeler blade between the centre crankshaft web and the thrustwashers **(see illustration)**. This will indicate whether new thrustwashers are required or not.

6 Unscrew the bolts and remove the main bearing caps complete with bearing shells. Recover the thrustwashers from the centre main bearing cap.

7 Lift the crankshaft from the crankcase and remove the remaining centre bearing thrustwashers **(see illustration)**.

8 Extract the bearing shells from the crankcase recesses and the caps, and identify them for location **(see illustration)**.

Examination

9 Examine the bearing surfaces of the crankshaft for scratches or scoring and, using a micrometer, check each journal and crankpin for ovality. Where this is found to be in excess of 0.001 in (0.0254 mm) the crankshaft will have to be reground and undersize bearings fitted.

10 Crankshaft regrinding should be carried out by an engineering works, who will normally supply the matching undersize main and big-end shell bearings.

11 If the crankshaft endfloat is more than the maximum specified amount, new thrustwashers should be fitted to the centre main bearing; these are usually supplied together with the main and big-end bearings on a reground crankshaft.

12 During 1982, modifications were made to the cylinder block and main bearing caps. The lower main bearing shells fitted to these modified units are plain, i.e. they have no central oil groove. Both engine sizes are affected.

13 Make sure that the correct type shells are obtained when engine overhaul is undertaken.

10.5 Checking the crankshaft endfloat with a feeler blade

10.7 Removing the crankshaft

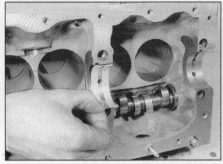

10.8 Removing a main bearing shell

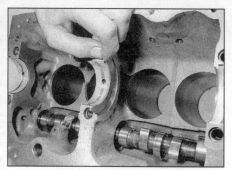

10.21 Installing the centre main bearing thrustwashers

10.22 Installing the centre main bearing cap and thrustwashers

10.23 Tightening the main bearing cap bolts

The new and old type bearings are not interchangeable.

14 Selective-fit main bearing shells are fitted to all later 1275 cc engine crankshafts, the journal diameters, main bearing bores and shell thickness' being grouped into three tolerance bands that are identified by Red, Green or Yellow colour codes.

15 The codes are in the form either of appropriately-coloured dye or of the stamped letter "R", "G" or "Y". The codes identifying each crankshaft journal are located on the adjacent web; note that all crankshafts supplied in service are coded Green. If dye is used to identify the bearing bores it is applied to the appropriate cap, while if letters are used they are stamped into the centre main bearing block, their location respective to each other showing the bearing to which they refer.

16 If the bearing shells are to be renewed and both the cylinder block and crankshaft are coded, select the shells according to the accompanying table.

17 If the bearing shells are to be renewed but the cylinder block is not coded, fit a set of Green-coded shells, temporarily refit the crankshaft and use Plastigage to check the bearing running clearance. If the clearance is excessive, fit a set of Red-coded shells; if it is too small, fit a set of Yellow-coded shells.

18 If the crankshaft is thought to need regrinding, seek the advice of a Rover dealer as to whether undersize shells are available.

Refitting

Note: *Read Section 11, before proceeding.*

19 Clean the backs of the bearing shells and the bearing recesses in both the cylinder block and main bearing caps.

20 Press the main bearing shells into the cylinder block and caps and oil them liberally.

21 Using a little grease, stick the thrustwashers to each side of the centre main bearings with their oilways facing away from the bearing **(see illustration)**. Similarly fit the thrustwashers to the centre main bearing cap.

22 Lower the crankshaft into position, then fit the main bearing caps in their previously noted locations **(see illustration)**.

23 Insert and tighten evenly the main bearing cap bolts to the specified torque (see "*Specifications*" in Chapter 2A) **(see illustration)**. Check that the crankshaft rotates freely, then check that the endfloat is within the specified limits by inserting a feeler blade between the centre crankshaft web and the thrustwashers.

24 Smear the front plate gasket with sealing compound and locate it on the front of the cylinder block. Fit the engine front plate and tighten the two lower retaining bolts.

25 With the engine upright, refit the timing cover, chain, and gears as described in Chapter 2A.

26 Refit the pistons and connecting rods as described in Section 9.

11 Cylinder block and crankcase - examination and overhaul

Examination

1 The cylinder bores must be examined for taper, ovality, scoring, and scratches. Start by examining the top of the bores: if these are worn, a slight ridge will be found which marks the top of the piston ring travel. If the wear is excessive, the engine will have had a high oil consumption rate accompanied by blue smoke from the exhaust.

2 If available, use an inside dial gauge to measure the bore diameter just below the ridge and compare it with the diameter at the bottom of the bore, which is not subject to wear. If the difference is more than 0.006 in (0.152 mm), the cylinders will normally require reboring with new oversize pistons fitted.

3 Provided the cylinder bore wear does not exceed 0.008 in (0.203 mm), however, special oil control rings and pistons can be fitted to restore compression and stop the engine burning oil.

Overhaul

4 If new pistons are being fitted to old bores, it is essential to roughen the bore walls slightly with fine glasspaper to enable the new piston rings to bed in properly.

5 Thoroughly examine the crankcase and cylinder block for cracks and damage and use a piece of wire to probe all oilways and waterways to ensure that they are unobstructed.

Cylinder block code	Crankshaft code cylinder block	Upper (grooved) bearing shell - bearing cap	Lower (plain) bearing shell -
Red	Red	Red	Red
Red	Green	Red	Green
Red	Yellow	Green	Green
Green	Red	Green	Red
Green	Green	Green	Green
Green	Yellow	Green	Yellow
Yellow	Red	Green	Green
Yellow	Green	Yellow	Green
Yellow	Yellow	Yellow	Yellow

Main bearing shell identification table - see paragraph 16

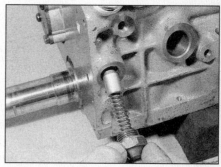

11.7 Removing the oil pressure relief valve

2B

6 Check the tappet bores for wear and scoring; if excessive, they can be reamed and oversize tappets fitted.

7 Unscrew the oil pressure relief valve cap and remove the valve and spring **(see illustration)**. Check the valve seating for excessive wear and check that the spring free length is as specified. Renew the valve and spring as necessary, and refit them to the cylinder block.

12 Engine - adjustment after major overhaul

Adjustment

1 With the engine/gearbox refitted to the car, make a final check to ensure that everything has been reconnected and that no rags or tools have been left in the engine compartment.

2 If new pistons or crankshaft bearings have been fitted, turn the carburettor slow running screw in about half a turn to compensate for the initial tightness of the new components.

3 Pull the choke fully out and start the engine. This may take a little longer than usual as the fuel pump and carburettor float chamber may be empty.

4 As soon as the engine starts, push in the choke until the engine runs at a fast tickover. Check that the oil pressure light goes out.

5 Check the oil filter, fuel hoses, and water hoses for leaks.

6 Run the engine until normal operating temperature is reached, then adjust the slow running as described in Chapter 4.

7 Drive the car for five to ten miles, then allow the engine to cool and remove the valve cover. Working in the order shown (see illustration 4.3 in Chapter 2A), loosen half a turn, then immediately tighten, each cylinder head nut to the specified torque (see *"Specifications"* in Chapter 2A). After the engine has completely cooled, readjust the valve clearances as described in Chapter 2A, then refit the valve cover.

8 If new pistons or crankshaft bearings have been fitted, the engine must be run-in for the first 500 miles (800 km). Do not exceed 45 mph (72 km/h), operate the engine at full throttle, or allow the engine to labour in any gear.

Chapter 3
Cooling, heating and ventilation systems

Contents

Degrees of difficulty

| Easy, suitable for novice with little experience | Fairly easy, suitable for beginner with some experience | Fairly difficult, suitable for competent DIY mechanic | Difficult, suitable for experienced DIY mechanic | Very difficult, suitable for expert DIY or professional |

Specifications

System type	Thermo-syphon with belt driven pump, pressurised front mounted radiator and electric cooling fan
Expansion tank cap pressure	15 lbf/in2 (1.05 kgf/cm2)
Thermostat opens at	88°C (190°F)
Drivebelt tension	0.16 in (4 mm) deflection between water pump and alternator pulleys under load of 7.5 to 8.2 lbf (33 to 36 Nm)
System capacity (including heater)	8.5 Imp pints (4.9 litres)

Torque wrench settings	lbf ft	Nm
MG Turbo		
Coolant drain plug	27	37
Coolant temperature transmitter	40	55
Other models		
Coolant temperature transmitter	14	20
Cylinder head outlet elbow nuts	8	11
Water pump bolts	16	22
Water pump pulley	8	11

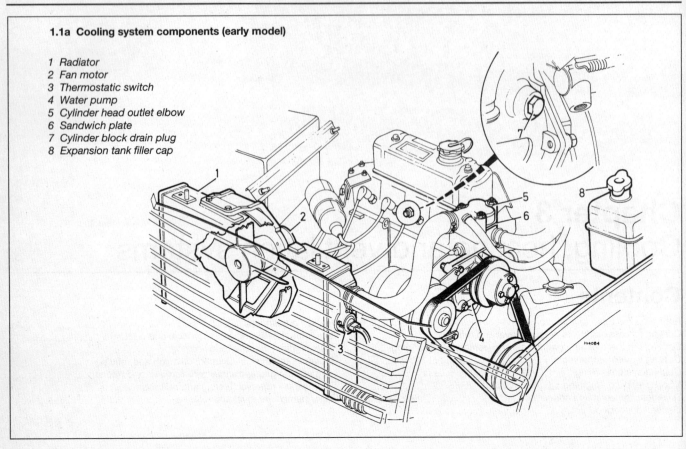

1.1a Cooling system components (early model)

1 Radiator
2 Fan motor
3 Thermostatic switch
4 Water pump
5 Cylinder head outlet elbow
6 Sandwich plate
7 Cylinder block drain plug
8 Expansion tank filler cap

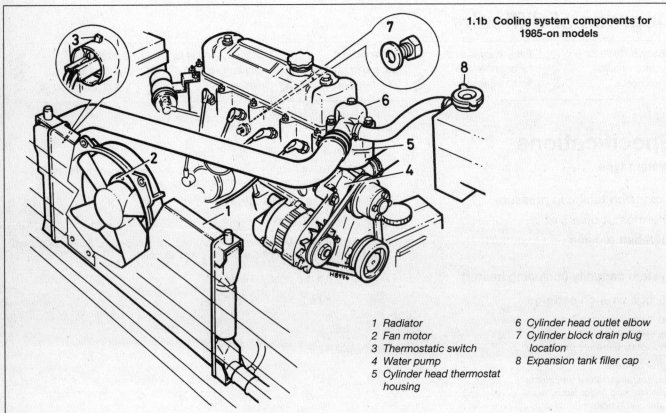

1.1b Cooling system components for 1985-on models

1 Radiator
2 Fan motor
3 Thermostatic switch
4 Water pump
5 Cylinder head thermostat housing

6 Cylinder head outlet elbow
7 Cylinder block drain plug location
8 Expansion tank filler cap

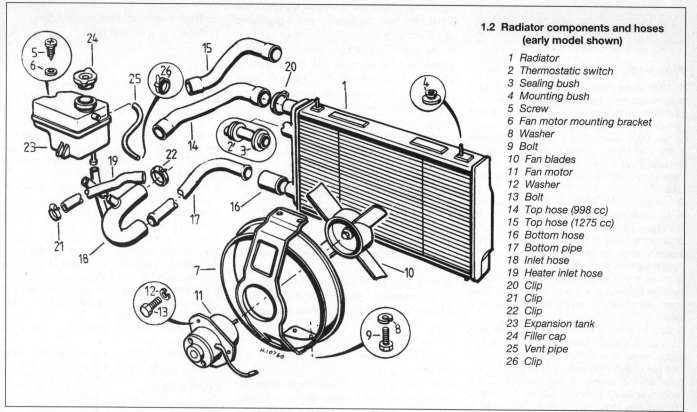

1. Radiator
2. Thermostatic switch
3. Sealing bush
4. Mounting bush
5. Screw
6. Fan motor mounting bracket
8. Washer
9. Bolt
10. Fan blades
11. Fan motor
12. Washer
13. Bolt
14. Top hose (998 cc)
15. Top hose (1275 cc)
16. Bottom hose
17. Bottom pipe
18. Inlet hose
19. Heater inlet hose
20. Clip
21. Clip
22. Clip
23. Expansion tank
24. Filler cap
25. Vent pipe
26. Clip

1 General description

1 The cooling system is of pressurised type and includes a front mounted radiator, belt driven water pump and an electric cooling fan. The thermostat is located in the water outlet at the front of the cylinder head. The radiator is of aluminium construction with plastic end tanks, and is not provided with a drain plug. On later models (1985-on) the radiator thickness has been reduced considerably, but its length has been increased. The radiator top hose inlet is now at the top right-hand side of the radiator (see illustrations). A drain plug is, however, provided at the rear right-hand side of the cylinder block.

2 The system functions as follows. Cold water in the bottom of the radiator circulates through the bottom hose and metal pipe to the water pump, where the pump impeller pushes the water around the cylinder block and head passages. After cooling the cylinder bores, combustion surfaces, and valve seats, the water reaches the underside of the thermostat which is initially closed, and is diverted through the heater inlet hose to the heater. After leaving the heater the water is returned to the water pump inlet hose. When the engine is cold, the thermostat remains closed and the water circulates only through the engine and heater. When the coolant reaches the predetermined temperature (see "Specifications"), the thermostat opens and the water passes

through the top hose to the top of the radiator. As the water circulates down through the radiator, it is cooled by the in-rush of air when the car is in forward motion, supplemented by the action of the electric cooling fan when necessary. Having reached the bottom of the radiator, the water is now cooled and the cycle is repeated (see illustration).

3 The electric cooling fan is controlled by a thermostatic switch located in the left-hand side radiator tank. Water temperature is monitored by a sender unit located beneath the thermostat in the cylinder head.

4 On some models where the radiator bottom hose incorporates a take-off point for the oil cooler and/or heater matrix, take care not to push the connecting pipe so far into the hose that the take-off point is blocked (see illustration).

1.4 Bottom hose with take-off for oil cooler

5 Correct fitting of this hose should be checked if problems are experienced with poor heater output.

2 Cooling system - draining

 Warning: Drain the cooling system when the engine has cooled.

Draining

1 It is preferable to drain the cooling system when the engine has cooled. If this is not possible, place a cloth over the expansion tank filler cap and turn it slowly in an anti-clockwise direction until the first stop is reached, then wait until all the pressure has been released.

2 Remove the filler cap.

3 Place a container beneath the left-hand side of the radiator.

4 Loosen the clip and ease the bottom hose away from the radiator outlet. Drain the coolant into the container.

5 Place a second container beneath the cylinder block drain plug located on the rear right-hand side next to the clutch slave cylinder. If necessary, remove the hot air stove from the exhaust manifold (Chapter 4), to improve access to the drain plug. Unscrew the plug and drain the coolant.

3

3 Cooling system - flushing

Flushing

1 After some time the radiator and engine waterways may become restricted or even blocked with scale or sediment, which reduces the efficiency of the cooling system. When this occurs, the coolant will appear rusty and dark in colour and the system should then be flushed. In severe cases, reverse flushing may be required as described later.

2 Disconnect the top hose from the cylinder head outlet elbow, and the bottom hose from the radiator outlet.

3 Insert a hose in the top hose, and allow water to circulate through the radiator until it runs clear from the outlet.

4 Insert the hose in the expansion tank filler neck and allow water to run out of the cylinder head outlet elbow and bottom hose until clear.

5 Disconnect the heater inlet hose from the front of the cylinder head, insert the hose, and allow water to circulate through the heater and out through the bottom hose until clear.

6 In severe cases of contamination, the system should be reverse flushed. To do this, remove the radiator, invert it, and insert a hose in the outlet. Continue flushing until clear water runs from the inlet.

7 If the engine is to be reverse flushed, remove the thermostat, and insert a hose into the cylinder head. Continue flushing until clear water runs from the cylinder block drain plug and bottom hose.

8 The use of any good proprietary cleaning agent may be necessary if the system is severely contaminated (always read manufacturers instructions). Reverse flushing is also recommended to cleanse the cooling system and restore maximum efficiency. To prevent contamination occurring in future, regular renewal of the antifreeze is necessary.

4 Cooling system - filling

Filling

1 Reconnect the radiator bottom hose and heater hose.

2 Refit the thermostat if removed, and reconnect the top hose to the outlet elbow.

3 Insert and tighten the cylinder block drain plug.

4 Pour coolant into the expansion tank filler neck until it reaches the level mark, then refit the cap.

5 Run the engine at a fast idling speed for three minutes, then stop the engine and check the level in the expansion tank. Top-up level as necessary, being careful to release pressure from the system before removing the filler cap if necessary.

5 Radiator - removal, inspection, cleaning and refitting

Removal

1 Disconnect the battery negative lead.

2 Drain the cooling system as described in Section 2.

3 Unscrew the bonnet lock cross panel securing screws and central bolt, and move the headlamp shrouds (if fitted). Remove the screws (early models) and lift the grille from its mountings **(see illustrations)**.

4 Position the bonnet lock cross panel to one side leaving the release cable still attached.

5 Loosen the clip and disconnect the top hose from the radiator.

6 Pull the plug connector from the thermostatic switch on the left-hand side of the radiator. Disconnect the plug and socket in the cooling fan motor supply leads.

7 Lift the radiator and fan assembly from the lower location pegs, and remove it from the car **(see illustrations)**.

8 Unbolt the electric cooling fan assembly from the radiator.

9 Release the thermostatic switch and sealing bush from the radiator.

Inspection

10 Radiator repair is best left to a specialist, but minor leaks may be repaired using a proprietary coolant additive, with the radiator *in situ* (always read the manufacturers instructions).

5.3a **Removing the front cross panel strut bolt**

5.3b **Removing the front cross panel mounting screws**

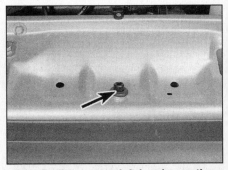

5.3c **Radiator upper left-hand mounting (arrowed)**

5.3d **Removing the front grille - lower mounting shown**

5.7a **Radiator lower location point (arrowed)**

5.7b **Radiator and cooling fan assembly**

Cleaning

11 Clear the radiator matrix of flies and small leaves with a soft brush or by hosing. Reverse flush the radiator as described in Section 3. Renew the top and bottom hoses and clips if they are damaged or deteriorated.

Refitting

12 Refitting is a reversal of removal, but always fit a new sealing bush to the thermostatic switch and extra care is necessary to ensure that the locating pins enter the mounting bushes **(see illustration)**. Fill the cooling system as described in Section 4.

6 Thermostat - removal, testing and refitting

Removal

1 Remove the expansion tank filler cap. If the engine is still hot, place a cloth over the cap and turn it slowly anti-clockwise until the first stop is reached, then wait until all the pressure has been released.
2 Place a clean container beneath the radiator outlet, then disconnect the bottom hose and drain approximately 4 pints (2.3 litres) of coolant. Reconnect the bottom hose and tighten the clip.
3 Unscrew the three nuts and lift the outlet elbow from the sandwich plate. Peel off the gasket **(see illustration)**.
4 Withdraw the thermostat from its seat in the sandwich plate **(see illustration)**.

Testing

5 To test whether the unit is serviceable, suspend it with a piece of string in a container of water. Gradually heat the water and note the temperature at which the thermostat starts to open. Remove the thermostat from the water and check that it is fully closed when cold.

5.12 Bonnet lock cross panel/radiator location pin

6 Renew the thermostat if the opening temperature is not as specified, or if the unit does not fully close when cold.
7 If the sandwich plate-to-cylinder head gasket has been disturbed, clean up the mating faces and fit a new gasket.

Refitting

8 Refitting is a reversal of removal, but use a new gasket and ensure that the spring support pillars do not obstruct the heater outlet in the sandwich plate. Top-up the cooling system with reference to Section 4.

7 Water pump - removal and refitting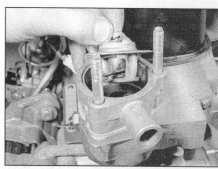

Removal

1 Disconnect the battery negative lead.
2 Remove the drivebelt as described in Chapter 1.
3 Remove the alternator adjustment nut and pivot bolts. Place the alternator to one side.
4 Remove the windscreen washer bottle and place it to one side. Unscrew the four bolts and remove the pulley from the water pump **(see illustration)**.

6.3 Removing the outlet elbow

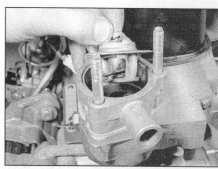

6.4 Removing the thermostat

5 Drain the cooling system as described in Section 2.
6 Loosen the clip and disconnect the inlet hose from the water pump.
7 Unscrew and remove the water pump retaining bolts, noting their length and location.
8 Using a soft-faced mallet, tap the water pump from the two locating dowels and remove it from the cylinder block **(see illustration)**. Remove the gasket.
9 If the water pump is faulty, renew it, as Rover do not supply individual components separately.

3

7.4 Removing the water pump pulley

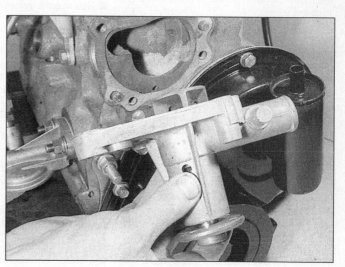

7.8 Removing the water pump

10 Clean the mating faces of the water pump and cylinder block.

Refitting

11 Refitting is a reversal of removal, but use a new gasket and tension the drivebelt as described in Chapter 1 **(see illustration)**. Fill the cooling system as described in Section 4.

8 Cooling fan assembly - testing, removal and refitting

Testing

1 Current supply to the cooling fan is direct from the battery, protected by a fuse. The circuit is completed by the cooling fan thermostatic switch, which is mounted in the left-hand side of the radiator.

2 If the fan does not appear to work, run the engine until normal operating temperature is reached, then allow it to idle. The fan should cut in within a few minutes (just before the temperature gauge needle enters the red section). If the fan does not operate, switch off the ignition, and disconnect the wiring plug from the cooling fan switch on the radiator. Bridge the two contacts in the wiring plug, using a length of spare wire. If the fan now operates, the switch is probably faulty, and should be renewed.

3 If the fan still fails to operate, check that the battery voltage is available at the feed wire to the switch; if not, then there is a fault in the feed wire (possibly due to a blown fuse). If there is no problem with the feed, check that there is continuity between the switch earth terminal and a good earth point on the body; if not, then the earth connection is faulty, and must be re-made.

4 If the switch and the wiring are in good condition, the fault must lie in the motor itself. The motor can be checked by disconnecting it from the wiring loom, and connecting a 12-volt supply directly to it.

Removal

5 Follow the initial radiator removal procedure described in Section 5, but do not drain the cooling system or disconnect the top and bottom hoses. Unbolt the cooling fan assembly.

6 Extract the C-clip and withdraw the fan blades from the motor spindle.

7 Remove the securing bolts and withdraw the motor from the mounting bracket. On later models (1985-on), to remove the fan motor from the cowl, drill out the three rivets.

8 Lubricate the armature shaft bearings with oil.

Refitting

9 Refitting is a reversal of removal, using new rivets (if applicable). Refer to Section 5 if necessary.

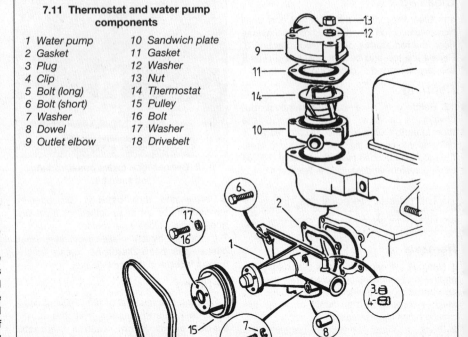

7.11 Thermostat and water pump components

1	Water pump	10	Sandwich plate
2	Gasket	11	Gasket
3	Plug	12	Washer
4	Clip	13	Nut
5	Bolt (long)	14	Thermostat
6	Bolt (short)	15	Pulley
7	Washer	16	Bolt
8	Dowel	17	Washer
9	Outlet elbow	18	Drivebelt

9 Cooling fan thermostatic switch - testing, removal and refitting

Testing

1 Testing of the switch is described in Section 8 as part of the cooling fan testing procedure.

Removal

2 Release the retaining plate and withdraw the switch and seal from the radiator **(see illustration)**.

Refitting

3 Refitting is a reversal of removal, but use a new seal and top-up the cooling system with reference to Section 4 **(see illustration)**.

10 Temperature gauge transmitter - removal and refitting

Removal

1 Remove the expansion tank filler cap. If the engine is hot, place a cloth over the cap, and unscrew it slowly to the first stop to allow all pressure to be released, before removing the cap.

2 Place a clean container beneath the radiator outlet, then loosen the clip and disconnect the bottom hose. Drain approximately 4 pints (2.3 litres) of coolant, then reconnect the bottom hose and tighten the clip.

9.2 Cooling fan thermostatic switch location

9.3 Thermostatic switch components

10.3 Temperature gauge transmitter location

11.2 Disconnecting the heater hoses

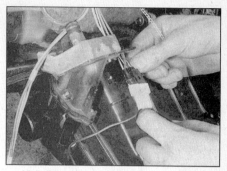

11.5 Disconnecting the heater wiring multi-plug

3 Disconnect the supply lead, and unscrew the transmitter from the front of the cylinder head **(see illustration)**.

Refitting

4 Refitting is a reversal of removal, but tighten the transmitter to the specified torque wrench setting. Top-up the cooling system with reference to Section 4.

11 Heater and heater radiator - removal and refitting

Removal

1 Drain the cooling system, and remove the air cleaner (see Chapter 4).
2 Identify the heater hoses on the engine side of the bulkhead, then disconnect them from the heater **(see illustration)**.

3 Remove the facia with reference to Chapter 11.
4 If fitted, remove the radio and cigar lighter (see Chapter 12 for details).
5 Remove the demister elbows and tubes, side and face vents (if fitted) and disconnect the heater multi-plug **(see illustration)**.
6 Remove the heater mounting bolts and the left-hand air inlet duct nut **(see illustrations)**.
7 Withdraw the heater unit from the car. Unbolt the air inlet duct and blanking plate and remove them by breaking the seal.
8 Pull off the heater control knobs, then unscrew the securing screws and withdraw the cover **(see illustrations)**.
9 Remove the screws and withdraw the inlet duct and blanking plate after releasing the sealant. Remove the radiator pipe seal and

drill out the rivets from the pipe flange, if applicable.
10 Withdraw the radiator pipe seal and drill out the rivets securing the flange.
11 Note the position of the air temperature control rod, then loosen the locking screws **(see illustration)**.
12 Remove the clips and screws retaining the two halves, loosen the control bracket screws, and withdraw the upper casing half **(see illustration)**.
13 Remove the screws, withdraw the retaining plate, and lift out the radiator and seals.

Refitting

14 Refitting is a reversal of removal, but it will be necessary to use a riveting tool to secure the pipe flange. Use sealing compound to seal

11.6a Removing the front heater mounting bolts

11.6b Removing the rear heater mounting bolt

11.8a Removing the heater control knobs

11.8b Removing the heater cover panel

11.11 Air temperature controls on the heater

11.12 Removing the heater case

3

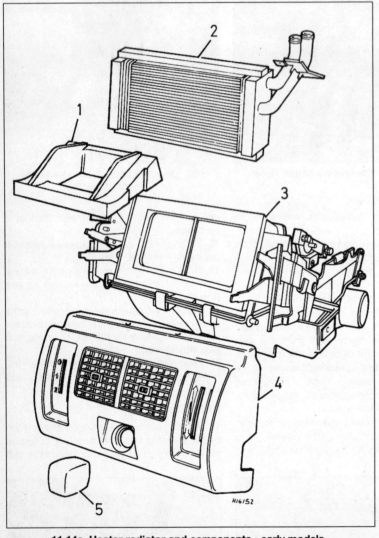

11.14a Heater radiator and components - early models

1 Seal   3 Heater assembly   5 Control knob
2 Radiator   4 Cover

11.14b Heater components for 1985-on models

1 Top case half   4 Bottom radiator retaining
2 Top radiator retaining plate   plate
3 Heater radiator   5 Bottom case half

---

the inlet duct and blanking plate to the housing. If necessary adjust the air temperature control as described in Section 12. Fill the cooling system with reference to Section 4 **(see illustrations)**.

12 Heater - adjustment

Note: *On some models the heater has preset cables that cannot be adjusted. Also removal of the fusebox cover will be necessary on later models.*

Air distribution

1 Position the air distribution control knob fully upwards **(see illustrations)**.

2 Loosen the rod-to-lever locking screw, and turn the lever fully clockwise.
3 Tighten the locking screw.

Temperature control and face level ventilation

4 Remove the facia as described in Chapter 11.
5 If fitted, remove the radio and cigar lighter as described in Chapter 12.
6 Pull off the heater control knobs, and remove the heater cover bottom screws.
7 Remove the heater mounting bolts and the left-hand air inlet duct nut.
8 Lower the heater sufficiently to remove the heater cover top screws and withdraw the cover.
9 Position the temperature control lever fully

upwards and loosen the control locking screws or clips if fitted. On 1985-on models the air distribution control should be moved fully down.
10 Turn the upper flap lever fully clockwise to close the flap, then tighten the upper screw or refit the adjuster clip to control rod, if fitted.
11 Turn the lower flap lever fully anti-clockwise then tighten the lower screw with the upper flap held fully clockwise.
12 Position the face level ventilation lever fully upwards and loosen the control linkage screw **(see illustration)**.
13 Turn the flap lever fully clockwise then tighten the locking screw.
14 Reverse the procedure given in paragraphs 4 to 8.

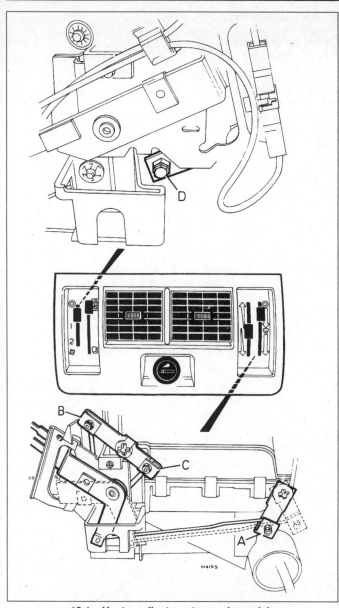

12.1a Heater adjustments - early models

A Air distribution
B Air temperature upper flap
C Air temperature lower flap
D Face level ventilation

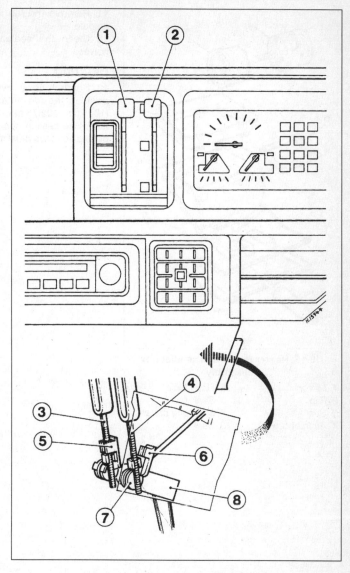

12.1b Heater controls for 1985-on models

1 Air temperature control
2 Air distribution control
3 Air temperature control rod
4 Air distribution control rod
5 Adjuster clip (locked)
6 Adjuster clip (unlocked)
7 Air temperature flap lever
8 Air distribution flap lever

12.12 Heater ventilation controls

13 Heater motor - removal and refitting

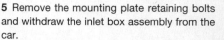

Removal

1 Disconnect the battery negative lead.

2 On right-hand drive models, remove the air cleaner (Chapter 4) and unbolt the cooling system expansion tank for access.

3 On left-hand drive models, unscrew the clutch hose bracket nut.

4 Disconnect the heater motor wiring multi-plug.

5 Remove the mounting plate retaining bolts and withdraw the inlet box assembly from the car.

6 Disconnect the wires from the heater motor, noting their locations.

7 Remove the screws and withdraw the mounting plate.

8 Unclip the drain tube and inlet seal, then remove the clips and screws retaining the inlet box halves.

9 Break the joint and separate the inlet box halves.

10 Withdraw the inlet baffle, heater motor and mounting strip.

3

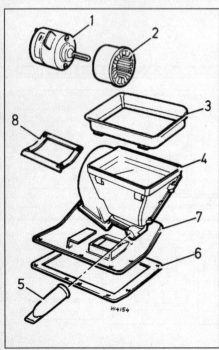

13.13 Heater motor and air inlet box assembly

1	Motor	5	Drain tube
2	Fan	6	Seal
3	Seal	7	Mounting plate
4	Air inlet box	8	Seal

11 Remove the fan from the heater motor spindle.

12 Clean the sealant from the inlet box halves.

Refitting

13 Refitting is a reversal of removal, but position the fan outer face 4.02 to 4.04 in (102.25 to 102.75 mm) from the motor tag rear face. Use sealing compound to seal the inlet box halves **(see illustration)**.

Chapter 4
Fuel and exhaust systems

Contents

Degrees of difficulty

Easy, suitable for novice with little experience	Fairly easy, suitable for beginner with some experience	Fairly difficult, suitable for competent DIY mechanic 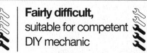	Difficult, suitable for experienced DIY mechanic	Very difficult, suitable for expert DIY or professional

Specifications

General

Air cleaner	Automatic air temperature control type, with renewable paper element
Air cleaner element:	See Chapter 1 Specifcations

Fuel tank capacity

Models up to 1986	6.6 Imp gals (30 litres)
1986-on models	7.8 Imp gals (35 litres)

Fuel pump

Type	Mechanical, diaphragm, operated by eccentric on camshaft
Fuel pump pressure (minimum)	6 lbf/in² (0.4 kgf/cm²)

Carburettor

998 cc

Type	HIF 38
Piston spring colour	Red
Jet size	0.090 in
Exhaust gas CO content	1.5 to 3.5%

1275 cc

Type	HIF 44
Piston spring colour	Red
Jet size	0.100 in
Exhaust gas CO content	1.5 to 3.5%

MG Turbo

Type	HIF44
Piston spring colour	Yellow
Jet size	0.100 in
Exhaust gas CO content	0.5 to 2.5%

4

Piston damper oil type
Specification . . . . Multigrade engine oil, viscosity SAE 15W/50 or 10W/40

Idling speeds (rpm)

	Idle	Fast Idle
998 cc		
Early models	750	1300
1982 1.0, L, City and Van	750	1300
1982 HLE	600 to 700	1100
1983 all models (except HLE)	750	1300
1983 HLE	650	1300
1984 Low comp., 1.0, L and Van	750	1300
1984 Std. comp., Eng. No. 99HA06P	650	1100
1984 Std. comp., Eng. No. 99HA07P	750	1300
1984 Low comp., City X and City	750	1300
1984 Std. comp., L, HLE and City X	650	1100
1985 Low and Std. comp., all models	700 to 800	1250 to 1350
1985 High comp., all models	600 to 700	1050 to 1150
1986 Low comp., all models	730 to 930	1250 to 1350
1986 Std. comp., all models	780 to 880	1250 to 1350
1986 High comp., all models	780 to 880	1050 to 1150
1987-on Low and Std. comp., all models (except unleaded)	780 to 880	1250 to 1350
1987-on High comp., all models (except unleaded)	780 to 880	1050 to 1150
Unleaded fuel specification (95 RON):		
1989-on Low comp., all models	780 to 880	1050 to 1150
1989-on Std. comp., all models	780 to 880	1050 to 1150
1275 cc		
Early models	750	1100
1982 Low comp., 1.3, L and Van	650	1100
1982 Std. comp., 1.3, L and Van	750	1100
1982 MG	850	1100
1982 Vanden Plas	750	1100
1983 Low comp. and HLE	650	1100
1983 All other models	750	1100
1984 Low comp., 1.3, L and Van	650	1100
1984 Std. comp., 1.3, L, automatic and Van	750	1100
1984 HLE	650	1100
1984 MG	850	1100
1984 Vanden Plas	750	1100
1985 Low and Std. comp., all models	600 to 700	1050 to 1150
1985 Automatic and Vanden Plas Automatic	750 to 850	950 to 1050
1985 MG and Vanden Plas manual:		
Engine 12HA83AA and 12HC14AA	800 to 900	1000 to 1100
Engine 12HB42AA and 12HC15AA	800 to 900	1100 to 1200
1986 Low comp., all models	830 to 930	1050 to 1150
1986 Std. comp., manual (except MG and Vanden Plas)	830 to 930	1050 to 1150
1986 Std. comp., automatic	830 to 930	950 to 1050
1986 MG and Vanden Plas:		
Engine 12HC14AA	830 to 930	1000 to 1100
Engine 12HC15AA	830 to 930	1100 to 1200
1987-89 1275 Sport, MG and Vanden Plas with manual gearbox:		
Engine 12HD24AA and 12HD17AA	830 to 930	1000 to 1100
Engine 12HD25	830 to 930	1100 to 1200
1989-on Unleaded fuel (95 RON), Low comp.	780 to 880	1050 to 1150
1989-on Unleaded fuel (95 RON), Std. comp.		
with automatic transmission	750 to 850	950 to 1050
with manual gearbox	780 to 880	1050 to 1150

Turbocharger
Boost pressure . . . . 4 to 7 lbf/in^2 (0.28 to 0.49 kgf/cm^2)
Wastegate operating pressure . . . . 4 lbf/in^2 (0.28 kgf/cm^2)
Permissible bearing clearance:
Radial . . . . 0.003 to 0.006 in (0.08 to 0.15 mm)
Axial . . . . 0.001 to 0.003 in (0.03 to 0.08 mm)

Fuel octane rating
Metro low compression . . . . 91 RON minimum
All other leaded type models . . . . 97 RON minimum
All Unleaded models . . . . 95 RON minimum

Torque wrench settings

	lbf ft	Nm
Carburettor nuts	16	22
Fuel pump nuts	16	22
Throttle damper	8	11
Turbocharger to exhaust manifold	28	38
Turbocharger to exhaust elbow	15	21
Oil drain adapter screws	16	22
Oil feed banjo bolts	11	15
Wastegate bracket screws	16	22
Plenum chamber to carburettor	16	22
Non-return valve to manifold	18	25

1 General description

 Warning: Many of the procedures in this Chapter require the removal of fuel lines and connections, which may result in some fuel spillage. Before carrying out any operation on the fuel system, refer to the precautions given in "Safety first!" at the beginning of this manual, and follow them implicitly. Petrol is a highly dangerous and volatile liquid, and the precautions necessary when handling it cannot be overstressed.

Fuel system

1 The fuel system comprises a rear mounted fuel tank, a fuel pump and an SU HIF (Horizontal, Integral Floatchamber) carburettor.

Fuel pump

2 The fuel pump is camshaft operated (except MG Turbo), and is located on the rear left-hand side of the cylinder block. It is of sealed construction. In the event of faulty operation, the pump should be renewed complete.

3 The fuel pump fitted to MG Turbo models is electrically operated. The pump is located next to the fuel tank, at the rear of the vehicle.

4 Electrical supply to the pump is through a relay energised by the starter motor solenoid when the engine is being started; thereafter the relay is controlled by the oil pressure warning switch. This means that the pump will stop if the engine stalls, or if there is a catastrophic fall in oil pressure when the engine is running.

5 The fuel pump output is at high pressure. The fuel pressure regulator valve in the engine bay reduces the fuel pressure according to the requirements of the carburettor.

Carburettor

6 The SU HIF carburettor is a variable choke, constant depression type. It incorporates a sliding piston. This automatically controls the mixture of air and fuel supplied to the engine, in relation to the throttle valve position and engine speed.

7 The carburettor functions as follows. With the engine stationary, the sliding piston remains in its lowest position due to its weight and the pressure of the piston spring. When the engine is started and is allowed to idle, the throttle valve passes a small amount of air. Because the piston is in a low position, it offers a large restriction, and the resultant pressure reduction draws fuel from the jet, and atomisation occurs to provide a combustible mixture. Since the inside section of the tapered needle is across the mouth of the jet, a relatively small amount of fuel is passed.

8 When the throttle valve is opened, the amount of air passing through the carburettor is increased, which causes a greater depression beneath the sliding piston. An internal passageway connects this depression with the suction chamber above the piston, which now rises. The piston now offers less of a restriction and the depression is reduced, with the result that a point is reached where the forces of depression, gravity, and spring tension balance out. The tapered needle has now been raised, and more fuel passes from the jet.

9 The overall effect of this type of carburettor is that the depression remains relatively constant, and the fuel/air mixture is controlled to a fine degree over the complete throttle valve movement.

10 Fuel enrichment for cold starting is provided by a choke cable-operated valve, which admits more fuel into the airstream passing through the carburettor.

11 The jet adjusting (mixture) screw mechanism incorporates a bi-metal strip, which alters the position of the jet to compensate for varying fuel densities resulting from varying fuel temperatures.

12 A throttle damper is fitted to certain models to retard the action of the throttle lever as it returns to the idling position. This prevents an over weak mixture during deceleration and reduces the emission of certain harmful gases from the exhaust system **(see illustration)**.

MG Turbo models

 Warning: This carburettor is sealed against atmospheric pressure, and must not be dismantled.

13 The SU HIF44 carburettor fitted to MG Turbo models works on the same principle as the normally-aspirated versions. However this carburettor is sealed against atmospheric pressure, and **must not** be dismantled. This is to maintain proper functioning throughout the range of boost pressures used, and to prevent fuel or fuel/air mixture being discharged into the engine compartment under conditions of high boost pressures. For this reason, at time of writing, there are no repair kits available. It cannot be emphasised too strongly that haphazard or ill-informed attempts at repair may result in dangerous fuel leakage.

Unleaded petrol

14 Models built up to October 1988 (as delivered from the factory) cannot use unleaded petrol; the valve seats fitted as standard will suffer serious premature wear without the protection of the petrol's lead content (see paragraph 18). Exceptions to this are those engines that have been modified as described in the next paragraph.

15 From October 1988 onwards (i.e. during the 1989 model year), improved components were gradually introduced at the factory to enable engines to run on 95 RON unleaded petrol. These vehicles can be identified by the green "95 RON unleaded" label attached to the bonnet lock platform. They can use unleaded petrol without modification or risk of damage.

16 If you own a 1989 model and suspect that the label has become detached, check first with a Rover dealer whether your vehicle can

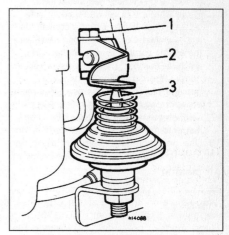

1.12 The throttle damper

1 Clamp bolt *3 Plunger*
2 Lever

1.23a MG Turbo engine compartment and rear of turbocharger

1 Turbocharger	10 Pressure reducing
2 Oil inlet pipe	valve and
2A Oil inlet pipe union	solenoid
3 Oil drain hose	11 Fuel pressure
4 Wastegate actuator	regulator
5 Wastegate	12 Electronic control
operating arm	unit
6 Pressure sensing	13 Carburettor
hose (to ECU and	14 Float chamber
fuel regulator)	venting valve (if
7 Plenum chamber	fitted)
8 Pressure hose (to	15 Idle speed
wastegate actuator)	adjustment screw
9 Pressure hose (to	16 Idle mixture
pressure reducing	adjustment screw
valve)	

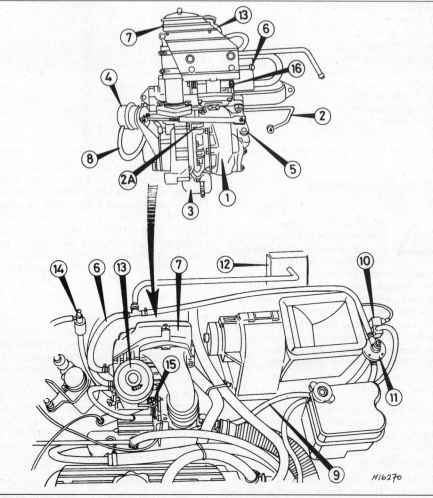

use unleaded petrol or not. The VIN will be required for positive identification. Note, however, that as a rule 998 cc engines that can use unleaded petrol have serial number prefixes of 99HE while 1275 cc equivalents have prefixes of 12HE or 12HF.

17 Do not attempt to use unleaded petrol in Turbo models; use only leaded four-star.

18 Leaded petrol will not be available anywhere in the EC from January 2000. A substitute known as 'lead-replacement petrol' (LRP) will be sold at the pumps. Anti-wear/lead replacement additives for use with unleaded petrol will also be available. If your car cannot be run on unleaded petrol, there are few courses of action:

a) *Use lead-replacement petrol (LRP) instead of leaded 4-star. No ignition timing adjustment should be necessary.*

b) *Use a petrol additive. These are available in a variety of forms – generally something solid which is placed in the fuel tank or in the fuel line to the engine, or a liquid which is added to the petrol. Some ignition timing adjustment may also be necessary.*

c) *Conversion kits are available (consisting of an exchange cylinder head) as "Green Packs" through Rover dealers only. Any vehicle which has had such a conversion will have the letter "U" stamped between the engine number prefix and the start of the serial number. These can use unleaded petrol without modification or risk of damage. Note: Apart from any adjustments made during the fitting of a "Green Pack" no alterations are required (or should be made) to the ignition timing or carburation.*

19 Use only unleaded petrol in any model fitted with a catalytic converter (see below).

Air cleaner

20 The air cleaner is of automatic air temperature control type and incorporates a disposable paper element. MG 1300 non-Turbo models, pre-1985 LHD Vanden Plas and 1985-on manual transmission Vanden Plas models are fitted with an air cleaner that has a vacuum-operated flap valve to control the inlet air temperature.

Manifolds

21 On most models the inlet and exhaust manifolds are manufactured as one integral casting. On 998 cc low compression models the exhaust manifold passageways converge into a single downpipe, but on all other models, the central siamesed exhaust manifold passageway is connected to a separate downpipe. MG 1300 and Turbo models are fitted with separate inlet and exhaust manifolds. The inlet manifold is heated by water from the cooling system. Pre-1985 LHD Vanden Plas and 1985-on manual transmission Vanden Plas models are also fitted with separate manifolds, the inlet manifold being coolant heated.

Exhaust system

22 The exhaust system is in two sections; the front section incorporates the downpipe(s) and front silencer, and the rear section incorporates the rear silencer and tailpipe. The exhaust system is suspended on rubber mountings although the front downpipe is attached rigidly to the right-hand side differential unit side cover. Twin downpipes are incorporated on all models except the low compression version.

Turbocharger

23 The turbocharger fitted to the MG Turbo model is of the "blow through" type, i.e. the compressor blows air into the carburettor. The turbocharger is made up of three housings; exhaust, centre and compressor. The exhaust housing is connected to the exhaust manifold. It contains the turbine wheel and the wastegate. The centre housing contains the shaft that connects the turbine and compressor wheels, together with the associated seals and bearings. Oil for bearing lubrication and heat transfer is fed to the centre housing from the engine's lubrication system **(see illustrations)**.

24 The compressor housing contains the compressor wheel. It is connected to the plenum chamber and thence to the carburettor. Boost pressure sensing connect-ions and a dump valve (to release excess pressure) are located in the plenum chamber. Exhaust gas flowing past the turbine wheel causes the wheel to rotate at speeds of up to 130 000 rpm. The compressor wheel, on the same shaft, compresses air into the engine's induction system at a pressure of up to 7 lbf/in² (0.5 kgf/cm²), thus improving efficiency and performance. Boost pressure is limited in several ways.

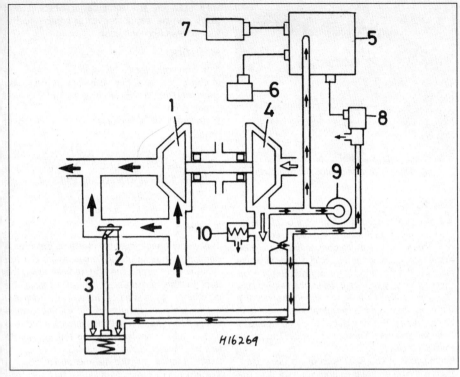

H16269

1.23b Schematic diagram of turbocharger control systems

1 Turbine wheel	5 Electronic control unit	8 Pressure reducing valve
2 Wastegate	6 Ignition amplifier	9 Fuel pressure regulator
3 Wastegate actuator	7 Boost gauge	10 Dump valve
4 Compressor wheel		

25 A device known as a wastegate diverts part of the exhaust gas flow away from the turbine wheel when boost pressure has reached a certain value. The pressure at which the wastegate operates is increased as engine speed rises; this is achieved by the electronic control unit (ECU), which opens a pressure reducing valve, thus reducing the pressure available for operating the wastegate. The dump valve, already mentioned, releases excess pressure from the plenum chamber.

26 The increased fuel demand at high speed and large throttle openings are catered for by the fuel pressure regulating valve. This valve increases fuel delivery in proportion to boost pressure. A boost gauge on the dashboard, linked to the ECU, displays to the driver the boost pressure being developed.

27 Although the turbocharger is a simple unit, it operates at very high speeds and high temperatures. Certain precautions should be observed, both for personal safety and to avoid damage to the unit. These are as follows:

28 *Do not* run the engine with the air inlet hose disconnected. The compressor rotates fast enough to cause grave personal injury, and there is a chance of foreign bodies being sucked in and damaging the compressor.

29 *Do not* rev the engine immediately after start-up. Wait a few seconds for oil pressure to become established at the turbine shaft bearings. This is especially important after an oil filter change, when the pressure may take a significant time to build up.

30 *Do not* switch the engine off without allowing it to idle for at least 10 seconds. Switching off immediately after a run can leave the turbine rotating at high speed with no oil pressure available at the bearings.

31 The above points also serve to stress the importance of regular oil and filter changes, and conscientious checking of the oil level between changes. Neglect of these items could prove very costly.

Catalytic converter

32 A catalytic converter was available as an optional extra for some 1990-on models. The converter consists of an element (or "substrate") of ceramic honeycomb. This is coated with a combination of precious metals (platinum and rhodium) in such a way as to produce a vast surface area over which the exhaust gases must flow. The assembly being mounted in a stainless-steel box in the vehicle's exhaust system. The precious metals act as catalysts to speed up the reaction between the pollutants and the oxygen in the car's exhaust gases, HC and CO being oxidised to form H_2O and CO_2.

33 The catalytic converter is a reliable and simple device that needs no maintenance in itself, but there are some facts of which an

owner should be aware if the converter is to function properly for its full service life:

a) *Do not* use leaded petrol in a vehicle equipped with a catalytic converter - the lead will coat the precious metals, reducing their converting efficiency and will eventually destroy the converter.

b) *Always* keep the ignition and fuel systems well maintained. In particular, ensure that the air cleaner filter element and spark plugs are renewed at the correct interval. If the inlet air/fuel mixture is allowed to become too rich due to neglect, the unburned surplus will enter and burn in the catalytic converter. This in turn will overheat the element and eventually destroying the converter.

c) If the engine develops a misfire, do not drive the vehicle at all or at least as little as possible until the fault is cured - the misfire will allow unburned fuel to enter the converter, which will result in its overheating.

d) *Do not* push or tow-start the vehicle - this will soak the catalytic converter in unburned fuel, causing it to overheat when the engine does start.

e) *Do not* switch off the ignition at high engine speeds, otherwise unburned fuel will enter the (very hot) catalytic converter, with the possible risk of its igniting on the element and damaging the converter.

f) *Do not* use fuel or engine oil additives - these may contain substances harmful to the catalytic converter.

g) *Do not* continue to use the vehicle if the engine burns oil to the extent of leaving a visible trail of blue smoke - the unburned carbon deposits will clog the converter passages and reduce its efficiency; in severe cases the element will overheat.

h) Remember that the catalytic converter operates at very high temperatures. *Do not* park the vehicle in dry undergrowth, over long grass or piles of dead leaves.

i) The catalytic converter is *fragile* - do not strike it with tools during servicing work and ensure that it is well clear of any jacks used to raise the vehicle. Do not drive the vehicle over rough ground, road humps, etc., in such a way as to ground the exhaust system.

j) In some cases, particularly when the vehicle is new and/or is used for stop/start driving, a sulphurous smell (like that of rotten eggs) may be noticed from the exhaust. Once the vehicle has covered a few thousand miles the problem should disappear - meanwhile a change of driving style or of the brand of petrol used may effect a solution.

k) The catalytic converter, used on a well-maintained and well-driven vehicle, should last for between 50 000 and 100 000 miles. From this point on, careful checks should be made at all specified service intervals of the CO level to ensure that the converter is still operating efficiently - if the converter is no longer effective it must be renewed.

4

2.1 Air cleaner vacuum hose connection

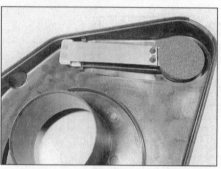

2.4 The air temperature control flap

2 Air cleaner and element (except MG Turbo) - removal and refitting

Removal

1 Unscrew and remove the two wing nuts on the top of the air cleaner. Disconnect the vacuum hose, if applicable **(see illustration)**.
2 Withdraw the air cleaner and at the same time, disconnect it from the hot air shroud tube.
3 The air cleaner element should be renewed as per service intervals shown in Chapter 1.

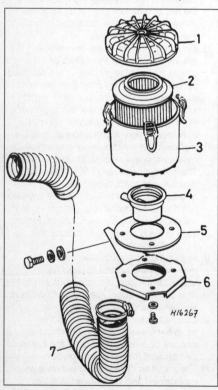

3.1 Air cleaner components - MG Turbo models

1 Cover	5 Seal
2 Element	6 Bracket
3 Housing	7 Supply hose
4 Adapter	

Refitting

4 Before refitting, clean the interior of the air cleaner with a fuel-moistened cloth, and wipe dry. The air temperature control flap should be in the open position when cold, to admit warm air from the heating stove. By heating the bi-metallic strap with a hair dryer, the flap should close the warm air aperture **(see illustration)**. If the operation of the temperature control is in doubt, renew the air cleaner body complete.
5 Install the new element and snap the cover onto the body.
6 Check that the seal is in good condition, then refit the air cleaner and connect it to the hot air shroud tube. Insert and tighten the two wing nuts and reconnect the vacuum hose, if fitted.

3 Air cleaner and element (MG Turbo models) - removal and refitting

Removal

1 The air cleaner on MG Turbo models is remote from the carburettor, being mounted on the left-hand side of the engine compartment **(see illustration)**.
2 To renew the air cleaner element, release the spring clips and take off the cover. Extract the element.
3 To remove the air cleaner unit complete, first disconnect the large supply hose and the small crankcase ventilation system hose. Then unbolt the air cleaner bracket from the car body and remove the air cleaner complete

4.2 Air cleaner temperature sensor (inside air cleaner body)

with bracket. The air cleaner bracket and body can be separated after removing the four screws from the case.

Refitting

4 If only renewing the element, clean the inside of the housing before fitting the new element. Refit the cover and secure with the spring clips.
5 Refitting is a reversal of the removal procedure.

4 Temperature control system (MG 1300 and Vanden Plas models) - testing

Testing

1 A visual check may be made to determine correct operation of the temperature control system. On starting the engine from cold, the flap in the air cleaner snout should be positioned so that air is drawn only from the hot air pick-up shroud. As the engine warms up, or if the vacuum hose is disconnected, the flap should move to close the hot air inlet in favour of the cold air.
2 Malfunction of the temperature control system may be due to a faulty temperature sensor **(see illustration)**, a faulty vacuum motor, or a failure in the vacuum supply (hose blocked or leaking). The temperature sensor is available separately from the air cleaner body, but the vacuum motor is not.

5 Fuel pump (except MG Turbo models) - testing, removal and refitting

Note: *Refer to the warning note in Section 1 before proceeding.*

Testing

1 Under certain conditions it is possible for the normal operation of the fuel pump to give rise to a knocking noise. From inside the car this noise may be mistaken for a sign of serious engine problems.
2 Diagnosis of fuel pump knock requires the help of an assistant. One person should sit in the car and hold the engine speed at the level where the knock is most pronounced, whilst another person squeezes and releases the fuel pump inlet flexible hose. If the noise changes or disappears when the hose is squeezed, this confirms that the fuel pump is the source of the noise.
3 Fuel pump knock can be eliminated by attention to the following points:
   a) *Make sure that the metal fuel pipe from the tank fits into its clip on the bulkhead without strain.*
   b) *Make sure that the flexible pipes are not touching the bulkhead, nor their clips.*
   c) *If the flexible pipes are under tension, fit longer pipes to relieve this.*

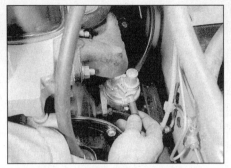

5.6a Disconnecting the feed pipe from the fuel pump

5.6b Disconnecting the outlet pipe from the fuel pump

5.7 Removing the fuel pump (except MG Turbo)

4 To test the operation of the fuel pump, remove the air cleaner (Section 2), then disconnect the fuel pipe from the carburettor. Disconnect the HT lead from the coil, and spin the engine on the starter while holding a wad of rag near the fuel pipe. Well-defined spurts of fuel should be ejected from the pipe if the fuel pump is operating correctly, provided there is fuel in the fuel tank.

Removal

5 To remove the fuel pump, disconnect the battery negative lead, and remove the air cleaner if not already removed.
6 Disconnect and plug the fuel feed pipe. Disconnect the fuel outlet pipe **(see illustrations)**.
7 Unscrew and remove the two retaining nuts and spring washers, and withdraw the fuel pump from the studs **(see illustration)**.
8 Remove the insulator block and gasket **(see illustration)**.

Refitting

9 Clean all traces of gasket from the crankcase, insulator block, and fuel pump flange.
10 Refitting is a reversal of removal, but fit new gaskets either side of the insulator. Locate the rocker arm on top of the camshaft eccentric, then push the pump onto the studs. Tighten the nuts to the specified torque.
Note: *When fitting a twin turret pump in place of an early single turret pump, ensure a thinner insulating block is also fitted. On automatic model, if the new fuel pump has a larger diameter body flange than the original, the kickdown rod may also need to be renewed.*

5.8 Fuel pump insulator block and gaskets

6 Fuel pump (MG Turbo models) - testing, removal and refitting

Note: *Refer to the warning note in Section 1 before proceeding.*

Testing

1 If the pump output is thought to be insufficient, this can be tested by disconnecting the oil pressure warning light switch, turning on the ignition and removing the fuel filler cap. Fuel should be coming out of the return line with a sufficient force to hit the far side of the filler neck. If not, check the pipes.
2 Before condemning the pump after testing, make sure that it is not the relay that is faulty. Disconnect the fuel pump relay multiplug (under the bonnet) and join the white/green and white/purple leads (relay terminals 85 and 30/51). If the pump output is now satisfactory, the relay is faulty.

Removal

3 Disconnect the battery earth lead, then raise and securely support the rear of the car. Temporarily remove the fuel filler cap to release any residual pressure in the tank, then refit it.
4 Disconnect the fuel hoses from the pump and plug them. Be prepared for some fuel spillage. Release the inlet hose from its clip.
5 Disconnect the electrical leads from the pump, identifying them if necessary.

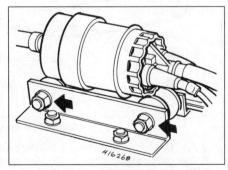

6.6 MG Turbo fuel pump. Remove nuts (arrowed) to release pump and mountings from support bracket

6 Remove the nuts that secure the fuel pump mountings to the support bracket. Work the pump over to the right-hand side of the car so that it can be extracted through the rear of the subframe **(see illustration)**.
7 Separate the pump from its mounting bracket. The pump cannot be repaired, but must be renewed if defective. If it is wished to renew the pump inlet and outlet hoses, the fuel tank must first be removed.

Refitting

8 Refitting the fuel pump is a reversal of the removal procedure. Position the pump in its mounting bracket so that the positive (+) connector will be vertically above the negative (-) connector when the pump is installed.
9 Run the engine and check for leaks on completion.

7 Fuel filter (MG Turbo models) - removal and refitting

Note: *Refer to the warning note in Section 1 before proceeding.*

> **⚠ Warning: Take precautions against fire when removing the filter, and do not smoke.**

Removal

1 The fuel filter is located in the fuel line between the pressure regulator and the carburettor. It should be renewed at the intervals specified in *"Routine maintenance and servicing"*, or more frequently if filter blockage is suspected.
2 Take precautions against fire when removing the filter, and do not smoke. Residual pressure in the fuel lines may lead to significant fuel spillage when the filter is removed.
3 Release the hose clamps on each side of the filter and carefully pull off the hoses. Inspect the hoses and clips; renew these too, if necessary. Mop up any fuel spilt.

Refitting

4 Fit the new filter. A directional arrow or an "OUT" marking should point towards the carburettor; an "IN" marking should face the pressure regulator. Without any markings the filter may be fitted either way round.

4

8.1 Fuel tank filler cap

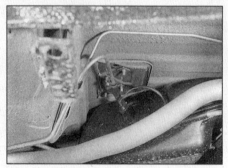

8.6 Fuel tank gauge sender unit location

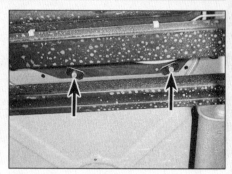

8.8 Fuel tank rear retaining bolt locations

5 Secure the new filter with the hose clamps. When all spilt fuel has been removed from the engine bay, start the engine and check for leaks.

8 Fuel tank - removal, servicing and refitting

Note: *In addition to the warning in Section 1, the fuel tank must always be removed in a well ventilated area, never over a pit.*

Removal

1 Disconnect the battery negative lead. Remove the tank filler cap **(see illustration)**.
2 Siphon or pump all the fuel from the fuel tank (there is no drain plug).
3 Jack up the rear of the car and support it on axle stands (see *"Jacking and vehicle support"*), but position the right-hand stand to allow for the removal of the tank and lowering the subframe. Chock the front wheels. Remove the fuel pump, if fitted.
4 On 3-door models only, detach the retaining strap from the right-hand rear Hydragas suspension unit. Unbolt the right-hand side of the rear subframe and lower the subframe sufficiently to remove the fuel tank.
5 On 5-door models, unscrew the nut from the exhaust system rear mounting and support the system on an axle stand. Loosen the filler hose clips and slide the hose off the fuel tank stub.
6 Loosen the clip and disconnect the short hose from the fuel tank gauge sender unit **(see illustration)**.

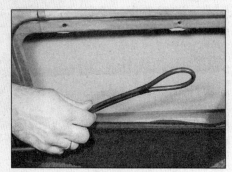

8.11a Fuel tank vent tube

7 Disconnect the supply lead from the gauge sender unit and unclip it from the fuel tank flange.
8 Loosen the two rear fuel tank retaining bolts **(see illustration)**. Unscrew and remove the two front retaining bolts.
9 Lower the fuel tank and disconnect the vent tube. Withdraw the fuel tank from under the car.

Servicing

10 If the tank is contaminated with sediment or water, remove the gauge sender unit as

described in Section 9 and swill the tank out with clean fuel. If the tank is damaged or leaks, it should be repaired by specialists, or alternatively renewed. *Do not under any circumstances solder or weld a fuel tank.*

Refitting

11 Refitting is a reverse of removal. Access to the vent tube is gained by removing the right-hand plastic pocket. On 5-door models, ensure that the filler hose is positioned equally on the tank stub and filler tube before tightening the clips **(see illustrations)**.

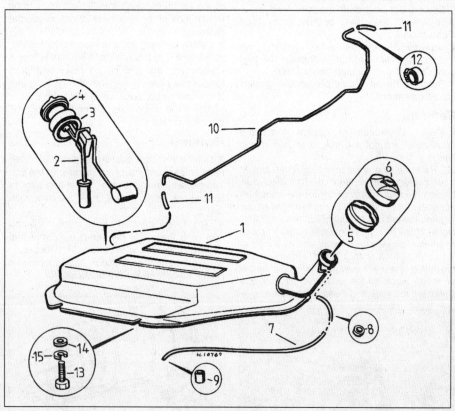

8.11b Fuel tank components

1 Fuel tank	6 Filler cap (locking)	11 Connector hose
2 Fuel gauge sender unit	7 Vent tube	12 Clip
3 Seal	8 Grommet	13 Bolt
4 Locking ring	9 Ferrule	14 Plain washer
5 Filler cap (non-locking)	10 Feed pipe	15 Spring washer

10.2 Choke cable - inner cable and clamp pin

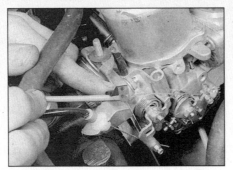

10.3 Removing the choke outer cable

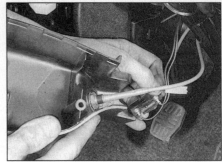

10.7 Choke warning switch and cable connection to steering column cowl

9 Fuel gauge sender unit - removal and refitting

Note: *In addition to the warning in Section 1, the fuel gauge sender unit must always be removed in a well ventilated area, never over a pit.*

Removal

1 Follow the procedure given in paragraphs 1 to 6 of Section 8.
2 Using two crossed screwdrivers, turn the locking ring to release it from the tank.
3 Withdraw the locking ring, seal, and sender unit.

Refitting

4 Refitting is a reversal of removal, but always fit a new seal.

10 Choke control cable - removal and refitting

Note: *On 1985-on models the choke control cable has been repositioned to the facia panel.*

Removal

1 Disconnect the battery negative lead.
2 Remove the air cleaner and with the choke now fully in, loosen the screw to release the inner cable from the carburettor lever **(see illustration)**. Remove the small clamp.
3 Release the outer cable at the carburettor end, by removing the clip **(see illustration)**.
4 Remove the screws retaining the steering column cowls to the outer column bracket.
5 Separate the cowls and withdraw the right-hand cowl.
6 Disconnect the lighting switch multi-plug and withdraw the left-hand cowl over the direction indicator switch.
7 Unclip the choke warning switch, remove the nut, and withdraw the choke cable through the bulkhead and cowl **(see illustration)**.

Refitting

8 Refitting is a reversal of removal, but before tightening the clamping pin, adjust the position of the inner cable to provide 0.08 in (2 mm) free movement **(see illustration)**.

11 Accelerator cable - removal and refitting

Removal

1 Disconnect the battery negative lead.
2 Remove the air cleaner, and loosen the screw to release the inner cable from the throttle lever.
3 Slide the outer cable from the carburettor bracket **(see illustration)**.
4 Working inside the car, prise the retaining clip from the top of the accelerator pedal, and disconnect the inner cable **(see illustration)**.
5 Prise the plastic bush from the bulkhead (engine side), and withdraw the complete accelerator cable from the engine compartment.

Refitting

6 Refitting is a reversal of removal, but before tightening the clamping pin, adjust the position of the inner cable to provide 0.16 in (4 mm) free movement. Check that with the accelerator pedal fully depressed, the throttle lever is fully open, and with the pedal fully released the lever is in the closed position.

12 Accelerator pedal - removal and refitting

Removal

1 Working inside the car, prise the retaining clip from the top of the accelerator pedal and pull the inner cable out of the slot.
2 Unbolt and remove the accelerator pedal.

Refitting

3 Refitting is the reverse of the removal procedure.

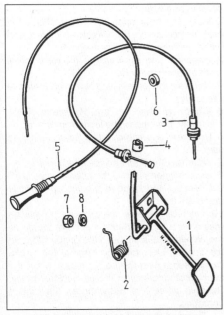

10.8 Choke and accelerator cables

1 Pedal assembly
2 Return spring
3 Accelerator cable
4 Retaining clip
5 Choke cable
6 Grommet
7 Locknut
8 Washer

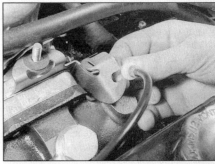

11.3 Removing the accelerator outer cable

11.4 Accelerator cable-to-pedal connection

4

13.12a Removing the carburettor elbow

13.12b Removing the carburettor

13 Carburettor (except MG Turbo models) - testing, removal and refitting

Note: *Refer to the warning note in Section 1 before proceeding.*

Testing

1 If a carburettor fault is suspected, always check first that the ignition timing is correctly set. Also check that the spark plugs are in good condition and correctly gapped. The accelerator and choke cables should be correctly adjusted. The air cleaner filter element needs to be clean. Refer to the relevant Chapters, for further details. If the engine is running very roughly, first check the valve clearances, then check the compression pressures as described in Chapter 2A, Section 1.

2 If careful checking of all the above produces no improvement, the carburettor must be removed for cleaning and overhaul.

3 In the rare event that a complete carburettor overhaul being necessary, it may prove more economical to renew the carburettor as complete assembly. Check also, the availability of component parts before starting work; note that most sealing washers, screws and gaskets are available in kits, as are some of the major sub-assemblies. In most cases, it may be sufficient to dismantle the carburettor and to clean the jets and passages.

Removal

4 Disconnect the battery negative lead.

5 Remove the air cleaner as described in Section 2.

6 Loosen the screws securing the choke and accelerator inner cables to their respective levers. Disconnect the outer cables and withdraw them from the carburettor.

7 Note the locations, then disconnect the vent tube and crankcase ventilation tube from the carburettor.

8 Disconnect and plug the fuel inlet pipe.

9 Disconnect the distributor vacuum pipe from the carburettor.

10 Unscrew and remove the carburettor mounting nuts and washers.

11 Disconnect the carburettor heater wires (where fitted to cold country models).

12 Withdraw the carburettor from the inlet manifold studs, and, if necessary, remove the air cleaner elbow and gasket by unscrewing the two cross head screws **(see illustrations)**.

13 Withdraw the gasket, control bracket complete with throttle damper, gasket, distance piece or heater (cold countries), and final gasket. If necessary, remove the throttle damper from the control bracket.

Refitting

14 Refitting is a reversal of removal, but tighten the mounting nuts to the specified torque in diagonal sequence (where applicable), and always fit new gaskets. Make sure that the mating faces of each component are clean.

15 Connect the choke and accelerator cables with reference to Sections 10 and 11. Adjust the throttle damper as described in Section 16. Adjust the idle and fast idle speeds as described in Chapter 1.

14 Carburettor (MG Turbo models) - testing, removal and refitting

Note: *Refer to the warning note in Section 1 before proceeding.*

Testing

1 Refer also to Section 13, paragraph 1.

2 If float chamber flooding is experienced, it may be possible to rectify the problem as follows.

3 Disconnect and plug the fuel inlet pipe at the carburettor. Also plug the carburettor fuel inlet. Mop up any spilt fuel.

4 Start the engine and run it until the fuel in the float chamber has been used up (indicated by the engine stopping).

5 Remove the plugs and reconnect the fuel inlet pipe to the carburettor, then restart the engine. The surge of fuel into the float chamber should clear the needle valve of dirt or grit which may have caused the flooding. If not, renew the carburettor.

Removal

6 Disconnect the battery earth lead.

7 Disconnect the pressure sensing hose from the plenum chamber and remove the heat shield. Release the inlet hose clip and unbolt and remove the plenum chamber.

8 Remove the compressor exit pipe and hose.

9 Disconnect the choke and throttle cables from the carburettor.

10 Disconnect the vacuum advance and the fuel supply pipes. Plug the fuel supply pipe. Disconnect the float chamber venting valve hose (if fitted).

11 Remove the nuts that secure the carburettor to the inlet manifold. Release the throttle cable bracket and remove the carburettor.

Refitting

12 Refitting is a reversal of the removal procedure, but note the following points:

a) *Use new gaskets and make sure that the mating surfaces are clean.*

b) *Adjust the choke and throttle cables as described in Sections 10 and 11.*

c) *Top-up the damper, then screw the damper cap firmly home and refit its clamp.*

15 Carburettor - dismantling, overhaul and reassembly

Note: *Refer to the warning note in Section 1 before proceeding. Refer also to `Testing`, in Section 13, before dismantling.*

Dismantling

1 Wash the exterior of the carburettor with paraffin and wipe dry.

2 Mark the float chamber cover about the carburettor body. Remove the screws and withdraw the cover and sealing ring.

3 Unscrew and remove the mixture screw and withdraw the seal.

4 Unscrew the jet retaining screw and remove the spring.

5 Withdraw the jet and bi-metal lever assembly. Disengage the lever from the jet.

6 Unscrew and remove the float pivot and seal.

7 Withdraw the float and the needle valve.

8 Unscrew and remove the needle valve seat.

9 Unscrew and remove the piston damper and drain the oil.

10 On later models the carburettor piston may have a circlip fitted to the tip of the guide rod. Where this is so, push the piston fully into the suction chamber and remove the circlip before separating the components. Mark the suction chamber with the carburettor body. Remove the screws and withdraw the suction chamber.

11 Remove the piston spring, and carefully lift the piston and needle assembly from the main body.

12 Unscrew the needle retaining grub screw. Remove the needle, guide, and spring from the piston.

15.27 Exploded view of the carburettor

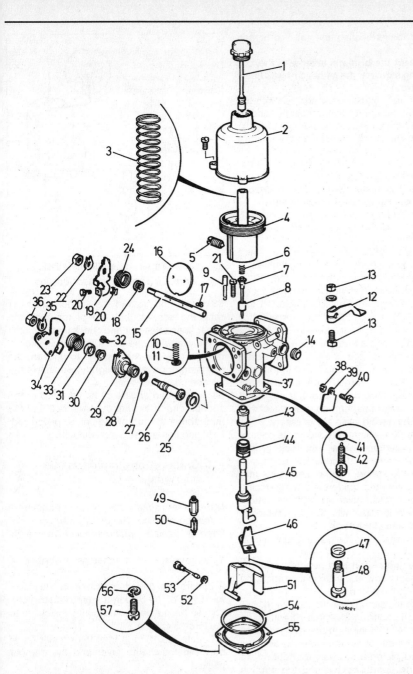

1	Piston damper	29 Retaining plate
2	Suction chamber	30 Seat
3	Spring	31 End cover
4	Piston	32 Screw
5	Grub screw	33 Return spring
6	Spring	34 Fast idle cam
7	Needle	35 Lockwasher
8	Guide	36 Nut
9	Lifting pin	37 Main body
10	Spring	38 Spring washer
11	Circlip	39 Identification tab
12	Throttle damper lever	40 Screw
13	Clamp bolt and nut	41 Seal
14	Seal	42 Mixture screw
15	Throttle spindle	43 Jet bearing
16	Throttle valve disc	44 Jet bearing nut
17	Screw	45 Jet assembly
18	Seal	46 Bi-metal lever
19	Throttle lever	47 Spring
20	Fast idle adjustment screw	48 Screw
21	Idle adjustment screw	49 Needle valve seat
22	Lockwasher	50 Needle valve
23	Nut	51 Float
24	Return spring	52 Seal
25	Cold start seal	53 Pivot
26	Cold start spindle	54 Seal
27	O-ring	55 Float chamber cover
28	Cold start body	56 Spring washer
		57 Screw

loosen the nut and bolt and remove the throttle damper lever.

26 Check the threaded end of the spindle and the main body with each other, then withdraw the spindle. Remove the two seals.

Overhaul

27 Clean all the components in fuel and allow to dry. Thoroughly examine the components for damage and excessive wear. In particular check the throttle spindle and bearings for wear. If excessive, renewal of the spindle may be sufficient, but if the bearings are worn it may be necessary to renew the complete carburettor, as new bearings are not always available. Check the needle valve and seating for excessive ridging. Examine the main body for cracks and for security of the brass fittings and piston key. Check the tapered needle, jet, and jet bearing for wear. Shake the float and listen for any trapped fuel that may have entered through a small crack or fracture. Renew the components as necessary and obtain a complete set of gaskets and seals, and two new throttle valve screws if necessary **(see liiustration)**.

28 Clean the inside of the suction chamber and the periphery of the piston with methylated spirit. Do not use any form of abrasive. Lubricate the piston rod with engine oil and insert it into the suction chamber. Hold the two components horizontal and spin the piston in several positions; the piston must spin freely without touching the suction chamber.

13 From beneath the main body, unscrew the jet bearing nut and withdraw the bearing.

14 Note how the spring is attached to the fast idle cam lever. Bend back the locktabs, then unscrew the nut and remove the washer.

15 Hold the return spring against the main body, and use a screwdriver to prise the cam lever from the end of the cold start spindle. Remove the spring.

16 Remove the end cover and spindle seat.

17 Remove the two screws and withdraw the retaining plate, cold start body, and gasket.

18 Remove the O-ring from the end of the cold start spindle, and withdraw the spindle from the main body. Remove the cold start seal.

19 Dismantling of the throttle spindle is not

recommended unless the components are damaged or excessively worn. If they are, first note how the return spring is attached to the throttle lever.

20 Mark the throttle valve with the spindle and main body.

21 Remove the throttle valve screws while supporting the spindle with a block of wood if necessary.

22 Open the throttle and withdraw the valve disc.

23 Remove any burrs from the spindle screw holes with a fine file.

24 Bend back the locktabs and unscrew the spindle nut. Remove the lockwasher, plain washer, throttle lever, and return spring.

25 From the opposite end of the spindle,

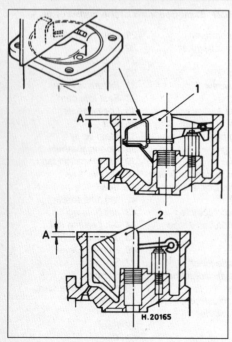

15.46 Float level checking dimension (A)
Arrows indicate checking point
Early float (1) = 0.40 ± 0.200 in (1.0 ± 0.5 mm)
Later float (2) = 0.80 ± 0.200 in (2.0 ± 0.5 mm)

Reassembly

29 Begin reassembly by fitting the throttle spindle and two seals to the main body. The seals must be slightly recessed in their housings.

30 Locate the return spring and throttle lever on the end of the spindle, and fit the plain washer, lockwasher, and nut. Tighten the nut while holding the lever, and bend over the locktabs to lock.

31 Engage the return spring with the throttle lever and main body, and tension the spring.

32 Fit the throttle valve disc to the spindle in its original position, and insert the new screws, tightening them loosely (coat the threads with a liquid locking agent).

33 Open and close the throttle several times to settle the disc, then tighten the screws while supporting the spindle on a block of wood. Using a small chisel, spread the ends of the screws to lock them.

34 Locate the throttle damper lever loosely on the end of the spindle.

35 Locate the cold start seal in the main body with the cut-out uppermost.

36 Insert the cold start spindle (hole uppermost), and fit the O-ring.

37 Fit the cold start body with the cut-out uppermost, and the retaining plate with the slotted flange facing the throttle spindle. Use a new gasket, then insert and tighten the retaining screws.

38 Fit the spindle seat and end cover, followed by the spring, cam lever, lockwasher, and nut. Make sure that the spring is correctly engaged, then tighten the nut and bend over the locktabs to lock.

39 Insert the jet bearing and nut, and tighten the nut.

40 Connect the bi-metal lever with the fuel jet, making sure that the jet head moves freely in the cut-out.

41 Insert the mixture screw and seal into the main body. Fit the jet to the bearing, and at the same time engage the slot in the bi-metal lever with the small diameter of the mixture screw.

42 Insert the jet retaining screw with the spring, and tighten the screw.

43 Adjust the mixture screw so that the top of the jet is flush with the venturi bridge.

44 Insert and tighten the needle valve seat, and with the carburettor inserted, insert the needle valve.

45 Position the float, then insert the pivot and seal through the body and float and tighten.

46 A modified float is fitted from early 1987, and the float level setting has been changed both for the early and modified floats. It can be checked by holding the carburettor inverted, with the float keeping the needle valve shut. Using a straight edge and feeler blade, check that the centre portion of the float is between 0.020 and 0.040 in (0.5 and 1.0 mm) below the surface of the float chamber face **(see illustration)**. If not, bend the brass tab (or float arm on later types) that contacts the needle valve as necessary.

47 Fit the float chamber cover in its original position together with a new sealing ring. Tighten the screws in diagonal sequence.

48 Insert the spring, needle, and guide into the piston with the guide etch marks facing the suction transfer holes and with the bottom face of the guide flush with the bottom face of the piston **(see illustration)**.

49 Insert and tighten the guide retaining grub screw.

50 Lower the piston and needle assembly into the main body, at the same time engaging the slot with the piston key.

51 Locate the spring over the piston rod.

52 Hold the suction chamber directly over the piston with its location mark aligned with the mark on the body, then lower it over the spring and piston rod. It is important not to tension the spring by twisting the suction chamber.

16.2 Throttle damper location

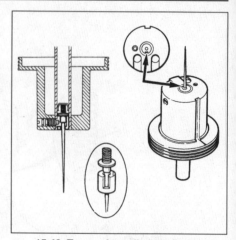

15.48 Tapered needle installation
Arrows indicate etch mark location

53 Insert and tighten the suction chamber retaining screws. Lift the piston with the finger, then release it and check that it returns to the venturi bridge without any assistance. If not, it may be necessary to loosen the retaining screws and slightly reposition the suction chamber.

54 Pour clean engine oil into the top of the suction chamber until the level is 0.5 in (13 mm) above the top of the hollow piston rod. Refit and tighten the piston damper.

16 Carburettor - throttle damper adjustment

Note: *Refer to the warning note in Section 1 before proceeding. The throttle damper is not fitted to vehicles manufactured from early 1982.*

1 Remove the air cleaner as described in Section 2.

2 Locate the throttle damper on the right-hand side of the carburettor **(see illustration)**. Loosen the nut and bolt securing the clamp to the throttle spindle.

3 Locate a 0.12 in (3 mm) thick feeler blade between the clamp lever and the damper plunger.

4 Depress the clamp lever until the plunger is fully compressed, then tighten the nut and bolt.

5 Release the clamp lever, and remove the feeler blade.

6 Refit the air cleaner with reference to Section 2.

17 Anti run-on valve (MG 1300 models) - removal and refitting

Removal

1 The anti run-on valve is mounted on a bracket on the bulkhead **(see illustration)**. Its function is to prevent the engine running-on

17.1 Anti-run-on valve is mounted on bulkhead

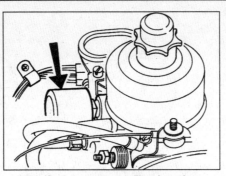

18.1 Carburettor vent filter location - 1.0 litre models with high compression economy engine

("dieseling") after the ignition is switched off. If it is disconnected or broken it may prevent the engine from idling or running at low speeds.

2 To remove the valve, disconnect the electrical connectors and the hose from it.

3 Undo the bracket securing nut and remove the valve complete with bracket.

Refitting

4 Refit in the reverse order, and check for correct operation on completion.

18 Carburettor vent filter - 1.0 litre economy models

The SU HIF carburettor requires an unrestricted flow of air to the float chamber through the vent pipe **(see illustration)**. If the pipe is becomes blocked, kinked or even incorrectly routed the mixture will be weakened, causing poor performance and difficult starting. On 1.0 litre models fitted with "economy" engines, a small air filter is fitted to the vent to improve carburettor calibration. This filter must

be renewed at the specified interval, or the mixture will become excessively weak during part-load running. The filter must never be omitted or the fuel consumption will increase.

19 Inlet and exhaust manifold - removal and refitting

Note: *Refer to the warning note in Section 1 before proceeding.*

> **HAYNES HINT** *Always fit a new manifold gasket. A little sealing paste will prevent the downpipe joint(s) from leaking.*

Removal

1 For Turbo models refer to Section 20. On some models, as described in Section 1, the manifold may be split into two **(see illustration)**.

2 To remove the manifold, first remove the carburettor as described in Sections 13 or 14.

3 Remove the clamp(s) securing the downpipe(s) to the manifold. Disconnect and plug the coolant hoses, if fitted.

4 Twist the plate on the heat stove, unscrew the nuts, and withdraw the stove **(see illustrations)**.

5 Unscrew the remaining nuts, remove the washers where fitted, and withdraw the manifold from the cylinder head **(see illustration)**. Although on some models, each manifold may be removed separately, both must be removed in order to renew the gasket.

6 Remove the gasket. Clean the mating faces of the manifold, cylinder head, and exhaust system downpipe.

7 Before refitting the inlet manifold on non-Turbo models make sure that the ferrules are positioned correctly in the cylinder head ports.

Refitting

8 Refitting is a reversal of removal. Always fit a new manifold gasket. Make sure that the downpipe is correctly located on the manifold before fitting the clamp. A little sealing paste will prevent the downpipe joint(s) from leaking. On completion top-up the cooling system as necessary.

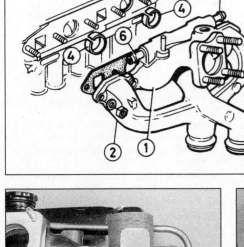

19.1 Inlet and exhaust manifolds with coolant heating for inlet - non-Turbo models

1 Inlet manifold
2 Exhaust manifold
3 Hot air shroud
4 Ferrules
5 Coolant inlet
6 Coolant outlet

19.4a Remove the retaining nuts . . .

19.4b . . . and withdraw the heat stove

19.5 Removing the manifold (1.3 HLS)

4

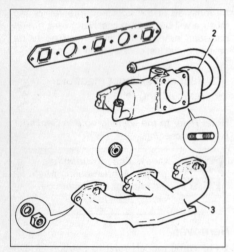

20.10 Inlet and exhaust manifolds with coolant heating for inlet - Turbo models

1 Manifold gasket
2 Inlet manifold
3 Exhaust manifold

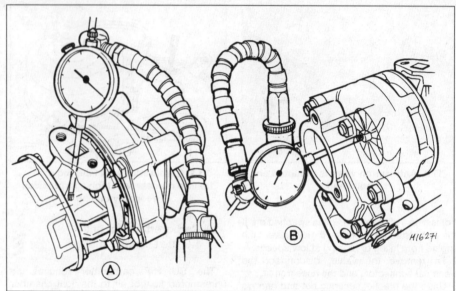

20.19 Measuring turbine bearing radial clearance (A) and axial clearance (B)

20 Turbocharger - removal, inspection and refitting

Note: Refer to the warning note in Section 1 before proceeding. Also note that, DIY repair to the turbocharger **is not** possible. If the bearings are worn, or some other malfunction is evident, it should be exchanged for a new one.

Note: Ensure that the air cleaner element is clean, the air inlet is unrestricted, that all pressure sensing connections are tight and that the engine itself is in good condition.

Removal

1 Disconnect the battery earth lead. Chock the rear wheels, then raise and securely support the front of the car.

2 Remove the U-bolt and clamp plate that secure the exhaust downpipe.

3 Release the hose clip that secures the oil drain hose to the turbochargers. Free the hose from the adapter.

4 Disconnect and plug the coolant hoses which supply the inlet manifold. Be prepared for some coolant spillage.

5 Disconnect and plug the fuel hose from the carburettor. Be prepared for some fuel spillage.

6 Disconnect the air pressure hose from the plenum chamber. Remove the heat shield from the plenum chamber, slacken the inlet hose clip, undo the two through-bolts and remove the plenum chamber.

7 Free the crankcase ventilation system oil trap from the flywheel housing. Disconnect the banjo union from the inlet manifold and the vacuum advance pipe from the carburettor. Move the hoses to one side.

8 Remove the heat shields from the clutch master cylinder and from the flywheel housing.

9 Release the manifold securing nuts. Unscrew the nuts that secure the inlet manifold as far as the ends of their studs.

10 Work the inlet manifold and carburettor free of the manifold gasket and off the studs. Move the assembly to one side **(see illustration)**.

11 Disconnect the air inlet hose and the boost control hose from the turbocharger housing.

12 Remove the clamp that secures the exhaust pipe to the turbocharger elbow.

13 Disconnect the oil supply pipe at the warning light switch adapter.

14 Support the engine/gearbox assembly with a jack (preferably a trolley jack), using a piece of wood to spread the load.

15 Remove the nut and washers from the rear right-hand engine mounting. Depending on the flexibility of the remaining mountings, the front right-hand mounting may also need to be disconnected.

16 Remove the nuts from the manifold studs. Raise the engine on the jack sufficiently to extract the exhaust manifold and turbocharger together, at the same time freeing the drain hose.

17 Separate the turbocharger from the exhaust manifold. If necessary, remove the oil feed pipe and drain elbow, and the exhaust pipe adapter.

Inspection

18 Do not immerse the turbocharger in solvent for cleaning purposes. Use solvent if necessary to clean the outside of the wastegate housing, and use a scraper or wire brush to remove carbon. Make sure that the wastegate moves freely.

19 If a dial gauge indicator is available, the radial and axial clearances of the turbine bearings may be measured **(see illustration)**.

The clearances must not exceed the values given in the Specifications.

20 If a regulated compressed air supply is available, apply air pressure to the wastegate actuator and check that the wastegate operates at 4 lbf/in^2 (0.28 kgf/cm^2).

Refitting

21 If a new turbocharger is being fitted, lubricate the bearings by pouring clean engine oil into the oil inlet port, rotating the compressor wheel at the same time. Drain the oil afterwards.

22 Refitting the turbocharger is a reversal of the removal procedure, but note the following points.

a) Use a copper-based anti-seize compound on all nuts, bolts and studs.

b) Use new gaskets for the inlet manifold-to-engine and manifold-to-carburettor joints (the latter only if it has been disturbed). Make sure that the mating faces are clean.

c) Make sure that the oil feed pipe is not strained or kinked, and that both its unions are tightened to the specified torque.

d) Remember to give the unit time to fill with oil before revving the engine.

21 Pressure reducing valve - testing, removal and refitting

Note: Refer to the warning note in Section 1 before proceeding.

Testing

1 The pressure reducing valve and solenoid (sometimes together referred to as the boost solenoid valve), are located next to the fuel pressure regulator. Access is improved by moving aside the expansion tank and the cooling fan relay **(see illustration)**.

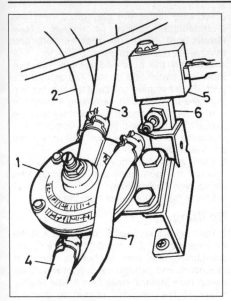

21.1 Fuel pressure regulator and pressure reducing valve

1 Fuel pressure regulator
2 Fuel outlet hose
3 Pressure sensing hose
4 Fuel inlet hose
5 Pressure reducing valve solenoid
6 Pressure reducing valve
7 Pressure hose

2 The solenoid may be tested *in situ* by applying the battery voltage directly to its terminals, when it should be heard to operate. It may be removed independently of the valve.

Removal

3 To remove the solenoid and valve together, unscrew the fuel regulator valve bracket. Turn the bracket on its side and unscrew the fuel regulator valve from the bracket.
4 Disconnect the pressure hose and unbolt the valve and solenoid.
5 Separate the solenoid and valve if wished. No repair is possible.

Refitting

6 Refitting is a reversal of removal. Make sure that the vent hole in the valve is clear. If fitting a new valve, a blanking plug may be fitted for protection in transit. This plug should be removed before fitting the valve.

22 Dump valve - removal and refitting

Removal

1 Disconnect the pressure hose from the plenum chamber and remove the heat shield.
2 Slacken the compressor hose clip, undo the bolts and remove the plenum chamber from the carburettor.
3 Remove the diffuser pipe from the plenum chamber (two bolts at the front and one nut at

the back). Be prepared for the dump valve piston and spring to be released **(see illustration)**.
4 Renew the piston and spring if the operation of the dump valve is suspect. There is no easy way of testing the components except by substitution.

Refitting

5 Refit in the reverse order to removal, using new gaskets throughout.

23 Wastegate actuator - testing

Testing

1 The wastegate actuator may be tested *in situ* by applying compressed air at 4 lbf/in² (0.28 kgf/cm²) to its pressure hose connection.
2 If the actuator fails to operate, temporarily remove its connecting rod and repeat the test. Continued failure means that the fault is in the actuator itself; if the actuator now operates, the fault is seizure of the wastegate, which may be rectified by removal and thorough cleaning. Refer to Section 20, paragraphs 11, through to 22.
3 At the time of writing, the actuator unit was not available separately from the complete turbocharger. Removal and refitting are self-explanatory, but take care not to alter the actuating rod adjustment.

24 Electronic control unit - removal and refitting

Removal

1 The electronic control unit (ECU) is reached from inside the vehicle. Begin by removing the glovebox (see Chapter 11), and pulling back the carpet.
2 Remove the closing panel and unscrew the mounting bracket from the front panel.
3 Unplug the electrical connector and disconnect the pressure hose, then remove the ECU complete with bracket.
4 No DIY testing procedures exist for the ECU, other than testing by substitution of a known good unit.

Refitting

5 Refitting is the reverse of removal.

25 Fuel pressure regulator - removal and refitting

Note: *Refer to the warning note in Section 1 before proceeding.*

Removal

1 Disconnect the battery earth lead.
2 Free the fuel pump relay and the expansion tank, and move them to one side.

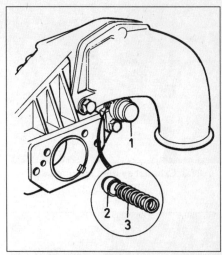

22.3 Dump valve components

1 Valve housing   *3 Spring*
2 Piston

3 Disconnect the pressure hose from the pressure reducing valve.
4 Unscrew the fuel pressure regulator bracket and turn the bracket to gain access to the regulator screws. Unscrew the regulator from the bracket.
5 Slide back the hose clips and disconnect the air pressure hose and the fuel hoses. Be prepared for some fuel spillage. Plug the fuel hoses.
6 No repairs to the fuel pressure regulator are possible. Do not attempt to alter the adjustment screw, which is preset and must not be moved.

Refitting

7 Refitting is the reverse of removal. Use new hoses and/or clips if the condition of the old items is in doubt.

26 Exhaust elbow gasket (if fitted) - removal and refitting

Removal

1 Chock the rear wheels, then raise and securely support the front of the vehicle.
2 Remove the U-bolt and clamp which secure the exhaust pipe to the transmission.
3 Unscrew the clutch damper bracket and move it to one side. Remove the heat shield and disconnect the brake servo hose.
4 Remove the clamp that secures the exhaust downpipe to the elbow.
5 Relieve the locking tabs, then remove the retaining bolts from the exhaust elbow.
6 Remove the exhaust elbow and gasket.

Refitting

7 Refitting is a reversal of removal. Use a new gasket and (ideally) new locktabs, and use high temperature anti-seize compound on the elbow bolts.

4

27.3 Exhaust system intermediate mounting

27.5a Exhaust system front downpipe clamp

27.5b Exhaust system front mounting clamp (1.3 HLS)

27 Exhaust system - removal and refitting

Removal

1 To remove the exhaust system, jack up the front and rear of the car and support it on axle stands (see *"Jacking and vehicle support"*). Alternatively, locate the front wheels on car ramps and jack up the rear and support with axle stands.

2 Lift the spare wheel cover in the luggage compartment and unscrew the rear exhaust mounting nut. Remove the lockwasher and plain washer.

3 Working under the car, disconnect the intermediate rubber mountings **(see illustration)**, lower the rear section, and remove the rear mounting.

4 Unscrew the nuts and remove the two mounting plates and U-bolt. Tap around the joint with a hammer, and twist the rear section from the front section, removing it from the rear of the car. If necessary, carefully heat the joint with a blowlamp to assist removal, but shield the fuel tank, fuel lines, and underbody adequately from heat.

5 Remove the front downpipe clamp(s), and remove the bolt from the front mounting clamp **(see illustrations)**.

6 Lower the front exhaust from the car.

Refitting

7 Refitting is a reversal of removal, but fit the downpipe(s) to the manifold before finally positioning the rear section to the rear mounting and tightening the intermediate clamp **(see illustrations)**. Use a little sealing paste at the manifold joint(s) to prevent leakage. Run the engine and check for leaks as described in Chapter 1.

28 Exhaust downpipes - modification

1 On cars subject to continual heavy use the exhaust downpipe may fracture just behind the first bend. To overcome this problem, a spring-tensioned balljoint is now fitted to allow slight flexing.

2 On MG Turbo models with a single downpipe, the balljoint is fitted with a single tensioning spring, but on twin downpipe models two springs are fitted.

3 The modified twin downpipe exhaust may be fitted instead of the earlier type, but it will be necessary to fit new exhaust mountings and new mounting brackets to the transmission and rear subframe. MG Turbo-type engine mountings should also be fitted.

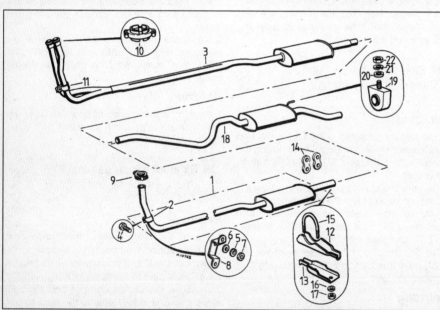

27.7a Exhaust system components (except MG Turbo)

1 Front exhaust system for 998 cc low compression engine	7 Nut	14 Mounting rubber
	8 Bracket	15 U-bolt
2 Clip	9 Clamp kit (998 cc low compression)	16 Washer
3 Front exhaust system for 998 cc high compression and 1275 cc engines	10 Clamp kit (998 cc high compression and 1275 cc engines)	17 Nut
		18 Rear exhaust system
4 Bolt	11 Clip	19 Rear mounting
5 Washer	12 Upper mounting bracket	20 Washer
6 Washer	13 Lower mounting bracket	21 Spring washer
		22 Nut

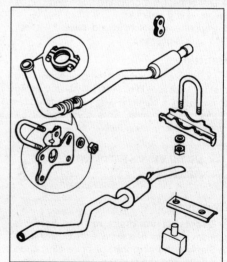

27.7b Exhaust system fitted to MG Turbo
Later type also has a spring-tensioned balljoint in the downpipe section

Chapter 5
Engine electrical systems

Contents

Degrees of difficulty

Easy, suitable for novice with little experience	Fairly easy, suitable for beginner with some experience	Fairly difficult, suitable for competent DIY mechanic	Difficult, suitable for experienced DIY mechanic	Very difficult, suitable for expert DIY or professional

Specifications

System type . . . . 12 volt battery (negative earth), coil and distributor

Battery
Capacity . . . . 30 amp hr or 40 amp hr
Type:
   Lucas . . . . 007 or 063
   Chloride . . . . 170/60/89 or 190/60/90
Charge condition:
   Poor . . . . 12.5 volts
   Normal . . . . 12.6 volts
   Good . . . . 12.7 volts

Coil
Type . . . . Lucas, Ducellier, Bosch, Unipart or AC Delco
Ballast resistance . . . . 1.3 to 1.5 ohms

Distributor
Type . . . . Lucas or Ducellier
   All 1985-on (except van) . . . . Lucas (electronic)
   All MG Turbo . . . . Lucas (electronic)
Air gap . . . . See Chapter 1 Specifications
Rotor rotation . . . . Anti-clockwise
Dwell angle . . . . See Chapter 1 Specifications
Contact breaker gap . . . . See Chapter 1 Specifications
Condenser capacity . . . . 0.18 to 0.25 mfd
Centrifugal advance (decelerating):
   998 cc - at 4800 rpm . . . . 22° to 26°
           - at 2800 rpm . . . . 14° to 18°
           - at 1500 rpm . . . . 10° to 14°
           - at 600 rpm . . . . 0° to 2°
   1275 cc - at 5200 rpm . . . . 24° to 28°
           - at 2800 rpm . . . . 23° to 27°
           - at 2500 rpm . . . . 16° to 20°
           - at 1600 rpm . . . . 8° to 12°
           - at 700 rpm . . . . 0° to 4°

5

Vacuum advance (maximum):
 998 cc (except HLE) . . . . 12° to 16° at 11 in (279 mm) Hg
 998 cc (HLE) . . . . 14° to 16° at 9 in (229 mm) Hg
 1275 cc . . . . 14° to 18° at 8 in (203 mm) Hg
Lubricant type/specification . . . . Multigrade engine oil, viscosity SAE 15W/50 or 10W/40

Firing order 1-3-4-2

Ignition timing at 1500 rpm (with vacuum disconnected)

998 cc
1980:
 HLE . . . . 8° ± 2° BTDC
 All other models . . . . 15° BTDC
1982:
 HLE . . . . 7° BTDC
 All other models . . . . 15° BTDC
1983:
 HLE . . . . 5° to 7° BTDC
 All other models . . . . 15° BTDC
1984:
 Engines 99HA06P and 99HA08P . . . . 5° to 7° BTDC
 All other models . . . . 15° BTDC
1985-on:
 High compression . . . . 5° to 7° BTDC
 All other models . . . . 14 to 16° BTDC
1989-on 95 RON unleaded fuel specification
 Low compression . . . . 15°± 1° BTDC
 Standard compression . . . . 5° ± 1° TDC

1275 cc
1980 . . . . 11° BTDC
1982:
 Low compression . . . . 13° BTDC
 Standard compression . . . . 11° BTDC
 MG . . . . 10° BTDC
 Vanden Plas . . . . 11° BTDC
1983:
 Low compression . . . . 13° BTDC
 HLE . . . . 9° BTDC
 All other models . . . . 11° BTDC
1984:
 Low compression . . . . 13° BTDC
 Standard compression . . . . 11° BTDC
 HLE . . . . 7° to 9° BTDC
 MG . . . . 10° BTDC
 Vanden Plas . . . . 11° BTDC
1985-on:
 Low compression . . . . 13° BTDC
 Standard compression . . . . 7° to 9° BTDC
 MG, Sport and Vanden Plas manual gearbox:
  Engines 12HA83AA, 12HC14AA, 12HD17AA and 12HD24AA . . . . 10° BTDC
  Engines 12HB42AA, 12HC15AA, 12HD25 . . . . 5° BTDC
1989-on 95 RON unleaded fuel specification:
 Low compression . . . . 13° ± 1° BTDC
 Standard and high compression . . . . 5° ± 1°

MG Turbo
1982 to 1984 . . . . 7° BTDC
1985-on . . . . 7° ± 1° BTDC

Alternator

Early models
Type . . . . Lucas or Motorola
Output at 14 volt and 3000 rpm . . . . 43 amp (Lucas), 45 amp (Motorola)
Minimum brush length . . . . 0.3 in (8 mm)

Later models
Type . . . . Lucas
Output at 14 volt and 6000 rpm . . . . 45 or 55 amps
Minimum brush length . . . . 0.4 in (10.0 mm)

Starter motor

Type .... Lucas inertia or pre-engaged

Torque wrench settings	lbf ft	Nm
Alternator adjusting link to alternator	9	12
Alternator adjusting link to front plate	27	37
Alternator bracket to crankcase	16	22
Alternator pulley nut	27	37
Alternator top fixings	16	22
Distributor clamp	16	22
Spark plugs	18	25
Starter motor retaining bolts	27	37

1 Mechanical ignition system - description

Note: *Although repair procedures are given in this Chapter, it may well be more economical to renew worn components as complete units.*

Description

The electrical system is of 12 volt negative earth type. The battery is charged by a belt-driven alternator which incorporates a voltage regulator. The starter motor is of inertia or pre-engaged type and incorporates four brushes and a face-type commutator. On the inertia type, the drive pinion is thrown into engagement with the flywheel ring gear by the movement of the starter motor. On the pre-engaged type, a solenoid moves the drive pinion into engagement before the starter motor is energised.

A conventional ignition system is fitted, comprising the battery, coil, distributor and spark plugs. The distributor is driven by a driveshaft in mesh with the camshaft.

In order that the engine can run correctly, it is necessary for an electrical spark to ignite the fuel/air mixture in the combustion chamber at exactly the right moment in relation to engine speed and load. The ignition system is based on feeding low tension voltage from the battery to the coil, where it is converted to high tension voltage. The high tension voltage is powerful enough to jump the spark plug gap in the cylinders many times a second under high compression, providing that the system is in good condition and that all adjustments are correct.

The ignition system is divided into two circuits, the low tension circuit and the high tension circuit. The low tension (sometimes known as the primary) circuit consists of the battery, lead to the ignition switch, lead from the ignition switch to the low tension or primary coil windings (terminal +), and the lead from the low tension coil windings (coil terminal -) to the contact breaker points and condenser in the distributor. The high tension circuit consists of the high tension or secondary coil windings, the heavy ignition lead from the coil to the distributor cap, the rotor arm, and the spark plug leads and spark plugs.

The system functions in the following manner. Low tension voltage is changed in the coil into high tension voltage by the opening and closing of the contact breaker points in the low tension circuit. High tension voltage is then fed via the carbon brush in the centre of the distributor cap to the rotor arm of the distributor, and each time it comes in line with one of the four metal segments in the cap, which are connected to the spark plug leads, the opening and closing of the contact breaker points causes the high tension voltage to build up, jump the gap from the rotor arm to the appropriate metal segment, and so via the spark plug lead to the spark plug, where it finally jumps the spark plug gap before going to earth. The ignition is advanced and retarded automatically, to ensure that the spark occurs at just the right instant for the particular load at the prevailing engine speed.

The ignition advance is controlled both mechanically and by a vacuum operated system. The mechanical governor mechanism comprises two weights, which move out from the distributor shaft as the engine speed rises due to centrifugal force. As they move outwards they rotate the cam relative to the distributor shaft, and so advance the spark. The weights are held in position by two light springs and it is the tension of the springs which is largely responsible for correct spark advancement.

The vacuum control consists of a diaphragm, one side of which is connected via a small bore tube to the carburettor, and the other side to the contact breaker plate. Depression in the inlet manifold and carburettor, which varies with engine speed and throttle opening, causes the diaphragm to move, so moving the contact breaker plate, and advancing or retarding the spark. A fine degree of control is achieved by a spring in the vacuum assembly.

The ignition system incorporates a resistive wire which is in circuit all the time that the engine is running. When the starter is operated, the resistance is bypassed to provide increased voltage at the spark plugs.

Early models were fitted with distributors with self-cleaning contact breaker points.

2 Electronic ignition system - description

Warning: Because of the high voltages generated, care should be taken to avoid receiving personal electric shocks from the HT system. This is particularly important for anyone fitted with an artificial cardiac pacemaker.

Description

The Lucas electronic ignition system consists of a distributor, an amplifier module and a coil. Externally, the distributor resembles a conventional type, but internally a reluctor and a pick-up unit take the place of the cam and contact breaker points.

Each time one of the reluctor teeth or arms passes through the magnetic field of the pick-up coil, an electrical signal is sent to the amplifier module which then triggers the coil in the same way as the opening of the points in a conventional system. Both centrifugal and vacuum advance are used in the same manner.

Because there are no contact breaker points to wear out, the electronic ignition system is extremely reliable. As long as the distributor is lubricated and the spark plugs inspected or renewed at the specified intervals, and leads and connections are kept clean and dry, it is very unlikely that trouble will be experienced.

3 Battery - removal and refitting

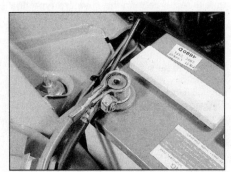

3.3 Battery positive terminal and lead

Removal

1 The battery is located on the right-hand side of the engine compartment.

2 Lift the plastic cover from the negative terminal, loosen the clamp bolt, and remove the lead.

3 Lift the plastic cover from the positive terminal, loosen the clamp bolt, and remove the lead **(see illustration)**.

4 Loosen the battery retaining bar nuts and completely remove the nuts from one side.

5 Swivel the bar to one side, and unhook the two rods.

6 Lift the battery from the carrier platform, taking care not to spill any electrolyte on the bodywork.

Refitting

7 Refitting is a reversal of removal, but make sure that the polarity is correct before connecting the leads, and do not overtighten the clamp bolts.

4 Battery - testing and charging

Testing

Standard and low-maintenance battery

1 If the vehicle covers a small annual mileage, it is worthwhile checking the specific gravity of the electrolyte every three months, to determine the state of charge of the battery. Use a hydrometer to make the check, and compare the results with the following table. Note that the specific gravity readings assume an electrolyte temperature of 15°C (60°F); for every 10°C (50°F) below 15°C (60°F), subtract 0.007. For every 10°C (50°F) above 15°C (60°F), add 0.007. However, for convenience, the temperatures quoted in the following table are ambient (outdoor air) temperatures, above or below 25°C (77°F):

	Above 25°C	Below 25°C
Charged	1.210 to 1.230	1.270 to 1.290
70% charged	1.170 to 1.190	1.230 to 1.250
Discharged	1.050 to 1.070	1.110 to 1.130

2 If the battery condition is suspect, first check the specific gravity of electrolyte in each cell. A variation of 0.040 or more between any cells indicates loss of electrolyte or deterioration of the internal plates.

3 If the specific gravity variation is 0.040 or more, the battery should be renewed. If the cell variation is satisfactory but the battery is discharged, it should be charged as described later in this Section.

Maintenance-free battery

4 In cases where a "sealed for life" maintenance-free battery is fitted, topping-up and testing of the electrolyte in each cell is not possible. The condition of the battery can therefore only be tested using a battery condition indicator or a voltmeter.

5 A battery with a built-in charge condition indicator may be fitted. The indicator is located in the top of the battery casing, and indicates the condition of the battery from its colour. If the indicator shows green, then the battery is in a good state of charge. If the indicator turns darker, eventually to black, then the battery requires charging, as described later in this Section. If the indicator shows clear/yellow, then the electrolyte level in the battery is too low to allow further use, and the battery should be renewed. Do not attempt to charge, load or jump-start a battery when the indicator shows clear/yellow.

6 If testing the battery using a voltmeter, connect the voltmeter across the battery, and compare the result with those given in the Specifications under "charge condition". The test is only accurate if the battery has not been subjected to any kind of charge for the previous six hours, including charging by the alternator. If this is not the case, switch on the headlights for 30 seconds, then wait four to five minutes after switching off the headlights before testing the battery. All other electrical circuits must be switched off, so check (for instance) that the doors and tailgate or boot lid are fully shut when making the test.

7 If the voltage reading is less than 12.2 volts, then the battery is discharged. A reading of 12.2 to 12.4 volts indicates a partially-discharged condition.

8 If the battery is to be charged, remove it from the vehicle (Section 3) and charge it as described in the following paragraphs.

Charging

Standard and low-maintenance battery

Note: *The following is intended as a guide only. Always refer to the manufacturer's recommendations (often printed on a label attached to the battery) before charging a battery.*

9 Charge the battery at a rate of 3.5 to 4 amps, and continue to charge the battery at this rate until no further rise in specific gravity is noted over a four-hour period.

10 Alternatively, a trickle charger charging at the rate of 1.5 amps can safely be used overnight.

11 Specially rapid "boost" charges which are claimed to restore the power of the battery in 1 to 2 hours are not recommended, as they can cause serious damage to the battery plates through overheating.

12 While charging the battery, note that the temperature of the electrolyte should never exceed 37.8°C (100°F).

Maintenance-free battery

Note: *The following is intended as a guide only. Always refer to the manufacturer's recommendations (often printed on a label attached to the battery) before charging a battery.*

13 This battery type requires a longer period to fully recharge than the standard type, the time taken being dependent on the extent of discharge, but it can take anything up to three days.

14 A constant-voltage type charger is required, to be set, where possible, to 13.9 to 14.9 volts with a charger current below 25 amps. Using this method, the battery should be usable within three hours, giving a voltage reading of 12.5 volts, but this is for a partially-discharged battery and, as mentioned, full charging can take considerably longer.

15 Use of a normal trickle charger should not be detrimental to the battery, provided excessive gassing is not allowed to occur, and the battery is not allowed to become hot.

5 Condenser - testing, removal and refitting

Testing

1 The condenser is fitted in parallel with the contact points, and its purpose is to reduce arcing between the points, and also to accelerate the collapse of the coil low tension magnetic field. A faulty condenser can cause the complete failure of the ignition system, as the points will be prevented from interrupting the low tension circuit.

2 To test the condenser, remove the distributor cap and rotate the engine until the contact points are closed. Switch on the ignition and separate the points. If this is accompanied by a *strong* blue flash, the condenser is faulty (a *weak* spark is normal).

3 A further test can be made, for short circuiting, by removing the condenser and using a test lamp and leads connected to the supply lead and body. If the test lamp lights, the condenser is faulty.

4 The most infallible test is to substitute a new unit and check whether the fault persists.

Removal

5 It will be easier to work on the distributor if it is removed (as described in Chapter 5), but this is not essential. On the Lucas distributor, release the clips and lift off the distributor cap, leaving the HT leads connected.

Lucas type

6 Remove the rotor arm, and push the low tension lead and grommet in through the hole in the body.

7 Press the moving contact spring from the insulator post, and slide out the low tension lead connector.

8 Remove the retaining screw and earth lead and withdraw the condenser **(see illustration)**.

Ducellier type

9 Pull the supply lead from the block on the side of the distributor.

10 Remove the retaining screw and withdraw the condenser.

Refitting - all types

11 Refitting is a reversal of the removal procedure.

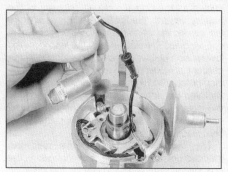

5.8 Removing the condenser (Lucas)

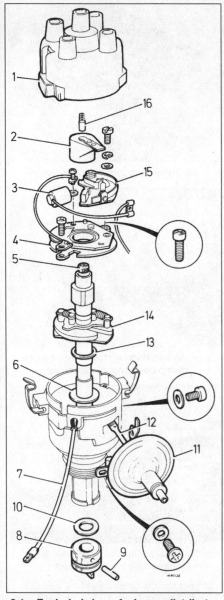

6.1a Exploded view of a Lucas distributor

1 Distributor cap	10 Thrustwasher
2 Rotor arm	11 Vacuum unit
3 Condenser	12 Arm
4 Baseplate assembly	13 Spacer
5 Felt pad	14 Centrifugal
6 Steel washer	advance mechanism
7 LT lead	15 Contact set
8 Drive dog	16 Pick-up brush
9 Roll pin	

6 Distributor - removal and refitting

Removal

Note: For better access to the distributor, the radiator may be temporarily moved to one side without disconnecting the top and bottom hoses, see Chapter 3 for details. This is

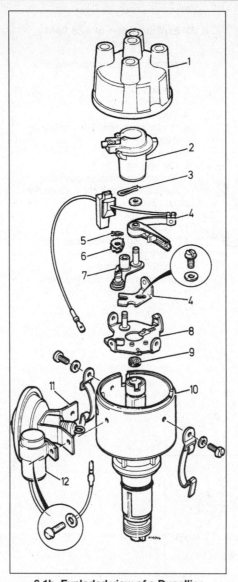

6.1b Exploded view of a Ducellier distributor

1 Distributor cap	7 Eccentric D-post
2 Rotor arm	8 Baseplate
3 Clip	9 Felt pad
4 Contact set	10 Body
5 Clip	11 Vacuum unit
6 Serrated cam	12 Condenser

particularly advantageous on 1985-on 1.3 engines where the electronic ignition amplifier module restricts access to the distributor clamp bolt. Also note that the distributor cap is retained with screws on 1985-on 1.3 models **(see illustrations)**. The distributor is designed to operate over very high mileage, and when wear eventually takes place, particularly between the shaft and body, the complete distributor should be renewed.

1 Disconnect the battery negative lead.

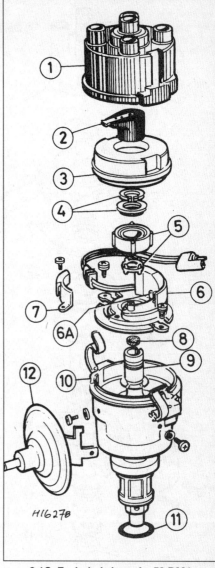

6.1C Exploded view of a 59 DM4 distributor

1 Distributor cap	6A Pick-up limb
2 Rotor arm	7 Wiring guide
3 Anti-flash shield	8 Felt pad
4 O-ring, washer and	9 Distributor shaft
circlip	10 Distributor body
5 Reluctor and	11 O-ring
coupling ring	12 Vacuum unit
6 Pick-up coil and	
baseplate assembly	

2 Remove No 1 spark plug (crankshaft pulley end) and place the thumb over the aperture.
3 Turn the engine in the normal running direction (clockwise from crankshaft pulley end) until pressure is felt in No 1 cylinder, indicating that the piston is commencing its compression stroke. Use a spanner on the crankshaft pulley bolt, or engage top gear and pull the car forwards.
4 Continue turning the engine until the V-notch in the crankshaft pulley is exactly in line

5

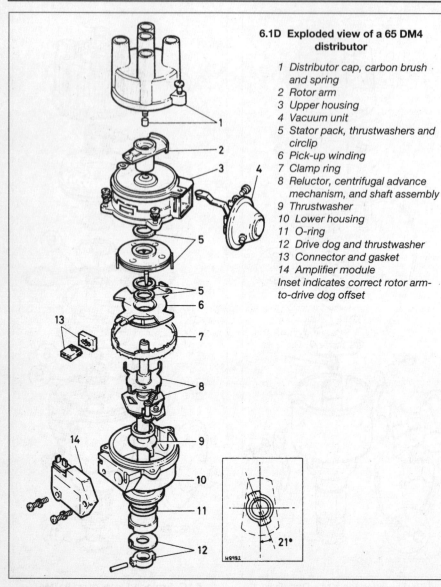

6.1D Exploded view of a 65 DM4 distributor

1 Distributor cap, carbon brush and spring
2 Rotor arm
3 Upper housing
4 Vacuum unit
5 Stator pack, thrustwashers and circlip
6 Pick-up winding
7 Clamp ring
8 Reluctor, centrifugal advance mechanism, and shaft assembly
9 Thrustwasher
10 Lower housing
11 O-ring
12 Drive dog and thrustwasher
13 Connector and gasket
14 Amplifier module

Inset indicates correct rotor arm-to-drive dog offset

6.5 Removing the distributor cap

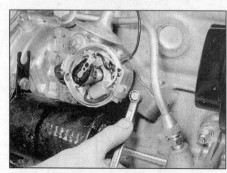

6.8A Unscrewing the distributor base clamp bolt (engine removed)

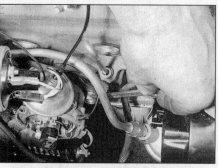

6.8B Unscrewing the distributor base clamp bolt (engine in car)

with the timing cover pointer top dead centre (TDC) mark. Note that the large pointer indicates TDC, and the remaining pointer peaks are in increments of 4° BTDC.

5 Make a mark on the distributor body in line with the No 1 spark plug HT lead terminal in the distributor cap. Remove the cap and check that the rotor arm is pointing to the mark **(see illustration)**.

6 Make a further mark on the cylinder block in line with the previous mark.

7 Disconnect the low tension lead and the vacuum advance pipe.

8 Remove the single base clamp bolt and withdraw the distributor from the cylinder block. Remove the clamp plate **(see illustrations)**.

Refitting

9 To refit the distributor, slide it into the cylinder block and engage the offset drive dog with the driveshaft **(see illustrations)**.

10 Turn the body to align the previously made marks on the body and cylinder block. Provided that the engine has not been turned, the rotor arm should also point towards the mark on the body.

11 Fit the clamp and tighten the securing bolt, then refit the distributor cap and

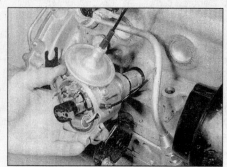

6.9A Installing the distributor (engine removed)

reconnect the low tension lead.

12 Refit the No 1 spark plug and HT lead. Reconnect the battery negative lead.

13 Check and, if necessary, adjust the ignition timing as described in Chapter 1, then refit the vacuum advance pipe.

6.9B Installing the distributor (engine in car)

7 Electronic ignition system - testing

Testing

Electronic ignition is normally very reliable; if it does fail, such failure tends to be complete. In cases of misfiring, or other intermittent faults, it is probably best to check the HT system first before proceeding to the table below.

An electrical multi-meter which can measure voltage and resistance (ohms) will be required for testing purposes. Such a meter need not be very expensive and is a useful addition to the electrically-minded mechanic's tool kit.

8 Thermostatically-operated vacuum switch - general, removal and refitting

General

1 Models fitted with catalytic converters have a thermostatically operated vacuum switch screwed into the cylinder head water outlet

Models fitted with 59 DM4 distributor

1 Is the reluctor air gap set to the specified dimension?

Yes: Proceed to Test 2
No: Adjust the gap, as described in Chapter 1, Section 16

2 Is the battery voltage greater than 11.5 volts?

Yes: Proceed to Test 3
No: Recharge the battery

3 Is the voltage at the coil "+" terminal more than 1 volt below battery voltage?

Yes: Faulty wiring or connector between ignition switch and coil, or faulty ignition switch
No: Proceed to Test 4

4 Is the voltage at the coil "-" terminal more than 2 volts?

Yes: Disconnect the wiring connector between distributor and ignition amplifier and proceed toTest 7
No: Disconnect the ignition amplifier lead at the coil "-" terminal and proceed to Test 5

5 Is the voltage at the coil "-" terminal now more than 2 volts?

Yes: Proceed to Test 6
No: Renew the ignition coil

6 Is the voltage at the ignition amplifier earth more than 0.1 volts?

Yes: Clean and/or repair the earth connection
No: Renew the ignition amplifier

7 Is the pick-up coil resistance measured at the wiring connector ignition terminals between 2.2k ohms and 4.8k ohms?

Yes: Reconnect the wiring connector between distributor and amplifier and proceed to Test 8
No: Renew the pick-up coil assembly in the distributor

8 Does the voltage at the coil "-" terminal drop when the starter motor is operated?

Yes: Check and adjust the ignition timing. If the fault still exists the problem may lie with the engine internal components
No: Renew the ignition amplifier

Models fitted with 65 DM4 distributor

1 Is the battery voltage greater than 11.7 volts?

Yes: Proceed to Test 2
No: Recharge the battery

2 Is the voltage at the coil "+" terminal within 1 volt of battery voltage?

Yes: Proceed to Test 3
No: Faulty wiring or connector between ignition switch and coil, or faulty ignition switch

3 Is the resistance between the ignition coil "+" and "-" terminals between 0.4 and 0.9 ohms?

Yes: Proceed to Test 4
No: Renew the ignition coil

4 Is the resistance between the ignition coil "+" and HT terminals between 5.0 and 15.0 k ohms?

Yes: Proceed to Test 5
No: Renew the ignition coil

5 Connect a low-wattage bulb across the ignition coil "+" and "-" terminals and spin the engine on the starter. Does the bulb flash?

Yes: Proceed to Test 6
No: Proceed to Test 10

6 Is the resistance of any HT lead greater than 20 k ohms?

Yes: Renew the HT lead
No: Proceed to Test 7

7 Are there signs of tracking on the ignition coil, distributor cap or rotor arm?

Yes: Renew the component as necessary
No: Proceed to Test 8

8 Is the ignition timing correct?

Yes: Proceed to Test 9
No: Adjust ignition timing

9 Are the spark plugs in good condition?

Yes: Check carburettor settings and engine mechanical condition
No: Renew the spark plugs

10 Are the module connections good?

Yes: Proceed to Test 11
No: Refer to Section 9, paragraphs 5 to 8

11 With the module removed, is the resistance of the distributor pick-up coil between 950 and 1150 ohms?

Yes: Refer to Section 9, paragraphs 5 to 8
No: Renew the distributor pick-up coil

5

elbow; the small-bore vacuum pipe being in two lengths that are connected from the carburettor to the switch and from the switch to the distributor. At coolant temperatures below 70°C (158°F) the switch prevents any vacuum advance from taking place, causing raised exhaust gas temperatures due to the retarded ignition timing, thus bringing the catalytic converter to its efficient operating temperature more quickly. Once coolant temperatures rise above this point, the switch opens and normal vacuum advance is restored.

2 To check the switch, first check the ignition timing (see Chapter 1). Unplug and reconnect the vacuum pipe at the distributor; the ignition timing should advance as the pipe is reconnected, retarding again when it is disconnected. If the ignition timing does not alter, check that the vacuum pipe is clear of blockages or kinks and that it is not leaking. Suck on the carburettor end of the pipe; if there is no effect on the ignition timing, then the vacuum unit or switch is faulty and must be renewed. The switch can be eliminated by connecting a vacuum pipe directly from the carburettor to the distributor; if the vacuum advance is then restored to normal the switch is proven faulty and must be renewed. Any more detailed tests must be left to a Rover dealer.

Removal

3 To remove the switch, either drain the cooling system (Chapter 3), or be prepared for some loss of coolant as the switch is unscrewed. If it is decided not to drain the cooling system, work quickly to minimise coolant loss. Disconnect and plug the vacuum pipes, then unscrew the switch and withdraw it; plug the opening to prevent the entry of dirt.

Refitting

4 Refitting is the reverse of the removal procedure, noting the following points:
  a) Wipe the threads of the switch and the elbow clean.
  b) If a sealing washer is fitted, renew it whenever it is disturbed to prevent leaks; if no sealing washer is fitted, apply a smear of sealant to the switch threads.
  c) Tighten the switch securely and reconnect the vacuum pipes.
  d) Refit any components removed to improve access.
  e) Refill or top-up the cooling system, as applicable (Chapter 3).

9 Electronic ignition amplifier - general, removal and refitting

Pre-1985 models

General

1 The ignition amplifier is mounted on the bonnet lock platform, near the ignition coil. The amplifier controls the function of the ignition coil in response to signals received from the pick-up coil in the distributor.

2 The amplifier may be tested using the procedure described in Section 7. If it is found to be faulty it should be renewed.

Removal

3 To remove the unit, disconnect the battery earth lead and then disconnect the wiring plug from the end of the amplifier. Undo the bracket retaining screws and remove the bracket complete with amplifier. The amplifier can then be removed if wished.

Refitting

4 Refitting is a reversal of removal. Make sure that there is good mechanical; and electrical contact between the amplifier and its bracket (which also serves as a heat sink) and between the bracket and its mounting area.

1985-on models

General

5 On later models the amplifier is attached to the distributor. If, after carrying out the test procedure described in Section 7, the amplifier module is diagnosed as being faulty, make sure that the wiring is intact and secure.

6 As a double-check remove the module, gasket and connector, and lightly squeeze together the terminals inside the connector. Clean the terminals in the module and distributor before refitting the module, and remember to apply heat-conducting silicone grease to the mounting face on the distributor.

7 Disconnect the wiring from the module, clean the terminals, and lightly squeeze together the terminals inside the connector before refitting it. Make sure that the connector is fully located over the base.

8 Check that the LT leads are correctly fitted to the ignition coil.

10 Coil - description and testing

Description

1 The coil is bolted to the front of the engine, and it should be periodically wiped down to prevent high tension (HT) voltage loss through possible arcing.

2 To ensure the correct HT polarity at the spark plugs, the LT coil leads must always be connected correctly. The LT lead from the distributor should be connected to the negative (-) terminal on the coil. Incorrect connections can cause bad starting, misfiring, and short spark plug life.

Testing

3 Accurate testing of the coil requires special equipment, and for the home mechanic the easiest test is by substitution of a new unit.

11 Alternator - testing

Note: *To carry out the complete test procedure, use only the following test equipment - 0 to 20 volt moving coil voltmeter, 0 to 100 amp moving coil ammeter.*

Testing

1 Check that the battery is at least 70% charged by using a hydrometer (Section 4).

2 Check the drivebelt tension (Chapter 1).

3 Check the security of the battery terminal leads, alternator multi-plug(s), and interconnecting wire.

4 To check the cable continuity, pull the multi-plug(s) from the alternator terminals and switch on the ignition, being careful not to crank the engine. Connect the voltmeter between a good earth and each of the terminals in the multi-plug in turn. If battery voltage is not indicated, there is an open circuit in the wiring, which may be due to a blown ignition warning light bulb if on the small terminal.

5 To check the alternator output, disconnect the multi-plug(s), and connect the ammeter between either of the large alternator output terminals and a bridging wire connector between the large terminals in the multi-plug. Connect a further bridging wire between the small terminals of the multi-plug and alternator **(see illustration)**. Run the engine at approximately 3000 rpm with the headlamps, heated rear window, and heater blower switched on, for one minute only. The ammeter should indicate the specified output of the alternator; if not, the alternator is faulty.

6 To check the charging circuit voltage drop, remove all previously fitted bridging wires and refit the multi-plug(s) to the alternator. Remove the cover from the multi-plug and connect the voltmeter between the battery positive terminal and either of the large alternator output terminals. Switch on the headlamps, heated rear window, and heater blower, and run the engine at approximately 3000 rpm. A dirty connection in the charging circuit is indicated if the voltmeter reads more than 0.5 volts.

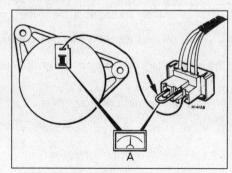

11.5 Checking the alternator output
Arrow shows bridging wire, 'A' indicates ammeter connections

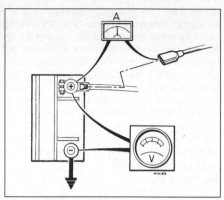

11.7 Checking the voltage regulator

'A' indicates ammeter connections
'V' indicates voltmeter connections

7 To check the alternator voltage regulator, refit the multi-plug cover, connect the voltmeter across the battery, and connect the ammeter between the positive battery lead and the main circuit supply lead as shown **(see illustration)**. If no terminal is fitted, unbolt the main circuit supply lead from the battery positive lead and connect the ammeter between them. With all accessories switched off, start the engine and run it at approximately 3000 rpm until the ammeter reads less than 10 amps: the voltmeter should read between 13.8 and 14.6 volts for a

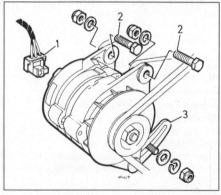

12.3 Alternator mounting

1 Multi-plug   3 Adjusting link
2 Pivot bolts

12.5 Removing the alternator

Motorola alternator, or between 13.6 and 14.4 volts for a Lucas alternator. If not, the voltage regulator is faulty.

12 Alternator - removal and refitting

Removal

1 Disconnect the battery negative lead.
2 Pull the multi-plug(s) from the alternator terminals **(see illustration)**.
3 Loosen the adjustment link nut and the mounting pivot bolts **(see illustration)**.
4 Swivel the alternator in towards the engine, and slip the drivebelt from the pulley.
5 Remove the adjustment link nut and washers. Remove the pivot bolts, nuts and washers. Withdraw the alternator from the engine **(see illustration)**.

Refitting

6 Refitting is a reversal of removal, but before tightening the mounting bolts and the adjustment nut, tension the drivebelt as described in Chapter 1.

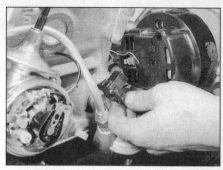

12.2 Removing the multi-plug from the alternator

13 Alternator brushes - removal, inspection and refitting

Removal and inspection

1 Remove the alternator (Section 12).

Lucas type

2 Disconnect and remove the interference suppression capacitor from the end cover (if fitted). Remove the securing screws and withdraw the end cover **(see illustrations)**.

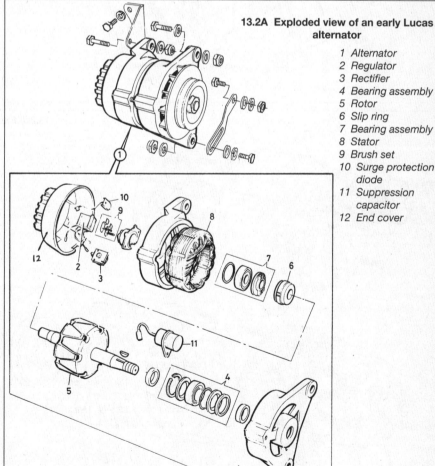

13.2A Exploded view of an early Lucas alternator

1 Alternator
2 Regulator
3 Rectifier
4 Bearing assembly
5 Rotor
6 Slip ring
7 Bearing assembly
8 Stator
9 Brush set
10 Surge protection diode
11 Suppression capacitor
12 End cover

5

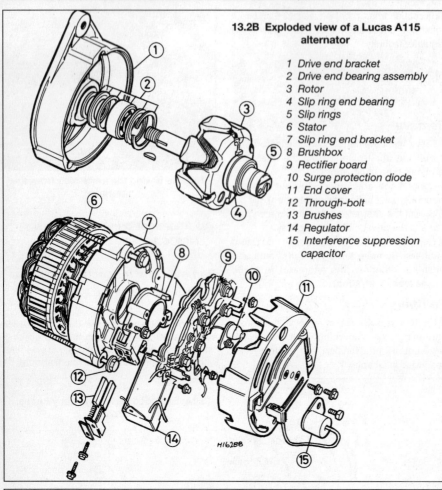

13.2B Exploded view of a Lucas A115 alternator

1 Drive end bracket
2 Drive end bearing assembly
3 Rotor
4 Slip ring end bearing
5 Slip rings
6 Stator
7 Slip ring end bracket
8 Brushbox
9 Rectifier board
10 Surge protection diode
11 End cover
12 Through-bolt
13 Brushes
14 Regulator
15 Interference suppression capacitor

3 Unscrew the surge protection diode securing screw. Either move the diode carefully out of the way, or disconnect it from the rectifier board and remove it. Disconnect the Lucar connector from the rectifier pack, and remove the brush moulding and regulator case retaining screws. Remove the brush moulding and regulator **(see illustrations)**.

4 Check that the brushes protrude from the moulding by more than the specified minimum amount. If not, remove the screws, withdraw them from the moulding, and renew them **(see illustration)**.

Motorola type

5 Remove the two screws securing the voltage regulator to the rear of the alternator. Withdraw the regulator and release the two wires **(see illustration)**.

6 Remove the screw and withdraw the brush holder, taking care not to damage the brushes.

7 Check that the brushes protrude from the moulding by more than the specified minimum amount. If not, renew the brushes by unsoldering them and fitting new ones.

Refitting

8 Refitting is a reversal of removal, but make sure that the brushes move freely in their holders. If necessary, clean them with petrol and, if this is not sufficient, use a fine file. Clean the slip rings with fine sandpaper and wipe them with a petrol-soaked cloth.

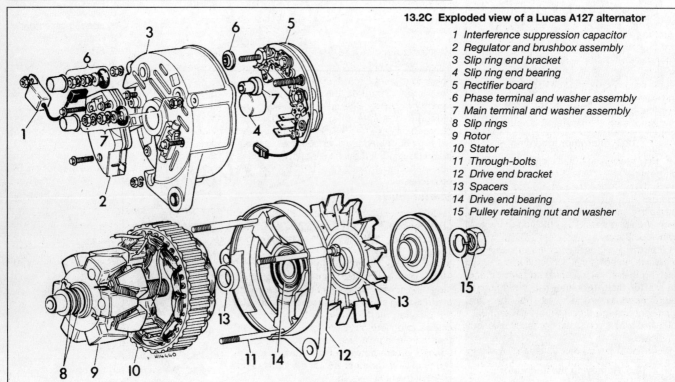

13.2C Exploded view of a Lucas A127 alternator

1 Interference suppression capacitor
2 Regulator and brushbox assembly
3 Slip ring end bracket
4 Slip ring end bearing
5 Rectifier board
6 Phase terminal and washer assembly
7 Main terminal and washer assembly
8 Slip rings
9 Rotor
10 Stator
11 Through-bolts
12 Drive end bracket
13 Spacers
14 Drive end bearing
15 Pulley retaining nut and washer

13.3A Undo the regulator and brushbox retaining screws

13.3B Withdraw the regulator and brushbox . . .

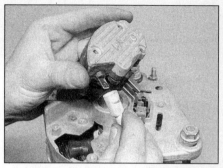

13.3C . . . and disconnect the wiring

13.4 Checking the alternator brush length

14 Starter motor - testing, removal and refitting

Testing

1 If the starter motor fails to operate, first check the condition of the battery by switching on the headlamps. If they glow brightly, then gradually dim after a few seconds, the battery is in an uncharged condition.

2 If the battery is in good condition, check the starter motor main terminal and the engine earth cable for security. Check the terminal connections on the starter solenoid located on the battery carrier (inertia starter) or over the starter (pre-engaged starter).

3 If the starter still fails to turn, use a voltmeter or 12 volt test lamp and leads to check that current is reaching the solenoid terminal with the Lucar terminals. Connect one lead to earth and the other to the terminal, when a reading should be obtained or the test lamp should glow.

4 With the ignition switched on and the ignition key in position III, check that current is reaching the remaining solenoid terminal and the starter main terminal. If a voltmeter is being used, there should not be any significant voltage drop at the main terminal, otherwise a bad connection or faulty solenoid is indicated.

5 If current at the correct voltage is available at the starter motor, yet it does not operate, the starter motor is faulty.

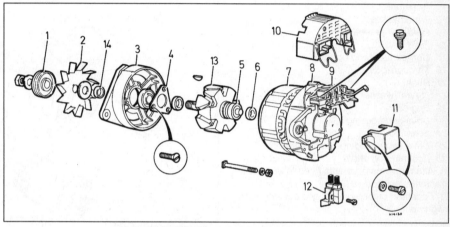

13.5 Exploded view of a Motorola alternator

1 Pulley	6 Bearing	11 Regulator
2 Fan	7 Stator	12 Brush holder
3 Drive end housing	8 Slip ring end housing	13 Rotor
4 Plate	9 Diode bridge	14 Spacer
5 Slip ring	10 Cover	

Starter solenoid (inertia starters)

6 Where an inertia starter motor is fitted, the solenoid is located on the battery carrier, and the circuit is earthed through the solenoid mounting bolts. Should the solenoid be defective the mounting bolts should be removed and cleaned, and the threads coated with a copper-based conductive grease before refitting. If the fault is not cured by this action, further investigation of the wiring will be necessary.

Starter relay

7 On all automatic transmission models, and other models from 1986 onwards, a relay is incorporated in the starter motor solenoid circuit.

8 The relay is located on the battery carrier, and is earthed via terminal 86 to the relay mounting screw. In the event of a malfunction, the mounting screw and battery carrier should be cleaned and coated with conductive grease to ensure good earthing. To establish that there is an earthing problem, temporarily connect a wire between the battery negative terminal and terminal 86 on the relay, and check if the fault persists.

Removal

9 Disconnect the battery negative lead.

10 On the inertia type starter, disconnect the supply cable from the starter main terminal **(see illustration)**.

11 On the pre-engaged type starter, disconnect the supply cables from the solenoid **(see illustrations)**.

12 Unscrew the bottom then top retaining bolts, and withdraw the starter motor from the engine **(see illustration)**. Remove the lead bracket.

14.10 Disconnecting the starter supply lead

5

Refitting

13 Refitting is a reversal of removal, but tighten the retaining bolts to the specified torque.

14.11A Exploded view of a Lucas 9M90 starter motor

1 *Housing retaining screws*
2 *Drive end housing*
5 *End cover*
6 *Solenoid*
7 *Jump ring*
8 *Thrust collar*
9 *Drive assembly*
10 *Engaging lever and bush*
11 *Armature*
12 *Thrustwasher*
13 *Field coil assembly*
14 *Field brush*
15 *Commutator end housing*
16 *Through-bolt*
17 *Bush*
18 *"Spire" washer*
19 *End cap*
20 *Drive end housing*
21 *Solenoid*
22 *Drive and engaging lever assembly*
23 *Eccentric pivot pin*
A *Alternative components fitted to automatic transmission models*
B *Eccentric pivot pin mark and housing arrow alignment*

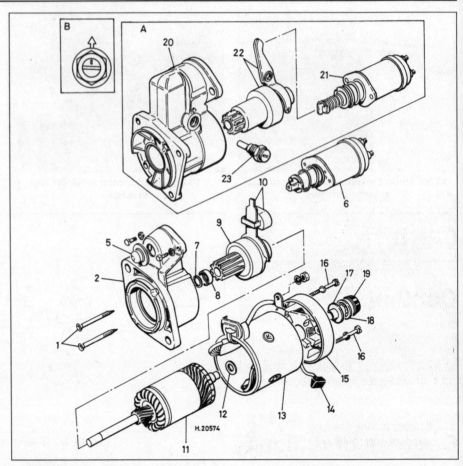

14.3B Exploded view of a Lucas M79 starter motor

1 *Solenoid and plunger*
2 *Commutator and bracket components*
3 *Brushes*
4 *Brush springs*
5 *Pivot and packing piece*
6 *Armature*
7 *Jump ring and thrust collar*
8 *Drive assembly*
9 *Field coils and yoke*
10 *Drive end bracket bush*
11 *Commutator end bracket bush*
12 *Drive end bracket*
13 *Insulation plate*
14 *Commutator end bracket*
15 *Circlip and washers*
16 *Sealing cap and gasket*

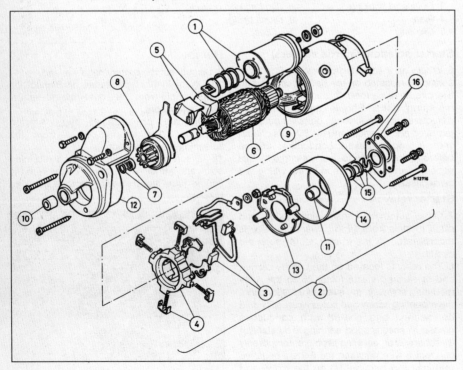

14.12 Removing the starter motor

Chapter 6
Clutch

Contents

Degrees of difficulty

Easy, suitable for novice with little experience	Fairly easy, suitable for beginner with some experience	Fairly difficult, suitable for competent DIY mechanic	Difficult, suitable for experienced DIY mechanic	Very difficult, suitable for expert DIY or professional

Specifications

Type:

Early models	Single dry plate and pressure plate located on inner face of flywheel; diaphragm spring and cover located on outer face of flywheel
Later models	Verto; single dry plate and pressure plate located on outer face of flywheel

Actuation:

Up to 1984	Hydraulic
1985-on	Cable with automatic adjustment

Clutch plate diameter .... 7.125 in (180.98 mm)

Diaphragm spring colour

Metro standard, Metro L and Metro HLE	Brown
Metro 1.3 S and Metro 1.3 HLS	Dark blue

Release lever clearance (where applicable) .... 0.040 in (1.016 mm)

Torque wrench settings

	lbf ft	Nm
Diaphragm spring cover to pressure plate	16	22
Dowel bolts	19	26
Driving strap to flywheel	19	26
Flywheel centre bolt	112	155
Pressure plate to flywheel	18	25

6

1.1 Exploded view of the clutch components. On models without a return stop, items 29 to 33 replace items 17, 19 and 21

1 Flywheel housing	12 Dowel bolt	23 Locknut
2 Primary gear oil seal	13 Keyplate	24 Release lever
3 Dust shield	14 Flywheel retaining bolt	25 Pivot pin
4 Pressure plate	15 Diaphragm spring	26 Return spring
5 Driven plate	16 Diaphragm spring cover	27 Release bearing housing
6 Primary gear locking ring	17 Thrust plate	28 Balance marks
7 C-thrustwasher	18 Spring clip	29 Thrust plate
8 Flywheel	19 Self-locking ring	30 Pushrod
9 Spacer	20 Release bearing	21 O-ring
10 Driving straps	21 Plunger	32 Bucket
11 Dowel bolt	22 Stop nut	33 Plunger

1 General description

General

1 On earlier vehicles the clutch is of a single dry plate type with a diaphragm spring. Actuation is by hydraulic master cylinder and slave cylinder. The driven plate and pressure plate are located on the inner face of the flywheel, and the diaphragm spring and cover are located on the outer face. The pressure plate protrudes through three apertures in the flywheel and is bolted to the diaphragm spring cover (see illustration).

2 The driven plate is free to slide along the splined primary gear, which runs on the crankshaft extension and transmits drive via the idler gear to the gearbox. Drive is transmitted from the flywheel to the pressure plate by six metal driving straps in groups of two. Friction lining material is riveted to the clutch driven plate on each side.

3 When the clutch pedal is depressed, the slave cylinder is actuated by hydraulic pressure, and the release lever moves the plunger and release bearing against the diaphragm spring cover. The diaphragm

spring flexes against the outer face of the flywheel, and the pressure plate is pushed away from the driven plate. Drive then ceases to be transmitted to the gearbox.

4 When the clutch pedal is released, the diaphragm spring, acting against the outer face of the flywheel, pulls the pressure plate into contact with the friction linings on the driven plate. The driven plate is also moved fractionally along the primary gear splines and into contact with the flywheel inner face. The driven plate is now firmly sandwiched between the pressure plate and flywheel, and so the drive is taken up.

5 As the friction linings wear, the pressure plate moves closer to the flywheel, and periodic adjustment of the release lever return stop clearance is therefore necessary where a return stop is fitted.

Verto clutch

6 The Verto clutch differs from all previous Metro clutches in that the pressure plate and friction plate are both on the "outside" of the flywheel, ie on the side furthest from the pistons. All references in this Chapter to the Verto clutch apply also to the factory supplied alternative manufactured by "Automotive" (AP) (see illustration).

7 A heavy duty version of the clutch, similar in external appearance, is fitted to MG Turbo models. The driven (friction) plate on these models does not have any damper springs fitted.

8 The principles of operation of the Verto clutch is the same as that of previous types. The friction plate is sandwiched firmly between the flywheel and pressure plate friction surfaces when the clutch pedal is released; when the pedal is depressed, the release components cause the diaphragm spring to flex and the grip of the pressure plate is relaxed.

9 The clutch is self-adjusting in use. Adjustment of the throw-out stop should only be necessary after dismantling has taken place.

10 This type of clutch was introduced as part of a complete package of changes, the external evidence of which is the three-point engine mounting system. Consult your Rover dealer or a clutch specialist if it is wished to fit the later clutch to an earlier model.

Clutch cable

11 From 1985 the clutch is engaged by means of a cable with automatic adjustment, instead of the hydraulic system.

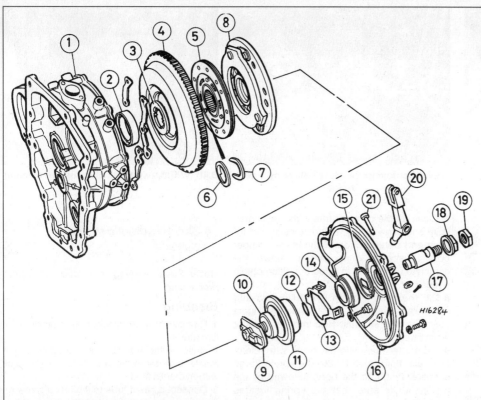

1 Flywheel housing
2 Oil seal (primary gear)
3 Dust shield
4 Flywheel
5 Driven plate
6 Primary gear locking ring
7 C-shaped thrustwasher
8 Pressure plate
9 Keyplate
10 Flywheel retaining bolt and
   lockwasher
11 Thrust sleeve
12 O-ring
13 Spring clip
14 Release bearing
15 Retainer plate
16 Clutch cover (release
   bearing housing)
17 Plunger
18 Throw-out stop
19 Locknut
20 Release lever
21 Pivot pin

2 Clutch master cylinder - removal, overhaul and refitting

Warning: Hydraulic fluid is both poisonous and acts as an effective paint stripper if spilt on the car paintwork. If spilt, wash off immediately with copious amounts of cold water. Hydraulic fluid for use in the hydraulic system must have been left unshaken for the previous 24 hours.

Removal

1 Disconnect the battery negative lead.
2 Remove the air cleaner with reference to Chapter 4.
3 Unscrew and plug the hydraulic pipe from the top of the master cylinder. Take care not to spill any hydraulic fluid on the surrounding paintwork as it acts as an effective paint stripper. If any is spilt, wash off immediately with copious amounts of cold water.
4 Working inside the car, remove the demister elbow, then extract the split pin and clevis pin, and disconnect the master cylinder pushrod from the clutch pedal.
5 Have an assistant hold the mounting bolts, then unscrew the nuts and remove the spring washers from under the bulkhead.
6 Withdraw the master cylinder and gasket from the bulkhead, taking care to keep it upright to prevent spilling of the hydraulic fluid.

Overhaul

7 Unscrew the filler cap and discard the hydraulic fluid, carefully.
8 Prise the boot from the mouth of the master cylinder. Extract the circlip and withdraw the pushrod assembly.
9 Tap the cylinder on the workbench to remove the piston assembly and spring. Note the location of the component parts.
10 Using the fingers only, remove the outer seal from the piston. Remove the spring seat, seal and washer.
11 Clean all the components with methylated spirit and allow to dry. Make a thorough examination for wear and deterioration. In particular check the master cylinder bore for scoring and corrosion. If evident, renew the complete master cylinder. If the bore is good, obtain a repair kit of seals.
12 Dip the outer seal in clean hydraulic fluid and manipulate it onto the piston using the fingers only. Dip the inner seal in clean hydraulic fluid, then fit the washer, seal, and spring seat to the end of the piston. The seal lips must face the spring end of the piston.
13 Lubricate the cylinder bore with clean hydraulic fluid, then locate the spring on the spring seat and insert the assembly into the master cylinder. Take care not to damage the seal lips as they enter the bore.
14 Insert the pushrod assembly and fit the circlip into the groove.
15 Smear the inner sealing surface of the rubber boot with rubber lubricant, then locate it over the mouth of the cylinder.

Refitting

16 Refitting is a reversal of removal, but fit a new mounting gasket and bleed the system as described in Section 4 before refitting the air cleaner **(see illustration)**.

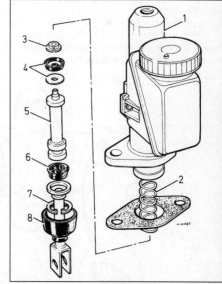

2.16 Exploded view of the clutch master cylinder

1 Master cylinder body	5 Piston
2 Spring	6 Seal
3 Spring seat	7 Circlip
4 Seal and washer	8 Rubber boot

6

3.1 Clutch slave cylinder return spring location

3.4a Removing the clutch slave cylinder bolts

3.4b Withdrawing the clutch slave cylinder

3 Clutch slave cylinder - removal, overhaul and refitting

Note: *Read warning in Section 2, before proceeding.*

Removal

1 Unhook the clutch release lever return spring and remove it **(see illustration)**.
2 Unscrew the clutch master cylinder filler cap, and tighten it down onto a piece of thin polythene sheeting. This will reduce hydraulic fluid loss in the subsequent procedure.
3 Loosen only the slave cylinder hose connection.
4 Unbolt the slave cylinder from the flywheel housing and withdraw it from the pushrod **(see illustrations)**.

Overhaul

5 Unscrew and remove the slave cylinder from the hose.
6 Prise the boot from the mouth of the cylinder, and tap out the piston and spring. Remove the bleed screw. Prise the seal from the piston using the fingers only.

7 Clean all the components with methylated spirit and allow to dry. Examine each part for wear and deterioration. If the slave cylinder bore is scored or corroded, renew the complete unit. If it is in good condition obtain a repair kit.
8 Dip the seal in clean hydraulic fluid and manipulate it onto the piston using the fingers only. The seal lip must face into the cylinder when fitted.
9 Lubricate the cylinder bore with clean hydraulic fluid, then locate the spring (large diameter first) into the bore, followed by the piston. Make sure that the spring locates centrally in the piston and that the seal lip is not damaged as it enters the bore.
10 Smear the inner sealing surfaces of the rubber boot with rubber lubricant, then locate it over the mouth of the cylinder.
11 Insert and tighten the bleed screw.

Refitting

12 Refitting is a reversal of removal, but bleed the system as described in Section 4. Do not leave the polythene sheeting under the filler cap **(see illustration)**.

4 Clutch hydraulic system - bleeding

Note: *Read warning in Section 2, before proceeding.*

Bleeding

1 Remove the air cleaner as described in Chapter 4.
2 Unscrew the filler cap and top-up the clutch master cylinder to the bottom of the filler neck with hydraulic fluid.
3 Connect a bleed tube to the bleed screw on the slave cylinder and place the free end in a jar.
4 Open the bleed screw three-quarters of a turn and have an assistant fully depress the clutch pedal slowly.
5 Tighten the bleed screw, then allow the clutch pedal to return to its stop. Pause for a moment, then repeat the procedure twice more. Top-up the master cylinder reservoir, and continue bleeding the system until the fluid entering the jar is free of air bubbles. The fluid must never drop more than half way down the reservoir.
6 Check the tightness of the bleed screw, and fit the filler cap after topping up the reservoir to the bottom of the filler neck.
7 Refit the air cleaner with reference to Chapter 4.

5 Clutch pedal - removal and refitting

Removal

1 Disconnect the battery negative lead.
2 Working inside the car, remove the demister elbow, then extract the split pin and clevis pin and disconnect the master cylinder pushrod from the clutch pedal. Retain the clevis pin washer.
3 Extract the circlip from the pedal point, and withdraw the pedal, return spring, and bush.
4 Examine the clutch pedal, bush, and footpad rubber for wear and renew them as necessary.

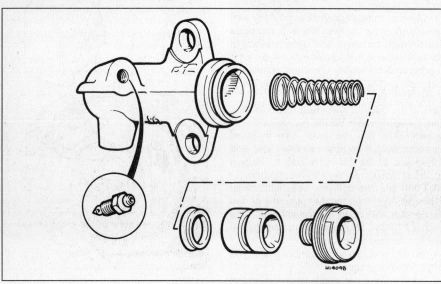

3.12 Exploded view of the clutch slave cylinder

Refitting

5 Refitting is a reversal of removal, but make sure that the return spring is correctly located over the pedal and bracket with the hooked end over the pedal **(see illustration)**.

6 Clutch (early models) - removal, inspection and refitting

Note: *Before starting work, it is essential to obtain tools 18G304 and 18G304N in order to release the flywheel from the crankshaft taper, A 1½ inch AF socket will also be required to unscrew the flywheel retaining bolt. The tools should be obtained from a tool hire agent. If the engine/gearbox unit is in the car, follow paragraphs 1 to 5.*

Removal

1 Remove the battery as described in Chapter 5, and remove the battery carrier.
2 Unhook the clutch release lever return spring.
3 Jack up the front of the car and support it with axle stands (see *"Jacking and vehicle support"*) positioned beneath the rear edges of the front subframe.
4 Support the engine/gearbox unit with a trolley jack and block of wood located beneath the transmission casing.
5 Unscrew the nut and remove the through-bolt and washer from the right-hand front engine mounting. Remove the buffer washer from the mounting.
6 Remove the starter motor as described in Chapter 5.

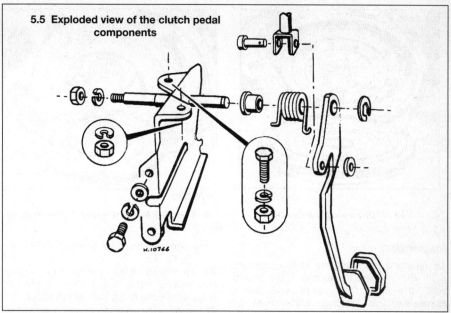

5.5 Exploded view of the clutch pedal components

7 Unbolt the clutch release bearing housing from the flywheel housing, and remove it complete with the mounting bracket. Note the fuel vent pipe bracket and engine mounting bracket locations **(see illustrations)**.
8 Mark the diaphragm spring cover and flywheel in relation to each other.
9 Progressively unscrew the three diaphragm spring cover-to-pressure plate dowel bolts to release the diaphragm spring. Withdraw the cover **(see illustration)**.

10 Turn the crankshaft with a spanner on the pulley centre bolt, until the slots in the flywheel and crankshaft are horizontal. This will prevent the primary gear C-washer falling out when the flywheel is removed.
11 Insert a wide-bladed screwdriver between the starter ring gear and the flywheel housing, then unscrew the flywheel retaining bolt. Make sure that the socket is fully engaged with the bolt as it is very tight.
12 Remove the keyplate and locking washer.
13 When separating the flywheel from the crankshaft taper, care must be taken not to screw the removal tool studs through the flywheel into the clutch driven plate. This is apparently possible with certain tools, resulting in damage to the driven plate. Using tools 18G304 and 18G304N, pull the flywheel from the crankshaft taper **(see illustration)**. It will be necessary to hold the flywheel stationary while tightening the puller centre bolt; strike the centre bolt with a hammer to help release the taper.
14 Withdraw the flywheel, clutch driven plate, and pressure plate **(see illustration)**.

6.7a Vent pipe location on the clutch release bearing housing

6.7b Engine mounting bracket location on the clutch release bearing housing

6.7c Removing the clutch release bearing housing

6.9 Removing the clutch diaphragm spring cover

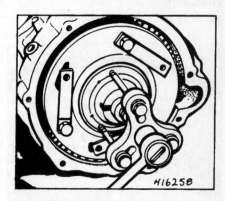

6.13 Using a puller to remove the flywheel

6

H16259

6.14 Withdrawing the flywheel

H16260

6.16 Withdrawing the clutch driven plate

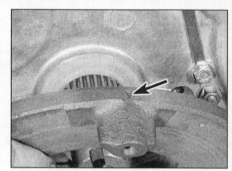

6.21 Fitting the pressure plate, showing location of "A" mark (arrowed)

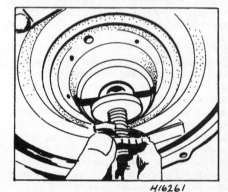

H16261

6.26 Fitting the flywheel retaining bolt

Inspection

15 Examine the surfaces of the pressure plate and flywheel for scoring. If this is only light, the parts may be re-used, but if excessive, the pressure plate must be renewed and the flywheel friction face ground flat, provided the amount of metal being removed is minimal. If any doubt exists, renew the flywheel.

16 Renew the driven plate if the linings are worn down to or near to the rivets. If the linings appear oil stained, the cause of the oil leak must first be put right; this is most likely to be a failed primary gear oil seal (refer to Chapter 7). Check the driven plate centre splines; if they are worn, renew the driven plate (**see illustration**).

17 Examine the diaphragm spring and cover for wear, and the driving holes for elongation. Check the dowel bolts for ridging, and the driving straps for elongated holes. Check the thrust plate for wear. Renew the components as necessary, renewing the dowel bolts and driving straps in complete sets.

18 Spin the release bearing and check it for roughness. Hold the outer race, and attempt to move it laterally against the inner race. If any excessive movement or roughness is evident, renew the release bearing as described in Section 8.

Refitting

19 Refer to Chapter 7A and check that the crankshaft primary gear endfloat is within the specified limits.

20 If removed, fit the driving straps, spacer, and locking plates to the flywheel, but only tighten the bolts finger tight at this stage.

21 Position the pressure plate in the flywheel housing, noting the location of the "A" mark on its periphery (**see illustration**).

22 Slide the driven plate, hub side first, onto the primary gear splines, at the same time locating it centrally within the pressure plate.

23 With the crankshaft slot still horizontal, fit the flywheel onto the crankshaft with the ¼ timing mark aligned with the "A" mark on the pressure plate.

24 Temporarily fit the three dowel bolts through the driving straps and into the pressure plate.

25 Turn the flywheel to align the keyplate slots, then fit the keyplate, locking washer, and flywheel retaining bolt. If the original bolt was of an encapsulated type, or secured with thread locking compound, the bolt hole threads should be thoroughly cleaned. Use a new bolt with a thread locking compound.

26 Have an assistant insert a wide-bladed screwdriver between the starter ring gear and the flywheel housing, then tighten the flywheel retaining bolt to the specified torque (**see illustration**).

27 Bend the locking washer over one flat of the retaining bolt and tap it flat.

28 Remove the three dowel bolts. Locate the diaphragm spring cover on the outer face of the flywheel with the "A" mark aligned with the flywheel ¼ timing mark (**see illustration**). Insert, but do not tighten, the three dowel bolts.

29 Hold the flywheel stationary, and tighten the driving strap bolts to the specified torque (**see illustration**). Bend the locking plates over one flat of each bolt and tap them flat.

30 Tighten the dowel bolts a few turns at a time making sure that they do not foul the driving straps. Finally tighten them to the specified torque.

31 On models with a return stop type release arm, check that the release bearing self-locking ring is correctly and securely positioned on the plunger (**see illustration**). Unscrew the return stop to position the shoulder of the plunger 0.188 in (5 mm) from

6.28 Fitting the diaphragm spring cover, showing the "A" mark (arrowed)

6.29 Tightening clutch cover driving strap bolts

6.31a Spring clip (arrowed), securing the clutch release bearing

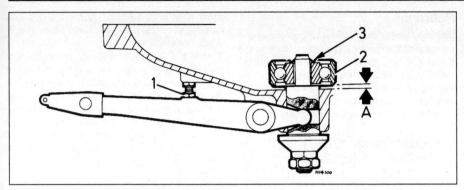

6.31b Cross sectional view of release bearing and lever showing setting "A" before fitting cover

1 Return stop   *2 Release bearing*   *3 Self-locking ring*

the inner face of the housing, shown as "A" **(see illustration)**. This will ensure that the release bearing centralizes on the clutch thrust plate.

32 On all models, check that the thrust plate is secured to the diaphragm spring cover by the spring clip **(see illustration)**.

33 Locate the release bearing housing on the flywheel housing, at the same time engaging the pushrod into the slave cylinder. Insert and tighten the securing bolts evenly in diagonal sequence, and refit the fuel vent pipe and engine mounting brackets.

34 Fit the starter motor with reference to Chapter 5.

35 If the engine/gearbox unit is in the car, carry out the procedure in the remaining paragraphs. Fit the buffer washer between the right-hand front engine mounting and the bracket. Insert the through-bolt and washer and, with the weight of the engine/gearbox unit on the mounting, tighten the nut.

36 Lower the car to the ground. Refit the clutch release lever return spring and screw in the return stop. Whenever the clutch is overhauled, the areas of the release

mechanism shown **(see illustration)**, should be lightly greased.

37 Adjust the return stop and throw-out stop as described in Chapter 1, Section 18.

38 Refit the battery carrier and battery as described in Chapter 5.

7 Clutch (Verto) - removal, overhaul and refitting

Note: *Read note in previous section.*

1 Special tools will be required to undertake this operation. They should be available from your Rover dealer or tool hire agent; details are as follows:

a) Spanner 18G 1303, or a deep socket spanner (30 mm AF) to undo the flywheel centre bolt.

b) Puller 18G 1381 (see illustration), or equivalent, to remove the flywheel clutch assembly from the crankshaft taper.

c) Clutch centring tool 18G 684. This tool is not essential and a way of avoiding its use is described in paragraph 20.

Removal

2 Disconnect and remove the battery, then remove the battery tray.

3 Place a jack and a piece of wood under the gearbox casing and take the weight of the engine/gearbox assembly.

6.32 Fitting the clutch cover thrust plate

4 On pre-1985 models, remove the anti-roll bar clamp bolt, which is located immediately below the right-hand front engine mountings.

5 Remove the nuts and washers from the right-hand front engine mounting rubber. Raise the engine slightly, then unbolt and remove the mounting bracket and spacer from the clutch cover.

6 Remove the starter motor as described in Chapter 5.

7 On pre-1985 models, undo the clutch slave cylinder mounting plate bolts, retrieving the spacer. Carefully withdraw the slave cylinder from its pushrod and place the assembly of slave cylinder, bracket and (if fitted) hydraulic damper to one side. On 1985-on models extract the C-clip from the cable self-adjusting spring, then remove the split pin, washer and pin from the clevis on the release lever and release the inner cable and buffer components from the clutch cover bracket **(see illustration)**.

8 Undo the clutch cover bolts and remove the cover. Remove the thrust bearing sleeve.

9 Make sure that the slots in the end of the crankshaft hub are horizontal. Lock the flywheel by jamming a wide-bladed screwdriver between the starter ring gear and the flywheel housing.

10 Relieve the lockwasher from the slots, then undo the flywheel centre bolt using spanner 18G 1303 or equivalent. Make sure the spanner fits well, as the bolt is very tight.

11 Remove the bolt and the keyplate from the crankshaft, then fit puller 18G 1381 or equivalent to the flywheel.

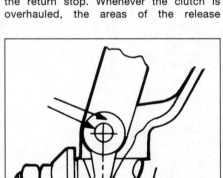

6.36 Clutch release mechanism greasing points (arrowed)

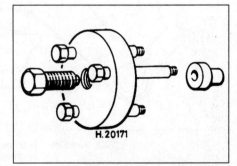

7.1 Puller 18G 1381 for removing the flywheel/clutch assembly from the crankshaft taper

7.7 Clutch cable and release lever fitted to 1985-on models

6

12 Screw in the puller centre bolt until the flywheel/clutch assembly is released from the crankshaft taper. If the unit seems reluctant to come off, strike the centre bolt sharply with a hammer to help release the taper.

13 Remove the flywheel/clutch unit. Unscrew the pressure plate bolts, half a turn at a time in criss-cross sequence, and remove the pressure plate and driven plate from the flywheel.

Overhaul

14 Inspect the components for wear and damage. The driven plate should be renewed as a matter of course unless it is nearly new. It must certainly be renewed if the linings are burnt, contaminated or badly worn, or if the centre splines are worn. The source of any contamination must be dealt with.

15 The flywheel and pressure plate are not sold separately, but must be renewed as a matched assembly if wear or damage is evident. Deep grooving, cracks or crazing of the friction surfaces are grounds for renewal.

16 Consideration should also be given to renewing the release bearing whilst it is easily accessible.

17 Before commencing reassembly, check the primary gear endfloat as described in Chapter 7A.

18 Fit the driven plate to the flywheel with the hub facing the flywheel. (The plate may be marked "FLYWHEEL SIDE" to confirm this orientation).

19 Fit the pressure plate to the flywheel and insert the retaining bolts. Only tighten the bolts finger-tight at this stage.

20 Offer the flywheel/clutch assembly to the crankshaft. Providing the pressure plate bolts are not too tight, the driven plate will be moved to the correct central position as it passes over the primary gear splines. Do not force the assembly onto the crankshaft if resistance is encountered, but remove it and check that the driven plate is just free to move, and approximately central. Use of the clutch centring tool 18G 684 will make this process easier.

21 When centralisation has been achieved, tighten the pressure plate retaining bolts in criss-cross sequence to the specified torque.

22 If a centralisation tool was used, remove it and fit the flywheel/ clutch assembly to the crankshaft.

23 If the flywheel centre bolt is of an encapsulated type, or was secured with thread locking compound, the bolt hole threads should be thoroughly cleaned. Fit the keyplate and the flywheel centre bolt. Renew the bolt if the original one was secured by any sort of thread lock, and apply a locking compound. Prevent the flywheel from rotating and tighten the centre bolt to the specified torque.

24 Stake the lockwasher into the slots in the hub, then fit the thrust bearing sleeve.

Refitting

25 The remainder of the refitting process is a reversal of the removal procedure. Adjust the throw-out stop on completion as described below. On 1985-on models, compress the self-adjusting spring in order to fit the C-clip, and finally depress the clutch pedal several times to operate the automatic cable adjuster.

8 Clutch release bearing (early models) - removal and refitting

Removal

1 Remove the clutch release bearing housing from the flywheel housing by following the procedure given in Section 6, paragraphs 1 to 7. However, do not remove the starter (ie omit paragraph 6). No special tools are required.

2 On models with a return stop type release arm, prise off the release bearing self-locking ring using a screwdriver. Pull the release bearing off the plunger.

3 On models without a return stop type release arm, extract the split pin and remove the washer, pivot pin and release arm. Unscrew the locknut and plunger stop, and withdraw the release bearing assembly from the housing. Using a drift through the holes provided, drive the release bearing and bucket from the plunger then remove the pushrod and O-ring and press the bucket from the bearing.

4 On all models, spin the bearing and check it for roughness. Attempt to move the outer race laterally against the inner race. If any excessive wear or roughness is evident, renew the bearing.

Refitting

5 To refit the bearing on models with a return stop type release arm, press the release bearing onto the plunger, making sure that it abuts the shoulder.

6 Using a length of tubing, press a new self-locking ring onto the plunger to secure the release bearing. Do not drive the ring on, but use hand pressure only, making sure that the ring is installed squarely and abuts the inner race. Do not overcompress the ring otherwise its locking action will be reduced.

7 To refit the remaining components, refer to Section 6, paragraphs 31 to 38, omitting paragraph 34.

8 To refit the bearing on models without a return stop type release arm, press the bucket into the bearing and insert the pushrod and O-ring with the O-ring 0.625 in (16.0 mm) below the face of the bucket. Press the bearing and bucket into the plunger, locate the assembly in the housing and fit the release arm, plunger stop, and locknut.

9 To refit the remaining components, refer to Section 6, paragraphs 32 to 38, omitting paragraph 34.

9 Clutch release bearing (Verto type) - removal and refitting

Removal

1 Proceed as described in Section 7, paragraphs 2 to 7, but do not remove the starter motor.

2 Undo the clutch cover bolts and remove the cover.

3 Pull the release bearing components off the plunger and retrieve the O-ring.

4 Separate the spring clip legs from the bearing retainer plate, then remove the bearing.

5 Examine the bearing for external damage,

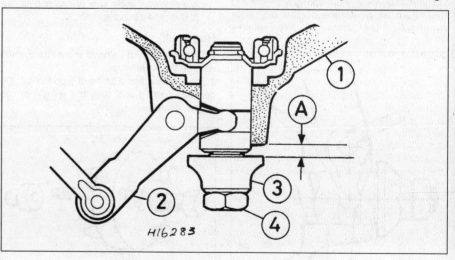

H16283

10.3 Verto clutch throw-out stop adjustment
A = 0.26 in (6.5 mm)

1 Clutch cover
2 Release lever

3 Throw-out stop
4 Locknut

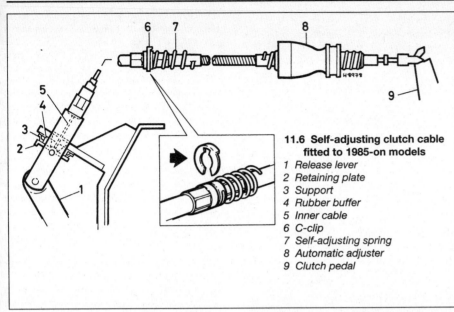

11.6 Self-adjusting clutch cable fitted to 1985-on models

1 Release lever
2 Retaining plate
3 Support
4 Rubber buffer
5 Inner cable
6 C-clip
7 Self-adjusting spring
8 Automatic adjuster
9 Clutch pedal

spin it to check for rough running and inspect it for grease leakage. If there is the slightest doubt as to its condition it should be renewed.

Refitting

6 Refitting is a reversal of removal, but note the following points:
   a) *The bearing seal faces away from the retaining plate.*
   b) *Do not forget to fit the O-ring on the plunger.*
   c) *Tighten fasteners to their specified torques, see "Specifications".*
   d) *Adjust the throw-out stop on completion.*
   e) *On 1985-on models depress the clutch pedal several times to operate the automatic cable adjuster.*

10 Verto clutch throw-out stop - adjustment

Adjustment

1 Unscrew the throw-out stop and locknut to the end of the thread.
2 Pull the release lever out (away from the clutch cover) by hand until you can feel the release bearing make contact with the thrust sleeve.
3 Screw the throw-out stop in until the clearance between the end of the stop and the face of the cover is as shown as "A", **(see illustration)**.
4 Tighten the locknut, taking care not to move the throw-out stop when doing so.

11 Clutch cable (1985-on models) - removal and refitting

Removal

1 For better access remove the battery and battery tray.
2 Extract the C-clip from the cable self-adjusting spring.
3 Remove the split pin, washer and pin from the clevis fork on the release lever.
4 Disengage the inner cable from the retaining plate, and remove the plate and rubber buffer.
5 Working inside the car, unhook the cable from the clutch pedal, then withdraw the cable from the engine compartment.

Refitting

6 Refitting is a reversal of removal, but first push the outer cable fully into the self-adjuster to reduce its overall length. To facilitate inserting the outer cable through the bulkhead, smear a little brake grease inside the inter-connecting tube. After refitting, compress the self-adjusting spring and insert the C-clip, then depress the clutch pedal several times to operate the automatic cable adjuster **(see illustration)**.

12 Clutch hydraulic damper - description, removal and refitting

Note: Read warning in Section 2, before proceeding.

Description

1 Certain models are fitted with a damper in the hydraulic line between the clutch master and slave cylinders. The function of the damper is to provide a steady re-engagement of the clutch, regardless of the rate at which the driver releases the pedal. This is supposed to reduce clutch judder. The clutch damper is mounted on a bracket next to the clutch slave cylinder **(see illustration)**.

Removal

2 Connect a length of tubing to the clutch slave cylinder bleed screw. Slacken the bleed screw and place the other end of the tubing in a jar then empty the clutch hydraulic system by pumping the pedal. Take care not to spill hydraulic fluid on the paintwork.
3 Disconnect the inlet hose at its union with the rigid pipe. Unscrew the outlet pipe from the damper, then release the inlet hose and unscrew it.
4 Unscrew the damper unit from its bracket and remove it. Be prepared for some spillage of hydraulic fluid.

Refitting

5 Refitting is a reversal of removal. Bleed the hydraulic system on completion, see Section 4 for details.

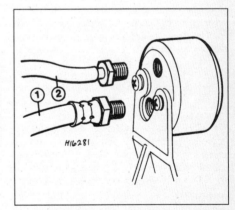

12.1 Clutch hydraulic damper unit

1 Inlet hose   2 Outlet hose

6

Chapter 7 Part A:
Manual gearbox

Contents

Degrees of difficulty

| Easy, suitable for novice with little experience | Fairly easy, suitable for beginner with some experience | Fairly difficult, suitable for competent DIY mechanic | Difficult, suitable for experienced DIY mechanic | Very difficult, suitable for expert DIY or professional |

Specifications

General

Type	Four forward speeds and reverse; synchromesh on all forward speeds

Oil capacity (as for engine) . . . . 8.5 pints (4.8 litres)

Primary gear

Endfloat . . . . 0.0035 to 0.0065 in (0.089 to 0.165 mm)

Idler gear

Endfloat . . . . 0.004 to 0.007 in (0.102 to 0.178 mm)

Torque wrench settings

	lbf ft	Nm
Bellcrank lever pivot pin nut	21	29
Drain plug	30	41
Flywheel housing nuts and bolts	18	25
Gearbox case stud nuts:		
⅜ in diameter	25	35
5⁄16 in diameter	18	25
Gearbox case studs:		
⅜ in diameter	8	11
5⁄16 in diameter	6	8
Gearbox case to crankcase	6	8
Speedometer gear housing bolts	6	8
Speedometer gear housing nuts	18	25

2.3 Removing the oil separator

2.6 Removing the flywheel housing

2.7 Removing the idler gear

1 General description

The manual gearbox incorporates four forward speeds and one reverse speed, with synchromesh engagement on all forward gears. Gearshift is by means of a floor mounted lever, connected by a remote control housing and extension rod to a selector shaft located in the bottom of the gearbox casing.

The final drive (differential) unit is attached to the rear of the gearbox casing. The final drive gear is in mesh with a splined pinion. This is on the end of the third motion shaft.

A drain plug incorporating a magnetic swarf collector is screwed into the right-hand side of the gearbox casing.

If a problem develops it is usually more economical to obtain a service exchange or good second-hand gearbox rather than to overhaul an existing gearbox.

2 Gearbox - removal and refitting

HAYNES HiNT *By wrapping adhesive tape around gear splines, you will protect oil seals inner faces from damage.*

Removal

1 Remove the engine and gearbox assembly as described in Chapter 2B, Section 3, and drain the oil.
2 Remove the clutch and flywheel as described in Chapter 6.
3 Unbolt the oil separator from the top of the flywheel housing, and remove the gasket **(see illustration)**.

4 Unscrew and remove the outer nuts and bolts from the flywheel housing. Remove the primary gear dust shield.
5 Flatten the locktabs, then unscrew and remove the inner nuts and bolts from the housing. Remove the lockwashers.
6 Wrap adhesive tape around the primary gear splines, then carefully tap the flywheel housing free and withdraw it with the gasket **(see illustration)**. The idler gear will probably remain with the housing so take care not to drop it.
7 Remove the idler gear and thrustwashers **(see illustration)**.
8 Unscrew the gearbox casing to crankcase nuts and bolts, and lift the engine from the gearbox **(see illustration)**.
9 Remove the two gaskets, main bearing caps oil seal, and the oil transfer hole O-ring **(see illustrations)**.

Refitting

10 Refitting is a reversal of the removal procedure, noting the following points:
  a) *Fit a new oil transfer hole O-ring, gearbox casing-to-crankcase gaskets, and flywheel housing* **(see illustration)***.*
  b) *Lubricate the new main bearing cap oil seal with engine oil before locating it on the timing chain end main bearing cap.*
  c) *If the flywheel housing is refitted with the primary gear in position, protect the oil seal by wrapping adhesive tape around the primary gear splines* **(see illustration)***.*

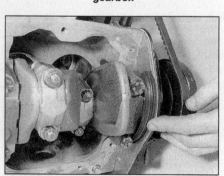

2.8 Separating the engine from the gearbox

2.9a Removing the gearbox-to-engine gaskets

2.9b Gearbox-to-main bearing cap oil seal

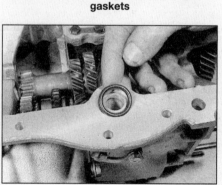

2.9c Oil transfer hole O-ring

2.10a Fitting the flywheel housing gasket

2.10b Adhesive tape used for protecting the flywheel housing oil seal

2.10c Locking a flywheel housing retaining nut

d) Tighten all nuts and bolts to the specified torque, and where applicable, bend the locktabs over one flat of the nuts and bolts to lock them (see illustration).

If either the idler gear, idler gear thrustwashers, flywheel housing, or gearbox casing have been renewed, one of the two methods given in paragraphs 11 to 20 must be followed to determine the idler gears thrustwasher thickness (see illustration). With either procedure, a selection of thrustwashers and an extra flywheel housing gasket should be obtained before starting work.

Method 1 - gearbox separated from engine

11 Fit the idler gear to the gearbox casing needle roller bearing, together with a medium size thrustwasher. Locate a small size thrustwasher on the outside of the idler gear.
12 Fit the flywheel housing with a new gasket to the gearbox casing, and tighten the nuts and bolts to the specified torque.
13 Using a feeler blade behind the flywheel housing, check the idler gear endfloat with the feeler blade between the inner thrustwasher and idler gear (see illustration). If the endfloat is not as specified, select a different outer thrustwasher of a thickness which will correct the endfloat.
14 Remove the flywheel housing and discard the gasket. Fit the correct outer thrustwasher, then fit the gearbox using a reversal of the removal procedure and using the remaining new gasket.

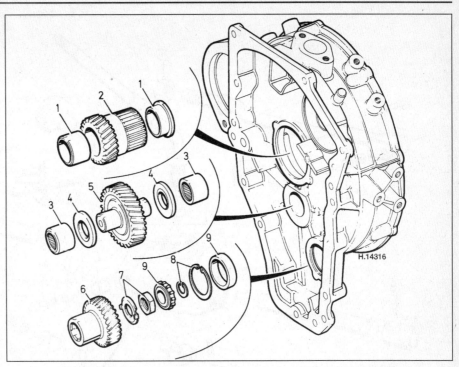

2.10d Exploded view of the transfer gears and flywheel housing

1 Primary gear bushes	4 Thrustwasher	7 Nut and lockwasher
2 Primary gear	5 Idler gear	8 Circlip
3 Needle roller bearing	6 First motion shaft gear	9 Spigot bearing

Method 2 - gearbox attached to engine

15 Fit the idler gear to the gearbox casing needle roller bearing together with a medium size thrustwasher.
16 Fit a thin washer followed by a wax washer and a further thin washer from tool 18G1089 to the flywheel side of the idler gear.
17 Fit the flywheel housing with a new gasket and tighten the nuts and bolts to the specified torque.
18 Unscrew the nuts and bolts and remove the flywheel housing and gasket.
19 Remove the thin washers and wax washer, and measure their thickness carefully with a micrometer. Subtract the specified endfloat, and fit a thrustwasher of the resulting thickness to the flywheel side of the idler gear.

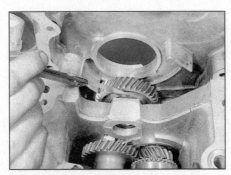

2.13 Checking the idler gear endfloat (gearbox separated from engine)

20 Discard the gasket just used, then fit the flywheel housing with the remaining new gasket.

3 Gearchange remote control - removal, overhaul and refitting

Removal and overhaul

1 Jack up the front of the car and support it on axle stands (see "Jacking and vehicle support"). Apply the handbrake.
2 Using a punch, drive out the roll pin securing the remote control extension rod to the selector shaft at the differential housing (see illustration).
3 Unscrew and remove the bolt securing the steady rod to the rear of the differential housing (see illustration).
4 Working inside the car, pull back the rear of the front carpet and disconnect the reversing light switch wiring.
5 Unscrew and remove the nuts securing the remote control bracket to the floor.
6 Working inside the car, twist the gear lever retaining dome anti-clockwise and release it from the housing.
7 Lower the remote control assembly and remove it from under the car (see illustrations).
8 If the assembly is to be overhauled, remove the upper and lower brackets and the bottom

7A

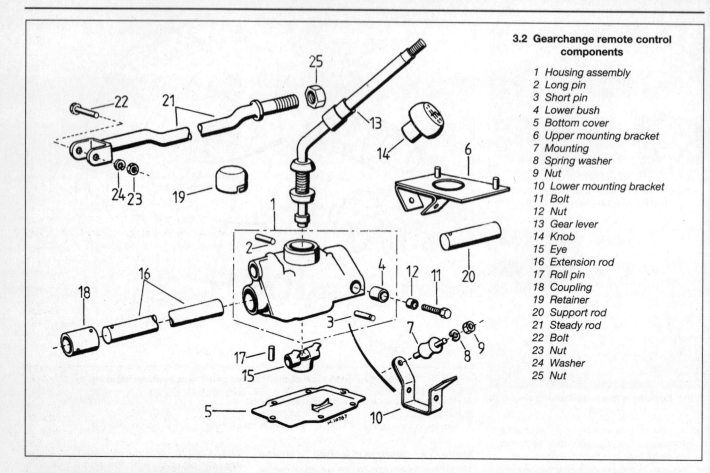

3.2 Gearchange remote control components

1 Housing assembly
2 Long pin
3 Short pin
4 Lower bush
5 Bottom cover
6 Upper mounting bracket
7 Mounting
8 Spring washer
9 Nut
10 Lower mounting bracket
11 Bolt
12 Nut
13 Gear lever
14 Knob
15 Eye
16 Extension rod
17 Roll pin
18 Coupling
19 Retainer
20 Support rod
21 Steady rod
22 Bolt
23 Nut
24 Washer
25 Nut

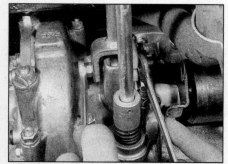

3.3 Removing the steady rod bolt

cover. Drive out the roll pins and remove the extension rod, eye and support rod. Drive the bushes from the housing.

9 Wash the components in paraffin and wipe them dry. Examine them for wear and damage, and check the bushes for deterioration. Renew all components as necessary.

Refitting

10 Refitting is a reversal of the removal procedure, noting the following points:

a) Lubricate the bearing surfaces with multi-purpose grease.
b) Make sure that the gear lever is correctly located before fitting the retaining dome.

4 Flywheel housing oil seal - removal and refitting

Removal

1 Remove the clutch and flywheel as described in Chapter 6.
2 Slide the dust shield from the primary gear, noting which way round it is fitted **(see illustration)**.
3 Remove the C-shaped thrustwasher and backing ring from the end of the crankshaft.
4 Pull the primary gear from the crankshaft; the oil seal will also be pulled from the flywheel housing **(see illustrations)**.

3.7a Gearchange remote control mountings

3.7b Gearchange remote control assembly

4.2 Removing the dust shield

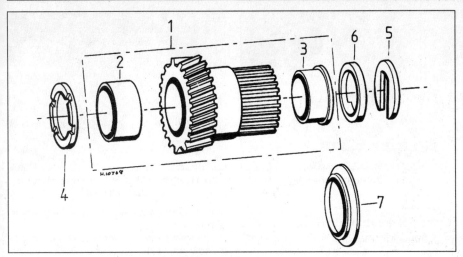

4.4b Removing the primary gear and oil seal

and must face the splined end of the primary gear. Use the clutch plate to push the shield fully home.

11 Fit the clutch and flywheel as described in Chapter 6.

4.4a Primary gear components

1 Primary gear assembly
2 Inner bush
3 Outer bush
4 Notched thrustwasher (selective)
5 C-shaped thrustwasher
6 Backing ring
7 Dust shield

Refitting

5 Make sure that the notched thrustwasher is located correctly on the crankshaft with its chamfer innermost **(see illustration)**.
6 Wrap adhesive tape over the primary gear splines, or alternatively use tool 18G1043. Lubricate the new oil seal with engine oil and locate it on the primary gear oil seal surface with the sealing lip facing the gear end **(see illustrations)**.
7 Slide the primary gear onto the end of the crankshaft until the oil seal contacts the housing.
8 Using a length of tubing, drive in the oil seal until it is flush with the flywheel housing **(see illustration)**.
9 Remove the tool or adhesive tape if fitted, then fit the backing ring and C-shaped thrustwasher.
10 Slide the dust shield onto the primary gear splines (inner flange side first). The outer stepped face is marked "FLYWHEEL SIDE"

5 Selector shaft oil seal - removal and refitting

Removal

1 Jack up the front of the car and support it on axle stands (see "Jacking and vehicle support"). Apply the handbrake.
2 Using a punch, drive out the roll pin securing the remote control extension rod to the selector shaft at the differential housing.
3 Separate the extension rod from the selector shaft and remove the rubber bellows **(see illustrations)**.

4.5 Correct fitting of the notched thrustwasher

4.6a Adhesive tape to protect the flywheel housing oil seal

4.6b Locating the oil seal on the primary gear

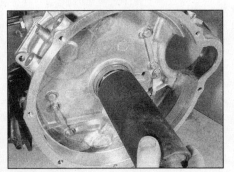

4.8 Installing the flywheel housing oil seal

5.3a Removing the extension rod . . .

5.3b . . . and rubber bellows

7A

5.5 Extracting the selector shaft oil seal

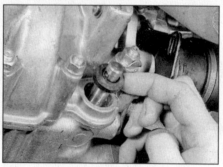

5.7 Fitting the new seal

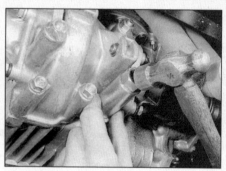

5.8 Using a socket to install the selector shaft oil seal

4 Unscrew the drain plug and drain the engine oil into a clean container. Refit the drain plug.

5 Using a small screwdriver, hook the selector shaft oil seal from the differential housing **(see illustration)**.

6 Clean the shaft and housing and wrap some adhesive tape around the shaft shoulder.

Refitting

7 Smear clean engine oil on the inner lip of the new oil seal and slide it over the tape onto the shaft **(see illustration)**. Remove the tape.

8 Using a socket, tap the seal into the differential housing until flush with the outer surface **(see illustration)**.

9 Refit the rubber bellows and locate the extension rod on the selector shaft.

10 Align the holes and drive in the roll pin **(see illustration)**.

11 Lower the car to the ground, and refill the engine with oil.

6 Manual gearbox overhaul - general information

Overhauling a manual gearbox unit is a difficult and involved job for the DIY home mechanic. In addition to dismantling and reassembling many small parts, clearances must be precisely measured and, if necessary, changed by selecting shims and spacers. Internal gearbox components are also often difficult to obtain, and in many instances, extremely expensive. Because of this, if the gearbox develops a fault or becomes noisy, the best course of action is to have the unit overhauled by a specialist repairer, or to obtain an exchange reconditioned unit.

Nevertheless, it is not impossible for the more experienced mechanic to overhaul the gearbox, provided the special tools are available, and the job is done in a deliberate step-by-step manner, so that nothing is overlooked.

The tools necessary for an overhaul include internal and external circlip pliers, bearing pullers, a slide hammer, a set of pin punches, a dial test indicator, and possibly a hydraulic press. In addition, a large, sturdy workbench and a vice will be required.

During dismantling of the gearbox, make careful notes of how each component is fitted, to make reassembly easier and more accurate.

Before dismantling the gearbox, it will help if you have some idea what area is malfunctioning. Certain problems can be closely related to specific areas in the gearbox, which can make component examination and replacement easier. Refer to the Fault Finding Section at the end of this manual for more information.

5.10 Installing the roll pin

Chapter 7 Part B:
Automatic transmission

Contents

Degrees of difficulty

Easy, suitable for novice with little experience	Fairly easy, suitable for beginner with some experience	Fairly difficult, suitable for competent DIY mechanic	Difficult, suitable for experienced DIY mechanic	Very difficult, suitable for expert DIY or professional

Specifications

General

Type .... AP four-speed with manual hold/change facility. Three element torque converter input with oil cooler on front of engine

Torque wrench settings

	lbf ft	Nm
Converter bolts	21	29
Converter centre bolt	112	155
Converter housing nuts and bolts	18	25
Drain plug	30	40
Input shaft nut	70	97
Transmission case to crankcase	12	17
Transmission case studs and nuts	(see Chapter 7A)	

7B

1 General description

The automatic transmission incorporates four forward speeds and one reverse speed; speeds 1, 2, and 3 may be selected and held independently of the automatic function. A three-element torque converter transmits drive from the engine to the transmission.

The transmission oil, which also circulates through the engine lubrication system, is cooled by an oil cooler mounted on the front of the engine. Oil pressure is provided by the engine oil pump driven by the camshaft.

Due to the complexity of the automatic transmission, work by the home mechanic should be limited to the procedures given in the following Sections. If the unit is faulty, do not remove the automatic transmission until the fault has been diagnosed by a Rover dealer or specialist.

2 Automatic transmission - removal and refitting

Removal

1 Remove the engine/transmission assembly as described in Chapter 2B, Section 3, and drain the oil.
2 Remove the torque converter and housing as described in Section 3.

3 Unscrew the union nut and disconnect the oil feed pipe from the transmission adapter.

4 Lever the main oil feed pipe from the oil pump and transmission casing.

5 Unscrew the bolts and lift the engine from the transmission.

6 Remove the two gaskets, the main bearing cap oil seal, and the O-ring from the top of the oil pick-up pipe.

Refitting

7 Refitting is a reversal of the removal procedure, noting the following points:

  a) *Fit a new O-ring and casing-to-crankcase gaskets.*

  b) *Lubricate the new main bearing cap oil seal with engine oil before locating it on the timing chain end main bearing cap.*

  c) *Tighten all nuts and bolts to the specified torque.*

  d) *Refer to Section 3 when refitting the torque converter and housing, and to Chapter 2B when refitting the engine/transmission assembly.*

3 Torque converter, oil seal and housing - removal and refitting

Note: *Before starting work it is essential to obtain converter assembly remover tool (i.e. tool no. 18G1086), and output gear holding tool (i.e. 18G 1088). A 1 ½inch AF socket will also be required to unscrew the torque converter retaining bolt.*

Note: *If the engine/transmission is in the car, follow paragraphs 1 to 6.*

Removal

1 Drain the engine/transmission oil into a container, then refit the drain plug.

2 Remove the battery as described in Chapter 5 and remove the battery carrier.

3 Jack up the front of the car and support it with axle stands positioned beneath the rear edges of the front subframe (see *"Jacking and vehicle support"*).

4 Take the weight of the engine/transmission with a hoist.

5 Unscrew the nut and remove the through-bolt and washer from the right-hand front engine mounting. Unscrew and remove the nut and washer from the right-hand rear engine mounting.

6 Unscrew the bonnet lock cross panel securing screws and central bolt, and move the headlamp shrouds (if fitted). Remove the screws and withdraw the grille, then position the bonnet lock cross panel and radiator carefully to one side.

7 Remove the starter motor (Chapter 5) and the oil filter assembly (Chapter 1).

8 Unbolt and remove the torque converter cover. If the engine is in the car, it will be necessary to move the carburettor drain pipe and earth cable to one side.

9 Turn the crankshaft with a spanner on the pulley centre bolt, until the slots in the torque

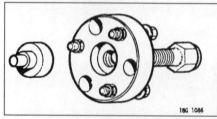

3.12 Converter remover tool (18G 1086)

converter and crankshaft are horizontal. This will prevent the output gear C-washer subsequently falling out.

10 Insert a wide-bladed screwdriver between the starter ring gear and the torque converter housing, then unscrew the torque converter retaining bolt. Make sure that the socket is fully engaged with the bolt as it is very tight.

11 Remove the keyplate and locking washer, then flatten the locktabs and unscrew three equally spaced bolts from the centre of the torque converter.

12 Using the remover **(see illustration)**, pull the torque converter from the crankshaft taper. It will be necessary to hold the torque converter stationary whilst tightening the puller centre bolt; strike the centre bolt with a hammer to help release the taper. Note that the torque converter will still retain some oil.

13 Using a hooked instrument as shown **(see illustration)**, extract the oil seal from the torque converter housing.

14 If removing the housing, continue with following paragraphs 15 to 21.

15 Remove the securing screws and detach the low pressure valve from the converter housing.

16 Attach the holding tool **(see illustration)**, to the converter output gear, remove the input gear nut. Disconnect the selector cable, unscrew the bellcrank pivot post and remove the bellcrank lever from the converter housing.

17 Remove the right-hand engine mounting. Apply tape to the output gear. Remove the nuts and screws securing the converter housing to the engine and partially withdraw the converter housing. Disconnect the oil feed pipe and withdraw the housing.

Refitting

18 Proceed to paragraph 22, if the housing is attached. Insert the oil feed pipe into its location in the transmission, fit a new gasket to the housing and, ensuring that the tape is still in place on the output gear, partially fit the housing. Connect the oil feed pipe, push the housing fully into place and remove the tape.

19 Fit the securing nuts and screws, ensuring that UNC screws secure the housing to the transmission and UNF screws secure the housing to the block. Tighten to the specifications shown.

20 Fit the input gear nut and using the holding tool tighten to the torque given.

21 Fit the bellcrank lever, connect the selector cable and fit the low pressure valve

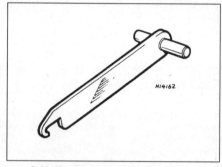

3.13 Tool for removing the torque converter oil seal

using a new gasket.

22 Continue refitting by using a micrometer or vernier calipers to measure the distance from the housing face to the end of the stator bush in the oil seal bore. If this dimension is less than 0.375 in (9.5 mm), deduct it from 0.375 in (9.5 mm) to obtain the oil seal protrusion from the housing face. If the dimension is equal to, or greater than 0.375 in (9.5 mm), the oil seal must be fitted flush with the housing face.

23 Using a length of tubing, install the oil seal into the housing to its correct position. Note that if the oil seal is not positioned correctly it may cover an important drain hole in the housing.

24 Fit new locking plates to the centre of the torque converter by removing and refitting the remaining bolts one at a time. Do not remove all the bolts at the same time. Insert and tighten all the bolts to the specified torque, then bend the locktabs onto one flat of each bolt.

25 With the crankshaft slot still horizontal, fit the torque converter onto the crankshaft and align the keyplate slots. Fit the keyplate, locking washer and retaining bolt.

26 Have an assistant insert a wide-bladed screwdriver between the ring gear and the housing, then tighten the torque converter retaining bolt to the specified torque. Bend the locking washer over one flat of the retaining bolt.

27 The remaining refitting procedure is a reversal of the removal procedure given in paragraphs 1 to 8. Fill the engine/transmission with the correct quantity of the specified oil.

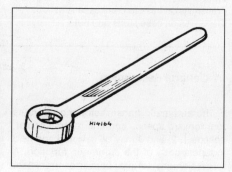

3.16 Input shaft holding tool (18G 1088)

4 Automatic transmission selector cable - removal, refitting and adjustment

Removal

1 Jack up the front of the car and support it with axle stands positioned beneath the rear edges of the front subframe (see "*Jacking and vehicle support*"). Apply the handbrake.

2 Unbolt the bellcrank cover plate from the transmission and unclip the selector cable from the subframe **(see illustration)**.

3 Extract one circlip, remove the pivot pin, and disconnect the cable clevis from the bellcrank lever.

4 Remove the locknut and washer, and withdraw the clevis from the cable.

5 Pull back the rubber covers, unscrew the outer cable locknut and remove the cable from the transmission.

6 Working beneath the selector housing, unscrew the cable retaining nut, then unscrew the adapter **(see illustration)**.

7 Using a split box spanner, loosen the locknut securing the cable to the plunger. Fit the fork and locknut to the inner cable and remove the inner cable from the plunger. Remove the fork and locknut together with the adapter olive and outer cable securing nut. Withdraw the cable.

Refitting

8 Refitting is a reversal of removal, but adjust the cable as follows.

9 With the bellcrank cover removed and the front of the car still supported on axle stands (see "*Jacking and vehicle support*"), loosen the large nut on the outer cable beneath the selector housing.

10 At the transmission end of the cable, turn the bellcrank lever fully anti-clockwise (from below) so that the transverse selector rod is in the "Park" position.

11 Have an assistant move the selector lever to the "P" position, making sure that the lever is in the notch at the left-hand side of the

4.2 Exploded view of the selector components

1	Selector lever	20	Lockwasher
2	Knob	21	Connector
3	Gate and side plate	22	Olive
4	Bias spring	23	Nut
5	Bolt	24	Gaiter
6	Nylon lock nut	25	Gaiter
7	Washer	26	Cable clip
8	Barrel	27	Reversing light
9	Pivot pin		switch
10	Pin retainers	28	Bracket
11	Mounting plate	29	Plug
12	Gasket	30	Stiffener plate
13	Screw	31	Seal
14	Washer	32	Nut
15	Selector housing	33	Washer
16	Selector plunger	34	Housing
17	Selector cable	35	Light unit
18	Locknut	36	Slide
19	Locknut	37	Light bulb

gate. If the notch cannot be felt, remove the selector lever nacelle and position the selector lever 0.035 in (0.9 mm) from the end of the gate slot.

12 With the bellcrank lever held still, pull the outer cable from the selector housing, then tighten the securing nut.

13 Refit the bellcrank cover and lower the car to the ground.

Adjustment

14 To check the adjustment, select "N" and start the engine. Move the lever to "R" and check that reverse is engaged, then slowly move the lever back to "N", the gear should disengage when the lever reaches the "N" position, or slightly before. Repeat the check but this time select "1".

15 When carrying out the adjustment check, it may be found that either first or reverse gear does not disengage when the selector lever reaches the "N" position.

16 If "R" remains engaged in position "N", reduce the gap at the end of the selector lever travel by 0.01 in (0.25 mm).

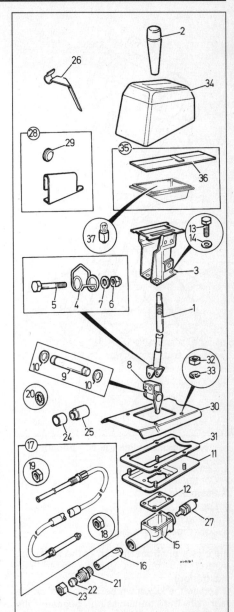

17 If "1" remains engaged in position "N", increase the gap at the end of the selector lever travel by 0.01 in (0.25 mm).

18 Recheck the adjustment and repeat paragraph 16 or 17 as necessary.

19 Check that the starter motor can be operated only in positions "P" and "N". Adjust the inhibitor switch if necessary as described in Section 6.

5 Kickdown linkage - adjustment

Adjustment

1 Run the engine to normal operating temperature and adjust the idling speed as described in Chapter 1.

2 Prise off the starlock washer and extract

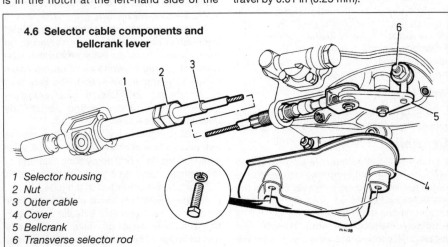

4.6 Selector cable components and bellcrank lever

1 Selector housing
2 Nut
3 Outer cable
4 Cover
5 Bellcrank
6 Transverse selector rod

7B

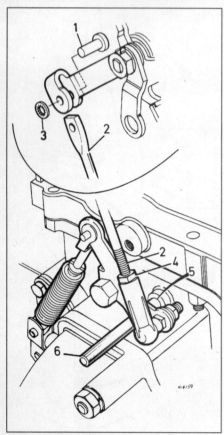

5.2 Kickdown linkage components

1 Clevis pin
2 Control rod
3 Starlock washer
4 Locknut
5 Casing hole
6 Dowel rod for checking

the clevis pin from the top of the kickdown control rod on the throttle lever **(see illustration)**.

3 Locate the kickdown bellcrank lever on the rear of the transmission beneath the manifolds. Insert a 6 mm (0.25 in) diameter rod through the hole in the lever and into the special hole in the transmission casing.

4 Check that the clevis pin can be inserted without removing the throttle lever. If not, loosen the locknut and turn the control rod as necessary.

5 Tighten the locknut, refit the clevis pin with a new starlock washer, and remove the dowel rod from the transmission casing.

6 Test drive the car and check that with the accelerator pedal fully depressed the gear changes occur according to the following:

1 to 2	29 to 37 mph (46 to 59 km/h)
2 to 3	43 to 51 mph (69 to 82 km/h)
3 to 4	61 to 69 mph (98 to 111 km/h)

7 If the changes occur at a lower speed, shorten the kickdown control rod by two complete turns and road test the car again. If the changes occur at a higher speed, lengthen the rod by two complete turns.

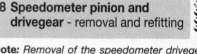

6 Starter inhibitor switch - removal, refitting, and adjustment

Removal

1 Jack up the front of the car and support it with axle stands positioned beneath the rear edges of the front subframe (see "*Jacking and vehicle support*"). Apply the handbrake.

2 Adjust the selector cable as described in Section 4. Move the selector lever to position "D".

3 Unbolt the guard plate from the front of the transmission, and disconnect the wiring from the inhibitor switch.

4 Either drain the engine/transmission oil or have ready a tapered plug, then loosen the locknut and unscrew the switch.

Refitting

5 Refitting is a reversal of removal, but top-up the engine/transmission oil as necessary. Before tightening the locknut, adjust the position of the switch as follows.

Adjustment

6 With the wiring disconnected, connect a test lamp and battery to the switch terminals. Screw in the switch until the test lamp just goes out, then screw it in a further three to four flats.

7 Tighten the locknut and check that the test lamp only lights up with the selector lever in positions "P" or "N".

8 Remove the test lamp and refit the wiring and guard plate.

9 Lower the car to the ground and check that the engine will only start with the selector lever in positions "P" or "N".

7 Reversing light switch - removal, refitting and adjustment

Removal

1 Jack up the front of the car and support it with axle stands positioned beneath the rear edges of the front subframe (see "*Jacking and vehicle support*"). Apply the handbrake.

2 Disconnect the wiring from the switch terminals, loosen the locknut, and unscrew the switch from the selector lever housing.

Refitting

3 Refitting is a reversal of removal, but adjust the switch as follows.

Adjustment

4 First move the selector lever to position "R". Connect a test lamp and battery to the switch terminals. Screw in the switch until the test lamp just lights up, then screw it in a further one and a half to three flats.

5 Tighten the locknut and remove the testlamp. Reconnect the wiring and lower the car to the ground.

6 Check that the reversing lights operate only with the selector lever in position "R".

8 Speedometer pinion and drivegear - removal and refitting

Note: *Removal of the speedometer drivegear on 1985-on models is not recommended for the home mechanic as it involves removal of the engine and transmission. The use of special tools to retain the forward clutch and align the oil feed pipe, will also be required.*

Removal

1 Disconnect the speedometer cable from the left-hand side of the transmission.

2 Unscrew the clamp bolt and withdraw the pinion assembly.

3 Unbolt the drive housing and withdraw the gasket and drivegear.

Refitting

4 Refitting is a reversal of removal, but always fit a new gasket.

9 Automatic transmission overhaul - general information

If there is a fault occurring with the transmission, it is first necessary to determine whether it is of an electrical, mechanical or hydraulic nature. To do this, special test equipment is required. It is therefore essential to have the work carried out by a Rover dealer if a transmission fault is suspected.

Do not remove the transmission from the car for possible repair before professional fault diagnosis has been carried out, since most tests require the transmission to be in the vehicle.

Owners of early Automatic Metros may experience slip or loss of drive when "R" is selected, and perhaps a condition known as "tie-up" (more than one gear selected) when engaging "D". These problems are not due to faults in the transmission, but to inaccuracies in the selector mechanism.

An improved selector cable with reduced backlash is now available. This cable can be distinguished from the initial production type by a dab of red or white paint on the cable outer at the transmission end. The improved cable should be fitted if gear selection problems exist, and attention paid to the adjustment procedures.

On later vehicles the selector gate slot is extended somewhat at the "D" end. Earlier vehicles can be modified by filing that end of the gate slot until the end of the slot is within 0.276 in (7 mm) of the end of the gate.

A revised selector valve is also fitted to later models. Consult your Rover dealer if you wish to fit a later type of valve to an early transmission. The operation is beyond the scope of this book.

Chapter 7 Part C:
Final drive

Contents

Degrees of difficulty

| Easy, suitable for novice with little experience | | Fairly easy, suitable for beginner with some experience | | Fairly difficult, suitable for competent DIY mechanic | 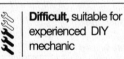 | Difficult, suitable for experienced DIY mechanic | 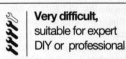 | Very difficult, suitable for expert DIY or professional | |

7C

Specifications

Differential bearing preload . . . . 0.004 in (0.102 mm)

Torque wrench settings	lbf ft	Nm
Differential housing nuts - ⁵⁄₁₆ in	18	25
Differential housing nuts - ³⁄₈ in	25	35
Final drive gear	48	66
Final drive pinion nut	150	207
Side cover bolts	18	25
Speedometer drivegear housing bolts	6	8
Speedometer drivegear housing nuts	18	25

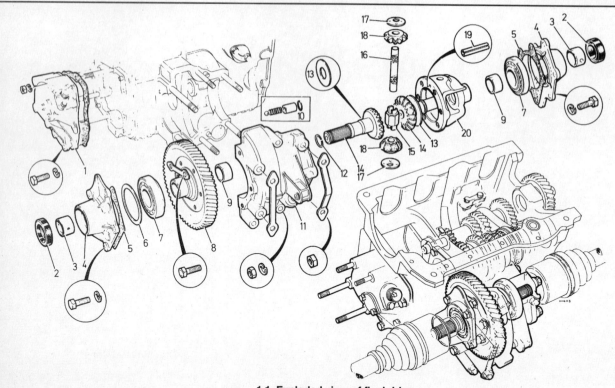

1.1 Exploded view of final drive

Note: *Except for item 10 the layout of the components fitted to automatic transmission models is identical.*

1 Speedometer drive housing	8 Final drive gear
2 Oil seal	9 Bush
3 Bush	10 Detent ball, spring, sleeve and O-ring
4 Side cover	(manual gearbox only)
5 Gasket	11 Differential housing
6 Shim	12 Spring ring
7 Bearing	13 Thrustwasher

14 Differential gear
15 Thrust block
16 Pinion pin
17 Thrustwasher
18 Differential pinion
19 Roll pin
20 Differential cage

1 General description

1 The final drive unit is located on the rear of the gearbox casing. The final drive gear is driven by a pinion that is splined to the gearbox third motion shaft on manual gearbox models, or to the top and reverse clutch hub on automatic transmission models **(see illustration)**.

2 The differential unit incorporates two pinions mounted on a single pin.

2 Differential unit - removal and refitting

Removal

1 Remove the engine and gearbox assembly as described in Chapter 2B, and place it on a workbench.

2 Unbolt and remove the left-hand side cover and gasket, and remove the adjustment shim(s). Place the shim(s) in a safe place, as they determine the differential bearing preload.

3 Unbolt and remove the right-hand side cover and gasket: note the exhaust bracket location.

4 On manual gearbox models, extract the selector shaft detent sleeve, O-ring, spring and ball from the gearbox casing on the right-hand side of the differential **(see illustrations)**.

5 Wrap adhesive tape over the selector shaft hole.

6 On all models, bend back the ends of the locktabs, then unscrew evenly in a diagonal sequence the differential housing securing nuts. Remove the locktabs and washers.

7 Withdraw the housing and gaskets (if fitted), followed by the differential unit **(see illustrations)**.

8 Prise the oil seals from the side covers and housing **(see illustration)**.

9 If a new or reconditioned differential unit is being fitted, the final drive pinion must also be renewed. See Section 3.

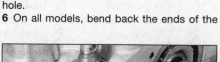

2.4a Removing the selector shaft detent spring and ball

2.4b Removing the selector shaft detent sleeve

2.7a Removing the differential housing

2.7b Removing the differential unit

2.8 Removing a side cover oil seal

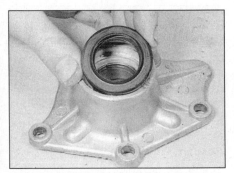

2.15a Installing a new side cover oil seal

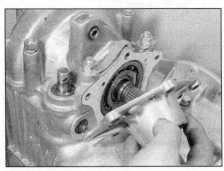

2.15b Installing the right-hand side cover

2.16 Exhaust bracket location on right-hand side cover

Refitting

10 Ensure that the differential housing and gearbox casing mating faces are clean.

11 Position the differential unit onto the gearbox casing and engage the final drive gear with the pinion. Push the unit slightly towards the right (flywheel) side of the casing to facilitate the subsequent preload adjustment. On manual gearbox models, wrap adhesive tape over the selector shaft to protect the oil seal.

12 If gaskets were originally fitted, fit new gaskets over the studs. If no gaskets were fitted, do not use any sealant at this stage.

13 Install the differential housing, locktabs and washers, and tighten the securing nuts evenly in diagonal sequence sufficiently to hold the differential unit firmly. However, it must be possible to move the unit when refitting the side cover to adjust the preload.

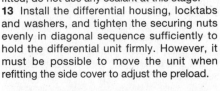

2.20 Differential bearing preload shim checking

14 On manual gearbox models, insert the selector shaft detent ball, spring, sleeve, and O-ring into the right-hand side of the gearbox casing.

15 Fit the right-hand (flywheel side) side cover together with a new gasket and oil seal, making sure that the oil holes in the cover and differential housing are aligned **(see illustrations)**.

16 Insert the securing bolts and washers and tighten them evenly in diagonal sequence to the specified torque after locating the exhaust bracket in position **(see illustration)**.

17 Fit the previously removed shims against the left-hand bearing outer race. If new components have been fitted, fit a nominal amount of shims.

18 Fit the left-hand side cover without a gasket, insert the securing bolts and washers, and tighten them evenly in diagonal sequence just sufficiently for the side cover to fully contact the bearing outer race. Do not overtighten the bolts, otherwise the side cover will be distorted.

19 If no gap exists between the side cover and the housing and casing, remove the side cover and add more shims.

20 Using a feeler blade, check the gap between the side cover and the housing **(see illustration)**. If the bolts have been tightened evenly, the gap will be identical at all points around the cover. Compare the measured gap with the preload figure plus the compressed gasket thickness. The compressed gasket thickness can be assumed to be 0.007 in (0.18 mm), therefore the figure to compare the

gap with is 0.011 in (0.28 mm). Calculate the shim thickness as follows:
a) *If the measured gap is greater than 0.011 in (0.28 mm), subtract 0.011 in (0.28 mm) from the measured gap to determine the thickness of shims to remove from the shim pack.*
b) *If the measured gap is less than 0.011 in (0.28 mm), subtract the measured gap from 0.011 in (0.28 mm) to determine the thickness of shims to add to the shim pack.*

21 Remove the left-hand side cover and adjust the shim pack as necessary.

22 If no gaskets are fitted between the differential housing and gearbox casing, remove the right-hand side cover and gasket, remove the nuts and withdraw the differential housing sufficiently to apply an unbroken bead of a sealant on each of the two mating faces. Do not disturb the position of the differential unit. After applying the sealant, the differential housing nuts must be fully tightened within twenty minutes. However, first refit the housing and install the locktabs washers and nuts. Tighten the nuts as described in paragraph 13, then refit the right-hand side cover and gasket, insert the securing bolts and washers, and tighten them evenly in diagonal sequence to the specified torque.

23 On gasket and non-gasket types grease the adjustment shims and locate them against the differential bearing outer race.

24 Fit the left-hand side cover together with a new gasket, making sure that the oil holes in the cover and differential housing are aligned.

7C

2.26 Tightening differential housing nuts

25 Insert the securing bolts and washers and tighten them evenly in diagonal sequence to the specified torque.
26 Tighten the differential housing nuts evenly and in diagonal sequence to the specified torque **(see illustration)**. Lock the nuts by bending up the locktabs.
27 Remove the tape and refit the engine and gearbox assembly as described in Chapter 2B.

3 Final drive pinion (manual gearbox models) - removal and refitting

Removal

Note: *If either final drive pinion or gear is worn, a new or reconditioned unit must be fitted.*

1 Remove the differential unit as described in Section 2.
2 Remove the bolt and clamp securing the speedometer pinion to the housing **(see illustration)**.
3 Withdraw the speedometer pinion together with the bushes and gasket **(see illustration)**.
4 Unscrew the speedometer pinion housing nuts and bolts evenly, noting the location of the engine mounting brackets.
5 Remove the engine mounting bracket, then withdraw the housing and gear from the gearbox casing **(see illustration)**. Remove the gasket.
6 Turn the gear selector shaft anti-clockwise

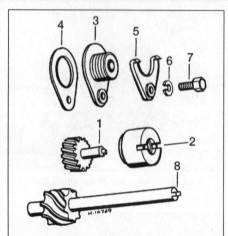

3.2 Speedometer drivegear components

1 *Speedometer pinion*
2 *Plain bush*
3 *Pinion bush with seal*
4 *Gasket*
5 *Clamp*
6 *Spring washer*
7 *Bolt*
8 *Speedometer gear*

to disengage the stub and interlock spool from the bellcrank levers.
7 Working through the differential aperture in the gearbox casing, use a screwdriver to push the centre bellcrank lever inwards to select 4th gear. Lever the 1st/2nd selector fork towards the final drive pinion to select 1st gear. The gears are now locked together.
8 Flatten the locktabs, then, using a 1 ½ inch AF socket, unscrew and remove the final drive pinion nut and lockwasher **(see illustration)**.
9 Mark the final drive pinion in relation to the third motion shaft, then slide it off **(see illustration)**. Note the line of notches on the pinion teeth to indicate the final drive gear mesh position.

Refitting

10 Fit the new final drive pinion on the third motion shaft, making sure that it is the correct way round.
11 Fit the locktab and nut and tighten the nut

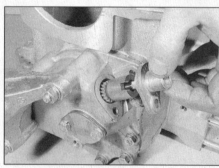

3.3 Removing the speedometer pinion

3.5 Removing the speedometer pinion housing and gear

to the specified torque **(see illustration)**. Bend the locktab onto one flat of the nut to lock it.
12 Lever the 1st/2nd selector fork into neutral. Pull the centre bellcrank lever outwards to select neutral.
13 Clean the speedometer gear housing and gearbox casing mating faces, and install the housing with a new gasket.
14 Install the engine mounting bracket, then fit and tighten the housing retaining nuts and bolts evenly and in diagonal sequence to the specified torque.
15 Turn the gear selector shaft clockwise to engage the stub and interlock spool with the bellcrank levers.
16 Insert the speedometer pinion together with the bushes and a new gasket. Fit the clamp to the housing and tighten the bolt.
17 Fit the differential unit as described in Section 2.

3.8 Removing the final drive pinion nut lockwasher

3.9 Removing the final drive pinion

3.11 Tightening the final drive pinion nut

Chapter 8
Driveshafts

Contents

Degrees of difficulty

Easy, suitable for novice with little experience		**Fairly easy,** suitable for beginner with some experience		**Fairly difficult,** suitable for competent DIY mechanic		**Difficult,** suitable for experienced DIY mechanic		**Very difficult,** suitable for expert DIY or professional	

Specifications

Type .... Solid shafts splined to constant velocity inner and outer joints

Torque wrench settings	lbf ft	Nm
Driveshaft-to-drive flange nut:		
Two split pin hole type	200	274
Single split pin hole type	193	264
Steering balljoint nut	22	30
Upper and lower balljoint nuts	37	51

1 General description

1 Drive is transmitted from the splined final drive differential gears to the inner constant velocity joints. Splined solid driveshafts are connected to the inner and outer constant velocity joints and drive is transmitted through the splined driving flange to the front wheels **(see illustration)**.

2 Overhaul of the constant velocity joints is not possible. However, it is possible to renew the gaiters that are available in repair kits. If the outer constant velocity joints are worn excessively, they will "click" loudly on full left or right turns under load.

2 Outer constant velocity (CV) joint and driveshaft - removal and refitting

Note: *Before starting work, obtain tool 18G1342 and a balljoint separator.*

Removal

1 Working beneath the front of the car, remove the cross-head screws and withdraw the square rebound rubber from under the upper suspension arm. Insert a large size nut or block of wood between the arm and

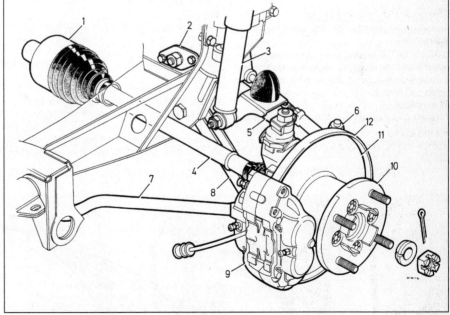

1.1 Left-hand side driveshaft and components

1 Inner joint	5 Upper suspension arm	9 Brake caliper
2 Suspension arm pivot plate	6 Steering balljoint	10 Drive flange
3 Shock absorber	7 Anti-roll bar	11 Disc
4 Driveshaft	8 Lower suspension arm	12 Shield

8

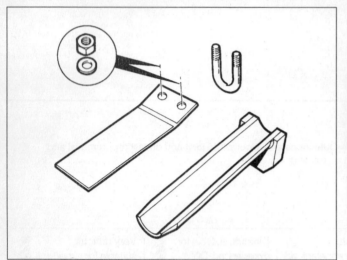

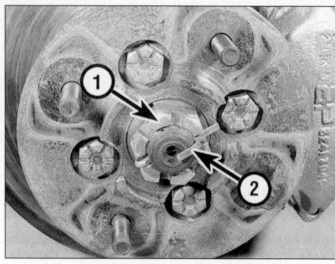

2.3 Tool 18G1342 for releasing driveshaft from inner CV joint

2.6 Drive flange nut and split pin

1 Nut   2 Split Pin

subframe to retain the front suspension in the normal running position.

2 Apply the handbrake, then jack up the front of the car and support it on axle stands (see "*Jacking and vehicle support*"). Remove the roadwheel.

3 Grease the tapered end of tool 18G1342 **(see illustration)**. Slide it along the top of the driveshaft and carefully insert it under the neck of the gaiter and into contact with the inner joint extension tube.

4 Fit the clamp and plate of the tool to the underside of the driveshaft so that it contacts the subframe. On the left-hand side, rest the tapered part of the tool on the U-bolt.

5 Drive the tapered part of the tool towards the differential to release the inner joint from the driveshaft spring ring. Remove the tool.

6 Have an assistant firmly apply the brake pedal, then remove the split pin and unscrew the drive flange nut. Note that this nut is **very** tight. Remove the split collar **(see illustration)**.

7 Refer to Chapter 9 and remove the brake caliper without disconnecting the hydraulic hoses. Suspend the caliper to one side without straining the hoses.

8 Pull the drive flange and the disc assembly from the driveshaft, using a puller if necessary.

9 Unscrew the self-locking nut from the steering balljoint. Using a separator tool, disconnect the balljoint from the steering arm.

10 Remove the disc brake shield from the swivel hub assembly.

11 Unscrew the nuts from the swivel hub upper and lower balljoints. Using a separator tool, disconnect the upper and lower suspension arms from the swivel hub.

12 Withdraw the swivel hub and driveshaft assembly from the inner constant velocity joint.

13 Drive the outer constant velocity joint from the swivel hub assembly using a soft metal drift. If the inner bearing inner race remains on the CV joint stubshaft, the ball-bearings will be displaced and should be examined for damage and wear. Renew the bearing if necessary, with reference to Chapter 10.

14 Tap the water shield from the CV joint.

15 Examine the outer CV joint gaiter for damage and splits and, if necessary, renew it as follows, provided the joint is in good

condition. If the joint is being renewed, note that it is serviced with the driveshaft as a complete assembly.

16 To renew the gaiter, first obtain a repair kit. Cut the old clips from the boot using snips.

17 Slide the gaiter off the driveshaft.

18 Hold the driveshaft vertically over the workbench with the outer CV joint downwards. Using a soft-faced mallet, strike the outer edge of the joint sharply and remove the joint from the driveshaft.

19 Extract the spring ring from the outer end of the driveshaft.

Refitting

20 Fit the new spring ring from the repair kit, and drive the driveshaft into the outer CV joint while compressing the ring to facilitate entry.

21 Pack the CV joint with the grease supplied with the repair kit. Smear some of the grease on the joint working surfaces and put the remainder in the gaiter.

22 Slide the new gaiter into position over the CV joint and driveshaft, making sure that the mating surfaces are clean.

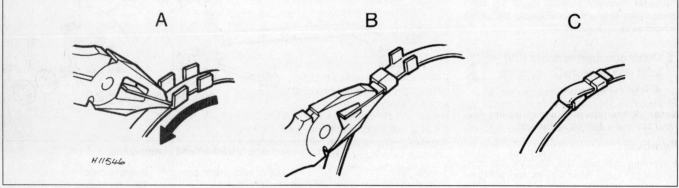

2.23 Method of securing clip to CV joint boot; arrow indicates forward rotation of shaft

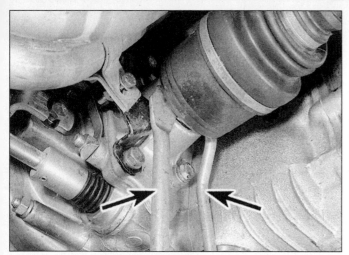

3.7 Using levers to remove the inner constant velocity joints (arrowed)

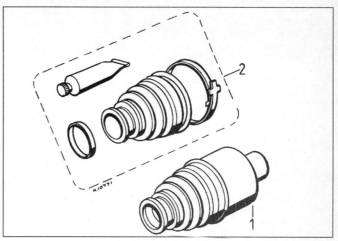

3.10 Inner constant velocity joint and repair kit

1 Constant velocity joint   *2 Repair kit*

23 The large retaining clip must be fitted with the fold facing the forward direction of rotation. Wrap the clip around the gaiter and pull the free end tightly between the front tabs. Flatten the tabs with a screwdriver, and bend the clip back between the rear tabs. Flatten the rear tabs to secure the clip **(see illustration).**

24 Check that the gaiter is not stretched or compressed, then secure it to the driveshaft with the small clip, using the method described in the previous paragraph.

25 Fit the water shield squarely onto the outer end of the CV joint and fill the sealing face with grease. Refer to Chapter 10 for the fitting dimension.

26 Insert the driveshaft through the swivel hub, and pull it fully into the hub without displacing the outer bearing. Rest the outer bearing inner race on a length of tubing and tap the driveshaft assembly down through the bearings.

27 Lubricate the inner joint gaiter, then insert the driveshaft and push it sharply to engage the spring ring.

28 Locate the swivel hub ball-pins into the upper and lower suspension arms and refit the tab washers and nuts. Tighten the nuts to the specified torque and bend up the tab washers to lock them.

29 Locate the disc brake shield on the swivel hub assembly.

30 Fit the steering balljoint to the steering arm, but do not fully tighten the self-locking nut at this stage.

31 Fit the drive flange and disc assembly, followed by the brake caliper (Chapter 9).

32 Place a plain washer over the end of the driveshaft. The washer dimensions should be: 50 mm (1.97 in) outside diameter, 25 mm (0.98 in) inside diameter, 6.5 mm (0.26 in) thickness. Fit the driveshaft nut and tighten it firmly - say to half the final specified torque - whilst an assistant applies the brake, then unscrew the nut and remove the washer. The purpose of this operation is to make sure that the shaft is fully home.

33 Oil the driveshaft threads.

34 Tighten the steering balljoint self-locking nut to the specified torque.

35 Fit the split collar and the driveshaft nut. Have an assistant apply the brake, or bolt a bar to two of the wheel studs, and tighten the driveshaft nut to the specified torque. If the split pin holes are not aligned at this torque, tighten further until the holes are aligned. Insert a new split pin and bend back the legs.

36 Refit the roadwheel and lower the car to the ground.

37 Remove the nut or wooden block, and refit the rebound rubber to the subframe.

3 Inner constant velocity (CV) joint - removal and refitting

Removal

1 Follow the removal procedure given in previous Section 2, paragraphs 1 to 5.

2 Refer to Chapter 9 and remove the brake caliper without disconnecting the hydraulic hoses. Suspend the caliper to one side without straining the hoses.

3 Unscrew the self-locking nut from the steering balljoint. Using a separator tool, disconnect the balljoint from the steering arm.

4 Unscrew the nuts from the swivel hub upper and lower balljoints. Using a separator tool, disconnect the upper and lower suspension arms from the swivel hub.

5 Withdraw the swivel hub and driveshaft assembly from the inner constant velocity joint and place it to one side.

6 Drain the oil from the engine/gearbox unit.

7 Using two levers as shown, lever the inner constant velocity joint from the differential side gear **(see illustration).**

8 Examine the inner CV joint gaiter for damage and splits, and if necessary, renew it as follows. First obtain a repair kit, then cut the old clip from the boot using snips.

9 Remove the gaiter from the joint.

Refitting

10 Pack the CV joint with the grease supplied with the repair kit **(see illustration).** Smear some of the grease on the joint working surfaces and put the remainder in the gaiter.

11 Clean the mating surfaces of the boot and joint, then slide the new gaiter in position.

12 Note that the clip must be fitted with the fold facing the forward direction of rotation. Wrap the clip around the gaiter and pull the free end tightly between the front tabs. Flatten the tabs with a screwdriver, and bend the clip back between the rear tabs. Flatten the rear tabs to secure the clip **(see illustration 2.23).**

13 Fit the ring over the small diameter end of the gaiter.

14 Smear the differential side cover oil seal clip with engine oil.

15 Wipe clean the CV joint oil seal surface, then fit the CV joint to the differential side gear and sharply push it in to engage the spring ring.

16 Lubricate the inner joint gaiter, then insert the driveshaft complete with swivel hub and push it sharply to engage the spring ring.

17 Locate the swivel hub ball-pins into the upper and lower suspension arms, and refit the tab washers and nuts. Tighten the nuts to the specified torque and bend up the tab washers to lock them.

18 Fit the steering balljoint to the steering arm, but do not fully tighten the self-locking nut at this stage.

19 Refit the brake caliper with reference to Chapter 9.

20 Tighten the steering balljoint self-locking nut to the specified torque.

21 Refit the roadwheel and lower the car to the ground.

22 Remove the wooden block, and refit the rebound rubber to the subframe.

23 Refill the engine/gearbox unit with oil.

8

Chapter 9
Braking system

Contents

Degrees of difficulty

Easy, suitable for novice with little experience		Fairly easy, suitable for beginner with some experience		Fairly difficult, suitable for competent DIY mechanic		Difficult, suitable for experienced DIY mechanic		Very difficult, suitable for expert DIY or professional	

Specifications

General

System type	Four wheel hydraulic, with discs on front and drums on rear. Dual hydraulic feeds with rear brake pressure regulating valve. Servo assistance on some models. Cable-operated handbrake on rear wheels. Ventilated discs fitted to MG Turbo and all 1985-on models (note that LH and RH are not interchangeable).
Servo boost ratio	2.04 : 1

Discs

Working diameter	8.35 in (213 mm)
Minimum pad thickness	0.125 in (3 mm)
Disc minimum thickness:	
Plain disc	0.34 in (8.6 mm)
Ventilated disc	0.74 in (18.7 mm)
Maximum allowable run-out	0.006 in (0.15 mm)
Maximum allowable thickness variation	0.0005 in (0.013 mm)

Drums

Internal diameter	7.0 in (177.9 in)
Minimum lining thickness	0.063 in (1.6 mm)

Torque wrench settings

	lbf ft	Nm
Backplate to radius arm	19	26
Caliper	38	53
Compensating valve end plug	40	54
Disc to flange	38	52
Master cylinder/brake servo mounting (1.3 litre)	9	12
Master cylinder mounting (1.0 litre)	19	26
Master cylinder reservoir flange	5	7
Master cylinder mounting plate to bulkhead	8.5	12

9

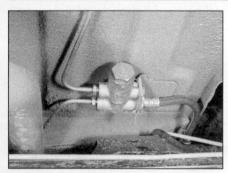

1.2a Pressure compensating valve (early models)

1 General description

1 The braking system is of four wheel hydraulic, dual circuit type with discs at the front and manually adjusted drum brakes at the rear. The dual circuit system is of the H-I type, where the primary circuit feeds both front and rear brakes, and the secondary circuit feeds the front brakes only. Each front brake caliper incorporates four pistons and two independent hydraulic feeds. A direct acting brake servo unit is fitted to 1.3 and later 1.0 models.

2 On early vehicles, a pressure compensating valve is installed in the rear hydraulic circuit to prevent the rear wheels locking before the front wheels during heavy applications of the brakes. 1985-on Saloon models are fitted with a pressure reducing valve in the rear brake hydraulic circuit that is located on the master cylinder. Vans built from 1984-on are fitted with an inertia/pressure regulating valve in the rear brake hydraulic circuit instead of the compensating valve **(see illustrations)**.

3 The handbrake operates on the rear wheels only, and incorporates a switch that illuminates a warning light on the instrument panel when the handbrake is applied. Driver warning lights are provided for the brake pad wear and brake fluid low level.

2 Precautions

Caution. Brake pads and linings must be renewed as a complete sets, i.e. BOTH left and right brake pad sets must be renewed at the same time. DO NOT renew the pads or linings on just one roadwheel, as unbalanced braking may occur, making the car unstable. Note that the dust created by wear of the pads or linings may contain asbestos, which is a health hazard. Do not use compressed air to blow out brake dust and debris - use a brush. Avoid inhaling any of the dust; wear an approved filtration mask. Use only proprietary brake cleaner fluid or methylated spirit to cleanse the brake components. DO NOT use petrol or any other petroleum-based product.

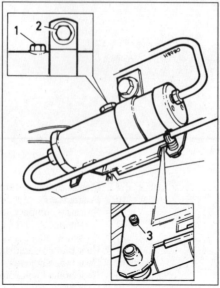

1.2b Inertia/pressure regulating valve fitted to 1984-on Vans

| 1 Vent plug | 3 Locating peg |
| 2 Clamp bolt | (where fitted) |

⚠ *Warning. Brake fluid is poisonous; thoroughly wash off spills from bare skin without delay. Seek immediate medical advice if any fluid is swallowed or gets into the eyes. Certain types of hydraulic fluid are inflammable, and may ignite when brought into contact with hot components. When servicing any hydraulic system, it is safest to assume that the fluid IS inflammable, and to take precautions against the risk of fire as though it is petrol that is being handled. Hydraulic fluid is an effective paint stripper, and will also attack many plastics. If spillage occurs onto painted bodywork or fittings, it should be washed off immediately, using copious quantities of fresh water. It is also hygroscopic (it can absorb moisture from the air); excess moisture content lowers the fluid boiling point to an unacceptable level, resulting in a dangerous loss of braking effectiveness. Old fluid may have suffered contamination, and should never be re-used. When topping-up or renewing the fluid, always use the recommended grade, and ensure that it comes from a freshly opened sealed container.*

3 Rear brakes - adjustment

1 Chock the front wheels, then jack up the rear of the car and support it on axle stands (see *"Jacking and vehicle support"*).
2 Fully release the handbrake and make sure that both rear wheels can be rotated freely.
3 Working beneath the car, turn the adjuster

3.3 Adjusting the rear brakes

on the rear face of one backplate clockwise until the wheel is locked **(see illustration)**.
4 Loosen the adjuster by two or three flats until the wheel can be rotated freely.
5 Repeat the procedure on the remaining rear wheel, then lower the car to the ground.

4 Disc pads - inspection and renewal

Note: *The instrument panel warning lamps should glow if either inner pad wears to the minimum thickness.*

Inspection

1 Apply the handbrake, then jack up the front of the car and support it on axle stands (see *"Jacking and vehicle support"*). Remove the roadwheels.
2 Using a screwdriver, move the anti-rattle spring upwards to release it from the bottom split pin, then withdraw it downwards from the upper split pin **(see illustration)**.
3 Measure the thickness of the lining material on each disc pad, and if either one is at or below the specified minimum, renew the complete set of front disc pads **(see illustration)**.
4 To remove the pads, straighten the split pins and extract them from the caliper.
5 Where fitted, disconnect the wear indicator wiring from the harness and detach the rubber clip **(see illustration)**.
6 Press each pad slightly against its pistons, then withdraw it from the caliper **(see illustration)**.

4.2 Removing the disc pad anti-rattle spring

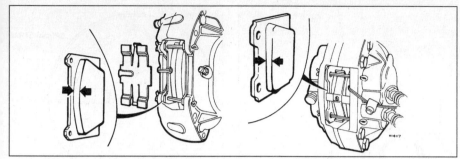

4.3 Alternative types of front brake pads - arrows indicate pad thickness measuring point

4.5 Disc pad wear indicator wiring connector

4.6 Removing a disc pad from the caliper

13 Insert the split pins through the caliper and pads. Bend the ends to lock them.
14 Fit the anti-rattle spring under the bottom split pin, then hook it under the top split pin.
15 Repeat the procedure on the remaining wheel, then refit the wheels and lower the car to the ground.
16 Depress the footbrake pedal several times to set the pads, then check and, if necessary, top-up the level of brake fluid in the master cylinder reservoir.

5 Rear brake shoes - inspection and renewal

Inspection

1 Chock the front wheel, then jack up the rear of the car and support it on axle stands (see *"Jacking and vehicle support"*). Remove the rear wheels. The rear brake backplate on 1985-on models incorporates an inspection hole through which the trailing shoe lining can be checked for thickness. The use of a torch will be helpful, and, after checking, always make sure that the rubber grommet is correctly fitted in the hole.
2 Release the handbrake. Remove the two cross-head screws and withdraw the brake drum from the wheel studs **(see illustration)**. If the drum is tight, release the adjuster one or two turns, and if necessary tap the periphery of the drum with a soft-faced mallet to release it from the studs.
3 Brush the dust from the brake drum, brake shoes, and backplate, *do not inhale the dust, see warning in Section 2.* Scrape any scale or rust from the drum.
4 Measure the brake shoe lining thickness. If it is worn down to the specified minimum amount, or if it is nearly worn down to the rivets, renew all four rear brake shoes. If the linings are in good condition, refit the drum and adjust the brakes as described in Section 3.
5 To remove the brake shoes, first note the location of the return springs, and to which holes they are fitted **(see illustrations)**.

7 Brush the dust and dirt from the caliper, pistons, disc and pads, *do not inhale the dust (see warning in Section 2)*. Scrape any scale or rust from the disc and pad backing plate.
8 When the front brake pads have to be renewed, it is a good idea to check the thickness of the brake disc. The minimum allowable thickness is given in the Specifications, refer to Section 7 if necessary.

Renewal

Note: *Check the level of brake fluid in the reservoir regularly to avoid spillage.*
9 Using a piece of wood, press the pistons back into the caliper. At the same time, check the level of brake fluid in the reservoir. If this is near the top of the reservoir, unscrew the

relevant bleed screw to release the fluid while the piston is being depressed. Tighten it immediately afterwards.
10 Smear special anti-squeal grease lightly on the metal-to-metal contact surfaces of each pad backing plate. The grease must not be allowed to contact the caliper piston seals, as may happen when the pistons are pushed back to receive the new pads. Before pushing the caliper pistons in wipe around the side of the pistons with a clean dry cloth.
11 Insert the pads into the caliper with the linings facing the disc. Note that only one pad has a wear indicator; fit this on the inner side of the disc.
12 Connect the wear indicator wiring and clip where fitted.

5.2 Removing the brake drum

5.5a Rear brake shoe upper return spring location and adjuster

9

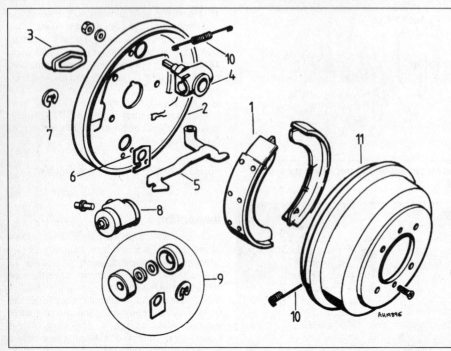

5.5b Exploded view of the rear brakes - left-hand side shown

1 Brake shoes	5 Lever assembly	9 Repair kit
2 Backplate	6 Gasket	10 Return springs
3 Rubber boot	7 Circlip	11 Brake drum
4 Adjuster	8 Wheel cylinder	

6 Release each shoe from the adjuster pegs using a screwdriver or adjustable spanner. Similarly release the shoes from the wheel cylinder pistons.

7 Disengage the handbrake levers and withdraw the shoes. Detach both return springs.

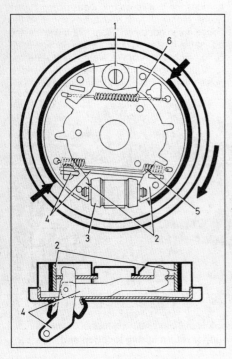

5.9 Sectional view of the rear brakes - right-hand side shown

1 Adjuster	5 Bottom return
2 Brake shoes	spring
3 Wheel cylinder	6 Top return spring
4 Handbrake lever	
assembly	

Arrows indicate brake shoe leading edges and forward rotation of drum

8 Clean the brake backplate. If there are any signs of loss of grease from the rear hub bearings, the oil seal should be renewed with reference to Chapter 10. If hydraulic fluid is leaking from the wheel cylinder, it must be repaired or renewed as described in Section 8. Do not touch the brake pedal or handbrake lever while the shoes are removed. Position an elastic band over the wheel cylinder pistons to retain them. To overcome rear brake squeal a spring strap (available from Rover dealers) can (or may already), be fitted under the brake backplate/anti-roll bar securing bolt so that the spring strap bears against the backplate **(see illustration)**.

Renewal

9 Lay the new shoes on a flat surface in their approximate fitted attitude. The leading edges must face in the opposite direction to forward movement of the drum **(see illustration)**.

10 Hook the bottom return spring to the shoes with the middle section to the bottom; this will ensure that it does not foul the hub when fitted.

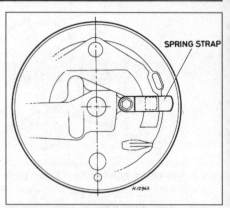

5.8 Position (A) on right-hand rear brake backplate for fitting self-adhesive wheel balance weight to counteract rear brake

11 Fit the shoes and spring to the handbrake levers. Remove the elastic band and locate the shoe webs in the wheel cylinder piston slots.

12 Hook the top return spring to the shoes from the rear, then lever the shoe webs into the adjuster peg slots.

13 Fully unscrew the adjuster. Tap the shoes so that they are located concentric to the hub.

14 Fit the drum and tighten the two screws.

15 Refit the roadwheel and adjust the rear brakes and handbrake as described in Sections 3 and 18.

16 Lower the car to the ground.

6 Disc caliper - removal, overhaul and refitting

Removal

1 Jack up the front of the car and support it on axle stands (see "*Jacking and vehicle support*"). Remove the roadwheel.

2 Remove the disc pads (Section 4).

3 Unscrew the two bolts securing the caliper and disc shield to the swivel hub. Remove the spring washers.

4 Withdraw the caliper and support it on a stand without straining the hydraulic hoses.

Overhaul

5 Clean the caliper thoroughly with methylated spirit and allow to dry.

6 Make a piece of hardwood of the shape as shown **(see illustration)**, and insert it into the caliper. Have an assistant slowly depress the footbrake pedal until the free piston is almost out of its bore. Remove the hardwood block and pull out the piston; soak up the released brake fluid with a piece of cloth.

7 Using a non-metallic instrument such as a plastic needle, prise the retainer and wiper seal from the mouth of the bore. Similarly remove the fluid seal from the groove inside the bore.

8 Clean the piston, bore and grooves with a lint-free cloth, then inspect their surfaces for damage, wear and corrosion. If the piston surface alone is unserviceable, it may be possible to obtain a new piston. However, it is

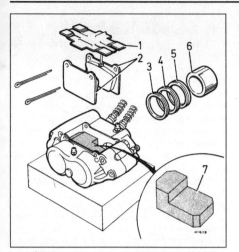

6.6 Exploded view of front brake caliper

1 Anti-rattle spring
2 Pads
3 Retainer
4 Wiper seal
5 Fluid seal
6 Piston
7 Wooden block for removing pistons

more common for both sealing surfaces to be affected, in which case the complete caliper must be renewed. If the components are in good condition, obtain a repair kit of new seals.

Refitting

9 Dip the new fluid seal in clean brake fluid and manipulate it into the bore groove using the fingers only. Note that the groove is designed to hold the inner edge of the seal slightly raised.

10 Fit the wiper seal to the retainer and press them both into the mouth of the bore.

11 Loosen the bleed screw for the piston removed (one screw is provided for both upper pistons). Then smear the piston with clean brake fluid and insert it into the bore leaving approximately 0.15 in (4 mm) projecting. Tighten the bleed screw and top-up the reservoir as necessary.

12 Repeat the procedure given in paragraphs 6 to 11 for the remaining pistons.

13 If the caliper is to be renewed, identify each brake fluid hose for position, then unscrew the unions. Note that two types of caliper are fitted, and it is important to fit the correct type: the information (type A or type B) is to be found on the bonnet lock crossmember. Also note that bleed nipples for both types are not interchangeable; the nipple taper must contact the seat before the hexagon contacts the body. *Do not separate the caliper halves.*

14 If necessary, the disc shield can be removed at this stage.

15 Reconnect the hoses to the caliper and tighten the unions.

16 Refit the caliper and disc shield to the swivel hub, and tighten the bolts to the specified torque.

17 Refit the disc pads (Section 4).

18 Refit the roadwheel and lower the car to the ground.

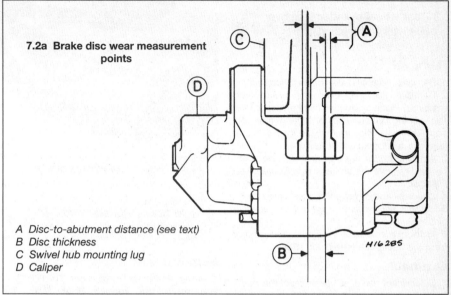

7.2a Brake disc wear measurement points

A Disc-to-abutment distance (see text)
B Disc thickness
C Swivel hub mounting lug
D Caliper

19 Bleed the complete brake hydraulic circuits as described in Section 17.

7 Brake disc - examination, removal and refitting

> ⚠ **Warning: Brake discs should always be renewed in pairs in order to maintain even braking.**

Examination

1 Jack up the front of the car and support it on axle stands (see "*Jacking and vehicle support*"). Apply the handbrake and remove the roadwheel.

2 Rotate the disc and examine it for deep scoring or grooving. Light scoring is normal, but, if excessive, the disc should be removed and either renewed or ground by a suitably qualified engineering works. A further check should be made by measuring the gap between the disc face and the caliper abutment on each side of the disc **(see illustration)**. If this dimension exceeds 0.110 in (2.8 mm) on either side, the disc must be renewed. Brake discs should always be renewed in pairs to maintain even braking. When fitting discs to MG Turbo and 1985-on models, note that the discs are "handed", i.e. left-hand and right-hand discs are different. The difference is in the angle of the cooling vanes, which are designed to function efficiently in one direction of rotation only. The manufacturers have provided an external means of distinguishing the discs. The edge facing the drive flange has a concave finish on the left-hand disc, where the right-hand disc is finished with a smooth taper **(see illustration)**.

Removal

3 To remove the brake disc, first refit the roadwheel and lower the car to the ground. Remove the split pin, and loosen the

driveshaft nut while an assistant depresses the footbrake pedal.

4 Jack up the front of the car again and support it on axle stands (see "*Jacking and vehicle support*"). Remove the roadwheel.

5 Remove the disc caliper as described in Section 6, leaving the hydraulic hoses connected and supporting the caliper on a stand.

6 Remove the driveshaft nut and the split collar from the end of the driveshaft.

7 Pull the drive flange and disc assembly from the driveshaft, using a puller if necessary.

8 Mark the drive flange and disc in relation to each other, then unscrew the special bolts and separate the two components.

Refitting

9 Refitting is a reversal of removal, but make sure that the mating faces of the disc and flange are clean, and tighten the bolts in diagonal sequence to the specified torque. Grease the hub outer oil seal before inserting the drive flange. Refer to Chapter 8 for details of driveshaft nut tightening.

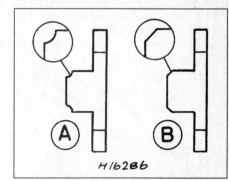

7.2b Ventilated disc identification

A Left-hand (concave edge)
B Right-hand (smooth edge)

9

8 Rear wheel cylinder - removal, overhaul and refitting

Removal

1 Remove the rear brake shoes (Section 5).
2 Remove the cap from the brake fluid reservoir. Place a sheet of thin polythene over the warning switch assembly, then tighten the cap. This will help prevent the loss of brake fluid in the subsequent procedure.
3 Working under the car, unscrew the union nut and remove the brake pipe from the wheel cylinder.
4 Unscrew and remove the bleed screw.
5 Using a screwdriver, prise out the retaining circlip.
6 Withdraw the wheel cylinder and gasket from the backplate (see illustration).

Overhaul

7 Disconnect the dust covers from the body, and withdraw the pistons. Identify the pistons side for side (see illustration).
8 Remove the dust covers and seals from the pistons.
9 Clean all the components in methylated spirit and allow to dry. Examine the surfaces of the pistons and cylinder bores for wear, scoring and corrosion. If evident, renew the complete wheel cylinder. If they are in good condition, discard the seals, retaining circlip and gasket, and obtain a repair kit.
10 Dip the inner seals in clean brake fluid, and fit them to the piston inner grooves, using the fingers only to manipulate them. Make sure that the larger diameter end faces the inner end of the piston.
11 Carefully insert the pistons half way into the cylinders.
12 Coat the sealing surfaces of the dust covers with rubber lubricant, then fit them into the groove on the pistons and wheel cylinder body.

Refitting

13 Refitting is a reversal of removal, but use the new gasket and circlip. Adjust the brakes as described in Section 3, and bleed the hydraulic system as described in Section 17. Do not forget to remove the polythene sheet from the brake fluid reservoir.

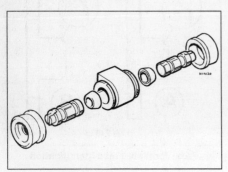

8.7 Exploded view of the rear wheel cylinder

8.6 Rear brake wheel cylinder

9 Rear brake adjuster - removal and refitting

Removal

1 Remove the rear brake shoes (Section 5).
2 Remove the rubber boot from the backplate.
3 Unscrew the two nuts and remove the spring washers.
4 Withdraw the adjuster from the backplate.
5 Remove the pegs and identify them side for side. Check that the adjuster screw moves freely and lubricate the threads with grease. Grease the pegs and reinsert them in the adjuster.

Refitting

6 Refitting is a reversal of removal, but adjust the brakes as described in Section 3. Note that the adjuster can only be fitted one way round.

10 Brake drum - inspection and renovation

Inspection

1 Whenever the brake drums are removed, they should be checked for wear and damage. Light scoring of the friction surface is normal, but if excessive, it is recommended that the drums are renewed as a pair.
2 To prevent water entering the rear brake drums, later models are fitted with a paper gasket between the brake drum and the flange.
3 If problems due to water entry are encountered on earlier models, obtain and fit the gaskets between the drums and their flanges. Clean off any rust on the friction surfaces and gasket mating surfaces, using fine grade abrasive paper.

Renovation

4 After a high mileage, the friction surface may become oval. Where this has occurred, it may be possible to grind the surface true, but this should only be carried out by a qualified engineering works. It is preferable to renew the drums as a pair.

11 Rear brake backplate - removal and refitting

Removal

1 Remove the rear brake shoes (Section 5).
2 Remove the rear wheel cylinder and adjuster as described in Sections 8 and 9.
3 Remove the hub assembly as described in Chapter 10.
4 Remove the clevis pin and disconnect the handbrake cable from the operating lever. Withdraw the lever assembly and rubber boot from the backplate.
5 Unscrew and remove the three nuts and washers, and withdraw the backplate from the radius arm.
6 If necessary, remove the bolts and cable bracket from the radius arm, noting the location of the spacers.

Refitting

7 Refitting is a reversal of removal, but make sure that the mating surfaces of the flange and radius arm are clean. Adjust the rear brakes and handbrake (Sections 3 and 18).

12 Master cylinder - removal, overhaul and refitting

Removal

1 If a servo unit is fitted, depress the footbrake pedal several times to dissipate the vacuum.
2 Working in front of the car, connect bleed tubes to the primary and secondary bleed nipples on the passenger-side brake caliper. The nipples are located on one side of the caliper.
3 Loosen the bleed nipples half a turn, and place the ends of the tubes in a jar.
4 Operate the footbrake pedal until the fluid reservoir is empty, then tighten the bleed screws and remove the tubes.
5 Pull the wiring connectors from the reservoir filler cap terminals (see illustration).
6 Unscrew the primary and secondary union nuts, and remove the hydraulic pipes from the master cylinder. Plug the ends of the pipes,

12.5 Brake master cylinder location (left) showing fluid level warning switch wires - clutch master cylinder on right

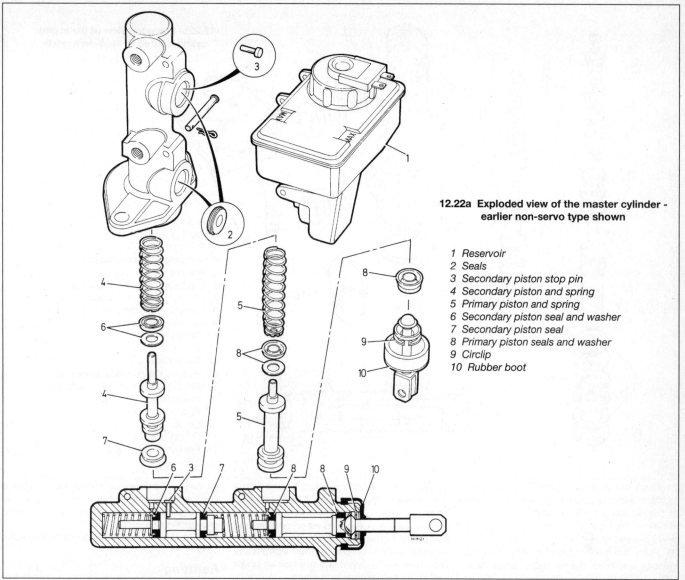

**12.22a Exploded view of the master cylinder -
earlier non-servo type shown**

1 *Reservoir*
2 *Seals*
3 *Secondary piston stop pin*
4 *Secondary piston and spring*
5 *Primary piston and spring*
6 *Secondary piston seal and washer*
7 *Secondary piston seal*
8 *Primary piston seals and washer*
9 *Circlip*
10 *Rubber boot*

and place cloth rags around the bottom of the master cylinder to protect the surrounding paintwork.

7 Where a servo unit is fitted, unscrew the retaining nuts and washers, and withdraw the master cylinder and gasket from the servo unit.

8 Where the master cylinder is mounted directly on the bulkhead plate, remove the clevis pin securing the pushrod to the brake pedal inside the car. Unbolt the master cylinder and remove it together with the gasket.

9 Do not spill any brake fluid on the paintwork otherwise repainting may be necessary. If accidentally spilt, swill off immediately with copious amounts of cold water.

10 Drain and discard the fluid remaining in the reservoir.

Overhaul

11 Clean the exterior of the master cylinder with methylated spirit, then mount it horizontally in a soft-jawed vice with the reservoir uppermost.

12 Unbolt the reservoir from the body (non-servo models) or remove the clips and pull out the pins (servo models).

13 Prise the sealing washers from the body with a screwdriver.

14 Push the pushrod/piston fully into the cylinder, and use long-nosed pliers to remove the secondary piston stop pin from the secondary inlet. Release the pushrod.

15 *On the non-servo type* prise the rubber boot from the end of the master cylinder.

16 *On both types* depress the piston and extract the circlip from the mount of the master cylinder using circlip pliers.

17 Remove the pushrod (where fitted), primary piston and primary spring. Place them on the bench in order of removal.

18 Remove the cylinder from the vice and tap it on a block of wood to remove the secondary piston and spring.

19 Note the position of each item, then remove the seals, washers and spring retainers from the pistons, keeping them in

their correct order of removal.

20 Clean all the components in methylated spirit and examine them for wear and damage. In particular check the surfaces of the pistons and cylinder bore for scoring and corrosion. If evident, renew the complete master cylinder, but if in good condition, discard the seals and washers and obtain a repair kit.

21 Check that the inlet and outlet ports are free and unobstructed. Dip the pistons and seals in clean brake fluid.

22 Fit the seals and washers to the pistons with the lips facing the directions shown **(see illustrations)**, use the fingers only to manipulate them into position.

23 Fit the spring retainers to the ends of the pistons, followed by the springs.

24 Insert the secondary piston and spring into the bore, taking care not to damage the seal lips. Similarly insert the primary piston and spring.

9

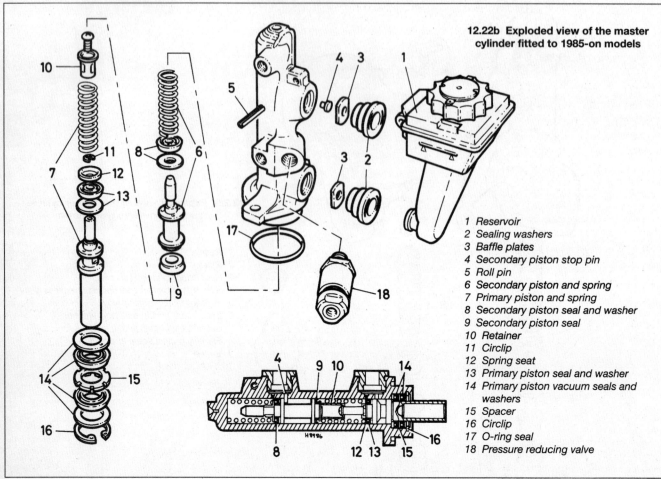

12.22b Exploded view of the master cylinder fitted to 1985-on models

1 Reservoir
2 Sealing washers
3 Baffle plates
4 Secondary piston stop pin
5 Roll pin
6 Secondary piston and spring
7 Primary piston and spring
8 Secondary piston seal and washer
9 Secondary piston seal
10 Retainer
11 Circlip
12 Spring seat
13 Primary piston seal and washer
14 Primary piston vacuum seals and washers
15 Spacer
16 Circlip
17 O-ring seal
18 Pressure reducing valve

25 Push the primary piston into the bore, together with the pushrod (where fitted), and fit the retaining circlip to the groove in the mouth of the bore. Refit the rubber boot on the non-servo type.

26 Push the pushrod/piston fully into the cylinder, and insert the secondary piston stop pin.

27 Locate the seals on the cylinder inlets and refit the reservoir according to type. Only tighten the screws (where fitted) to the specified torque.

Refitting

28 Refitting is a reversal of removal, but use a new mounting gasket, and bleed the hydraulic system as described in Section 17.

13 Pressure compensating valve (except Vans) - removal, overhaul and refitting

Removal

1 The pressure compensating valve is located to the left of the fuel tank on the underbody.

2 To remove the valve, jack up the rear of the car and support it on axle stands (see "Jacking and vehicle support"). Chock the front wheels, and remove the left-hand rear wheel.

3 Remove the brake fluid reservoir filler cap and place a sheet of thin polythene over the warning switch assembly, then tighten the cap. This will help prevent the loss of brake fluid in the subsequent procedure.

4 Unscrew the union nut securing the left-hand rear rigid brake pipe to the flexible hose at the bracket on top of the radius arm.

5 Unscrew the nut, remove the washer, and detach the flexible hose from the bracket.

6 Unscrew the flexible hose from the compensating valve.

7 Unscrew the two union nuts securing the rigid brake pipes to the compensating valve.

8 Remove the mounting bolt and withdraw the compensating valve.

Overhaul

9 Clean the exterior of the valve with methylated spirit.

10 Mount the valve in a soft-jawed vice, and unscrew the end plug. Remove the washer.

11 Remove the small diameter spring, piston, bearing, large diameter spring and seals, keeping them in the order of removal.

12 Clean all the components with methylated spirit and examine them for wear and damage. If excessive, renew the complete compensating valve, but if the components are in good condition, discard the old seals and obtain a repair kit.

13 Dip the seals and piston in clean brake fluid.

Refitting

14 Reassemble the valve in the reverse order to dismantling. Tighten the end plug to the specified torque. Fit the valve to the bracket and insert the mounting bolt and flexible hose, then tighten them both **(see illustration)**.

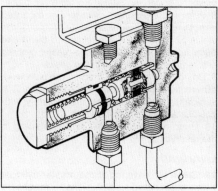

13.14 Cutaway view of the pressure compensating valve

15 The remaining refitting procedure is a reversal of removal, but when completed bleed the brakes as described in Section 17. Do not forget to remove the polythene sheet from the brake fluid reservoir.

14 Pressure reducing valve (1985-on models) - removal and refitting

Removal

1 To remove the valve, place a container and rag beneath the master cylinder.
2 Unscrew the two secondary pipe unions then pull out and plug the pipes.
3 Unscrew the pressure reducing valve from the master cylinder and remove the washer.

Refitting

4 Refitting is a reversal of removal, but bleed the hydraulic system on completion.

15 Inertia/pressure regulating valve (Van models) - removal and refitting

Removal

1 To remove the valve, chock the front wheels, then jack up the rear of the van and support on axle stands (see "*Jacking and vehicle support*").
2 Remove the brake fluid reservoir filler cap and place a sheet of thin polythene over the warning switch assembly, then tighten the cap. This will prevent unnecessary loss of brake fluid in the subsequent procedure.
3 Unscrew the union nuts from the valve then remove and plug the hydraulic pipes.
4 Unscrew the clamp bolt, prise open the clamp, and withdraw the valve.

Refitting

5 Refit the valve with the vent plug uppermost and, where fitted, make sure that the valve is located on the special peg. Tighten the clamp bolt and union nuts.
6 During the bleeding of the hydraulic circuit, loosen the vent plug two or three times to release any trapped air. Finally lower the van to the ground.

16 Hydraulic brake lines and hoses - inspection, removal and refitting

Inspection

1 It is important to note that two types of fittings are in use as shown **(see illustration)**. The metric fittings are coloured gold or black and generally have the letter "M" stamped on them. If there is any doubt about the compatibility of fittings, check that they can be fully screwed together using the fingers only.

16.1 Unified and Metric fittings used in the braking system
A - *Metric pipe nuts, unions, bleed screws and hose ends are coloured black or gold. Most are also identified by the letter M*
B - *The correct Unified or Metric pipe flares must be used*
C - *The end of a Metric hose is coloured black or gold*
D - *Metric fittings are not counterbored. Some Unified fittings may also not be counterbored. If the thread type is not known on a fitting, screw the item in by finger pressure only. If the fit is slack, or the item will not screw fully in, the threads may be of different types*
E - *A Metric hose seals against the bottom of the port, with a gap between the cylinder or caliper and the hose hexagon*

2 At the intervals given in Chapter 1, clean the rigid brake lines and flexible hoses and check them for damage, leakage, chafing and cracks. If the rigid pipes are corroded excessively, they must be renewed. Check the retaining clips for security, and clean away any accumulations of dirt and debris.

Removal

3 To remove a rigid brake line, unscrew the union nuts at each end, and where necessary remove the line from the clips.
4 To remove a flexible brake hose, unscrew the union nut securing the rigid brake line to the end of the flexible hose. Remove the nut and washer, and withdraw the hose from the bracket. Unscrew the remaining end from the component or rigid pipe according to position.

Refitting

5 Refitting of either of the above is a reversal of removal.
6 Bleed the complete hydraulic system as described in Section 17 after fitting a rigid brake line or flexible brake hose.

17 Hydraulic system - bleeding

Note: Read the warning in Section 2 before proceeding.
1 The correct functioning of the brake hydraulic system is only possible after the removal of all air from the components and circuit; this is achieved by bleeding the system. Note that only clean unused brake fluid, which has remained unshaken for at least 24 hours, must be used.
2 If there is any possibility of incorrect fluid being used in the system, the brake lines and components must be completely flushed with uncontaminated fluid and new seals fitted to the components.
3 *Never* re-use brake fluid that has been bled from the system.

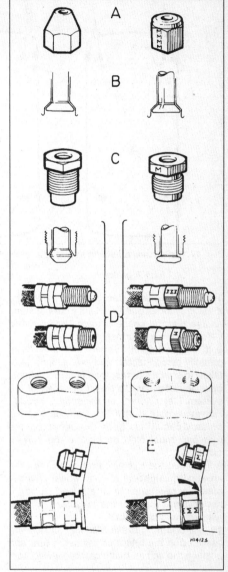

4 During the procedure, do not allow the level of brake fluid to drop more than half way down the reservoir.
5 Before starting work check that all pipes and hoses are secure, unions tight, and bleed screws closed. Take great care not to allow hydraulic fluid to come into contact with the car paintwork, otherwise the finish will be seriously damaged. Wash off any spilled fluid immediately with cold water.
6 There are a number of one-man, do-it-yourself, brake bleeding kits currently available from motor accessory shops. It is recommended that one of these kits is used wherever possible, as they greatly simplify the bleeding operation, and reduce the risk of expelled air and fluid being drawn back into the system. If one of these kits is not available, it will be necessary to obtain, a clean jar and two lengths of clear plastic tubing that is a tight fit over the bleed screw. Also engage the help of an assistant.

9

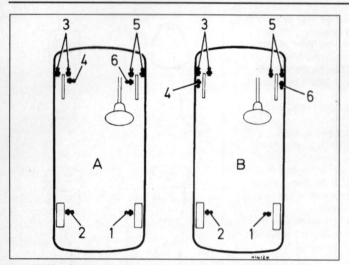

17.12a Brake bleeding sequence for right-hand drive cars

A - type A brakes   *B - type B brakes*

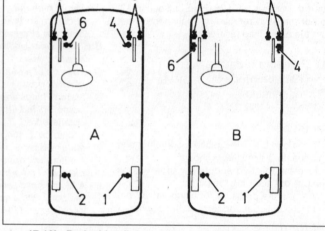

17.12b Brake bleeding sequence for left-hand drive cars

A - type A brakes   *B - type B brakes*

7 If hydraulic fluid has been lost from the master cylinder due to a leak in the system, ensure that the cause is traced and rectified before continuing further.

8 If the hydraulic system has only been partially disconnected and precautions were taken to prevent further loss of fluid, it should only be necessary to bleed that part of the system (i.e. primary or secondary circuit). However, note that if the front part of the primary circuit has been disconnected, the rear part must also be bled in the correct order.

9 To bleed the system, first clean the area around the right-hand rear wheel cylinder bleed screw and fit the bleed tube. If necessary, top-up the master cylinder reservoir with brake fluid.

10 *If a one-man brake bleeding kit is being used,* open the bleed screw half a turn and position the unit so that it can be viewed from

the car. Depress the brake pedal to the floor and slowly release it; the one-way valve in the kit will prevent expelled air from returning to the system. Repeat the procedure then top-up the brake fluid level. Continue bleeding until clean hydraulic fluid, free from air bubbles, can be seen coming through the tube. Now tighten the bleed screw and remove the tube.

11 *If a one-man brake bleeding kit is not available,* immerse the free end of the bleed tube in the jar and pour in sufficient brake fluid to keep the end of the tube submerged. Open the bleed screw half a turn and have your assistant depress the brake pedal to the floor and then slowly release it. Tighten the bleed screw at the end of the down stroke to prevent the expelled air and fluid from being drawn back into the system. Repeat the procedure then top-up the brake fluid level. Continue bleeding until clean hydraulic fluid,

free from air bubbles, can be seen coming through the tube. Now tighten the bleed screw and remove the tube.

12 Repeat the procedure described in paragraphs 9 to 11 on the left-hand rear wheel cylinder, then follow the order shown **(see illustrations)**, dependent on brake system type - see label on bonnet lock crossmember. Note that the lower pair of pistons in the front brake calipers must be bled simultaneously, and therefore two bleed tubes are necessary. This also applies to one-man brake bleeding kits **(see illustration)**, therefore two bleed tubes must be obtained.

13 When completed, recheck the fluid level in the reservoir, top-up if necessary, and refit the cap. Depress the brake pedal several times; it should feel firm and free from "sponginess" that would indicate air still present in the system.

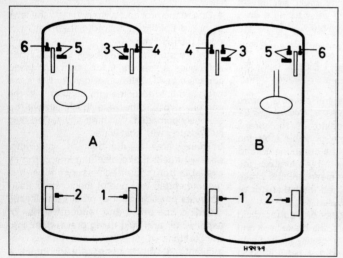

17.12c Brake bleeding sequence for 1985-on models

A Left-hand drive models   *B Right-hand drive models*

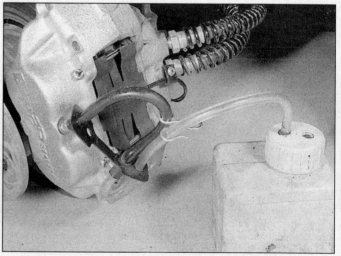

17.12d Typical brakes bleeding kit connected to front brake caliper - note that two tubes are required for lower circuit

18 Handbrake - adjustment

1 Chock the front wheels, then jack up the rear of the car and support it on axle stands (see "*Jacking and vehicle support*").
2 Apply the handbrake four times to settle the compensator and cable positions.
3 Adjust the rear brakes (Section 3).
4 Apply the handbrake six notches on an old cable, or four notches on a new cable, then check that both rear wheels are locked.
5 To adjust the handbrake, loosen the cable locknut using a spanner through the access slot in the carpet behind the handbrake. Turn the adjusting nut until the correct tension is achieved, then tighten the locknut.
6 Release the handbrake and check that the wheels rotate freely, then lower the car to the ground.

19 Handbrake cable - removal and refitting

Removal

1 Remove one front seat with reference to Chapter 11.
2 Unbolt the central seat belt arms from the underbody tunnel.
3 Lift the rear carpet, move the cable guide aside and remove the seal.
4 Remove the clevis pin and disconnect the cable from the handbrake lever (**see illustration**).

19.7 Handbrake cable backplate location

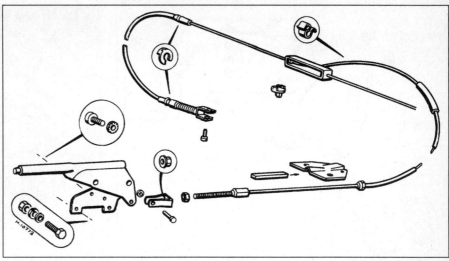

19.4 Handbrake cable components

5 Jack up the rear of the car and support it on axle stands (see "*Jacking and vehicle support*"). Chock the front wheels.
6 Working beneath the car, remove the cable from the underbody bracket and fuel tank, and pull the cable through the floor.
7 Remove the clevis pins and disconnect the cables from the rear brake levers (**see illustration**).
8 Release the cables from the radius arm brackets, abutment brackets and subframe.
9 Lift the compensator link from its guide, and withdraw the cable assembly (**see illustration**).

Refitting

10 Refitting is a reversal of removal, but adjust the handbrake (Section 18).

20 Handbrake lever and switch - removal and refitting

Removal

1 Remove one front seat with reference to Chapter 11.
2 Unbolt the central seat belt arms from the underbody tunnel.

3 Lift the rear carpet. Remove the clevis pin and disconnect the cable from the handbrake lever.
4 Pull off the wires from the switch terminals, remove the securing screws, and withdraw the switch (**see illustration**).
5 Unbolt the handbrake lever from the floor bracket.

Refitting

6 Refitting is a reversal of removal, but adjust the handbrake as described in Section 18.

21 Footbrake pedal - removal and refitting

Removal

1 Disconnect the battery negative lead.
2 Working inside the car, remove the clevis pin and disconnect the pushrod from the pedal.
3 Pull the wires from the stoplight switch, then unscrew the switch from the bracket (**see illustration**).
4 Unbolt the end pedal bracket from the bulkhead and unhook the return spring.
5 Unscrew the pivot nut, then withdraw the bracket, spring and pedal.

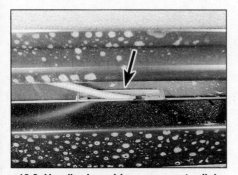

19.9 Handbrake cable compensator link location (arrowed)

20.4 Handbrake lever switch location (arrowed)

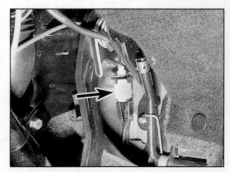

21.3 Stoplight switch location (arrowed)

9

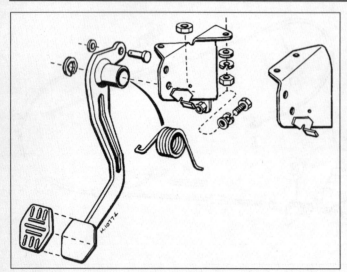

21.6 Footbrake pedal components

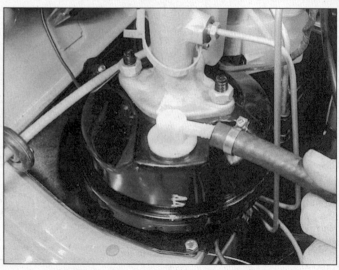

23.2 Removing the vacuum hose from the servo

Refitting

6 Refitting is a reversal of removal **(see illustration)**.

22 Vacuum servo unit - description

The vacuum servo unit provides assistance to the driver when the brake pedal is depressed.

The unit operates by vacuum from the inlet manifold and comprises a booster diaphragm and non-return valve.

With the brake pedal released, vacuum is channelled to both sides of the diaphragm, but when the pedal is depressed, one side is opened to the atmosphere. The resultant unequal pressures are harnessed to assist in depressing the master cylinder pistons.

Under normal operating conditions the vacuum servo unit is very reliable, and when a fault does occur the first action should be renewal of the non-return valve. If this does not help, the servo should be renewed. If there is a failure, the hydraulic system is in no way affected, except that higher pedal pressure will be necessary.

23 Vacuum servo unit - removal and refitting

Removal

1 Remove the master cylinder as described in Section 12.

2 Disconnect the vacuum hose from the non-return valve **(see illustration)**.

3 Working inside the car, remove the clevis pin and disconnect the pushrod from the brake pedal.

4 Unscrew the mounting nuts and remove the servo unit from the engine compartment.

Refitting

5 Refitting is a reversal of removal, with reference to Section 12.

Chapter 10
Suspension and steering

Contents

Degrees of difficulty

Easy, suitable for novice with little experience	Fairly easy, suitable for beginner with some experience 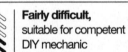	Fairly difficult, suitable for competent DIY mechanic	Difficult, suitable for experienced DIY mechanic	Very difficult, suitable for expert DIY or professional

Specifications

Front suspension
Type . . . . Independent, unequal length upper and lower arms, anti-roll bar, Hydragas spring units, telescopic shock absorbers

Rear suspension
Type . . . . Independent, trailing arms, operating interconnected Hydragas spring units via arms and pushrods

Suspension ride heights
Front - all models . . . . 12.87 ± 0.59 in (327 ± 15 mm)
Rear:
    Turbo - up to 1984 . . . . 12.44 ± 0.59 in (316 ± 15 mm)
    Van up to 1984, Turbo - 1985 on, GTa, Advantage . . . . 13.03 ± 0.59 in (331 ± 15 mm)
    Van - 1985 on . . . . 13.62 ± 0.59 in (346 ± 15 mm)
    All other models - up to 1984 . . . . 12.64 ± 0.59 in (321 ± 15 mm)
    All other models - 1985 on . . . . 13.23 ± 0.59 in (336 ± 15 mm)
    Maximum permissible side-to-side difference . . . . 0.39 in (10 mm)

Note: *Ride heights measured VERTICALLY (seen from front and side of vehicle) from wheel arch lip to roadwheel hub centre, engine cold and car unladen but with full fuel tank and all lubricants and fluids. If fuel tank is only half full, increase specified heights by adding 1 mm to front height and 3 mm to rear to compensate for reduced vehicle weight. Specified heights correct at nominal ambient temperature of 17°C - above this temperature add 0.6 mm for every 1°C temperature difference, below it subtract 0.6 mm for every 1°C temperature difference.*

Hydragas unit nitrogen nominal pressures

Front .... 315 lbf/in² ± 3% (2172 kN/m² ± 3%)
Rear .... 230 lbf/in² ± 3% (1586 kN/m² ± 3%)

Suspension grease points

Grease type .... Multi-purpose lithium based grease

Steering

Type .... Rack-and-pinion, flexible coupling
Number of turns lock-to-lock 3.3
Rack pinion bearing preload .... 0.001 to 0.004 in (0.025 to 0.102 mm)
Pinion bearing shim gap .... 0.011 to 0.013 in (0.28 to 0.33 mm)
Pinion bearing standard shim .... 0.092 in (2.337 mm)
Pinion bearing shims available .... 0.005 in, 0.0075 in, 0.010 in (0.127 mm, 0.1905 mm, 0.254 mm)
Yoke-to-cover plate clearance .... 0.002 to 0.005 in (0.05 to 0.12 mm)
Yoke-to-cover plate shims available .... 0.0024 in (0.061 mm)
Rack ball-pin centre dimension .... 44.2 to 44.3 in (112.2 to 112.5 mm)

Front wheel alignment (models up to 1985) - at correct ride heights

Toe-out .... 0 to 0.125 in (0 to 3 mm)
Inner wheel angle (with outer wheel at 20°) .... 23.75° ± 1.5°
Camber angle .... 0° ± 0030'
Caster angle .... 2° 6' positive ± 1°

Front wheel alignment (all models 1986-on)

Front wheel toe .... Parallel to 0° 25' toe-out
Inner wheel angle (except those below) with outer wheel at 20° ...... 20° 40'
Inner wheel angle (MG Turbo, GTa, Advantage) with outer
  wheel at 29° 48' .... 31° 50
Caster angle .... 2° 6' positive 2° 0'
King pin inclination .... 10° 38'

Rear wheel alignment - at correct ride heights

Toe-in/out .... 0°30 toe-in to 0°30' toe-out
Camber angle .... 1° negative ± 30'

Rear suspension (MG Turbo, GTa, Advantage)

Type .... As other models, plus anti-roll bar
Rear wheel alignment .... Parallel ± 0° 15'

Wheels

Size and type:

Pre-1984 (all models) .... 4.50B x 12 pressed steel
1984-on (all models) .... 315 x 105 mm pressed steel
MG Metro 1986-on .... 13 x 120
MG Turbo 1986-on .... 13 x 5 ½in
MG Turbo, GTa, Advantage and Metro Sport 1989-on .... 13 x 5 ½in
MG Turbo .... 5.50J x 13 alloy
MG 1300 (pre-1984) .... 5J x 12 pressed steel
MG 1300 (1984) .... 12 in x 5J alloy
MG 1300 (1985-on) .... 315 x 120 mm alloy
1.0 and 1.3 Van .... 12 in x 4.5B pressed steel

Tyres

Size:

1982 to 1983 models:
  1.0 models .... 135 SR x 12 radial
  1.3 models, except MG Turbo .... 165/70R x 12 radial
  MG Turbo .... 165/60 HR x 13 radial
1984 models:
  1.0 Saloon models .... 150/65 R315 radial
  1.0 and 1.3 Vans .... 155/70 SR12 radial
  1.3 Moritz .... 150/65 R315 radial
  MG 1300 .... 155/70 SR 12 radial
  MG Turbo .... 165/65 HR 13 radial
  All other 1.3 models .... 160/65 R315 radial

Size (continued):
    1985-on models:

MG Turbo	165/60 HR 13 radial	
All other models	160/65 R315 radial	

    1989-on:

MG Turbo, GTa, Advantage and Metro Sport	185 x 55 radial	

Note: *Refer to "Weekly checks" (on page 0•16) for tyre pressures*

Torque wrench settings

	lbf ft	Nm
Front suspension		
Anti-roll bar to subframe	19	26
Anti-roll bar end nut (see text)	30 to 80	41 to 111
Hub balljoint socket	75	103
Hub balljoint nut to arm	37	51
Lower arm pivot	75	103
Shock absorber upper nut	27.5	38
Shock absorber lower nut	35	48
Upper arm pivot	55	76
Hydragas unit charging valve	12	17
Anti-roll bar U-bolt clamp nuts	16	22
Rear suspension		
Hub nut	60	83
Radius arm pivot	53	73
Steering		
Column clamp to bracket	19	26
Column clamp to column	8.5	12
Coupling cover to body	6.5	9
Flexible coupling to pinion	11	15
Flexible coupling to column	19	26
Column bracket to shelf	19	26
Coupling to pinion	19	26
Column to bracket	19	26
Column lock shear bolt (minimum)	14	19
Steering arm to hub	38	45
Rack U-bolts	19	26
Steering wheel	35	48
Tie-rod end	22	30
Tie-rod to rack	35	48
Upper steering column	8.5	12

Wheels

Alloy wheel nuts:		
1985-on models	42	58
All other models	36	50
Steel wheel nuts	42	58

1 General description

1 The front suspension is of independent, upper and lower arm type incorporating separate Hydragas spring units on each side, telescopic shock absorbers and an anti-roll bar. From 1985, with exception of MG Turbo models, front shock absorbers are no longer fitted **(see illustration)**.

2 The rear suspension is of independent, trailing arm type incorporating interconnected Hydragas spring units, which are operated via pushrods from the trailing arms. The rear Hydragas units are each preloaded with a coil spring **(see illustration)**.

3 The Hydragas units comprise a chamber of pressurised nitrogen gas contained by a rubber diaphragm, and a further chamber of pressurised fluid consisting of water, alcohol and additives. Movement of the suspension causes the pushrod to compress the fluid, which causes the intermediate diaphragm to deflect into the nitrogen chamber. The unit acts as a variable rate gas spring.

4 Although the front and rear Hydragas units function in an identical manner, the rear units incorporate an internal damper flap valve, whereas the front units are dampened by separate telescopic shock absorbers. The front units are not interconnected but the rear units are via a pipe containing a flow restrictor. The front and rear ride heights are set by pressurising the fluid in the Hydragas units.

5 Due to the high pressures involved and the special equipment required, the Hydragas units must only be depressurised, evacuated and pressurised by a Rover dealer. In the event of loss of pressure, the car may be driven to the place of repair over metalled roads at up to 20 mph (32 kph).

6 The steering is of rack-and-pinion type mounted on the rear of the front subframe. The steering column is attached to the rack pinion by a flexible coupling. Note that a minor steering column modification was carried out on all cars early in 1981; if in doubt as to whether this modification has been carried out on your vehicle, consult your dealer. 1985 and 1986-on models are fitted with modified steering columns and rack and pinions. All service procedures should remain basically unchanged.

10

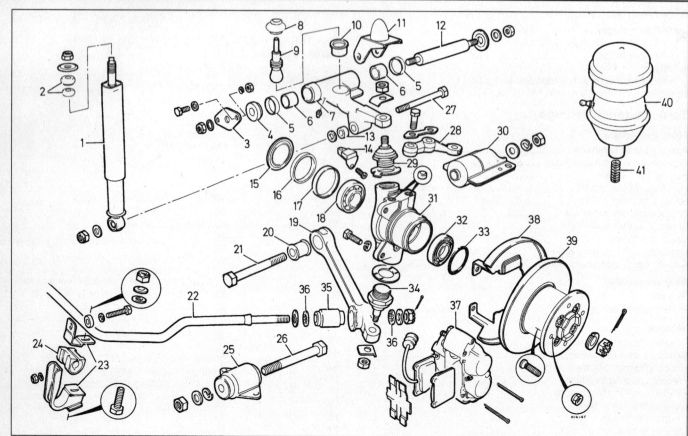

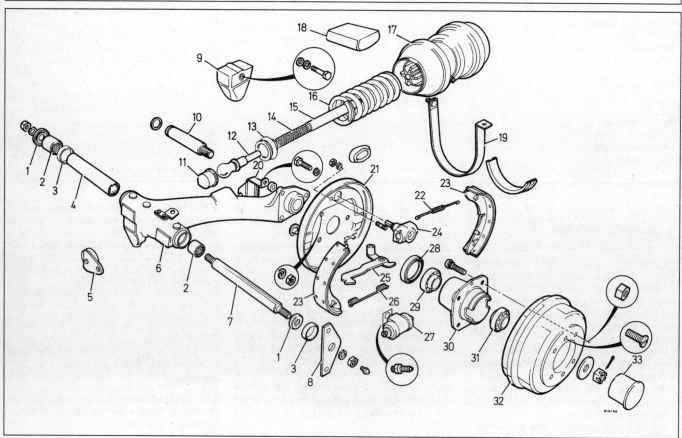

1.1 Exploded view of the front suspension

1 Shock absorber	22 Anti-roll bar
2 Rubber bushes	23 Bracket
3 Plate	24 Bearing
4 Thrustwasher	25 Subframe front
5 Sealing ring	mounting
6 Needle roller	26 Bolt
bearing	27 Shock absorber
7 Upper suspension	lower mounting
arm	bolt
8 Boot	28 Steering arm
9 Ball-pin (and spacer	29 Upper balljoint
where fitted)	30 Subframe rear
10 Socket	mounting
11 Bump rubber	31 Swivel hub
12 Pivot shaft	32 Outer bearing
13 Spacer	33 Oil seal
14 Rebound rubber	34 Lower balljoint
15 Water shield	35 Bush
16 Oil seal	36 Plastic washer
17 Spacer	37 Caliper
18 Inner bearing	38 Disc shield
19 Lower suspension	39 Driving flange and
arm	disc
20 Bush	40 Hydragas unit
21 Pivot bolt	41 Return spring

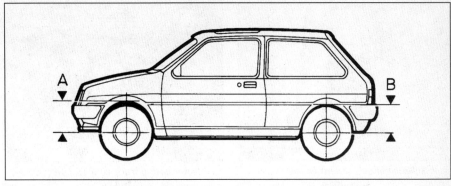

2.1 Suspension ride height measuring points
Measure VERTICALLY (seen from the front and side of vehicle) from wheel arch lip to roadwheel hub centre - see Specifications for dimensions

1.2 Exploded view of the rear suspension

1 Thrustwasher	19 Reaction strap
2 Needle roller	20 Handbrake cable
bearing	mounting bracket
3 Sealing ring	21 Backplate
4 Lubricating tube	22 Upper return
5 Rebound rubber	spring
6 Radius arm	23 Brake shoe
7 Pivot shaft	24 Brake adjuster
8 Retaining plate	25 Handbrake levers
9 Bump rubber	26 Lower return
10 Stub shaft	spring
11 Socket	27 Wheel cylinder
12 Ball-pin	28 Oil seal
13 Boot	29 Inner bearing
14 Return spring	30 Hub
15 Strut	31 Outer bearing
16 Helper spring	32 Brake drum
17 Hydragas unit	33 Grease retaining
18 Mounting pad	cap

2 Hydragas units - testing

Testing

1 A fault in a Hydragas unit can be determined by checking the car ride height as shown **(see illustration)**. If the measurements are less than those specified, first check the units and rear interconnecting pipe for signs of leakage, which will appear as a slight residue left after the fluid has evaporated.

2 If the cause is a union, tighten the nut and have the system repressurised by a Rover dealer.

3 Where a leak in a Hydragas unit is suspected, clean the area around the charging valve threads to determine whether the valve is the source of the leak.

> **HAYNES HiNT** *Talcum powder dusted around the clean valve may be helpful in tracing a leak..*

4 If it is established that the leak is occurring round the valve threads, have the system depressurised by your Rover dealer, then unscrew the valve.

5 Screw in a new valve, using a sealant on the threads (Loctite 270 or equivalent). Tighten the valve to the specified torque. Have the system recharged by your Rover dealer on completion, and check for leaks.

3.3 Front Hydragas unit

6 If it is determined that a Hydragas unit is leaking fluid, renew the unit and again have it repressurised by a Rover dealer.

7 If no fluid leak can be found, it is possible that nitrogen has leaked from the unit. To check this, the car must be taken to a Rover dealer and the unit checked with the pressure pump. The fluid pressure should increase rapidly to the pressure of the nitrogen, and thereafter increase at a noticeably slower rate. If nitrogen has been leaking, the pressure will have dropped and the fluid pressure will increase rapidly above the normal nitrogen pressure. The nitrogen pressures are as follows:

Front Hydragas unit   325 lbf/in² ± 6.5 lbf/in²
                       (2241 kN/m² ± 44.8 kN/m²)
Rear Hydragas unit   230 lbf/in² ± 4.6 lbf/in²
                       (1586 kN/m² ± 31.7 kN/m²)

Note that the rear Hydragas units must be checked for a nitrogen leak separately, by removing the interconnecting pipe and using an adapter.

8 If it is determined that a Hydragas unit has leaked nitrogen, renew it and have the suspension repressurised by a Rover dealer.

3 Front Hydragas unit - removal and refitting

Removal

1 Have the Hydragas unit depressurised by a Rover dealer.

2 Apply the handbrake, then jack up the front of the car and support it on axle stands (see *"Jacking and vehicle support"*). Remove the roadwheel.

3 Unbolt the outer bracket from the subframe tower, and withdraw the Hydragas unit together with its return spring **(see illustration)**.

4 Remove the piston spacer(s) from the knuckle joint on the driver's side.

Refitting

5 Refitting is a reversal of removal, but have the Hydragas unit pressurised by a Rover dealer.

10

4.3 Front shock absorber and lower mounting

5.1 Removing a front suspension rebound buffer

5.4 Anti-roll bar-to-lower suspension arm joint

4 Front shock absorber - removal, overhaul and refitting

Removal

1 If the left-hand shock absorber is being removed, remove the retaining screws and place the cooling system expansion tank to one side.

2 For both left and right-hand sides unscrew the self-locking nut from the upper mounting, and remove the cup washer and large diameter rubber bush.

3 Turn the steering to allow access from the front, then unscrew the bottom mounting nut and remove the washer **(see illustration)**.

4 Slide the shock absorber, washer and distance sleeve from the bottom mounting bolt, leaving the bolt and bump stop in position.

5 Withdraw the shock absorber from the upper mounting together with the small diameter rubber bush.

Overhaul

6 The rubber bush in the front shock absorber lower mounting eye may be renewed separately to the shock absorber if necessary. If so, drive the metal sleeve from the centre of the bush.

7 Using a metal tube, long bolt, thick washers and nut, pull the bush from the mounting eye. If necessary, cut the bush with a small hacksaw before removing it.

8 Dip the new bush in soapy water before pressing it into the eye, then refit the shock absorber.

9 Note that the shock absorber must be stored in an upright position.

Refitting

10 Before fitting, grip the shock absorber lower mounting in a vice with the unit upright, then compress and extend it at least six times until there is no free travel when changing the direction of stroke. This will remove any trapped air from the internal fluid.

11 Refitting is a reversal of removal, but tighten the self-locking mounting nuts to the specified torque.

5 Anti-roll bar - removal, overhaul and refitting

Removal

1 Turn the steering as necessary to allow access from the front, and remove the rebound buffers from the subframe on both sides. The buffers are located beneath the suspension upper arms and are secured by two cross-head screws **(see illustration)**.

2 Insert distance pieces such as nuts in place of the buffers to retain the suspension in the normal running position.

3 Apply the handbrake, jack up the front of the car, and support it on axle stands (see "*Jacking and vehicle support*"). Remove both front wheels.

4 Extract the split pin from one end of the anti-roll bar and unscrew the nut **(see illustration)**. Remove the plain washer and plastic washer. Similarly remove the nut and washers from the remaining end of the anti-roll bar.

5 Unbolt the bearing brackets from the front of the subframe, noting the position of the components **(see illustration)**.

6 Unbolt and detach one of the subframe rear mountings.

7 Remove the nut, spring and plain washer from the mounting pivot bolt, then drive the bolt through the mounting and lower suspension arm.

8 Pull the lower suspension arm from the subframe and detach the anti-roll bar from both lower suspension arms. Withdraw the anti-roll bar from the car. Remove the washers.

Overhaul

9 Check the anti-roll bar bushes for deterioration. Renew them if necessary. Lubricate the new bushes with a grease.

10 Clean any grease from the anti-roll bar itself in the area next to the bushes.

11 If not already so equipped, fit clamps and U-bolts on the inboard side of each bush as shown **(see illustration)**. The correct clamps are available from your Rover dealer.

5.5 Anti-roll bar and front bearing bracket

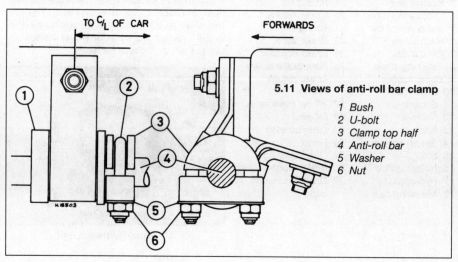

5.11 Views of anti-roll bar clamp

1 Bush
2 U-bolt
3 Clamp top half
4 Anti-roll bar
5 Washer
6 Nut

5.12 U-bolt and clamp next to anti-roll bar bush

12 Tighten the U-bolts evenly to the specified torque, making sure that the clamps are pulled down evenly and that the clamps are firmly up against the bushes, thus preventing sideways movement of the anti-roll bar **(see illustration)**.

Refitting

13 To refit the anti-roll bar, first fit one steel washer against the shoulder on each end of the bar, followed by one plastic washer.
14 Insert the bar in the fixed lower suspension arm, then in the free lower suspension arm.
15 Locate the lower suspension arm in the subframe and insert the pivot bolt through the arm and mounting from the front. Fit the plain washer and spring washer and tighten the nut finger tight.
16 Fit the mounting to the underbody and tighten the bolts.
17 Fit the bearing brackets to the front of the subframe and tighten the nuts finger tight.
18 Fit one plain washer on the ends of the bar against the lower arms, followed by the steel washers and nuts. Tighten the nuts finger tight.
19 Fit the roadwheels and lower the car to the ground.
20 Remove the distance pieces and fit the rebound buffers to the subframe.
21 With the weight of the car on the suspension, tighten the lower arm pivot bolts and the anti-roll bar bracket bolts to the specified torque.
22 Tighten the anti-roll bar end nuts to the lower of the torque wrench settings specified.

6.5 Hydragas unit-to-upper arm knuckle joint

Application of spacers for front Hydrogas units			
Model	LH side	RH side	Thickness i n (mm)
MG Turbo	1	3	0.09 (2.29)
MG and Vanden Plas (manual)	0	2	0.09 (2.29)
MG and Vanden Plas (manual - alternative fitting	1	1	0.05 (1.27)
Automatic models	1	4	0.09 (2.29)
All other models except Van	0	2	0.09 (2.29)
Van	0	0	-

Tighten further if necessary to align the split pin holes, but do not exceed the higher specified torque. Insert new split pins and bend over the ends to secure.

6 Front suspension upper arm - removal, overhaul and refitting

Removal

1 Have the relevant Hydragas unit depressurised by a Rover dealer.
2 Jack up the front of the car and support it on axle stands (see "*Jacking and vehicle support*"). Apply the handbrake and remove the roadwheel.
3 Unscrew the shock absorber lower mounting nut, and remove the shock absorber, washers and distance sleeve.
4 Remove the bolt and bump stop.
5 Remove the knuckle joint from the upper arm and extract it from the Hydragas unit together with the return spring **(see illustration)**.
6 Support the driving flange and disc assembly with a trolley jack or block of wood.
7 Flatten the tab washer and unscrew the swivel hub upper balljoint nut. Remove the tab washer.
8 Using a separator tool, release the upper arm from the balljoint.
9 Unscrew the upper arm shaft rear nut, and unbolt the front retaining plate from the subframe **(see illustration)**.
10 If removing the left-hand side upper arm, move the windscreen washer reservoir to one side.
11 Withdraw the pivot shaft assembly from the front of the subframe and recover the rear washers.
12 Lift the suspension upper arm from the subframe and recover the sealing rings and rear thrustwasher.

Overhaul

HAYNES HINT *Clean all the components in paraffin and wipe dry.*

13 To overhaul the upper arm, unscrew the grease nipple and grip the arm in a soft-jawed vice.

14 Remove the needle roller bearings with a soft metal drift.
15 Examine the needle roller bearings and the pivot shaft for damage, wear and pitting. If evident, renew the bearings and shaft. Make sure that the grease nipple lubrication drilling is unobstructed.
16 Drive the needle roller bearings into the upper arm with the marked ends facing outwards. Lubricate the bearings with multi-purpose lithium based grease, then refit the grease nipple.

Refitting

17 The number and thickness of the spacer(s) fitted between the front Hydragas units and their knuckle joint varies according to model.
18 Incorrect fitting of spacers will make the suspension seem firmer on one side of the car than on the other. Correct applications are as shown in the table at the top of this page.
19 Refitting is a reversal of removal, but note the following additional points:
  a) *The thrustwashers must be fitted with their grooved sides against the upper arm. Initially, fit the sealing rings and locate the rear thrustwasher in the ring.*
  b) *Lubricate the knuckle joint with a multi-purpose lithium based grease*
  c) *Tighten all nuts to the specified torque, and lock the swivel hub upper balljoint nut by bending the tab washer over the upper arm and nut.*
  d) *After having the Hydragas unit pressurised by a Rover dealer, fully loosen the shock absorber lower mounting nut and retighten it to the specified torque with the weight of the car on the suspension.*

6.9 Front suspension upper arm pivot front retaining plate

10

7 Front suspension lower arm - removal, overhaul and refitting

Removal

1 Turn the steering as necessary to allow access from the front, and remove the rebound buffer from the subframe on the relevant side. The buffer is located beneath the suspension upper arm and is secured by two cross-head screws.
2 Insert a distance piece such as a suitably sized nut in place of the buffer to retain the suspension in the normal running position.
3 Apply the handbrake, jack up the front of the car, and support it on axle stands (see *"Jacking and vehicle support"*). Remove the roadwheel.
4 Extract the split pin from the end of the anti-roll bar and unscrew the nut. Remove the plain washer and plastic washer abutting the lower arm.
5 Unbolt the anti-roll bar bearing brackets from the front of the subframe, noting the position of the components.
6 Flatten the tab washer and unscrew the swivel hub lower balljoint nut. Remove the tab washer.
7 Using a separator tool, release the lower arm from the balljoint.
8 Unbolt and detach the relevant subframe rear mounting.
9 Remove the nut, spring and plain washer from the pivot bolt, then drive the bolt through the mounting and lower suspension arm.
10 Pull the lower suspension arm from the subframe, and remove it from the anti-roll bar. Recover the plastic and steel washers from the anti-roll bar.

Overhaul

11 To overhaul the lower arm, the pivot bush and anti-roll bar bush should be renewed. To remove the bushes, use a length of metal tubing, a long bolt, nut and packing pieces. Tighten the nut to draw out the bush. To fit the new bushes, dip them in a soapy water solution or use a rubber lubricant. Pull them into the lower arm using a nut and bolt and packing pieces.

Refitting

12 Refitting is a reversal of removal, but note the following additional points:
 a) *The anti-roll bar plastic washers must be fitted against the lower arm*
 b) *Tighten all nuts and bolts to the specified torque; the lower arm pivot bolt and the anti-roll bar mounting nuts and bolts should be fully tightened with the weight of the car on the suspension*
 c) *Lock the swivel hub lower balljoint nut by bending the tab washer over the lower arm and nut.*
 d) *Lock the anti-roll bar-to-lever arm retaining nut with a new split pin.*

8 Front suspension upper or lower balljoint - removal and refitting

Removal

1 To prevent problems by not being able to unscrew the balljoint socket, it is recommended that tool 18G1341 is obtained from a tool hire agent.
2 Turn the steering as necessary to allow access from the front, and remove the rebound buffer from the subframe on the relevant side. The buffer is located beneath the suspension upper arm and is secured by two cross-head screws.
3 Insert a distance piece such as a suitably sized nut in place of the buffer to retain the suspension in the normal running position.
4 Apply the handbrake, jack up the front of the car, and support it on axle stands (see *"Jacking and vehicle support"*). Remove the roadwheel.
5 Flatten the tab washer and unscrew the swivel hub upper or lower balljoint nut (as applicable). Remove the tab washer.
6 Using a separator tool release the balljoint from the suspension arm. If removing the upper balljoint, support the swivel hub assembly with a trolley jack.
7 Flatten the lockwasher tabs, and if available fit tool 18G1341 to the balljoint socket, retaining it in position with the balljoint nut.
8 Hold the driving flange and swivel hub stationary, then unscrew the balljoint socket and remove the lockwasher. Remove the tool if used.

Refitting

9 Fitting a new balljoint is a reversal of the removal procedure. Apply two beads of Loctite 245 or equivalent compound, diametrically opposite each other, to the thread **(see illustration)**. Tighten the balljoint and nut to the specified torques within 15 minutes of Loctite application. Lock the balljoint by bending two opposite tabs of the lockwasher over the sides of the swivel hub. Lock the balljoint nut by bending the tab washer over the suspension arm and nut.

9 Front hub assembly - removal, overhaul and refitting

Removal

1 Turn the steering as necessary to allow access from the front, and remove the rebound buffer from the subframe on the relevant side. The buffer is located beneath the suspension upper arm and is secured by two cross-head screws.
2 Insert a distance piece such as a nut in place of the buffer to retain the suspension in the normal running position.
3 Extract the split pin from the end of the

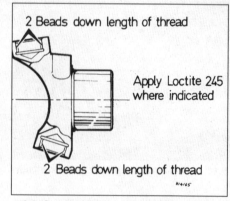

8.9 Sectional view of swivel hub upper balljoint, showing application of thread locking compound

driveshaft and loosen the nut while an assistant depresses the footbrake pedal.
4 Apply the handbrake, jack up the front of the car, and support it on axle stands (see *"Jacking and vehicle support"*). Remove the roadwheel.
5 Remove the brake caliper as described in Chapter 9, but leave the hydraulic hoses connected, and support the caliper on a stand without straining the hoses.
6 Unscrew the driveshaft nut and remove the split collar.
7 Slide the drive flange and disc assembly from the driveshaft, using a puller.
8 Flatten the tab washers and unscrew the swivel hub upper and lower balljoint nuts **(see illustration)**. Remove the tab washers.
9 Unscrew and remove the tie-rod end nut. Remove the disc shield.
10 Using a separator tool, release the tie-rod end from the steering arm, and the suspension arms from the balljoints.
11 While tapping the end of the driveshaft with a mallet, withdraw the swivel hub assembly. Use a puller to remove the inner bearing inner race from the driveshaft.
12 If necessary, remove the water shield from the driveshaft.
13 Prise out the inner oil seal and remove the spacer.
14 Prise out the outer oil seal.
15 Using a soft metal drift, drive out one of the bearing inner races, then invert the hub

9.8 Swivel hub upper balljoint

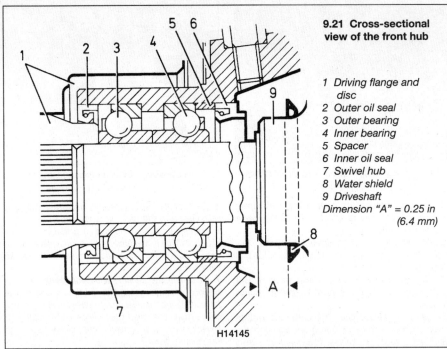

9.21 Cross-sectional view of the front hub

1 Driving flange and disc
2 Outer oil seal
3 Outer bearing
4 Inner bearing
5 Spacer
6 Inner oil seal
7 Swivel hub
8 Water shield
9 Driveshaft
Dimension "A" = 0.25 in (6.4 mm)

H14145

and drive out the complete opposite bearing. Invert the hub again and drive out the remaining outer race.

Overhaul

Note: *The inner oil seal has an extended flange that fits into the water shield.*

16 Clean the hub, bearings and driveshaft stub with paraffin and wipe dry. The inner bearing will almost certainly be damaged upon removal, therefore replacement will be necessary. The bearings are only available in a complete kit, along with all the seals, spacers grease and split pins required.

17 Lubricate the bearings with the grease supplied, then drive them into the swivel hub with the marked ends facing outwards. Use a length of tubing on the outer races only.

18 Fit the spacer against the inner bearing.

19 Dip the oil seals in engine oil, then press them into the swivel hub with their lips facing inwards. Use a block of wood to locate the outer seal flush with the hub, and use a length of metal tubing to locate the inner seal against the spacer.

20 Press grease into the spaces between the bearings and oil seals.

21 Press the water shield onto the driveshaft with reference to dimension "A" **(see illustration)**. Fill the water shield groove with grease.

22 Locate the swivel hub over the end of the driveshaft and, using a length of metal tubing against the outer bearing inner race, tap the inner races fully onto the driveshaft.

Refitting

23 The remaining refitting procedure is a reversal of removal, but tighten the nuts to the specified torque. Lock the balljoint nuts by bending the tab washers over the suspension arms and nuts. Refer to Chapter 8 for the driveshaft nut tightening procedure.

10 Rear Hydragas unit - removal and refitting

Removal

1 Have the rear Hydragas units depressurised by a Rover dealer.

2 Chock the front wheels, jack up the rear of the car and support it on stands. Remove the roadwheel.

3 Disconnect and plug the interconnecting pipe from the Hydragas unit.

4 Unbolt the bump rubber and reaction strap from the body **(see illustrations)**.

5 Unbolt the shield and clamp plate from the subframe.

6 Withdraw the Hydragas unit, helper spring and strut, together with the return spring from the subframe and knuckle joint.

7 Prise the knuckle joint assembly from the radius arm.

8 Note that if the three-way connector in front of the left-hand rear wheel is removed, it must always be refitted with the restricted drilling in the line between the two rear Hydragas units **(see illustration)**.

9 Check the knuckle joint for wear, and renew it if necessary.

Refitting

10 Refitting is a reversal of removal, but lubricate the knuckle joint with a multi-purpose lithium based grease. Have the rear Hydragas units pressurised by a Rover dealer.

11 The struts must be located in the centre hole within the units, and where helper springs are fitted, these must locate on the split collars welded to the subframe. If the split collars are loose, have them re-welded in position.

10.4a Rear suspension bump rubber (arrowed) . . .

10.4b . . . Hydragas unit . . .

10.4c . . . and reaction strap inner mounting nut (arrowed)

10.8 Rear Hydragas interconnecting pipe and three-way connector

10

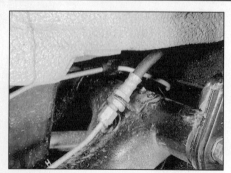

11.4 Brake pipe and hose connection on rear suspension radius arm

11.5a Rear suspension arm pivot shaft inner nut

11.5b Rear suspension arm outer mounting

11 Rear suspension radius arm - removal, overhaul and refitting

Removal

1 Remove the rear Hydragas unit as described in Section 10.

2 Release the handbrake, then remove the clevis pin and disconnect the handbrake cable from the backplate and bracket.

3 Remove the brake fluid reservoir filler cap, wrap thin polythene over the level warning switch and tighten the cap onto the polythene. This will help prevent brake fluid from being lost in the subsequent procedure.

4 Unscrew the rigid brake pipe union, then unscrew the nut and remove the flexible hose from the bracket in the radius arm **(see illustration)**.

5 Unscrew the nuts from each end of the pivot shaft, and unbolt the retaining plate from the subframe **(see illustrations)**. Remove the outer thrustwasher.

6 Support the radius arm with a jack, then tap out the pivot shaft from the inside.

7 Withdraw the radius arm and collect the inner thrustwasher and both sealing rings.

8 If necessary, remove the brake shoes and backplate as described in Chapter 9.

9 If the bearings are to be renewed, drive them out of the radius arm and remove the lubricating tube.

Overhaul

10 Clean all the components with paraffin and examine them for wear and damage. Renew them as necessary and obtain new sealing rings. Make sure that the lubricating drillings in the shaft are unobstructed.

11 Drive one needle roller bearing into the outer end of the radius arm with its stamped end outwards and to a depth of 0.2 in (5 mm).

12 Insert the lubricating tube with the splined end towards the outer bearing, and drive the second needle roller bearing into the radius arm with the stamped end facing outwards.

13 Locate the large thrustwasher with its grooved side against the inner end of the radius arm, and fit the wide sealing ring over it.

14 Fit the narrow sealing ring to the outer end of the radius arm.

15 Support the radius arm in the subframe, and insert the pivot shaft with the grease nipple outwards.

16 Fit the small thrustwasher with the chamfer against the shaft, install the retaining plate, and tighten the bolts.

17 Fit the spring washers and nuts to the pivot shaft and tighten them to the specified torque.

18 Using a grease gun, lubricate the radius arm bearings with the recommended grease.

19 Reconnect the brake flexible hose and rigid pipe to the bracket. Reconnect the handbrake cable.

20 Remove the polythene from the brake fluid reservoir, then adjust and bleed the brakes as described in Chapter 9.

Refitting

21 Spacers are now fitted between the rear struts and Hydragas units as shown below:

Model	LH side	RH side	Thickness in (mm)
MG Turbo	1	1	0.145 (3.68)
All other 3-door models (except van)	1	1	0.05 (1.27)
Van and 5-door models	0	0	-

22 Refit the rear Hydragas unit as described in Section 10.

12 Rear hub assembly - removal, overhaul and refitting

Note: *From chassis number 631497 (early 1982), nearside hub nut and shaft has left-hand thread. All replacement nearside hub nut and shaft assemblies have left-hand thread regardless of year.*

Removal

1 Chock the front wheels, jack up the rear of the car, and support it on axle stands (see *"Jacking and vehicle support"*). Remove the roadwheel and release the handbrake.

2 Remove the securing screws and withdraw the brake drum; loosen the adjuster if necessary.

3 Brush clean the backplate, but *do not inhale the brake dust as it is injurious to health.*

4 Using a soft metal punch, tap the grease cap on alternate sides, and remove it **(see illustration)**.

5 Extract the split pin and unscrew the hub nut. Remove the plain washer.

6 Using a puller, remove the hub from the stub shaft. If the inner bearing inner race remains in the stub shaft, use a puller to remove it.

7 Prise out the oil seal with a screwdriver.

8 Using a soft metal drill, drive out one of the bearing inner races, then invert the hub and drive out the complete opposite bearing. Invert the hub again and drive out the remaining outer race.

Overhaul

9 Clean all the components in paraffin and examine them for damage and wear. Check the bearing balls and races for wear and pitting. Renew the components as necessary and obtain a new oil seal. If the wheel studs are worn or damaged, drive them out and install new ones.

10 Lubricate the bearings with multi-purpose lithium based grease, then drive them into the hub with their marked ends outwards, using a length of metal tube on the outer races.

11 Dip the oil seal in engine oil, then press it into the hub with the lip facing inwards.

12 Wipe clean the stub shaft and oil seal bearing surface. Locate the hub on the stub shaft and use a length of metal tube to drive the inner races onto the shaft.

13 Fit the plain washer and tighten the nut to the specified torque.

14 Lock the nut with a new split pin and tap the grease cap into the hub.

Refitting

15 Refit the brake drum and wheel, adjust the brakes, and lower the car to the ground.

12.4 Removing the rear hub grease cap

13 Rear anti-roll bar (MG Turbo) - removal and refitting

Removal

1 Chock the front wheels, slacken the rear wheel nuts and raise and support the rear of the vehicle. Remove the rear wheels.
2 Undo the nut and bolt on each side which hold the ends of the anti-roll bar to the suspension links.
3 Remove the mounting clamps from the central section of the anti-roll bar. The bar and mounting rubbers can now be removed.
4 Renew any mounting components which have deteriorated. Renew the anti-roll bar if it is distorted or damaged.

Refitting

5 Commence refitting by connecting the ends of the bar to the suspension links. Fit the nut and bolt on each side but do not tighten them yet.
6 Fit the mounting clamps over the mounting rubbers and secure them to their brackets.
7 Tighten the mounting clamp bolts and then the end link nuts and bolts.
8 Refit the roadwheels and lower the car to the ground.

14 Steering wheel - removal and refitting

Removal

1 Set the front wheels in the straight-ahead position.
2 Prise the cover from the centre of the steering wheel (see illustration).
3 Unscrew and remove the retaining nut and mark the steering wheel and inner column in relation to each other.
4 Withdraw the steering wheel from the inner column splines.

Refitting

5 Refitting is the reversal of removal, but align the previously made marks, and tighten the retaining nut to the specified torque.

15.3 Steering column and wiring multi-plug

14.2 Removing the steering wheel central cover

15 Steering column - removal and refitting

Note: *The top bush for 1986-on models is a press fit in the top of the outer column, and should be coated with graphite grease before fitting.*

Removal

1 Remove the steering wheel (Section 14).
2 Lift the carpet, remove the coupling cover, and unbolt the inner column from the flexible coupling. Carefully note how the bolts are positioned to ensure that they are refitted correctly.
3 Remove the steering column cowls with reference to Chapter 12. Disconnect the multi-plugs (see illustration).
4 Unscrew the top and bottom mountings and withdraw the steering column assembly from the car.
5 Remove the switch assembly. Unbolt the upper column, withdraw the inner column, and remove the top bush halves.

6 Clean the components in paraffin and wipe dry. Examine the bush for wear and renew it if necessary.

Refitting

7 To reassemble, insert the inner column in the outer column then bolt the top bush and upper column to the outer column. The top bush for 1986-on models is a press fit in the top of the outer column, and should be coated with graphite grease before fitting.
8 Fit the combination switch assembly and tighten the clamp screw.
9 Centralise the inner steering column and roadwheels, and engage the pinion coupling with the flexible coupling. Align the column and fit the top mounting bracket bolts finger tight.
10 Fully tighten the coupling nuts. The flexible coupling, on later models incorporate a support plate which must contact the pinion coupling with the lugs located over the studs.
11 Position the coupling cover as shown (see illustration), centralise the inner column in the outer column, then insert and tighten the coupling cover bolts. Fit the circular grommet.
12 Fully tighten the top mounting bracket bolts. When refitting the steering column, make sure that there is a clearance between the bottom of the steering wheel and the cowls. If not, loosen the outer column mounting bolts, lower the column slightly, then retighten the bolts. Note that the adjustment is only possible on 1986-on models.
13 Reconnect the ignition switch multi-plug and combination switch bulbholder, and refit the fusebox cover.
14 Reconnect the wiring multi-plugs.
15 Refit the steering column cowls and steering wheel.
16 Reconnect the battery negative lead.

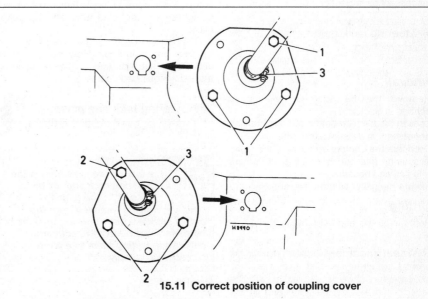

15.11 Correct position of coupling cover

1 *Right-hand drive coupling cover bolts*
2 *Left-hand drive coupling cover bolts*
3 *Clamp bolt*

10

16 Steering column lock/ignition switch - removal and refitting

Removal

1 Remove the steering column (Section 15).
2 Drill out the shear bolt heads from the lock clamp, and remove the lock ignition switch from the outer column.
3 Locate the lock body centrally over the slot in the outer column, and lightly bolt the clamp into position without shearing the heads.

Refitting

4 Refit the steering column, but before fitting the cowls, check that the lock and ignition switch operate correctly.
5 Tighten the clamp bolts until the bolt heads shear off, then refit the cowls.

17 Tie-rod end balljoint - removal and refitting

Removal

1 Apply the handbrake, jack up the front of the car, and support it on axle stands (see "*Jacking and vehicle support*"). Remove the roadwheel.
2 Loosen the tie-rod end adjustment locknut a quarter of a turn.
3 Unscrew the balljoint nut and detach the balljoint from the steering arm using a separator tool **(see illustrations)**.
4 Unscrew the tie-rod end from the tie-rod.

Refitting

5 Refitting is a reversal of removal, but tighten the nuts to the specified torque and check the front wheel alignment, making any adjustment as necessary as in Section 19.

18 Steering rack gaiter - removal and refitting

Removal

1 Remove the tie-rod end balljoint as described in Section 17.
2 Loosen the clips on the tie-rod and steering gear housing, and remove the gaiter.
3 Lubricate the contact surfaces of the gaiter with steering gear grease, then locate it over the tie-rod and housing.
4 Secure the gaiter with the two clips.

Refitting

5 Refit the tie-rod end balljoint (Section 17).

19 Wheel alignment - checking and adjusting

Checking

1 Accurate wheel adjustment is essential for good steering and slow tyre wear. Before

17.3a Steering tie-rod end balljoint

checking it, make sure that the car is only loaded to kerbside weight (i.e. with a full fuel tank), the tyres are correctly inflated, and the suspension ride heights are correct; check the latter as described in Section 2, and specifications at the beginning of this chapter.
2 Place the car on level ground with the wheels in the straight-ahead position, then roll the car backwards 12 ft (4 metres) and forwards again.
3 Using a wheel alignment gauge, check that the front wheel toe-out dimension is as given in the Specifications.

Adjustment

4 If adjustment is necessary, loosen the tie-rod end locknuts on both tie-rods and release the small gaiter clips.
5 Rotate each tie-rod by equal amounts until the alignment is correct. Ideally, there should be an equal number of exposed threads on each tie-rod, but note that the setting procedure used by the factory means that there can be up to six threads difference in tie-rod lengths with the wheel alignment still within tolerances; if this is found to be the case on any vehicle, care must be taken to alter the length of both tie-rods by exactly the same amount so that the factory setting is preserved.
6 Tighten the locknuts and refit the gaiter clips.
7 Camber and castor angles are preset and cannot be adjusted. However, if their accuracy is suspect, they can be checked by a suitably equipped dealer.

20 Steering rack and pinion - removal, overhaul and refitting

HAYNES HiNT *Where difficulty is experienced in removing the steering rack and pinion assembly, the pinion coupling may be removed from the pinion splines after removing the clamp bolt. Mark the pinion and coupling before separating them to ensure correct reassembly.*

Removal

1 Disconnect the battery negative lead.
2 Jack up the front of the car and support it on stands (see "*Jacking and vehicle support*").

17.3b Using a separator tool to release the tie-rod end balljoint

Apply the handbrake and remove both front wheels. Centralise the steering.
3 Lift the carpet, remove the coupling cover, and disconnect the pinion coupling from the flexible coupling. Unbolt the steering column from the top mounting bracket (1985 on models). Note how the bolts are positioned to ensure that they are refitted correctly.
4 Unscrew the tie-rod end balljoint nuts and use a separator tool to detach the balljoints from the steering arms.
5 Unscrew the nuts and bolts and remove the U-bolt and mounting pad and clamp **(see illustration)**.
6 Rotate the rack assembly and withdraw it from the driver's side of the subframe.
7 Remove the tie-rod ends, locknuts, gaiters and clips with reference to Sections 17 and 18.

Overhaul

8 Examine the steering gear assembly for signs of wear or damage, and check that the rack moves freely throughout the full length of its travel, with no signs of roughness or excessive free play between the steering gear pinion and rack. It is possible to overhaul the steering gear assembly housing components, but this task should be entrusted to a Rover dealer. The only components which can be renewed easily by the home mechanic are the steering gear gaiters, the tie rod balljoints and the tie rod ends **(see illustrations)**.

Refitting

9 Refitting is a reversal of removal, but tighten all nuts and bolts to the specified torque, and adjust the front wheel alignment as described in Section 19.

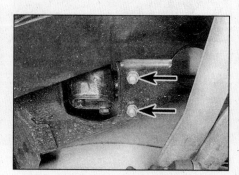

20.5 Steering rack and pinion U-bolt mounting nuts (arrowed)

20.8a Exploded view of the steering components (early models)

1 Tie-rod end
2 Locknut
3 Tie-rod
4 Rubber gaiter
5 Ball housing
6 Ball seat
7 Locking pin
8 Locking ring
9 Rack
10 End cover
11 Gasket
12 Shims
13 Bearing
14 Pinion
15 Bearing
16 Oil seal
17 Pinion coupling
18 Flexible coupling
19 Inner column
20 Mounting bracket
21 Cowl assembly
22 Steering wheel
23 Upper column
24 Top bush
25 Steering lock and ignition switch
26 Outer column
27 Clip
28 Ring
29 Cover
30 Plastic bush
31 Clamp
32 Centralising hole seal
33 U-bolt
34 Rack housing
35 Mounting pad
36 Yoke
37 Spring
38 Shims
39 Gasket
40 End cover

20.8b Exploded view of the steering components on 1985 models

1 Tie-rod ends
2 Locknuts
3 Tie-rods
4 Rubber gaiters
5 Rack housing
6 U-bolt
7 Mounting pad
8 Centralising hole seal
9 Clamp
10 Pinion coupling
11 Flexible coupling
12 Inner column
13 Coupling cover
14 Retaining ring
15 Outer column
16 Top mounting bracket
17 Top bush
18 Upper column
19 Steering wheel
20 Ignition switch/steering lock assembly
21 Steering column cowl

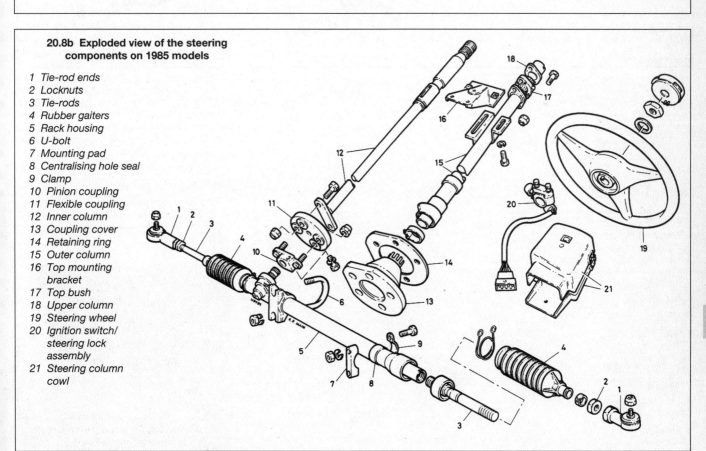

20.8c Exploded view of the steering components on 1986-on models

1 Tie-rod ends
2 Locknuts
3 Tie rods
4 Rubber gaiters
5 Rack housing
6 U-bolt
7 Mounting pad
8 Centralising hole seal
9 Clamp
10 Pinion coupling
11 Flexible coupling
12 Inner column
13 Coupling cover
14 Retaining ring
15 Outer column
16 Top mounting bracket
17 Top bush
18 Steering wheel
19 Ignition switch/steering lock assembly
20 Steering column cowl

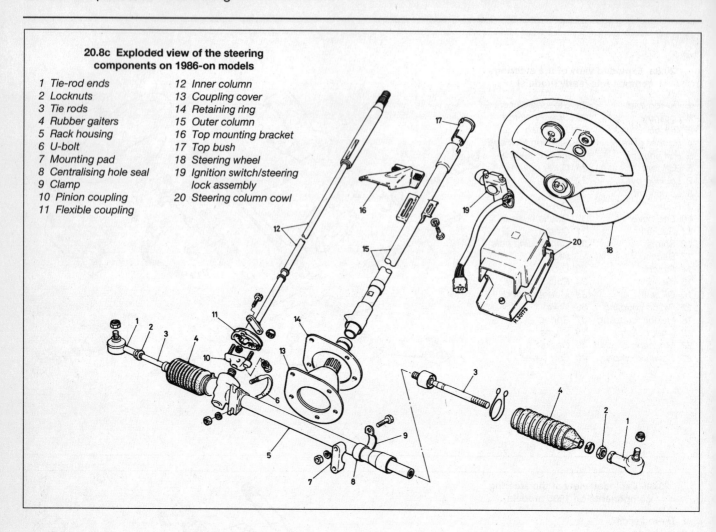

Chapter 11
Bodywork and fittings

Contents

Degrees of difficulty

Easy, suitable for novice with little experience	Fairly easy, suitable for beginner with some experience	Fairly difficult, suitable for competent DIY mechanic	Difficult, suitable for experienced DIY mechanic	Very difficult, suitable for expert DIY or professional

1 General description

The bodyshell and underframe are of all-steel welded construction and of computer based design. The assembly and welding of the main body unit is completed entirely by computer controlled robots, and the finished unit is checked for dimensional accuracy using modern computer and laser technology.

The front wings are bolted in position and are detachable should renewal be necessary after a front end collision.

2 Minor body damage - repair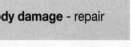

Note: *For more detailed information about bodywork repair, the Haynes Publishing Group publish a book called, The Car Bodywork Repair Manual. This incorporates information on such aspects as rust treatment, painting and glass fibre repairs, as well as details on more ambitious repairs involving welding and panel beating.*

Repair of minor scratches in bodywork

If the scratch is very superficial, and does not penetrate to the metal of the bodywork, repair is very simple. Lightly rub the area of the scratch with a paintwork renovator or a very fine cutting paste or compound, to remove loose paint from the scratch and to clear the surrounding bodywork of wax polish. Rinse the area with clean water.

Apply touch-up paint, or a paint film to the scratch using a fine paint brush. Continue to apply fine layers of paint until the surface of the paint in the scratch is level with the surrounding paintwork. Allow the new paint at least two weeks to harden: then blend it into the surrounding paintwork by rubbing the scratch area with a paintwork renovator or a very fine cutting paste, or compound. Finally, apply wax polish.

Where the scratch has penetrated right through to the metal of the bodywork, causing the metal to rust, a different repair technique is required. Remove any loose rust from the bottom of the scratch with a penknife, then apply rust inhibiting paint to prevent the formation of rust in the future. Using a rubber or nylon applicator fill the scratch with bodystopper paste or putty. If required, this paste can be mixed with cellulose thinners to provide a very thin paste that is ideal for filling narrow scratches. Before the stopper-paste in the scratch hardens, wrap a piece of smooth cotton rag around the top of a finger. Dip the finger in cellulose thinners, and then quickly sweep it across the surface of the stopper-paste in the scratch; this will ensure that the surface of the stopper-paste is slightly hollowed. The scratch can now be painted over as described earlier in this Section.

Repair of dents in bodywork

When deep denting of the vehicle's bodywork has taken place, the first task is to pull the dent out, until the affected bodywork almost attains its original shape. There is little point in trying to restore the original shape completely, as the metal in the damaged area will have stretched on impact and cannot be reshaped fully to its original contour. It is better to bring the level of the dent up to a point that is about ⅛ in (3 mm) below the level of the surrounding bodywork. In cases where the dent is very shallow anyway, it is not worth

11

trying to pull it out at all. If the underside of the dent is accessible, it can be hammered out gently from behind, using a mallet with a wooden or plastic head. Whilst doing this, hold a block of wood firmly against the outside of the panel to absorb the impact from the hammer blows. This will prevent a large area of the bodywork from being belled-out.

Should the dent be in a section of the bodywork that has a double skin or some other factor making it inaccessible from behind, a different technique is called for. Drill several small holes through the metal inside the area - particularly in the deeper section. Then screw long self-tapping screws into the holes just sufficiently for them to gain a good purchase in the metal. Now the dent can be pulled out by pulling on the protruding heads of the screws with a pair of pliers. The next stage of the repair is the removal of the paint from the damaged area, and from an inch or so of the surrounding "sound" bodywork. This is accomplished most easily by using a wire brush or abrasive pad on a power drill, although it can be done just as effectively by hand using sheets of abrasive paper. To complete the preparation for filling, score the surface of the bare metal with a screwdriver or the tang of a file, or alternatively, drill small holes in the affected area. This will provide a good "key" for the filler paste.

Repair of rust holes or gashes in bodywork

Remove all paint from the affected area and from an inch or so of the surrounding "sound" bodywork, using an abrasive pad or a wire rush on a power drill. If these are not available a few sheets of abrasive paper will do the job just as effectively. With the paint removed you will be able to gauge the severity of the corrosion and therefore decide whether to renew the whole panel (if this is possible) to repair the affected area. New body panels are not as expensive as most people think and it is often quicker and more satisfactory to fit a few panel than to attempt to repair large areas of corrosion.

Remove all fittings from the affected area except those which will act as a guide to the original shape of the damaged bodywork (i.e. headlamp shells, etc.). Then, using tin snips or a hacksaw blade, remove all loose metal and any other metal badly affected by corrosion. Hammer the edges of the hole inwards to create a slight depression for the filler paste.

Wire brush the affected area to remove the powdery rust from the surface of the remaining metal. Paint the affected area with rust inhibiting paint. If the back of the rusted rear is accessible treat this also.

Before filling can take place it will be necessary to block the hole in some way. This can be achieved by aluminium or plastic mesh, or aluminium tape.

Aluminium or plastic mesh or glass fibre matting is probably the best material to use on a large hole. Cut a piece to the approximate size and shape of the hole to be filled, then position it in the hole so that its edges are below the level of the surrounding bodywork. It can be retained in position by several blobs of filler paste around its periphery.

Aluminium tape should be used for small or very narrow holes. Pull a piece off the roll and trim it to the approximate size and shape required. Then pull off the backing paper (if used) and stick the tape over the hole; it can be overlapped if the thickness of one piece is sufficient. Burnish down the edges of the tape with the handle of a screwdriver or similar, to ensure that the tape is securely attached to the metal underneath.

Bodywork repairs - filling and re-spraying

Before reading these instructions, read from the beginning of this Section about dent, deep scratch, rust holes and gash repairs.

Many types of bodyfiller are available, but generally those proprietary kits that contain a tin of filler paste and a tube of resin hardener are best for this type of repair. Some can be used directly from the tube. A wide, flexible plastic or nylon applicator will be found invaluable for imparting a smooth and well-contoured finish to the surface of the filler.

Mix up a little filler on a clean piece of card or board - measure the hardener carefully (follow the maker's instructions on the pack) otherwise the filler will set too rapidly or too slowly. Using the applicator apply the filler paste to the prepared area; draw the applicator across the surface of the filler to achieve the correct contour and to level the filler surface. When a contour that approximates to the correct one is achieved, stop working the paste. If you carry on too long the paste will become sticky and begin to "pick up" on the applicator. Continue to add thin layers of filler paste at twenty-minute intervals until the level of the filler is just proud of the surrounding bodywork.

Once the filler has hardened, excess can be removed using a metal plane or file. From then on, progressively finer grades of abrasive paper should be used, starting with a 40 grade production paper and finishing with 400 grade wet-and-dry paper. Always wrap the abrasive paper around a flat rubber, cork, or wooden block - otherwise the surface of the filler will not be completely flat. During the smoothing of the filler surface the wet-and-dry paper should be periodically rinsed in water. This will ensure that a very smooth finish is imparted to the filler at the final stage.

At this stage the "dent" should be surrounded by a ring of bare metal, which in turn should be encircled by the finely "feathered" edge of the good paintwork. Rinse the repair area with clean water, until all the dust produced by the rubbing-down operation has gone.

Spray the whole repair area with a light coat of primer - this will show up imperfections in the surface of the filler. Repair these imperfections with fresh filler paste or bodystopper, and again smooth the surface with abrasive paper. If bodystopper is used, it can be mixed with cellulose thinners to form a thin paste that is ideal for filling small holes. Repeat this spray and repair procedure until you are satisfied that the surface of the filler, and the feathered edge of the paintwork are perfect. Clean the repair area with clean water and allow to dry fully.

The repair area is now ready for final spraying. Paint spraying must be carried out in a warm, dry, windless and dust free atmosphere. This condition can be created artificially if you have access to a large indoor working area, but if you are forced to work in the open, you will have to pick your day very carefully. If you are working indoors, dousing the floor in the work area with water will help to settle the dust that would otherwise be in the atmosphere. If the repair area is confined to one body panel, mask off the surrounding panels; this will help to minimise the effects of a slight mismatch in paint colours. Bodywork fittings (i.e. chrome strips, door handles, etc.), will also need to be masked off. Use genuine masking tape and several layers of newspaper for the masking operations.

Before starting to spray, agitate the aerosol can thoroughly, then spray a test area (an old tin, or similar) until the technique is mastered. Cover the repair area with a thick coat of primer; the thickness should be built up using several thin layers of paint rather than one thick one. Using 400 grade wet-and-dry paper, rub down the surface of the primer until it is smooth. While doing this, the work area should be thoroughly doused with water, and the wet-and-dry paper periodically rinsed in water. Allow to dry before spraying on more paint.

Spray on the top coat again building up the thickness by using several thin layers of paint. Start spraying in the centre of the repair area and then work outwards, with a side-to-side motion, until the whole repair area and about 2 inches of the surrounding original paintwork is covered. Remove all masking material 10 to 15 minutes after spraying on the final coat of paint.

Allow the new paint at least two weeks to harden, then, using a paintwork renovator or a very fine cutting paste blend the edges of the paint into the existing paintwork. Finally, apply wax polish.

3 Major body damage - repair

Where serious damage has occurred or large areas need renewal due to neglect, it means certainly that completely new sections or panels will need welding in and this is best left to professionals. If the damage is due to impact, it will also be necessary to completely check the alignment of the bodyshell structure. Due to the principle of construction, the strength and shape of the whole car can be affected by damage to one part. In such instances the services of a Rover dealer with specialist checking jigs are essential. If a body is left misaligned, it is firstly dangerous as the car will not handle properly. Secondly, uneven stresses will be imposed on the steering, engine and transmission, causing abnormal wear or complete failure. Tyre wear may also be excessive.

4 Door rattles - tracing and rectification

1 Check first that the door is not loose at the hinges, and that the latch is holding the door firmly in position. Check also that the door lines up with the aperture in the body. If the door is out of alignment, adjust it as described in Sections 16 and 17.
2 If the latch is holding the door in the correct position but the latch still rattles, the lock mechanism is worn and should be renewed.
3 Other rattles from the door could be caused by wear in the window operating mechanism, interior lock mechanism, or loose glass channels.

5 Bonnet - removal and refitting

Removal

1 Support the bonnet in its open position, and place some cardboard or rags beneath the corners by the hinges.
2 Mark the location of the hinges with a pencil, then loosen the four retaining nuts and bolts **(see illustration)**.
3 With the help of an assistant, release the stay, unscrew and remove the retaining bolts, and withdraw the bonnet from the car.

Refitting

4 Refitting is a reversal of removal, but adjust the hinges to their original positions. The bonnet rear edge should be flush with the scuttle and the gaps at either side equal.

6 Front wing - removal and refitting

Removal

1 Support the bonnet in its open position.
2 Pull the bulb holder from the side repeater lamp.
3 Unscrew the bolt from behind the wing and remove the bumper end capping. Remove the aerial where applicable.
4 Loosen the wing retaining bolt in the top of the door shut, and remove the remaining bolts.
5 Withdraw the front wing from the car.

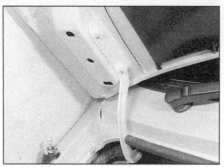

5.2 Bonnet hinge and bolts

Refitting

6 Refitting is a reversal of removal, but use a sealer compound to seal the wing to the body.

7 Tailgate - removal and refitting

Removal

1 Disconnect the battery negative lead.
2 Unhook the parcel shelf support cords.
3 Prise out the tailgate trim pad.
4 Disconnect the washer tube from the jet and the wiper wires from the multi-plug, tape them together, and tie a draw cord to them.
5 Prise out the rubber grommet and pull the wires and tube through the tailgate until the cord emerges, then untie the cord but leave it in the tailgate.
6 Disconnect the wire from the heated rear window and attach a cord to it. Prise out the grommet and pull the wire through, then untie the cord but leave it in position.
7 Using a pencil, mark the position of the hinges.
8 With the help of an assistant, support the tailgate, then prise out the locking pegs and detach the support struts from the tailgate.
9 Using an impact screwdriver, remove the hinge screws from the tailgate, then withdraw the tailgate from the car **(see illustration)**.

Refitting

10 Refitting is a reversal of removal, but adjust the hinges to their original positions and if necessary adjust the striker **(see illustration)**.

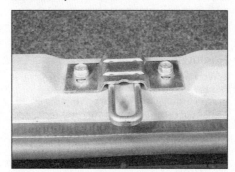

7.10 Tailgate striker

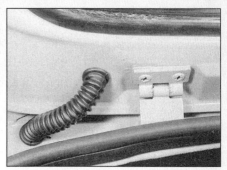

7.9 Tailgate hinge and bellows

8 Tailgate lock - removal and refitting

Removal

1 Prise out the trim pad.
2 Unclip the operating rod from the private lock then unbolt the lock from the door **(see illustration)**.
3 If necessary, the private lock may be removed by pulling out the clip. Note the location of the sealing washer.

Refitting

4 Refitting is a reversal of removal.

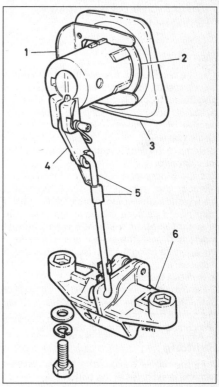

8.2 Tailgate lock components

1 Clip	5 Operating rod and
2 Sealing washer	clip
3 Retainer	6 Lock
4 Private lock lever	

11

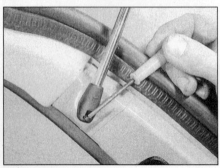

9.2a Releasing the tailgate strut locking peg

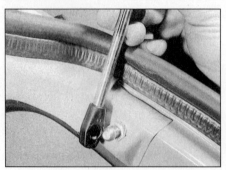

9.2b Removing the tailgate strut

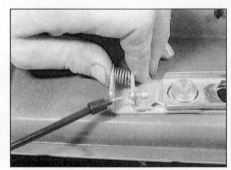

13.2 Removing the bonnet release cable

9 Tailgate support strut - removal and refitting

Removal

1 With the tailgate open, unhook the parcel shelf support cords and have an assistant support the tailgate.
2 Using a small screwdriver, prise out the locking pegs and detach the support strut from the tailgate and body **(see illustrations)**.

Refitting

3 Refitting is a reversal of removal.

10 Windscreen glass - removal and refitting

Removal

1 If the windscreen has shattered, cover the facia panel and air vents with a large sheet of polythene to catch the pieces of glass. If available, adhesive sheeting will facilitate the removal of the shattered windscreen. Remove all the glass.
2 Remove the windscreen wiper arms and the interior mirror.
3 If the windscreen is to be removed intact, release the rubber surround from the bodywork with a blunt screwdriver, taking care not to damage the paintwork. Have an assistant support the windscreen, then sit inside and push the screen and rubber from the aperture using the feet (suitably padded) if necessary.
4 Remove the rubber surround.
5 Examine the rubber surround for damage or deterioration and renew it if necessary. Clean the sealer from the body aperture and repair any damage or distortion of the flange.

Refitting

6 Fit the rubber surround to the windscreen with the drain holes at the bottom.
7 Obtain a length of strong cord and insert it into the flange groove of the rubber surround with the free ends overlapping at the bottom.
8 Locate the windscreen on the aperture and have an assistant press gently from the outside.

9 From inside the car, pull each end of the cord in turn to locate the rubber surround onto the flange. Tap the glass with the palm of the hand to make sure that it is fully seated.
10 Fit the interior mirror and wiper arms.

11 Tailgate glass - removal and refitting

Removal

1 The procedure is similar to that for the windscreen described in Section 10, except that it is necessary to unhook the parcel shelf support cords. Disconnect the heated rear window feed wire and earth strap, and remove the wiper arm and rubber grommet.

Refitting

2 Refitting is a reversal of removal.

12 Rear quarterlight glass - removal and refitting

Removal

1 The procedure is similar to that for the windscreen described in Section 10, except that it is necessary to fold the relevant rear seat forwards.

Refitting

2 When fitting the glass, apply sealer between the outer part of the rubber surround and the glass and flange.

13 Bonnet release cable - removal and refitting

Removal

1 Working inside the car, remove the bonnet release lever and disconnect the cable.
2 Working in the engine compartment, disconnect the cable from the lock and release the cable straps **(see illustration)**.
3 Withdraw the cable and grommet from the scuttle.

Refitting

4 Refitting is a reversal of removal.

14 Bonnet lock - adjustment

1 Adjustment is only possible at the lock pin mounted on the bonnet **(see illustration)**.
2 Loosen the locknut and use a screwdriver to adjust the length of the lock pin so that the bonnet closes easily and is held firmly in place.
3 Tighten the locknut.

15 Door trim pad - removal and refitting

Removal

1 Remove the screws and withdraw the armrest, interior door handle surround, door pull and door pocket where fitted. On 5 door models, prise out the plastic cap, then remove the interior handle surround screw and withdraw the surround **(see illustrations)**.
2 Fully close the window and note the fitted position of the window regulator handle. Remove the screw and withdraw the handle and bezel. Ideally the screw should be removed with a special splined tool, but an Allen key may be used instead **(see illustrations)**.
3 On the front door, remove the screws from the door pocket and disconnect the wiring plugs to the speaker and electric window switch, as applicable.
4 With a wide-bladed screwdriver, release the trim pad retaining clips from the door inner

14.1 The bonnet lock pin

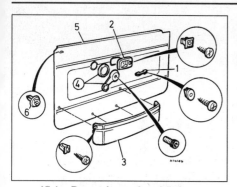

15.1a Door trim pad and fittings

1 Armrest
2 Door handle
   surround
3 Pocket
4 Window regulator
   handle
5 Trim pad
6 Clip

panel starting at the bottom rear corner. Withdraw the trim pad **(see illustration)**.

Refitting

5 Refitting is a reversal of removal.

16 Door - removal and refitting

Removal

1 Remove the trim pad (Section 15).
2 Carefully pull off the polythene sheet. Disconnect the wiring multi-plugs if fitted, and release the rubber gaiter and pull the wiring through the body.

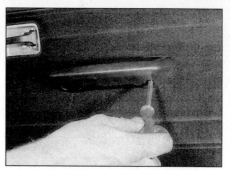

15.1b Removing the armrest

15.1d . . . and surround

3 On the rear door, if applicable, remove the lower trim panel and seat belt reel from the centre post.
4 Using a pencil, mark the position of the hinges on the door **(see illustrations)**.

15.1c Removing the interior door handle surround screw . . .

15.1e Removing the plastic cap from the interior door handle surround - later models

5 With the help of an assistant, support the door. On the front door, prise out the plug and remove the lower hinge nuts and bolt. Remove the top hinge bolts, withdraw the door and recover the lower hinge plate.

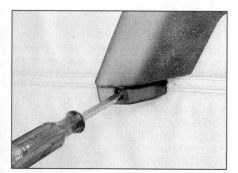

15.1f Removing the front door pull lower screw on 5-door models

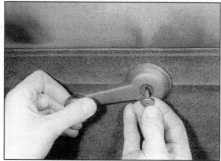

15.2a Removing the window regulator handle - early models

15.2b Removing the plastic cap from the window regulator handle - later models

15.4 Removing the trim pad

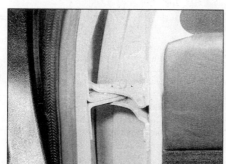

16.4a Front door upper hinge

16.4b Front door lower hinge

11

6 On the rear door, if applicable, remove the lower hinge nuts and recover the hinge plate. Remove the top hinge bolts, withdraw the door and recover the upper hinge plate.

Refitting

7 Refitting is a reversal of removal, but locate the hinges in their original positions. Check that the front edge of the door is flush or slightly recessed to the front wing, and if necessary adjust the hinges.

17 Door lock - removal and refitting

⚠ **Warning: On vehicles with central locking, it is important to first disconnect the battery negative lead.**

Removal

1 Remove the trim pad as described in Section 15.
2 Carefully pull off the polythene sheet.
3 Unscrew the locking button, then refit the handle and fully raise the window.
4 Unclip the control rods from the outer door handle and private lock **(see illustration)**.
5 Remove the cross-head screw from the inner door handle, pull the control rod from the clip and disconnect it from the lock **(see illustrations)**.
6 Remove the screw from the rear window channel.
7 Remove the lock assembly screws and withdraw the lock from the door aperture. Unbolt the lock motor and disconnect the operating rod, if fitted.

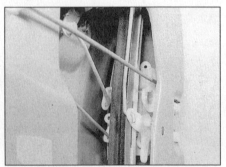

17.4 Door lock and control rods

Refitting

8 Refitting is a reversal of removal, but adjust the lock striker pin as follows.
9 Check that the latch disc is in the open position, then loosen the striker pin nut and position the pin so that the door can be closed easily and is held firmly. Close the door gently but firmly when making the adjustment.
10 Tighten the striker pin nut.

18 Door private lock - removal and refitting

Removal

1 Remove the trim pad (Section 15).
2 Carefully pull off the polythene sheet.
3 Refit the handle and fully raise the window.
4 Working through the aperture, unclip the control rod from the private lock and slide out the retaining clip.
5 Withdraw the private lock from the outside of the door.

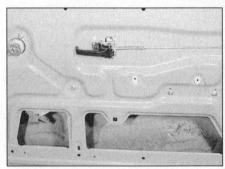

17.5a Inner door handle and rod

Refitting

6 Refitting is a reversal of removal.

19 Central locking door lock motor - removal and refitting

Removal

1 Disconnect the battery negative lead.
2 Remove the trim pad and, except for on the tailgate, peel off the polythene sheet.
3 Disconnect the wiring multi-plug(s) to the motor.
4 On the tailgate, remove the mounting bracket screws, unclip the mounting bracket from the private lock and unclip the operating rod from the lock lever. Remove the private lock then remove the mounting bracket and motor, and unbolt the motor.
5 On the front or rear door, unbolt the motor and disconnect the operating rod.

Refitting

6 Refitting is a reversal of removal.

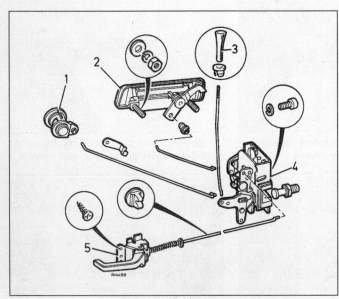

17.5b Front door lock components

1 Private lock
2 Outer door handle
3 Locking button
4 Lock assembly
5 Interior door handle

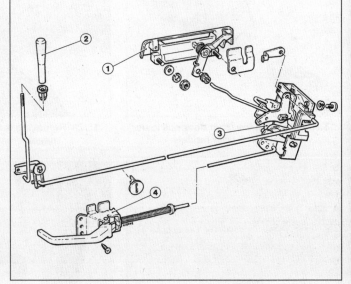

17.5c Rear door lock components

1 Outer handle assembly
2 Locking button
3 Lock assembly
4 Inner handle assembly

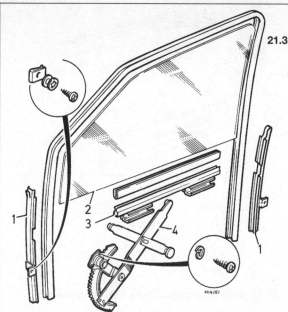

21.3 Window regulator and glass components

1 Window channel
2 Glass
3 Lower channel
4 Regulator

20 Interior rear view mirror - general

Note: *Ensure that both the mirror's mounting surface and the area on the glass, are spotlessly clean before mounting.*

1 The mirror is stuck to the windscreen by a double-sided adhesive pad. Do not disturb it unless absolutely necessary as it is very difficult to achieve a reliable bond.
2 Clean both surfaces.
3 Remove the protective foil from one side of the pad. Attach the pad to the mirror's mount. Remove the other foil. Line the mirror up to the windscreen. Firmly press the mirror in place.

21 Door glass - removal and refitting

Removal

1 Remove the trim pad as described in Section 15.
2 Carefully pull off the polythene sheet.
3 Remove the cross-head screw retaining the window channel guides, and door lock if fitted **(see illustration)**.
4 Remove the window regulator with reference to Section 22.
5 Fully lower the glass to the bottom of the door and release it from the channel.
6 Remove the outer weatherstrip, lift the rear edge of the glass, and withdraw it from the door.

Refitting

7 Refitting is a reversal of removal, referring to Section 22, if necessary.

22 Window regulator - removal and refitting

Removal

1 Remove the trim pad as described in Section 15.
2 Carefully pull off the polythene sheet.
3 Refit the handle and raise the window to 2 inches (50 mm) from the top. Wedge the window in this position.
4 Remove the regulator securing screws and the regulator channel securing screws.
5 Slide the regulator arms from the glass lower channel, then withdraw the regulator from the door aperture.

Refitting

6 Refitting is a reversal of removal.

23 Electric window motor - removal and refitting

Removal

1 Fully close the window then disconnect the battery negative lead.
2 Remove the door trim panel and peel off the polythene sheet.
3 Wedge the window in the closed position.
4 Disconnect the wiring multi-plug to the motor.
5 Unscrew the window regulator bolts.
6 Remove the front window channel bolt, unclip the top of the channel, and withdraw it from the door.
7 Unbolt the motor and withdraw it from the door together with the regulator **(see illustration)**.

Refitting

8 Refitting is a reversal of removal, but the window channel should be positioned so that the window movement is smooth.

24 Seats - removal and refitting

Removal

1 Ideally a special splined tool should be obtained to remove the seat mounting screws, but it may be possible to remove them using an Allen key.

Front seat

2 Adjust the seat as necessary for access, remove the rotating screws, and withdraw the seat through the door aperture.

Rear seat

3 Unhook the parcel shelf support cords and fold down the rear seat. Remove the shelf.
4 Detach the carpet from the seat, then remove the mounting screws.
5 Withdraw the seat assembly through the tailgate aperture.

Refitting

6 Refitting front or rear seats are a reversal of removal, but before tightening the rear seat mounting screws, secure the squabs to ensure correct alignment.

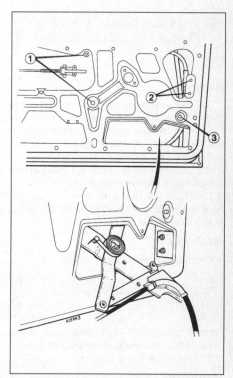

23.7 Electric window motor components

1 Regulator mounting components
2 Electric motor mounting bolts
3 Window channel bolt

11

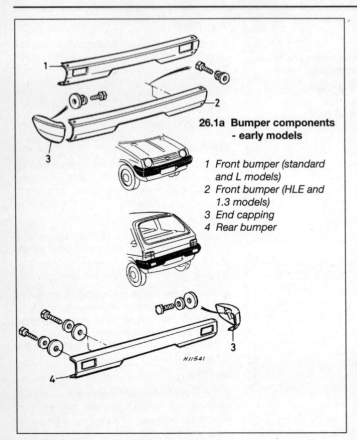

26.1a Bumper components - early models

1 Front bumper (standard and L models)
2 Front bumper (HLE and 1.3 models)
3 End capping
4 Rear bumper

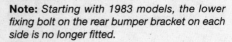

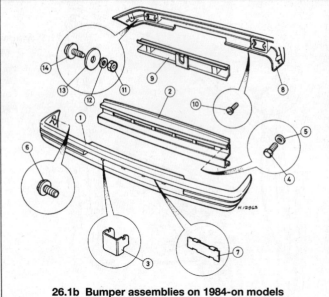

26.1b Bumper assemblies on 1984-on models

1 Bumper cover (front)	8 Bumper cover (rear)
2 Bumper reinforcement	9 Bumper reinforcement
3 Cover-to-reinforcement clip	10 Cover-to-reinforcement screw
4 Cover-to-wing screw	11 Bumper-to-body nut
5 Washer	12 Washer
6 End fixing screw and washer	13 Distance piece
7 Front blanking plate	14 End fixing screw and washer

25 Front seat release lever cable (3-door models) - removal and refitting

Removal

1 Pull the plastic clip from the bottom of the front seat backrest. If the cables on each side have been broken, reach through the rear of the seat and release the pawls from each side so that the seat back may be folded forward.
2 On 1985-on models, prise out the plug and unbolt the protection plate from the lever.
3 Carefully roll the seat covering up the backrest sufficiently to disconnect the cable from the lever and pawls.

Refitting

4 Refitting is a reversal of removal.

26 Bumpers - removal and refitting

Note: *Starting with 1983 models, the lower fixing bolt on the rear bumper bracket on each side is no longer fitted.*

Removal

1 The bumper is in sections for the earlier models as shown. The outer cover on 1984-on models are one piece **(see illustrations)**.

2 To remove a front bumper, it will probably be necessary to remove the radiator (Chapter 3) to gain access to the mounting bolts.
3 To remove either a front or rear bumper, first remove the end cappings, which are each retained in place by a single bolt.
4 Where applicable, disconnect the wiring from the fog lamps, front sidelamps, and rear number plate lamps.
5 Unscrew the mounting bolts and withdraw the bumper from the car.

Refitting

6 Refitting is the reversal of removal.

27 Radiator grille (1984-on) - removal and refitting

Removal

1 Open the bonnet.
2 Using a flat bladed screwdriver depress the three plastic clips along the lower edge of the grille, one after the other at the same time pulling upward on the grille to release the clips.
3 Pull the grille further up to release the three upper clips then tilt the grille forward to release it.

Refitting

4 Refit in reverse order ensuring that the upper clips engage before pushing the grille downward to engage the lower clips.

28 Headlamp surrounds (1984-on) - removal and refitting

Removal

1 Remove the radiator grille as described earlier.
2 Undo the two screws securing each surround to the front cross-rail.
3 Tilt the surround forward and lift upward to disengage the lower clips and withdraw the surrounds.

Refitting

4 Refit in reverse order.

29 Facia - removal and refitting

Removal

Pre 1985 models

1 Remove the instrument panel as described in Chapter 12.
2 Open the glovebox, remove the two pivot screws and bushes, and withdraw the glovebox **(see illustration)**.
3 Remove the two screws and pull back the carpet from the top of the glove compartment area.

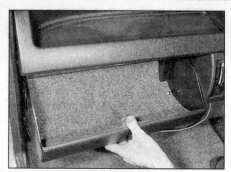

29.2 Removing the glovebox

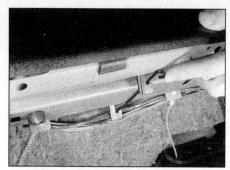

29.4 Facia retaining rod location

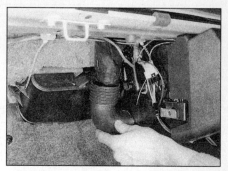

29.5 Disconnecting the vent duct tubes

29.6a Removing the ashtray

29.6b Removing the centre facia retaining screw

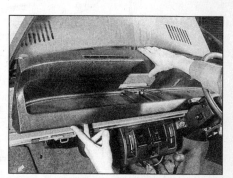

29.7 Removing the facia

4 Unclip and remove the three facia retaining rods (see illustration).
5 Disconnect the tubes from the vent ducts (see illustration).
6 Prise out the ash tray and remove the centre facia retaining screw (see illustrations). Remove the remaining retaining screws from under the shelf.
7 Pull the facia from the bulkhead, starting at the top, and withdraw it through the passenger door aperture (see illustration).
8 If necessary, prise out the speaker grille and detach the demister ducts (1 screw each).

1985-on models

9 Remove the steering column, as described in Chapter 10.
10 Disconnect the choke cable from the carburettor and pull it through the bulkhead.
11 Disconnect the heater control rods from the flap levers.

12 Prise out the plastic covers and remove the upper screws. Also remove the screws securing the facia to the heater.
13 Remove the facia side mounting screws.
14 Withdraw the facia rearwards, disconnect the multi-plugs and aerial, and remove the facia from the car.

Refitting

15 Refitting is a reversal of removal.

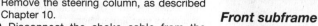

30 Subframes - removal and refitting

Front subframe

Removal

1 Remove the front Hydragas units as described in Chapter 10.
2 Remove the engine and gearbox assembly, and the engine mountings as described in Chapter 2B.
3 Remove the steering rack and pinion as described in Chapter 10.
4 Remove the swivel hub assemblies as described in Chapter 10, together with the driveshafts.
5 Remove the exhaust system, gearchange rod and support stay, and disconnect the shock absorber lower mountings.
6 Support the rear of the subframe and remove the lower suspension arms, anti-roll bar, and rear subframe mountings (see illustration).

7 Support the front of the subframe and remove the front subframe mountings (see illustration).
8 Withdraw the subframe from under the car, and remove the upper suspension arms with reference to Chapter 10.

Refitting

9 Refitting is a reversal of removal (see illustration).

Rear subframe

Removal

10 Chock the front wheels. Jack up the rear of the car and support on axle stands (see "Jacking and vehicle support") leaving a clear space beneath the rear subframe.
11 Remove both rear wheels.

30.6 A front subframe rear mounting

30.7 A front subframe front mounting

11

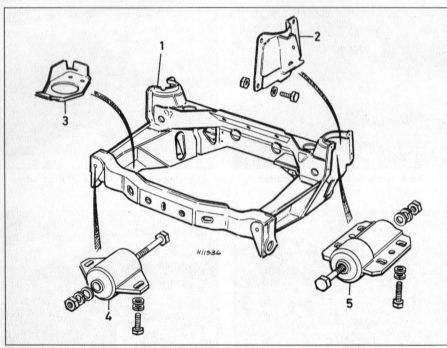

30.9 Front subframe components

| 1 Front subframe | 3 Engine mounting | 4 Front mounting |
| 2 Tower bracket | bracket | 5 Rear mounting |

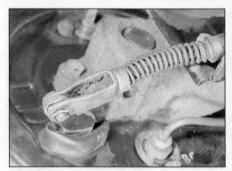

30.12 Handbrake cable end fitting and clevis pin

30.13 Plastic strap (arrowed) holding handbrake cable to rear radius arm

12 Release the handbrake, then disconnect the cable end fittings from the rear brake levers by extracting the split pins and removing the clevis pins **(see illustration)**.

13 Cut the plastic straps holding the handbrake cable to each rear radius arm **(see illustration)**.

14 Fit brake hose clamps to the flexible brake hoses attached to the radius arms **(see illustration)**. If clamps are not available,

tighten the brake fluid reservoir cap onto a piece of polythene to help reduce the loss of fluid when the hoses are disconnected.

15 Working on each side in turn, unscrew the rigid pipe union nuts, then unscrew the locknuts and disconnect the flexible hoses from the brackets on the radius arms.

16 Support the rear subframe on axle stands or trolley jacks.

17 Unbolt the Hydragas straps from the underbody. If preferred, the outer bolts only can be unscrewed and the straps uncurled to release the Hydragas units, otherwise unscrew the inner strap mountings accessible within the spare wheel well **(see illustrations)**.

18 Unbolt the front of the subframe from the mountings **(see illustration)**.

19 Disconnect the handbrake cables from the radius arm brackets by pulling out the clips and sliding the inner cables through the bracket slots **(see illustrations)**.

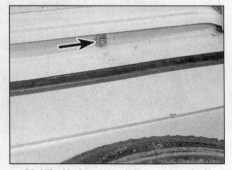

30.14 Clamp fitted to rear brake hose

30.17a Hydragas unit outer strap bolt (arrowed)

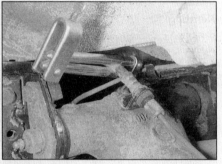

30.17b Hydragas unit inner strap bolt viewed from the spare wheel well

30.18 Unbolting the subframe from the front mountings

30.19a Pull out the clip (arrowed) . . .

30.19b . . . and disconnect the handbrake cable from the radius arm bracket

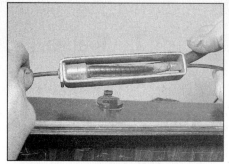

30.20 Releasing the equaliser from the plastic clip on the front of the subframe

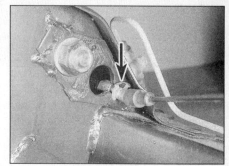

30.21a Pull out the clip (arrowed) . . .

30.21b . . . and withdraw the handbrake cable ends through the access holes

30.22 Rear subframe removed from the car

30.23 Hydragas Schrader valve and union (arrowed)

20 Lower the rear subframe three or four inches, then unclip the handbrake equaliser from the plastic clip on the front of the subframe **(see illustration)**.

21 Disconnect the handbrake cables from the front of the subframe by pulling out the clips, removing the rubber covers and withdrawing the cable ends through the access holes **(see illustrations)**.

22 Lower the rear subframe to the ground and withdraw it from under the car **(see illustration)**.

23 To dismantle the radius arms and Hydragas units, depressurise the units and follow the procedure given in Chapter 10. Unbolt the Schrader valve and union, and unclip the fluid pipes **(see illustration)**.

24 Unbolt the subframe mountings from the body and examine them for deterioration and damage **(see illustrations)**. Renew them if necessary.

Refitting

25 Refitting is a reversal of removal **(see illustration)**. Have the Hydragas units pressurised by a Rover dealer, bleed the brake hydraulic system and adjust the handbrake cable, as detailed in Chapter 9. Attach the handbrake cables to the radius arms with new plastic straps.

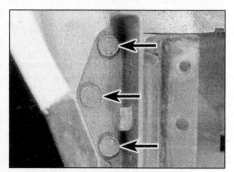

30.24a Unscrew the bolts (arrowed) . . .

30.24b . . . and remove the rear subframe mounting

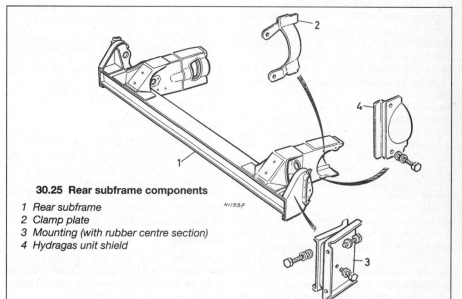

30.25 Rear subframe components
1 Rear subframe
2 Clamp plate
3 Mounting (with rubber centre section)
4 Hydragas unit shield

H11537

11

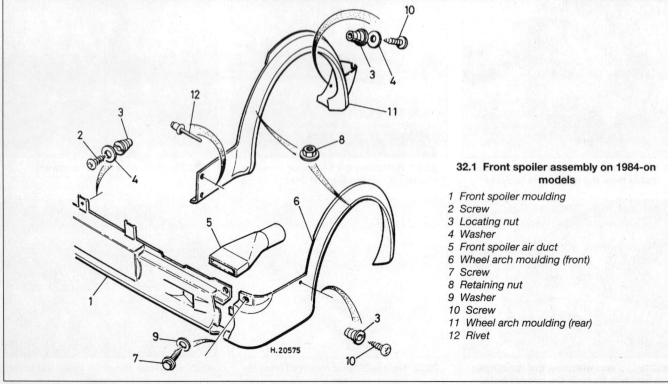

32.1 Front spoiler assembly on 1984-on models

1 Front spoiler moulding
2 Screw
3 Locating nut
4 Washer
5 Front spoiler air duct
6 Wheel arch moulding (front)
7 Screw
8 Retaining nut
9 Washer
10 Screw
11 Wheel arch moulding (rear)
12 Rivet

H.20575

31 Plastic components

With the use of more and more plastic body components by the vehicle manufacturers (e.g. bumpers, spoilers, and in some cases major body panels), rectification of more serious damage to such items has become a matter of either entrusting repair work to a specialist in this field, or renewing complete components. Repair of such damage by the DIY owner is not feasible owing to the cost of the equipment and materials required for effecting such repairs. The basic technique involves making a groove along the line of the crack in the plastic using a rotary burr in a power drill. The damaged part is then welded back together by using a hot air gun to heat up and fuse a plastic filler rod into the groove. Any excess plastic is then removed and the area rubbed down to a smooth finish. It is important that a filler rod of the correct plastic is used, as body components can be made of a variety of different types (e.g. polycarbonate, ABS, polypropylene).

Damage of a less serious nature (abrasions, minor cracks, etc.) can be repaired by the DIY owner using a two-part epoxy filler repair material. Once mixed in equal proportions (or applied direct from the tube), this can then be used in similar fashion to the bodywork filler used on metal panels. The filler is usually cured in twenty to thirty minutes, ready for sanding and painting.

Standard paints, generally, will not bond to plastic or rubber satisfactorily, but special paints to match any plastic or rubber finish can be obtained from dealers. However, it is now possible to obtain a plastic body parts finishing kit that consists of a pre-primer treatment, a primer and coloured top coat. Full instructions are normally supplied with a kit, but the method of use is to first apply the pre-primer to the component concerned and allow it to dry for up to 30 minutes. Then the primer is applied and left to dry for about an hour before finally applying the special coloured top coat. The result is a correctly coloured component where the paint will flex with the plastic or rubber, a property that standard paint does not normally possess.

32 Front spoiler - removal and refitting

Note: *On 1985-on models completely remove the front bumper.*

Removal

1 Remove the front bumper end caps, and remove the end fastenings from the spoiler. On 1985-on models completely remove the front bumper **(see illustration)**.
2 Remove the screws that secure the top and bottom of the spoiler. Remove the spoiler and (if wished) take off the air ducts.

Refitting

3 Refitting is a reversal of the removal procedure. Fit all fastenings loosely at first and check the spoiler alignment before tightening.

33 Wheel arch finishers - removal and refitting

Note: *Raise and support the vehicle at the quarter being worked on. Remove the wheel if wished to improve access.*

Front finisher

Removal

1 Remove the front bumper and cap. On 1985-on models completely remove the front bumper, see previous section.
2 Remove the screws that secure the front and rear of the finisher.
3 Remove the securing nuts from inside the wheel arch.
4 The finisher can now be removed.

Refitting

5 Refitting is a reversal of the removal procedure. Fit the fastenings finger-tight at first. Check the fit of the finisher before finally tightening.

Rear finisher

Removal

6 Drill out the rivets that secure the finisher to the wheel arch (where applicable).
7 Follow paragraphs 1 to 4 and remove the finisher.

Refitting

8 Refit the finisher using the nuts and screws. When alignment is correct, either drill new rivet holes or use the existing ones to fit new pop rivets.

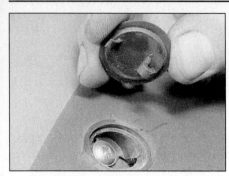

34.1 Rear spoiler screw cover plug

34 Rear spoiler (MG and 1985-on models) - removal and refitting

Removal

1 Prise out the screw cover plugs from the top edge of the spoiler **(see illustration)**.
2 Disconnect the tailgate support struts from the tailgate.
3 From inside the tailgate, remove the two long securing screws (one below the strut attachment, the other in the same position on the opposite side) and the two securing nuts (one above the strut attachment, and the corresponding position opposite).
4 From outside the tailgate, remove the four securing screws from the top edge of the spoiler.
5 Disconnect the washer tube from the washer jet.
6 Remove the spoiler from the tailgate. Some effort may be needed to free it from the sealer.
7 Remove the washer jet and the sealing washers.

Refitting

8 Refitting is a reversal of the removal procedure. Make sure that the spoiler is correctly aligned before tightening the screws and nuts **(see illustration)**.
9 Note that replacement tailgates are not supplied ready drilled to accept a spoiler. Consult your Rover dealer concerning the components and tools needed to prepare the tailgate for spoiler fitting.

35 Opening rear quarterlight - removal and refitting

Removal

1 Protect the vehicle's paintwork during the following operations by covering the area between the quarterlight hinges with masking tape.
2 Open the quarterlight. Have an assistant support the window whilst you remove the screws that secure the catch to the rear pillar.
3 Carefully open the quarterlight until the hinge tabs can be withdrawn from their grommets in the middle pillar.
4 Detach the catch from the clip by drilling out the hollow rivet.
5 Remove the frame and rubber surround by drilling out the rivet that secures the frame to the channel.

Refitting

6 Refitting is a reversal of the removal procedure. Use new rivets where these had to be removed. In the absence of a riveting tool for use with hollow rivets, it may be possible to use a small nut and bolt instead. Lubricate the hinge tabs with liquid soap or washing-up liquid before inserting them in the grommets.

36 Sunroof - general, removal and refitting

General

1 A removable panel type sunroof is available as an option on some models.
2 To open the sunroof, push the handle forwards and upwards until it locks. Close by reversing this operation.

Removal

3 To remove the sunroof, open it and then disconnect the handle by squeezing its arms together **(see illustration)**. Unhook the safety spring and lift the roof panel rearwards until the two front lugs are free. The wind deflector will automatically spring upwards.

Refitting

4 Refit the sunroof in the reverse order to removal.

37 Remote control door mirror - removal and refitting

Removal

1 Remove the adjusting knob.
2 Remove the inner cover then unbolt the assembly and remove the seal.

Refitting

3 Refitting is a reversal of removal.

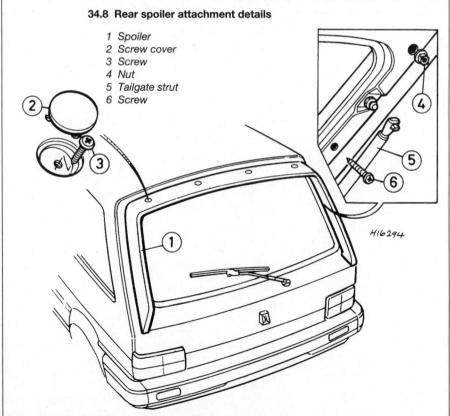

34.8 Rear spoiler attachment details

1 Spoiler
2 Screw cover
3 Screw
4 Nut
5 Tailgate strut
6 Screw

H16294

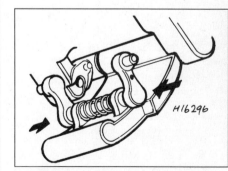

36.3 Squeeze arms of sunroof catch together at points arrowed to release

H16296

11

Chapter 12
Body electrical systems

Contents

Degrees of difficulty

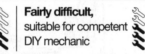

Easy, suitable for novice with little experience	Fairly easy, suitable for beginner with some experience	Fairly difficult, suitable for competent DIY mechanic	Difficult, suitable for experienced DIY mechanic	Very difficult, suitable for expert DIY or professional

Specifications

Fuses

	Current rated
Fuse 1	17 amp
Fuse 2	12 amp
Fuse 3	8 amp
Fuse 4	8 amp
Line fuse, rear fog lamps	15 amp
Line fuse, other	35 amp

Bulbs

	Wattage
Direction indicators	21
Footwell lamp	5
Glovebox lamp	5
Headlamps - Metro and Metro L	45/40
Headlamps - all other models	60/55
Heated rear window switch	1.2 or 0.36
Instrument panel lamps	1.2 or 1.12
Ignition (no-charge) warning light (from VIN 388652)	2
Interior lamp	10 (bayonet), 5 (festoon)
Loadspace lamp - Van	5
Luggage area lamp - Car	6
Rear fog lamp	21
Rear number plate lamp	6 (wedge), 10 (bayonet)
Reverse lamps	21
Sidelamps	4 (bayonet), 5 (wedge)
Side repeater lamps	5
Stop and tail lamps	21/5
Switch illumination lamps	0.75, 0.36 or 1.2

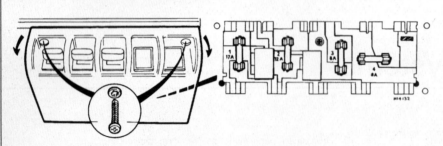

2.1a Fuse locations - early models

2.1b Switch board and fuses - early models

1 General description

 Warning: Before carrying out any work on the electrical system, read through the precautions given in "Safety first!" at the beginning of this manual, and in Chapter 5.

The electrical system is of 12-volt negative earth type. Power for the lights and all electrical accessories is supplied by a lead/acid type battery, which is charged by the alternator.

This Chapter covers repair and service procedures for the various electrical components not associated with the engine. Information on the battery, alternator and starter motor can be found in Chapter 5.

It should be noted that, prior to working on any component in the electrical system, the battery negative terminal should first be disconnected, to prevent the possibility of electrical short-circuits and/or fires.

2 Fuses - general

Early models

1 The fuses are located behind the switch panel on the right-hand side of the dash panel. Access to them, is gained by removing the two screws from the front of the switch panel, and pivoting the panel downwards **(see illustrations)**.
2 The fuse locations are numbered together with the respective current rating, and the circuits protected are as follows:

Fuse 1 17 amp Direction indicators, stop lamps, reverse lamps, heated rear window and warning light
Fuse 2 12 amp Interior lamp, hazard warning, lighter
Fuse 3 8 amp Sidelamps, tail lamps, number plate lamps, panel lamps, automatic gear selector lamp (if applicable)
Fuse 4 8 amp Heater control, tailgate wiper and washer motor

3 In addition to the main fuses, in-line fuses are provided to protect the following circuits:
Rear fog lamps line fuse is normally located behind the switch panel.
Wiper, washer and heater motor lines fuses are normally located in the engine compartment on the right-hand wing valance.
4 Always renew a fuse with one of identical rating, and never renew it more than once without finding the source of the trouble (usually a short circuit).

1985-on models

5 On 1985-on models the fusebox is located below the right-hand side of the facia **(see illustration)**. To remove the cover, twist the retainers using a coin. Each fuse is colour coded as follows:
3 amp   Violet   10 amp   Red
5 amp   Tan   15 amp   Blue
6 1985-on models are also fitted with three fusible links in the first part of the battery "+" cable. If a number of circuits fail to work, check for battery voltage at the fusebox input side.
7 If a fusible link has failed, disconnect both battery terminals. Carefully cut back the binding and remove the sleeve from the "+" cable. Unsolder the failed fusible link and renew it with one of the same size. Cover the joints with insulating tape and reconnect the battery.

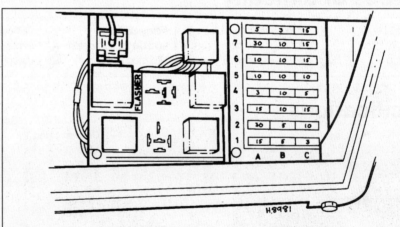

2.5 Inside view of the fusebox on 1985-on models

Circuit	Location	Rating (amp)
Heated rear window	A1	15
Electric front windows	A2	30
Central door locking	A3	15
Instruments	A4	3
Direction indicators, hazard lights	A5	10
Interior lamps	A6	10
Left-hand side and tail lights	B1	5
Right-hand side and tail lights, and number plate lights	B2	5
Left-hand dipped headlight	B3	10
Right-hand dipped headlight	B4	10
Left-hand main beam headlight	B6	10
Radio	C1	3
Heater blower	C2	10
Screen wiper and washers	C3	15
Rear foglamps	C4	5
Stop and reverse lights	C5	10
Rear wiper and washer	C6	15
Electric cooling fan	C7	15

5.4 Removing the right-hand steering column cowl

3 Direction indicator and hazard flasher system - general

1 The flasher units are located on the fuseboard behind the switch panel on the right-hand side of the dash panel.

2 To remove either one of them, disconnect the battery negative lead, then remove the two screws and pivot the switch panel downwards. The direction indicator flasher unit is located on the left of the fuseboard, and the hazard flasher unit is located to the right of it. Pull the required unit directly from the fuseboard to remove it.

3 Should the flashers become faulty in operation, check the bulbs for security and make sure that the contact surfaces are not corroded. Check all the relevant wiring and terminals. If the flashers are still faulty and the relevant fuse has not blown, renew the flasher

7.2a Removing the switch panel screws - early models

7.2c Remove the instrument panel surround upper screws . . .

unit. If the fuse has blown, a short circuit may be the cause of the failure.

4 Ignition switch/steering column lock - removal and refitting

The ignition switch is an integral part of the steering column lock, and removal and refitting procedures are given in Chapter 10.

5 Combination switches - removal and refitting

Removal

Pre-1985 models

1 Remove the steering wheel (Chapter 10).
2 Disconnect the battery negative lead.
3 Remove the screws retaining the steering column cowls together and to the outer column bracket.
4 Separate the cowls and withdraw the right-hand cowl over the wash/wipe switch **(see illustration)**.
5 Disconnect the multi-plug connectors to the wash/wipe switch, direction indicator switch and lighting switch.
6 Remove the left-hand cowl over the direction indicator switch, leaving the choke cable attached.
7 Loosen the securing screw, and withdraw the combined switches from the upper column.

1985-on models

8 Remove the steering wheel (Chapter 10).

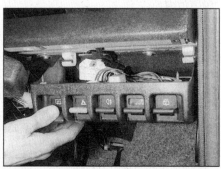

7.2b Lowering the switch panel - early models

7.2d . . . and lower screws . . .

6.6 Lighting switch and multi-plug

9 Disconnect the battery negative lead.
10 Remove the screws and withdraw the steering column cowl lower half, followed by the top half.
11 Lift the clips and pull the fibre optic guides from each side of the switch.
12 Depress the retainers and withdraw the switch. Disconnect the wiring multi-plug.

Refitting

13 Refitting is a reversal of removal, but after tightening the switch assembly clamp screw, position the striker bush with the arrow pointing towards the direction indicator switch.

6 Lighting switch - removal and refitting

Removal

1 Remove the steering wheel (Chapter 10).
2 Disconnect the battery negative lead.
3 Remove the screws retaining the steering column cowls together and to the outer column bracket.
4 Separate the cowls and withdraw the right-hand cowl over the wash/wipe switch.
5 Disconnect the multi-plug connector to the lighting switch.
6 Remove the left-hand cowl over the direction indicator switch. The lighting switch can now be removed from the cowl by depressing the plastic ears **(see illustration)**.

Refitting

7 Refitting is a reversal of removal, but make sure that the switch is fully entered into the cowl.

7 Instrument panel switches - removal and refitting

Removal

1 Disconnect the battery negative lead.
2 Remove the two screws from the front of the switch panel, and pivot the panel downwards - on early models. Remove the five screws, withdraw the surround and switch panel - on later models. Disconnect the wiring multi-plugs **(see illustrations)**.

12

7.2e . . . then disconnect the multi-plugs (later models)

7.3 Removing a switch from the instrument panel surround

9.2 Removing the courtesy light switch

3 Depress the plastic ears of the relevant switch, push it from the fuseboard, and remove it from the switch panel **(see illustration)**.

Refitting

4 Refitting is a reversal of removal, but make sure that the switch is fully entered into the panel.

8 Electric window switch and relay - removal and refitting

Removal

1 Disconnect the battery negative lead.
2 Prise the switch from the door pocket and disconnect the wiring; after noting the terminal locations.
3 The electric window relay is located on the

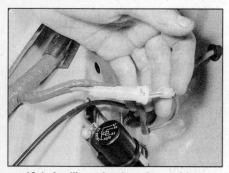

10.1 Auxiliary circuits relay and fuse

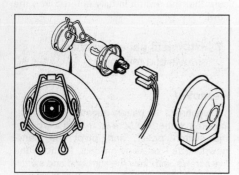

11.1 Headlamp bulb components for Metro and Metro L models

fusebox, No 2 (centre) on the bottom row. Access is gained by removing the fusebox cover.

Refitting

4 Refitting is a reversal of removal.

9 Courtesy light switch - removal and refitting

Removal

1 Disconnect the battery negative lead.
2 Open the door and locate the courtesy light switch on the front door pillar. Remove the single screw and withdraw the switch **(see illustration)**.
3 Disconnect the supply wire and tie a loose knot in it to prevent it dropping into the pillar. Remove the switch.

Refitting

4 Refitting is a reversal of removal.

10 Auxiliary circuits relay and circuit diode - description

1 An auxiliary circuits relay is fitted in the wiring harness on all models, and is located on the right-hand side wheel arch on right-hand drive models and on the left-hand side wheel arch on left-hand drive models. The relay and line fuse are connected in the heater and wiper circuit and protects the ignition switch from overloading **(see illustration)**.
2 All models are equipped with a circuit junction diode to protect the various instruments fitted with semi-conductors devices.

11 Headlamps and headlamp bulbs - removal and refitting

Note: *From late 1986, all models were fitted with a headlamp dim-dip system which prevents the vehicle from being driven with the sidelamps only illuminated. A unit mounted in the right-hand front of the engine compartment controls a resistor fastened behind the radiator grille and right-hand headlamp surround, so that whenever the*

sidelamp and ignition are switched on at the same time, the headlamp dip beams light at one-sixth of their normal output.

Removal

Metro and Metro L models

1 With the bonnet open, pull the socket connector from the rear of the headlamp, and withdraw the rubber cover **(see illustration)**.
2 Release the clip and remove the headlamp bulb.
3 To remove the headlamp unit, first remove the plastic radiator grille. Prise off the mounting clips and lower the unit from the adjustment screws **(see illustration)**.

Metro HLE, 1.3S and 1.3 HLS models

4 With the bonnet open, pull the rubber cover from the rear of the headlamp **(see illustration)**.
5 Pull the socket connector from the bulb **(see illustration)**.
6 Release the clip and remove the headlamp bulb **(see illustration)**.
7 To remove the headlamp unit, first remove the plastic radiator grille.
8 Remove the sidelamp and direction indicator bulbs.

11.3 Headlamp unit components for Metro and Metro L models

11.4 Headlamp rear cover (1.3 HLS)

11.5 Removing the headlamp bulb socket (1.3 HLS)

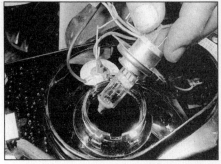

11.6 Removing the headlamp bulb (1.3 HLS)

9 Unscrew the four mounting nuts, one of which is located under the front wing **(see illustration)**. Remove the washers.

10 Withdraw the headlamp unit from the front of the car **(see illustration)**.

Refitting

11 Refitting is a reversal of removal, but make sure that the lug on the bulb flange engages with the notch on the reflector, and adjust the headlamp alignment as described in Section 13.

12 Do not touch the bulb glass; if touched, clean it with methylated spirit.

12 Lamp bulbs - renewal

Note: *Lamp bulbs should always be renewed with ones of similar type and rating as listed in the Specifications.*

Sidelamps and front indicator lamps

Metro and Metro L models

1 Remove the lens from the front bumper (2 screws) **(see illustration)**.

2 Push and twist the bulbs to remove them.

Metro HLE, 1.3 S, and 1.3 HLS models

3 To remove the sidelamp bulb, pull back the rubber cover and pull out the bulb holder **(see illustration)**. Push and twist the bulb or pull it straight out (as applicable) to remove it.

4 To remove the indicator bulb, pull back the rubber cover and turn the bulb holder anti-clockwise from the headlamp reflector. Push and twist the bulb to remove it **(see illustration)**.

Side repeater lamp

5 Reach up under the front wing, and pull the bulb holder from the lamp body.

6 A wedge type bulb is fitted; pull it straight from the bulb holder.

7 When refitting the bulb holder, support the lamp body and lens from the outside. If the lamp body is displaced, use adhesive to stick it to the wing **(see illustration)**.

11.9 Removing the headlamp retaining nuts (1.3 HLS)

11.10 Removing the headlamp unit (1.3 HLS)

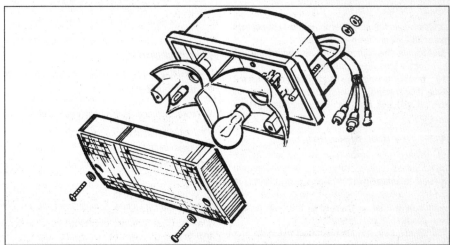

12.1 Sidelamp and front indicator lamp components for Metro and Metro L models

12.3 Removing the front sidelamp bulb holder (1.3 HLS)

12.4 Removing the front direction indicator bulb (1.3 HLS)

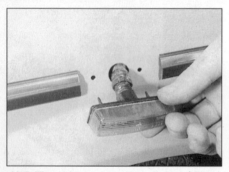

12.7 The side repeater lamp being refitted with adhesive

12.8 Removing the rear lamp cluster air vent

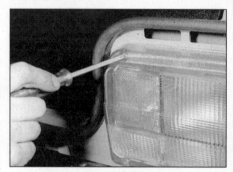

12.9a Removing the screws . . .

12.9b . . . and rear lamp lens

12.10 Removing a stop light bulb

12.11 Rear number plate lamp

Rear lamp cluster

8 Open the tailgate. Remove the two screws and the air vent **(see illustration)**.

9 Remove the four screws and withdraw the lamp lens **(see illustrations)**.

10 Push and twist the faulty bulb to remove it **(see illustration)**. Note that the stop/tail bulb has offset pins and can only be fitted in one position.

Rear number plate lamp

11 Where twin lamps (secured by screws) are fitted, press and twist the lamp lens to remove it **(see illustration)**. Where a single lamp is fitted, squeeze together the grips and withdraw the lamp, then twist the bulb holder anti-clockwise to release it.

12 Where twin lamps are fitted the bulb is a wedge type; pull it straight from the bulb holder **(see illustration)**. Where the single

lamp is fitted, press in the bulb and twist it anti-clockwise to remove it from the bulb holder.

Rear foglamp

13 Remove the two screws and withdraw the lens **(see illustration)**.

14 Push and twist the bulb to remove it.

15 Note that the lens is tapered; the narrow end must face the side of the car.

Interior lamp

16 Prise the lamp from the roof **(see illustration)**.

17 Where the lamp is part of the clock, prise the bulb from its clips; where the bulb only is fitted, press it in and twist it anti-clockwise to release it.

18 Do not trap the wires when refitting the lamp.

Switch illumination

19 Disconnect the battery negative lead.

20 Remove the switch panel, (Section 7).

21 Remove the bulb holder from the switch. A wedge type bulb is fitted; pull it straight from the bulb holder.

Instrument panel warning lamps

22 Remove the instrument panel as described in Section 14.

23 Twist the relevant bulb holder anti-clockwise and remove it.

24 A wedge type bulb is fitted; pull it straight from the bulb holder.

Ignition warning light bulb wattage

25 The wattage of the ignition warning light bulb has been increased from 1.2W to 2W on later models. This has the effect of lowering

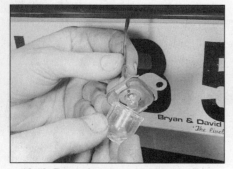

12.12 Removing the rear number plate lamp lens (lamp removed for clarity)

12.13 Removing the rear foglamp lens

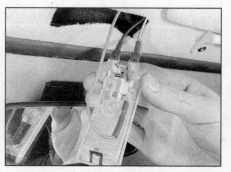

12.16 Interior lamp

the engine speed at which the warning light goes out (alternator cut-in speed).

26 If it is wished to lower the alternator cut-in speed on earlier models, a 2W bulb may be substituted for the existing one.

Luggage area/loadspace, glovebox and footwell lamps

27 On Van models, squeeze together its sides and unclip the loadspace lamp lens to reach the bulb; on all other types gently prise the lamp from its location (having first removed any retaining screws).

28 The bulb is a festoon type; prise it out of its clips.

Heater control illumination bulb - removal and refitting

29 Carefully work the heater control lamp free of its retainer.

30 Separate the bulbholder from the lens and extract the bulb from the holder **(see illustration)**.

31 Fit a new bulb and reassemble the lamp, then press it back into position.

Automatic transmission selector illumination bulb - removal and refitting

32 Unscrew the gear selector knob and lift the cover off the selector.

33 Remove the selector slide to expose the bulbholder **(see illustration)**.

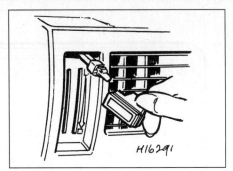

12.30 Heater control illumination bulb

34 Pull the bulb out of the holder and press in a new one.

35 Reassemble the selector unit.

13 Headlamps - alignment

1 The headlamp alignment should be checked every 12 000 miles (20 000 km) or 12 months, whichever occurs first.

2 It is recommended that the alignment is carried out by a Rover dealer using modern beam setting equipment. However, in an emergency, the following procedure will provide an acceptable light pattern.

3 Position the car on a level surface with the ride heights correct, the car normally laden and the tyres correctly inflated, approximately 10 metres (33 feet) in front of, and at right-angles to, a wall or garage door.

4 Draw a horizontal line on the wall or door at headlamp centre height. Draw a vertical line corresponding to the centre line of the car, then measure off a point either side of this, on the horizontal line, corresponding with the headlamp centres.

5 Switch on the main beam and check that the areas of maximum illumination coincide with the headlamp centre marks on the wall. If not, turn the plastic knobs located on the rear of the headlamps; turn both knobs to raise or lower the beam, and one knob (either will do) to move the beam horizontally.

14 Instrument panel and instruments - removal and refitting

Note: *Later models may be fitted with instrument panels made by Veglia instead of by Smiths. The two makes can be distinguished without dismantling. The mileage recorder window edges are chamfered on the Smiths panel, but square on the Veglia panel. Instruments and components are not interchangeable between the two makes. It is therefore important to specify which is required if spare parts are needed. Because of the different internal design of its instruments, the Veglia panel is not fitted with a voltage stabiliser.*

Removal

Early models, except MG

1 Disconnect the battery negative lead.

2 Prise out the speedometer cable grommet from the bulkhead, and pull out the cable to release it from the speedometer head.

3 Remove the switch panel, described in Section 7. Pull the pivots from the supports and allow the panel to hang by its harness.

4 Unscrew the nuts securing the instrument panel housing to the facia. Withdraw the housing and at the same time disconnect the multi-plug connectors from the printed circuit board **(see illustrations)**.

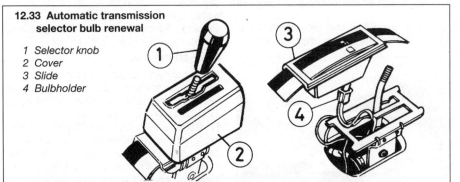

12.33 Automatic transmission selector bulb renewal

1 Selector knob
2 Cover
3 Slide
4 Bulbholder

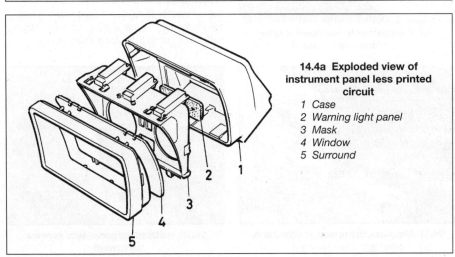

14.4a Exploded view of instrument panel less printed circuit

1 Case
2 Warning light panel
3 Mask
4 Window
5 Surround

14.4b Disconnecting the instrument panel multi-plugs

12

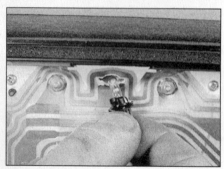

14.5a Removing a bulb holder from the instrument panel - early model

5 From the rear of the housing, twist the three upper bulb holders, anti-clockwise and remove them (see illustrations).

6 Remove the screws securing the three instrument panel sections, noting that the centre section screws are shorter (see illustration).

7 Carefully withdraw the instrument panel sections and printed circuit, taking care not to damage the latter (see illustration).

8 Each individual instrument can now be removed by removing the nuts or screws securing it to the panel. On 1.3 models, the digital clock can be removed from the tachometer by loosening the dial screws and withdrawing the clock reset control. If necessary, remove the front panel (see illustration).

Pre-1985 MG Turbo models

9 Remove the instrument panel (as from paragraph 1 to 4, this section).

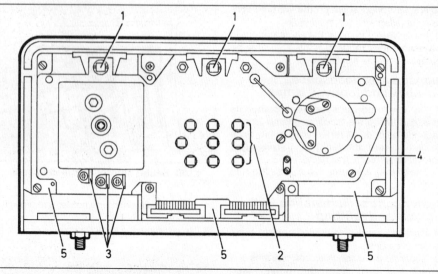

14.5b Rear view of the instrument panel - early model

1 Panel illumination lamps
2 Warning lamps
3 Voltage stabilizer connections
4 Printed circuit
5 Instrument panel sections

10 Undo the securing screws to release the instrument cluster from its housing. Release the clips to separate the instruments from the lens unit. *Do not touch the instrument faces with the fingers.*

11 If it is wished to remove the temperature gauge, the speedometer must be removed first.

12 When removing the tachometer, first release it from the casing, then extract the boost gauge and unplug the printed circuit.

13 If it is wished to remove the fuel gauge, the tachometer must first be removed as described above.

14 With all the instruments removed, the printed circuit may be renewed if wished, as described in Section 15.

Note: *The higher wattage of the ignition warning light bulb - this should be distinguished by having a red holder.*

1985-on models

15 Disconnect the battery negative lead.

16 Remove the switch panel, as described in Section 7, sufficiently to disconnect the wiring multi-plugs. Remove the panel.

17 Remove the air cleaner (Chapter 4), then prise out the speedometer cable grommet. Disconnect the cable by pulling it from the speedometer. If the cable is tight, remove the fusebox cover, reach up behind the instrument panel and squeeze the outside of the connector to release it (see illustration).

18 Remove the remaining screws, taking care not to drop them (see illustration).

14.6 Removing an instrument panel section screw - early model

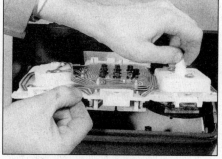

14.7 Removing the instrument panel sections - early model

14.8 Removing the instrument panel front

14.17 Squeeze the speedometer cable connector to release it

14.18 Instrument panel side screws (arrowed)

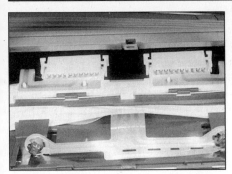

14.19a Disconnecting the multi-plugs

14.19b Removing the instrument panel

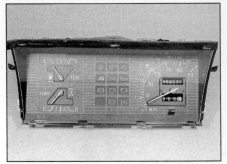

14.19c Front view of the 1985-on instrument panel

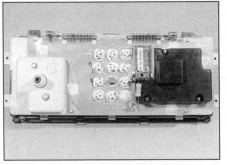

14.19d Rear view of the 1985-on instrument panel

14.20a Removing a panel light bulb

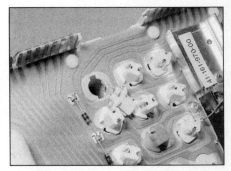

14.20b Removing a warning light bulb

19 Move the panel down and rotate it to release it from the facia. Disconnect the wiring multi-plugs and withdraw the instrument panel through the steering wheel **(see illustrations)**.

20 The warning and illumination bulbs may be removed by twisting the bulbholder anti-clockwise, but note that the "no-charge" bulb in the red bulbholder is the only bulb which can be separated from its holder **(see illustrations)**.

21 The multi-function unit incorporating the fuel and temperature gauges may be removed after withdrawing the cover (3 nuts) and unit retaining nuts **(see illustration)**.

22 To remove the printed circuit, first remove all the bulbs and the multi-function unit. Peel off the tape and remove the connector pegs.

23 To remove the speedometer head, remove the illumination bulb holders and the tape from the printed circuit. Free the wires

and remove the shroud and window assembly. Release the face plate from the case and remove the trip reset control. Remove the screws and withdraw the speedometer head.

24 Removal of the tachometer is similar to the procedure for the speedometer head, but the fuel and temperature gauges must first be removed.

Refitting

25 Refitting is a reversal of removal, but make sure that the reset controls, where fitted, pass through the holes in the instrument panel window. When fitting the multifunction unit, if applicable, tighten the nuts evenly to ensure good contact with the printed circuit.

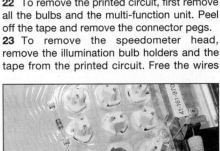

14.20c Removing the "no-charge" warning light bulb

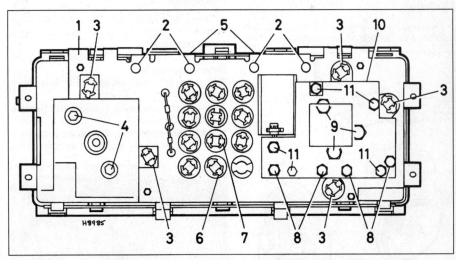

14.21 Component location on the instrument panel fitted to 1985-on models

1 Printed circuit
2 Retaining pegs
3 Illumination bulbs
4 Speedometer head screws
5 Multi-plug connectors
6 Warning light bulbs
7 No-charge warning light bulb
8 Fuel and temperature gauge nuts
9 Tachometer nuts
10 Multi-function unit
11 Multi-function unit nuts

12

15.3 Extracting the voltage stabilizer

16.5 Removing the cigar lighter

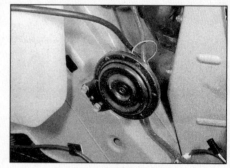

17.1 Horn location

15 Instrument panel printed circuit and voltage stabilizer - removal and refitting

Removal

1 Remove the instrument panel as described in Section 14.
2 Remove all the bulb holders from the rear of the housing.
3 Pull the voltage stabilizer from the blade connectors (see illustration).
4 Remove the cross-head screws and withdraw the blade connectors from the printed circuit.
5 Unscrew the retaining nuts and prise out the plastic retainers from the printed circuit.
6 Where a digital clock is fitted in the base of the tachometer, remove the brass screw, lift the printed circuit, then refit the screw to retain the clock.
7 Remove the remaining screws and withdraw the printed circuit.

Refitting

8 Refitting is a reversal of removal, with reference to Section 14 as necessary.

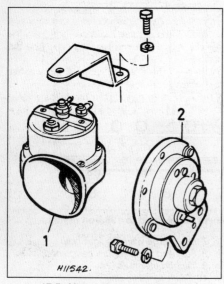

H11542.

17.5 Alternative types of horn
1 Mixo   2 Lucas

16 Cigar lighter - removal and refitting

Removal

1 Disconnect the battery negative lead.
2 If a radio is fitted, disconnect the supply and earth leads, and the aerial. Remove the rear mounting bolt and two side screws, and place the radio to one side.
3 Remove the cigar lighter button.
4 Pull the supply wire from the cigar lighter terminal.
5 Unscrew and remove the cigar lighter and earth lead (see illustration).

Refitting

6 Refitting is a reversal of removal.

17 Horn - removal and refitting

Removal

1 The single-note horn is located in the engine compartment on the left-hand side (see illustration).
2 To remove the horn, first disconnect the battery negative lead.
3 Disconnect the wires from the horn terminals.
4 Unbolt the mounting bracket and remove the horn.
5 If the horn emits an unsatisfactory sound, it may be possible to adjust it, assuming the

18.3 Removing the speedometer cable from the head

internal circuit and contact points are in good condition. The adjustment is best made with the horn mounted on the car. Turn the hexagon head (Mixo type) or screw (Lucas type) until the best sound is achieved (see illustration).

Refitting

6 Refitting is a reversal of removal.

18 Speedometer cable - removal and refitting

Removal

1 Prise the speedometer cable grommet from the engine compartment side of the bulkhead.
2 On 1985-on models, the fusebox cover and if necessary, the air cleaner.
3 Pull the cable straight out of the bulkhead to release it from the speedometer head (see illustration).
4 Unclip the cable from the swivel clip.
5 Remove the windscreen washer bottle and place it to one side.
6 Unscrew the knurled nut and pull the cable from the pinion housing on the left-hand side of the gearbox.
7 Withdraw the speedometer cable, and if necessary remove the inner cable and grommet. If either the inner or outer cable is damaged or worn, renew the complete assembly.

Refitting

8 Refitting is a reversal of removal.

19 Wiper blades - renewal

1 The wiper blades should be removed when they no longer clean the windscreen or tailgate window effectively.
2 Lift the wiper arm away from the windscreen or tailgate window.
3 Lift the spring retainer, then separate the blade from the wiper arm (see illustration).
4 Insert the new blade into the arm and make sure that the spring retainer is engaged correctly.

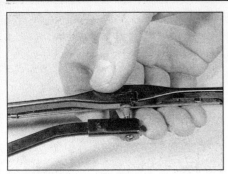

19.3 Disconnecting the windscreen wiper blade

20 Windscreen wiper motor - removal and refitting

Removal

1 Disconnect the battery negative lead.
2 Remove the air cleaner (Chapter 4).
3 Extract the clip from the linkage pivot on the motor crank lever.
4 Remove the bushes, washer and links from the crankpin.
5 Unscrew the nut and remove the washer and crank lever from the motor spindle.
6 Unscrew the motor mounting screws and disconnect the wiring multi-plug.
7 Disconnect the earth lead and withdraw the wiper motor.

Refitting

8 Refitting is a reversal of removal, but before fitting the crank lever, temporarily reconnect

the battery and switch on the ignition (wiper switch "off") to set the motor in the "parked" position. Fit the crank lever horizontally and facing the driver's side of the car. Lubricate the linkage bushes, crankpin and linkages with a molybdenum disulphide based grease.

21 Windscreen wiper linkage - removal, overhaul and refitting

Removal

1 Disconnect the battery negative lead.
2 Remove the air cleaner (Chapter 4).
3 Lift the hinged covers on the wiper arms and unscrew the nuts **(see illustration)**. Prise the wiper arms from the spindles with a screwdriver.
4 From each pivot housing, unscrew the nut and remove the washer and spacer.
5 Disconnect the wiring multi-plug and the earth lead.
6 Slide the rubber mounting from the bottom of the bracket, noting which slot engages the bracket.
7 Remove the wiper motor and linkage together from the car.

Overhaul

8 Extract the clips from the crankpin and pivot arms, and remove the links, bushes and washers, noting their relative positions.
9 Remove the wiper motor as described in Section 20.
10 Remove the bottom spacers from the pivot housings, drill out the rivets, and remove the housings from the bracket.

21.3 Unscrewing the wiper arm spindle nut

11 Press the bushes out of the links.
12 Examine the bushes and pivot housings for wear, and if worn excessively, obtain a kit of bushes and clips.

Refitting

13 Refitting is a reversal of removal, but note the following additional points:
a) *Lubricate the pivots and bushes with a molybdenum disulphide based grease.*
b) *Press the bushes into the links in the direction as shown* **(see illustration)**, *note that the rounded ends of the links must face outwards.*
c) *Fit the pivot housings (with the longer lever to the driver's side of the bracket), using new rivets.*
d) *Tighten the pivot housing nuts to 11.5 lbf ft (17Nm).*
e) *With the motor in the parked-position, fit the wiper arms to the spindles so that the blades are parallel to the lower edge of the windscreen.*

22 Tailgate wiper motor and gearbox - removal and refitting

Removal

1 Disconnect the battery negative lead.
2 Lift the hinged cover on the wiper arm and unscrew the nut. Prise the wiper arm from the spindle with a screwdriver, together with the spacer.
3 Unscrew the nut and remove the washer and spacer from the motor spindle.
4 Prise the trim panel from the tailgate inner panel using a wide-bladed screwdriver **(see illustration)**.

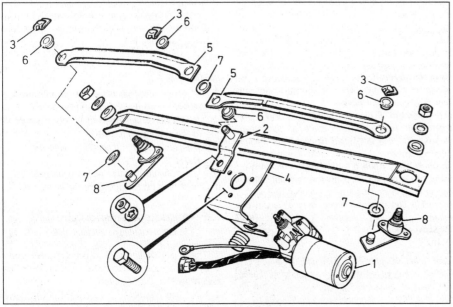

21.13 Windscreen wiper motor and linkage

1 Wiper motor	5 Link
2 Crank lever	6 Bush
3 Clip	7 Washer
4 Mounting bracket	8 Pivot housing

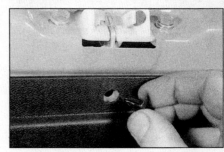

22.4 Removing a tailgate trim panel fastener

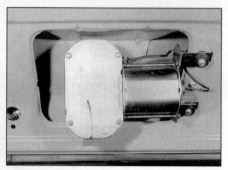

22.6 Tailgate wiper motor and gearbox

5 Disconnect the earth lead and the wiring multi-plug.

6 Remove the mounting bracket screws, and withdraw the wiper motor and gearbox **(see illustration)**.

7 Note the location of the wires in the multi-plug, then depress the tags and remove the pins.

8 Remove the insulating sleeve, and detach the pins from the wires.

9 Unscrew the through-bolts and withdraw the motor from the gearbox.

10 The motor and gearbox can be renewed separately if necessary.

Refitting

11 Reassembly and refitting are a reversal of the removal procedure, but note the following additional points:

a) *Make sure that the lug on the motor is engaged with the notch on the gearbox* **(see illustration)**.

b) *Adjust the armature endfloat by loosening the locknut on the gearbox, turning the screw to eliminate the endfloat, then loosening the screw very slightly to give a small endfloat. Tighten the locknut.*

c) *Before fitting the wiper arm, switch on the ignition and operate the motor to set the spindle in the "parked" position. Fit the wiper arm to the spindle so that the blade is parallel to the lower edge of the tailgate window.*

d) *Note that the tailgate washer bottle and motor are located on the left-hand rear inner panel* **(see illustration)**.

22.11b Tailgate washer bottle and motor

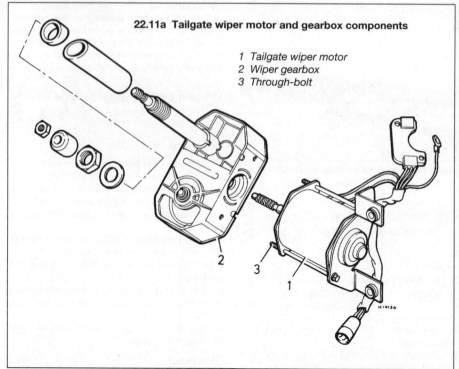

22.11a Tailgate wiper motor and gearbox components

1 *Tailgate wiper motor*
2 *Wiper gearbox*
3 *Through-bolt*

23 Windscreen and tailgate window washers - general

1 On all MG Turbo models, a combined reservoir is mounted in the left-hand rear of the luggage compartment, with two remote pumps located on the inner panel. The two identical pumps are connected to a single tube leading from the reservoir, and incorporate non-return valves in the outlet tubes to the windscreen and tailgate window.

2 For non-Turbo models, separate reservoirs for the windscreen and tailgate window are fitted to early models, being located on the left-hand front of the engine compartment and the left-hand rear of the luggage compartment. From VIN 556719, models with front and rear washers have a combined reservoir in the left-hand front of the engine compartment. Models with windscreen washers only have a single reservoir with an integral pump, located on the left-hand front of the engine compartment (except MG Turbo models). The integral pump is retained in the reservoir by a rubber grommet **(see illustration)**.

24 Screen washer pumps (MG Turbo models) - removal and refitting

Removal

1 Both the windscreen and the tailgate washer pumps are located at the rear of MG Turbo models, and they share a common reservoir **(see illustration)**.

2 Open the tailgate, remove the washer reservoir and release the left-hand quarter trim.

3 Identify the pump to be removed. (The windscreen washer feed tube is blue). Unscrew the pump mounting screws and disconnect the tubes and wires from the pump. Be prepared for some fluid spillage.

4 Release the pump bracket from the mounting rubber, but do not remove the bracket from the pump. The pump cannot be overhauled, and should be renewed if defective.

Refitting

5 Refitting is a reversal of the removal procedure. Note the following points:

a) *A new pump will need to be pop-riveted to the mounting rubber.*

b) *The pump inlet is marked "-" and the outlet "+".*

c) *The non-return valve outlet is marked "-".*

6 Check for correct operation on completion.

25 Windscreen washer tube (MG Turbo models) - removal and refitting

Removal

1 Open the tailgate and release the left-hand quarter trim.

2 Disconnect the windscreen washer tube (the blue one) from the non-return valve.

3 Secure a length of stout string to the tube, using sticky tape or some similar means. The string must be longer than the tube.

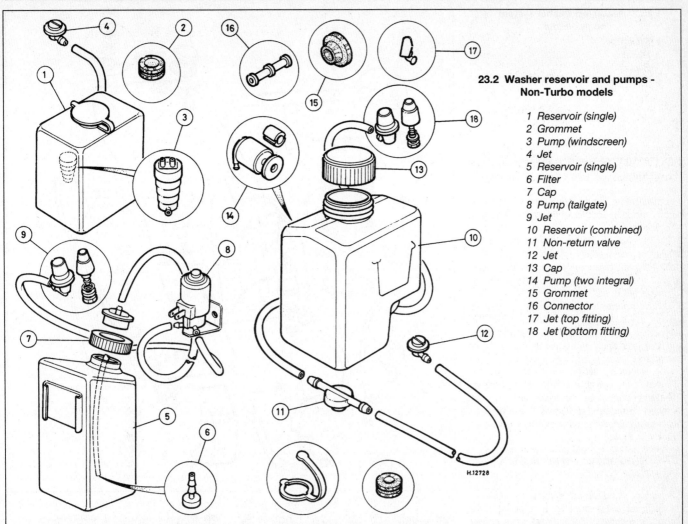

23.2 Washer reservoir and pumps -
Non-Turbo models

1 Reservoir (single)
2 Grommet
3 Pump (windscreen)
4 Jet
5 Reservoir (single)
6 Filter
7 Cap
8 Pump (tailgate)
9 Jet
10 Reservoir (combined)
11 Non-return valve
12 Jet
13 Cap
14 Pump (two integral)
15 Grommet
16 Connector
17 Jet (top fitting)
18 Jet (bottom fitting)

H.12728

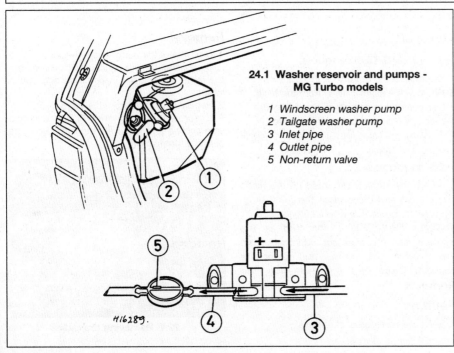

24.1 Washer reservoir and pumps -
MG Turbo models

1 Windscreen washer pump
2 Tailgate washer pump
3 Inlet pipe
4 Outlet pipe
5 Non-return valve

H16289.

4 Open the bonnet and extract the windscreen washer jet. Disconnect the tube from the jet and from any clips. Disconnect the battery earth lead.

5 Partially withdraw the facia, as described in Chapter 11, to gain access to the aperture in the left-hand front pillar. Pull the tube through from the engine compartment, then pull the other end of the tube (with string attached) through from the rear of the car.

6 Remove the string from the old tube and secure it to the new tube. Carefully draw the new tube through from the front to the back of the car.

7 Remove the string and connect the tube to the non-return valve.

8 Feed the tube into the engine compartment, refitting the grommet if this has become displaced. Connect the tube to the jet and engage any clips.

Refitting

9 Refit the disturbed trim, reconnect the battery and check the windscreen washer for correct operation. Remember that it will take a second or two for the pump to fill the new tube.

12

26.3 Headlamp washer system components

1 Reservoir
2 Pump
3 Relay
4 Overrider with jet

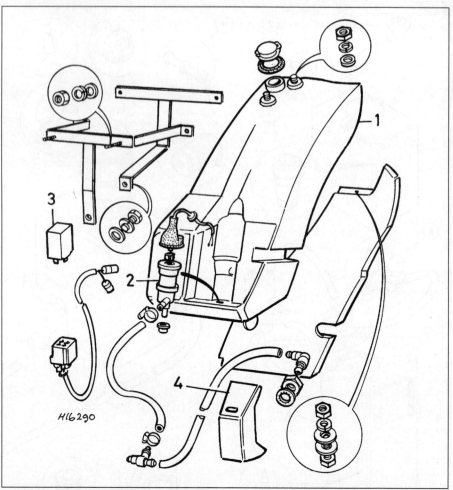

26 Headlamp washer system - general

1 A headlamp washer system is fitted to certain models, according to territory and trim level specified.
2 The system is similar in principle to the familiar screen washer systems, but a relay is included in the headlamp washer pump circuit so that the pump does not operate when the lights are not in use.
3 The components of the headlamp washer system are as shown **(see illustration)**. The reservoir is mounted under the left-hand wing, and the jets are positioned in the bumper overriders.
4 No specific dismantling or overhaul information is available at the time of writing. The pump cannot be repaired, and must be renewed complete if defective. It is a push fit into a grommet at the base of the reservoir.

27 Trip computer - general

1 A factory-fitted trip computer is available as an optional extra on certain models. The computer receives information from a speed transducer in the speedometer cable and from a fuel flow transducer in the fuel supply line. From these data and from its internal clock, the computer is able to display information relating to journey time, average speed, average and instantaneous fuel consumption and distance covered.
2 Very little is possible for the home mechanic by way of testing or repair of the computer and its transducers. In the event of malfunction, check first that all electrical connections are secure and that the battery is fully charged.
3 A faulty speed transducer (or speedometer cable) can be deduced if the trip computer fails to display distance (DIST) information. Obviously this will also affect the fuel consumption (INST and AVE) functions, but so will a faulty fuel transducer.
4 A faulty fuel transducer can be deduced if the fuel used (FUEL) information is grossly incorrect.
5 Testing of suspect transducers. or of the computer itself, is by substitution of a known good unit. No repair is possible.

28 Clock - removal and refitting

Removal

Pre-1985 MG Turbo models

1 Disconnect the battery earth lead.
2 Remove the ashtray away from the facia.
3 Carefully prise the clock mounting out of the facia and disconnect the multi-plug.
4 Press the retaining lugs to release the clock from its mountings.

1985-on models

5 Where the clock is mounted on the facia, prise it out and disconnect the multi-plug. Reverse the procedure when refitting.
6 Where the clock is mounted in the overhead console, prise out the interior lamp then remove the screws and lower the console. Disconnect the multi-plug and remove the clock.

Refitting

7 Refitting is a reversal of removal.

29 Radio - removal and refitting

Removal

1 Disconnect the battery negative lead.
2 Disconnect the supply and earth wires from the radio, leaving the in-line fuse and choke intact.
3 Remove the aerial from the radio.
4 Unscrew the rear mounting bolt and two side screws and withdraw the radio from the car **(see illustration)**.

29.4 Removing the radio

5 Using a small hooked instrument (a length of welding rod will do), pull out the bottom of the radio grille and remove it.

6 Remove the cross-head screws and withdraw the speaker and wiring from the facia.

7 If necessary, remove the radio earth wire from the speaker compartment.

Refitting

8 Refitting is a reversal of removal.

---

30 Radio/cassette player (electronic) - removal and refitting

Note: *The radio/cassette player is retained with DIN clips and it is necessary to make a tool using dowel rod, but the ends of the rods must be shaped to contact the clips.*

Removal

1 Disconnect the battery negative lead. If the unit has a security code, temporarily de-activate the code and re-activate it when the battery is re-connected; refer to the instructions and code supplied with the unit.

2 Prise the plastic covers from each side of the unit (**see illustration**).

3 Insert the special tool rods into the holes until they engage the clips (**see illustration**).

4 Press the ends of the rods outwards so that the clips are compressed, then pull out the unit from the facia.

5 Disconnect the multi-plug and aerial and remove the tool rods.

Refitting

6 Refitting is a reversal of removal, but make sure that the rubber support pads are in place before pushing the unit into the facia until the clips are engaged.

---

31 Central locking door lock motor - removal and refitting

Removal

1 Disconnect the battery negative lead.

2 Remove the trim pad and, except for on the tailgate, peel off the polythene sheet.

3 Disconnect the wiring multi-plug(s) to the motor.

4 On the tailgate, remove the mounting bracket screws, unclip the mounting bracket from the private lock and unclip the operating rod from the lock lever. Remove the private lock then remove the mounting bracket and motor, and unbolt the motor.

5 On the front or rear door, unbolt the motor and disconnect the operating rod.

Refitting

6 Refitting is a reversal of removal.

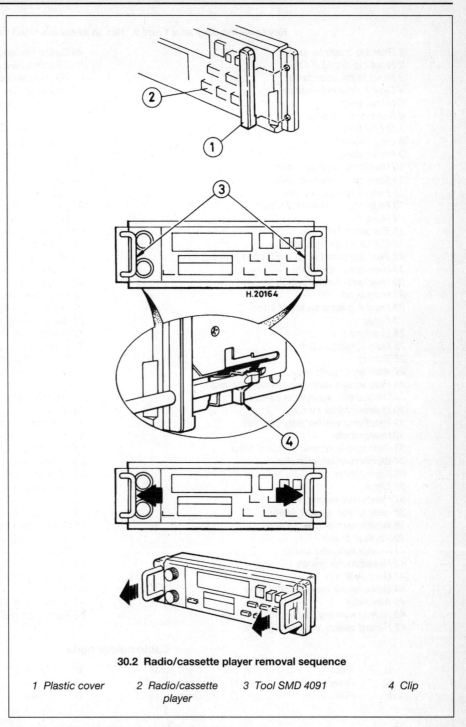

30.2 Radio/cassette player removal sequence

| 1 Plastic cover | 2 Radio/cassette player | 3 Tool SMD 4091 | 4 Clip |

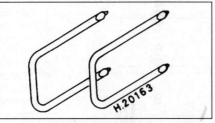

30.3 Tool SMD 4091 for removal of the radio/cassette player

12

Key to wiring diagrams 1 and 2. Not all items are fitted to all models

1 Rear fog guard lamps
2 Front fog lamps (if fitted)
3 Panel illumination lamp
4 Cigar lighter illumination
5 LH tail lamp
6 Number plate lamp
7 RH tail lamp
8 LH sidelamp
9 RH sidelamp
10 Headlamp dipped beams
11 Main beam warning lamp
12 Headlamp main beams
13 Front fog lamp relay (if fitted)
14 Horn
15 Starter motor
16 Starter motor solenoid
17 Rear fog guard lamp switch and warning light
19 Headlamp dipswitch
20 Headlamp flasher switch
21 Horn push
22 Front fog lamp switch (if fitted)
23 Fuses
24 Line fuses
25 Main lighting switch
26 Battery
27 Auxiliary circuits relay
28 Rear screen wash/wipe switch (if fitted)
29 Windscreen wash/wipe switch
30 Ignition/starter switch
31 Headlamp washer relay (if fitted)
32 Heater motor
33 Rear screen washer motor (if fitted)
34 Windscreen wiper motor
35 Cigar lighter
36 Clock
37 Headlamp washer motor
38 Rear screen washer motor
39 Windscreen washer motor
40 Radio (if fitted)
41 Interior light and switch
42 Heater motor switch
43 Door switches
44 Brake failure warning lamp relay
45 Alternator
46 Hazard warning flasher unit
47 Hazard switch and warning light

49 Ballast resistor cable
50 Direction indicator flasher unit
51 Heated rear screen switch and warning lamp
53 Brake fluid level sensor
54 Direction indicator switch
55 Brake failure warning light
56 Reversing lamp switch
57 Stop-lamp switch
58 Voltage stabilizer
59 Brake pad wear warning light
60 Ignition warning light
61 Tachometer (if fitted)
62 Ignition coil
63 Brake pad wear sensors
64 Choke warning light
65 Oil pressure warning light
66 Handbrake warning light
67 Seat belt warning light
68 Fuel gauge
69 Water temperature gauge
70 Induction heater and thermostat (if fitted)
71 Suction chamber heater (if fitted)
72 Direction indicator repeater lamps
73 RH front indicator lamp
74 RH rear indicator lamp
75 Indicator warning light
76 LH rear indicator lamp
77 LH front indicator lamp
78 Heated rear screen
79 Reversing lamps
80 Gearbox selector panel illumination (Automatics only)
81 Stop-lamps
82 Choke warning light switch
83 Oil pressure light switch
84 Handbrake warning light switch
85 Passenger seat switch
86 Passenger seat belt switch
87 Driver's seat belt switch
88 Fuel gauge tank unit
89 Water temperature transducer
90 Radiator cooling fan
91 Radiator cooling fan thermostat
92 Distributor
93 Heater control illumination
94 Panel switch illumination

Cable colour code

B	Black	LG	Light green	P	Purple	U	Blue
G	Green	N	Brown	R	Red	W	White
K	Pink	O	Orange	S	Slate	Y	Yellow

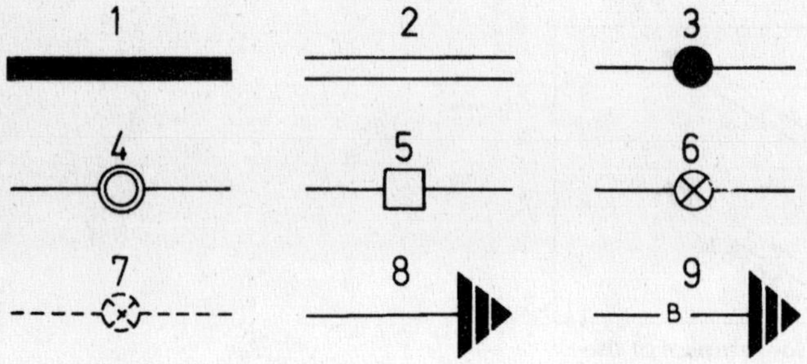

Symbols used in wiring diagrams

1 Fuse board printed circuit
2 Instrument printed circuit
3 Sealed joint
4 Instrument printed circuit connector
5 Fuse board printed circuit connector
6 Other connector
7 When fitted
8 Component earthed via mounting
9 Component earthed via cable

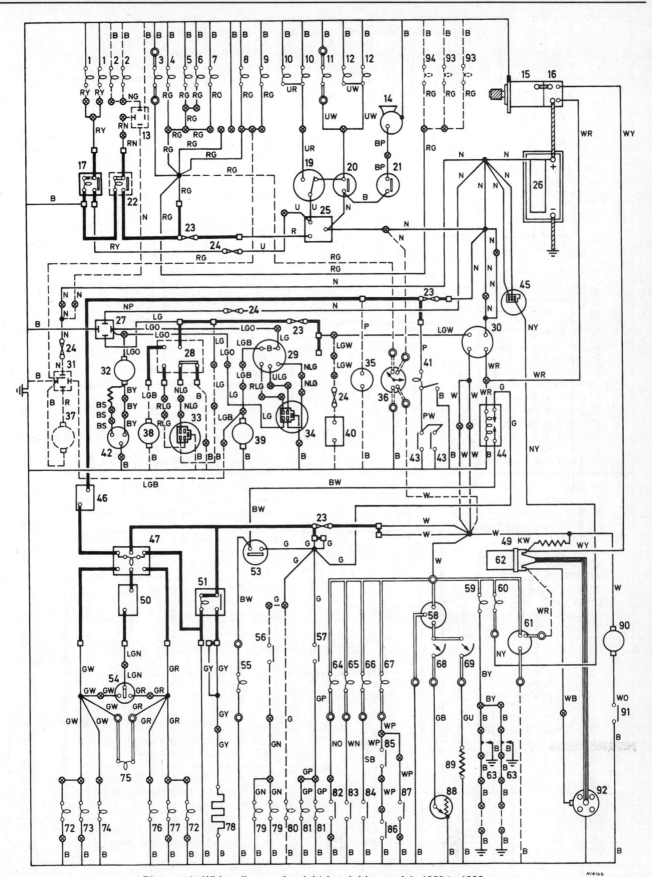

Diagram 1: Wiring diagram for right-hand drive models 1980 to 1982

WD

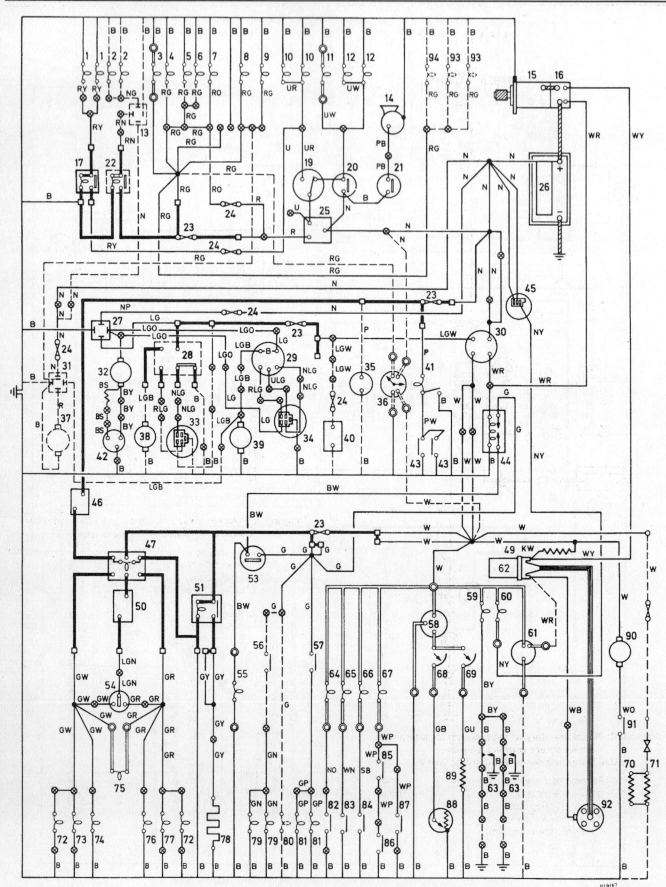

Diagram 2: Wiring diagram for left-hand drive models 1980 to 1983

H14167

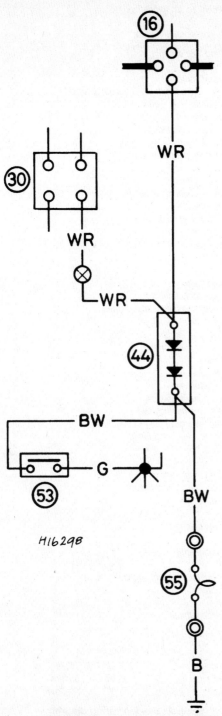

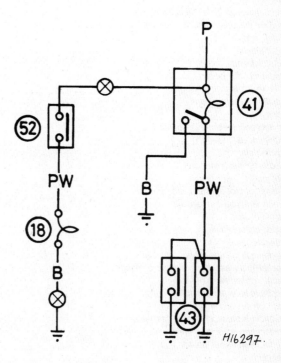

Diagram 4: Supplementary wiring diagram for load area light. Use in conjunction with Diagrams 1 or 2

18 Load area light
41 Passenger interior light and switch
43 Door switches
52 Load area light switch

Diagram 3: Supplementary wiring diagram for alternative brake failure warning system. Use in conjunction with Diagrams 1 or 2

16 Starter motor solenoid
30 Ignition/starter switch
44 Double blocking diode
53 Brake fluid level switch
55 Brake failure warning light

WD

Key to wiring diagrams 5 and 6. Not all items are fitted to all models

1 Rear foglamp(s)
2 Foglamps *
3 Cigar lighter illumination lamp
4 LH tail lamp
5 Rear foglamp switch and warning lamp
6 Foglamps switch and warning lamp*
7 Front foglamps relay *
8 Auxiliary circuits relay
9 Heater motor
10 Rear screen wash/wipe switch
11 Number plate illumination lamp(s)
12 RH tail lamp
13 LH sidelamp
14 R H sidelamp
15 Headlamp dip beam
16 Main beam warning lamp
17 Headlamp main beam
18 Horn(s)
19 Windscreen wash/wipe switch
20 Headlamp dip switch
21 Lighting switch
22 Headlamp flash switch
23 Horn push
24 Heater control illumination
25 Switch illumination lamp(s)
26 Starter motor
27 Starter solenoid
28 Battery
29 Headlamps washer relay
30 Headlamps wash high-pressure motor
31 Heater motor switch
32 Rear screen washer motor
33 Rear screen wiper motor
34 Direction indicator/hazard flasher unit
35 Windscreen washer motor
36 Windscreen wiper motor
37 Fuel pump
38 Fuel pump protection relay *
39 Radio or radio/cassette unit
40 Cigar lighter
41 Interior lamp(s)
42 Interior lamp door switch
43 Load space lamp switch
44 Load space lamp
45 Clock
46 Ignition/starter switch
47 Carburettor vent valve *

48 Double diode
49 Alternator
50 Hazard warning switch
51 Ballast resistor cable $
52 Direction indicator switch
53 Heated rear screen switch and warning lamp
54 Brake fluid level sensor switch
55 Direction indicator warning lamp
56 RH rear direction indicator lamp
57 Direction indicator repeater lamps
58 RH front direction indicator lamp
59 LH rear direction indicator lamp
60 Panel illumination lamp(s)
61 LH front direction indicator lamp
62 Heated rear screen
63 Brake failure warning lamp
64 Reverse lamp switch
65 Reverse lamp(s)
66 Stoplamp switch
67 Stoplamps
68 Choke warning lamp
69 Choke warning lamp switch
70 Oil pressure warning lamp or indicator
71 Oil pressure switch
72 Handbrake warning lamp
73 Handbrake warning lamp switch
74 Voltage stabiliser
75 Fuel level indicator
76 Fuel level indicator tank unit
77 Water temperature indicator
78 Water temperature transducer
79 Brake pad wear warning lamp
80 Ignition no charge warning lamp
81 Tachometer
82 Ignition coil
83 Radiator cooling fan motor
84 Radiator cooling fan thermostat
85 Ignition module *
86 Distributor
87 Brake pad wear sensor
88 Valve solenoid *
89 Electronic control unit *
90 Boost gauge *
91 Automatic gearbox selector indicator lamp
92 Anti-run-on valve
Aa Line fuses
Bb Fusebox printed circuit

$ Non-Turbo models   * Turbo models

Cable colour code

B	Black	LG	Light green	P	Purple	U	Blue
G	Green	N	Brown	R	Red	W	White
K	Pink	O	Orange	S	Slate	Y	Yellow

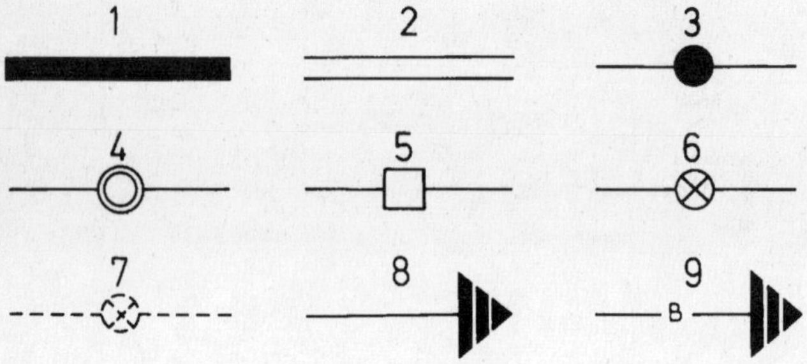

1
2
3
4
5
6
7
8
9

Symbols used in wiring diagrams

1 Fuse board printed circuit
2 Instrument printed circuit
3 Sealed joint
4 Instrument printed circuit connector
5 Fuse board printed circuit connector
6 Other connector
7 When fitted
8 Component earthed via mounting
9 Component earthed via cable

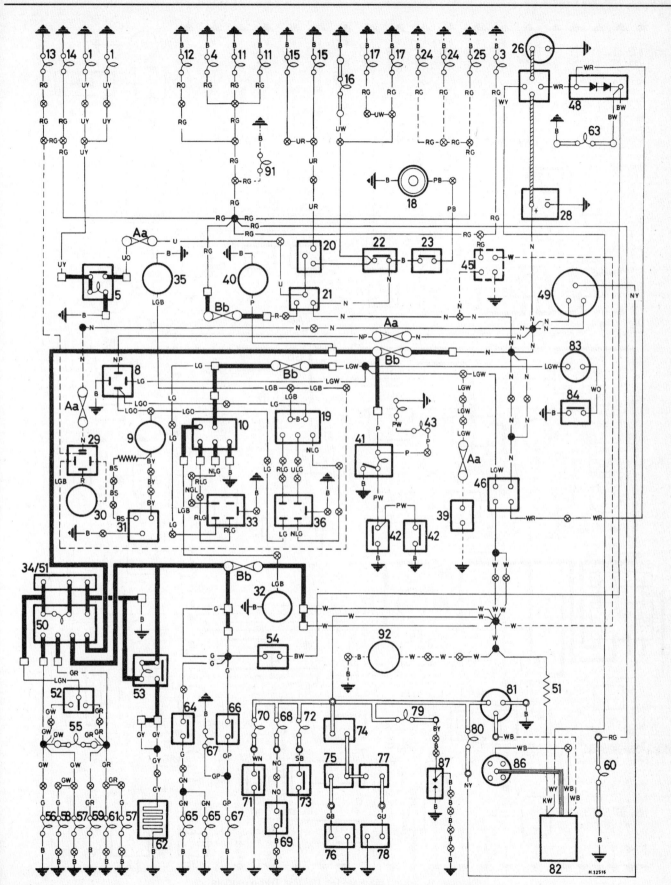

Diagram 5: Wiring diagram for 1983/84 models (except Turbo)

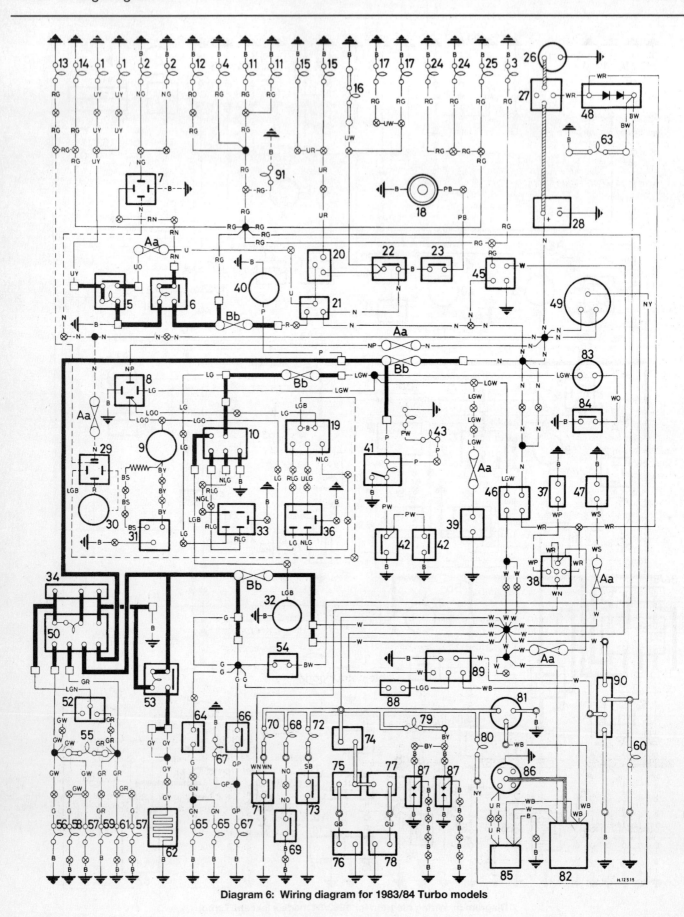

Diagram 6: Wiring diagram for 1983/84 Turbo models

Key to wiring diagrams 7 and 8. Not all items are fitted to all models

1 Alternator
3 Battery
4 Starter solenoid
5 Starter motor
6 Lighting switch
7 Headlamp dip switch
8 Headlamp dip beam
9 Headlamp main beam
11 RH side lamp
12 LH side lamp
15 Number plate illumination lamp(s)
16 Stop lamp(s)
17 RH tail lamp
18 Stop lamp switch
19 Fusebox
20 Interior lamp
21 Interior lamp door switch
22 LH tail lamp
23 Horn
24 Horn push
25 Direction indicator flasher unit
26 Direction indicator switch
28 RH front direction indicator lamp
29 LH front direction indicator lamp
30 RH rear direction indicator lamp
31 LH rear direction indicator lamp
32 Heater motor switch
33 Heater motor
35 Fuel level indicator tank unit
37 Windscreen wiper motor
38 Ignition/starter switch
39 Ignition coil
40 Distributor
41 Fuel pump *
42 Oil pressure switch
45 Headlamp flash switch
47 Water temperature transducer
49 Reverse lamp switch
50 Reverse lamp(s)
56 Clock $
57 Cigar lighter
60 Radio or radio cassette unit
76 Automatic gearbox selector indicator lamp $
77 Windscreen washer motor
82 Switch illumination lamp(s)
110 Direction indicator repeater lamps

115 Heated rear screen switch
116 Heated rear screen
118 Windscreen washer/wiper switch
150 Heated rear screen warning lamp
152 Hazard warning lamp
153 Hazard warning switch
165 Handbrake warning lamp switch
178 Radiator cooling fan thermostat
179 Radiator cooling fan motor
182 Brake fluid level switch
208 Cigar lighter illumination lamp
211 Heater control illumination
212 Choke warning lamp switch
216 Window lift switch
220 Window lift motor
231 Headlamp relay
240 Heated rear screen relay
246 Glovebox illumination lamp
247 Glovebox illumination switch
270 Rear screen wiper motor
271 Rear screen washer motor
286 Fog rearguard lamp switch
287 Fog rearguard warning lamp
288 Fog rearguard lamp(s)
296 Fuel pump relay *
298 Windscreen wiper delay
300 Ignition switch relay
314 Header console
326 Brake pad wear sensor
336 Speaker
342 Rear screen wiper switch
343 Rear screen wash switch
344 Door lock motor
345 Door lock control unit
347 Electronic control unit
349 Turbo boost gauge *
350 Control valve solenoid *
351 Load space lamp/switch
363 Carburettor vent valve
364 Window lift relay
389 Column switch illumination
396 Footwell illumination
397 Fusebox illumination
403 Auxiliary ignition relay
413 Fusible links
428 Mechanical instruments

$ Non-Turbo models   * Turbo models

Cable colour code

B	Black	LG	Light green	P	Purple	U	Blue
G	Green	N	Brown	R	Red	W	White
K	Pink	O	Orange	S	Slate	Y	Yellow

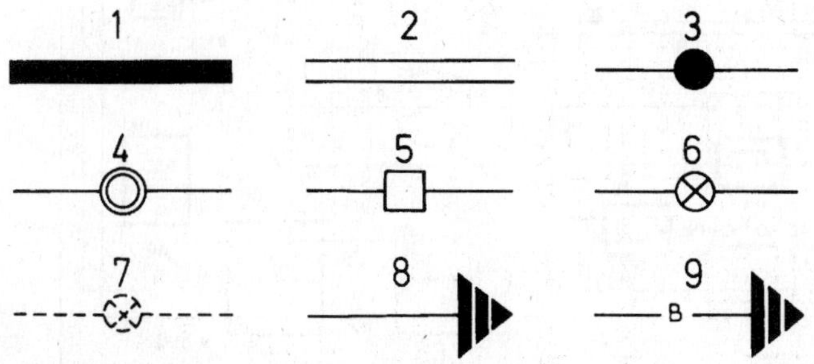

Symbols used in wiring diagrams

1 Fuse board printed circuit
2 Instrument printed circuit
3 Sealed joint
4 Instrument printed circuit connector
5 Fuse board printed circuit connector
6 Other connector
7 When fitted
8 Component earthed via mounting
9 Component earthed via cable

WD

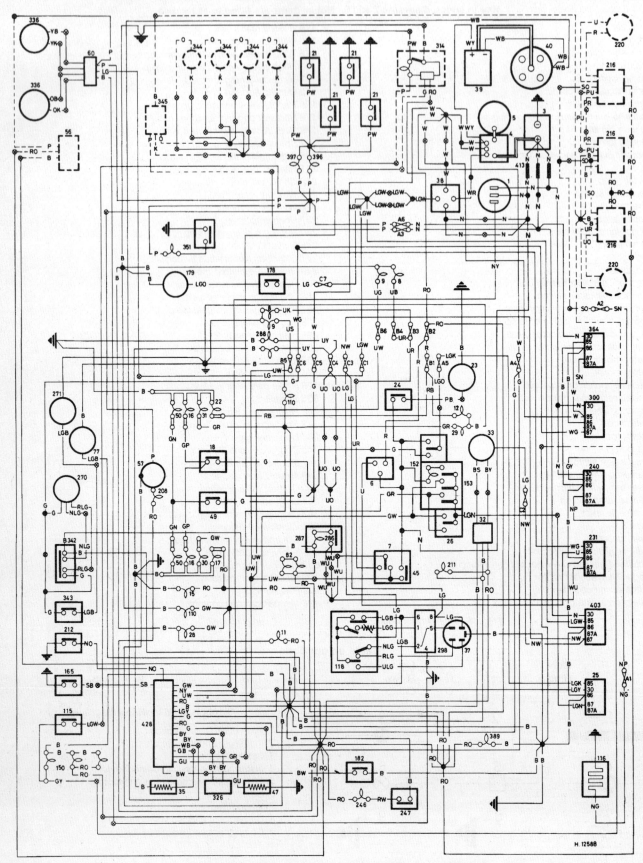

Diagram 7: Wiring diagram for 1985 models (except Turbo)

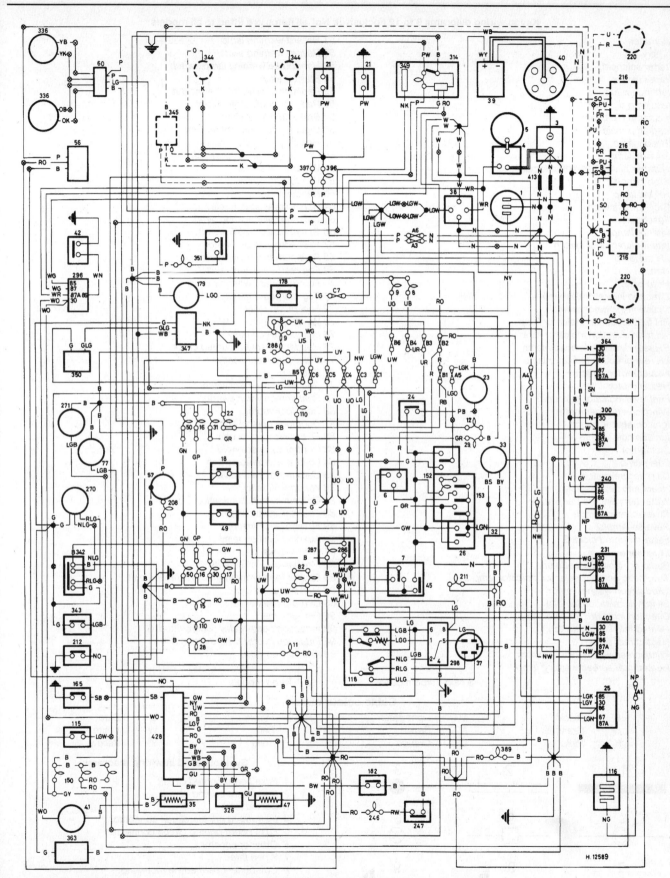

Diagram 8: Wiring diagram for 1985 Turbo models

WD

Key to wiring diagrams 9 to 12 (inclusive). Not all items are fitted to all models

1 Alternator
2 Battery
3 Starter solenoid
4 Starter motor
5 Lighting switch
6 Headlamp dip switch
7 Headlamp dip beam
8 Headlamp main beam
9 RH side lamp
10 LH side lamp
11 Number plate illumination lamp(s)
12 Stop-lamp(s)
13 RH tail lamp
14 Stop-lamp switch
15 Fusebox
16 Interior lamp
17 Interior lamp door switch
18 LH tail lamp
19 Horn
20 Horn push
21 Direction indicator flasher unit
22 Direction indicator switch
23 RH front direction indicator lamp
24 LH front direction indicator lamp
25 RH rear direction indicator lamp
26 LH rear direction indicator lamp
27 Heater motor switch
28 Heater motor
29 Fuel level indicator tank unit
30 Windscreen wiper motor
31 Ignition/starter switch
32 Ignition coil
33 Distributor
34 Fuel pump *
35 Oil pressure switch
36 Headlamp flash switch
37 Water temperature transducer
38 Reverse lamp switch
39 Reverse lamp(s)
40 Facia-mounted clock $
41 Cigar lighter
42 Radio or Radio/Cassette unit
43 Automatic gearbox selector indicator lamp $
44 Windscreen washer motor
45 Switch illumination lamp(s)
46 Direction indicator repeater lamps
47 Heated rear screen switch
48 Heated rear screen
49 Windscreen washer/wiper switch
50 Heated rear screen warning lamp

51 Hazard warning lamp
52 Hazard warning switch
53 Handbrake warning lamp switch
54 Starter relay
55 Radiator cooling fan thermostat
56 Radiator cooling fan motor
57 Brake fluid level switch
58 Cigar lighter illumination lamp
59 Heater control illumination
60 Choke warning lamp switch
61 Window lift switch
62 Window lift motor
63 Headlamp relay
64 Heated rear screen relay
65 Glovebox illumination lamp
66 Glovebox illumination switch
67 Rear screen wiper motor
68 Rear screen washer motor
69 Fog rearguard lamp switch
70 Fog rearguard warning lamp
71 Fog rearguard lamp(s)
72 Fuel pump relay *
73 Windscreen wiper delay
74 Ignition switch relay
75 Header console-mounted clock
76 Brake pad wear sensor
77 Speaker
78 Rear screen wiper switch
79 Rear screen wash switch
80 Door lock motor
81 Door lock control unit
82 Electronic control unit *
83 Control valve solenoid *
84 Load space lamp/switch
85 Carburettor vent valve *
86 Window lift relay
87 Column switch illumination
88 Footwell illumination
89 Fusebox illumination
90 Auxiliary ignition relay
91 Fusible links
92 Mechanical instruments
93 Rear screen programmed wash/wipe unit
94 Fuel pump resistor *
95 Dim-dip resistor
96 Dim-dip unit
97 Induction heater relay (where fitted) $
98 Induction heater (where fitted) $
99 Anti-run-on valve

$ Non-Turbo models   * Turbo models

Cable colour code

B	Black	LG	Light green	P	Purple	U	Blue
G	Green	N	Brown	R	Red	W	White
K	Pink	O	Orange	S	Slate	Y	Yellow

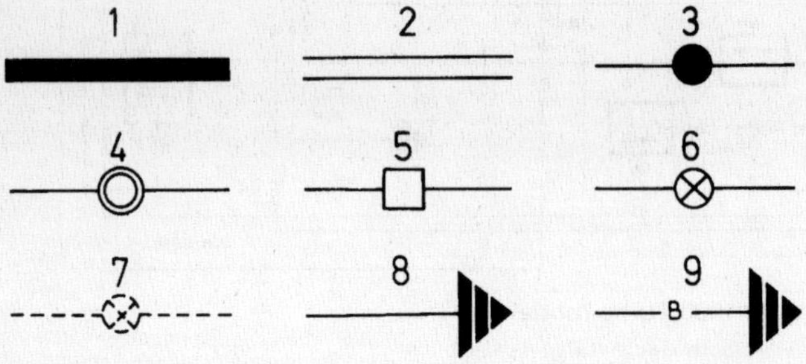

Symbols used in wiring diagrams

1 Fuse board printed circuit
2 Instrument printed circuit
3 Sealed joint
4 Instrument printed circuit connector
5 Fuse board printed circuit connector
6 Other connector
7 When fitted
8 Component earthed via mounting
9 Component earthed via cable

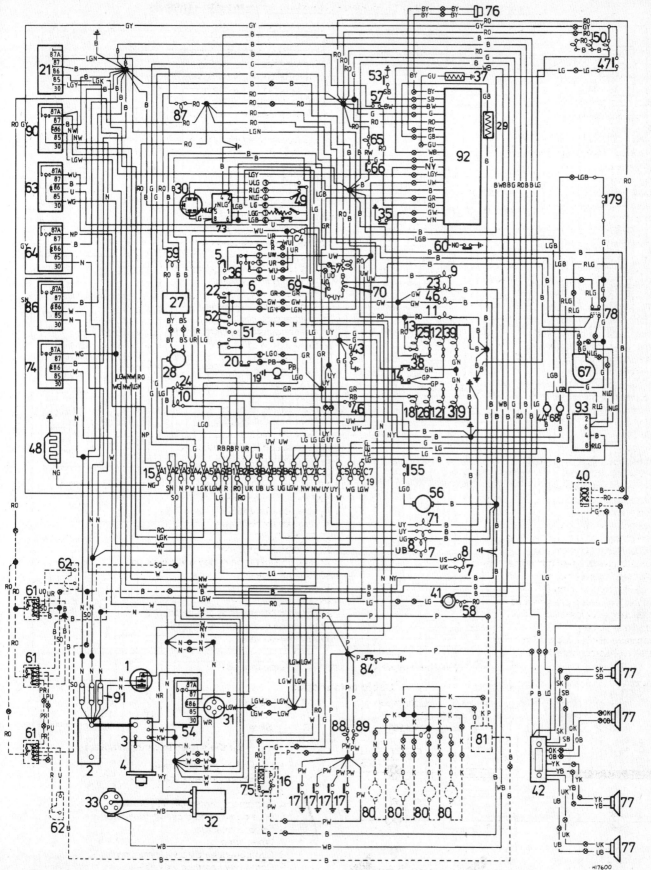

Diagram 9: Wiring diagram for 1986 models (except Turbo)

HI7600

WD

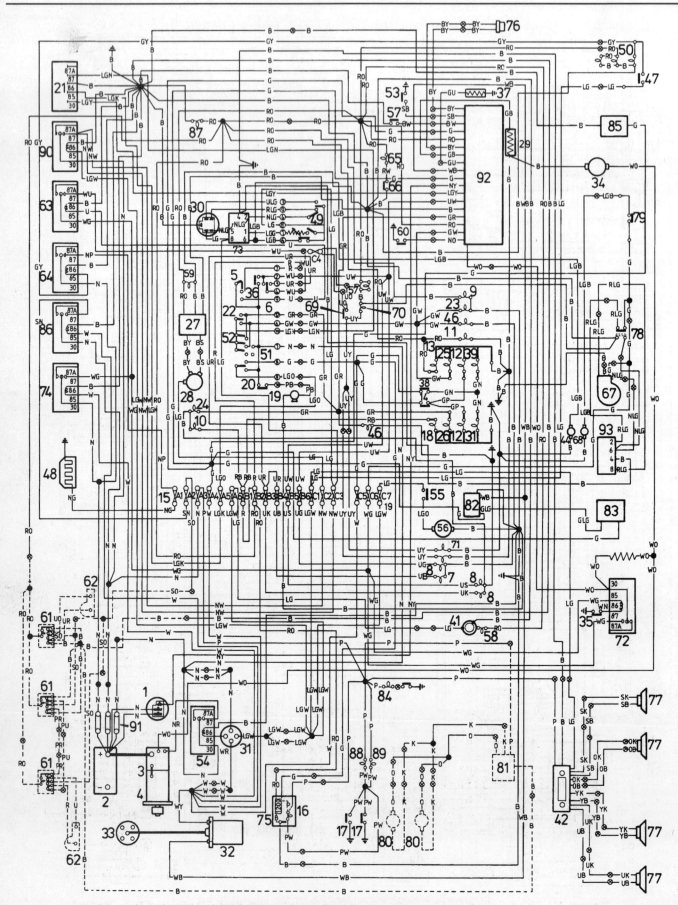

Diagram 10: Wiring diagram for 1986 Turbo models

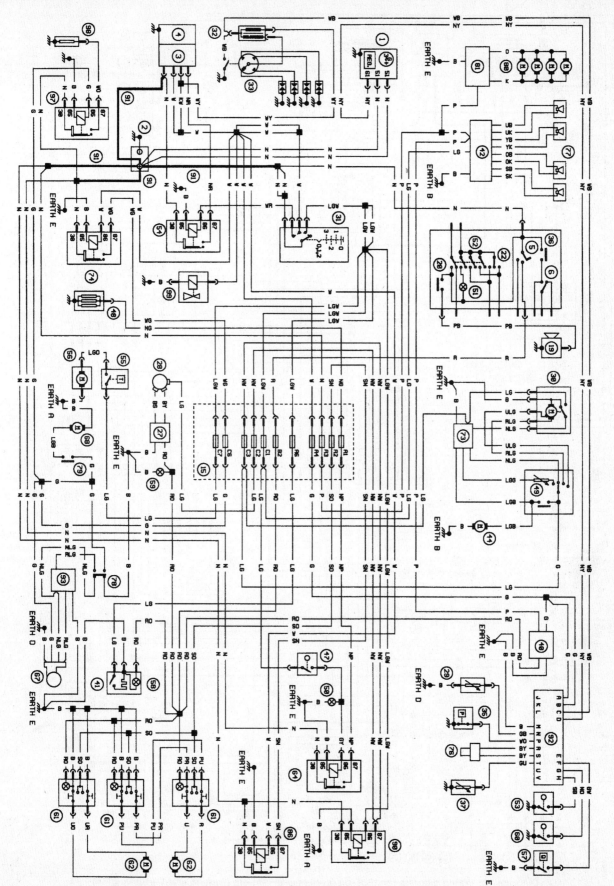

Diagram 11: Wiring diagram for 1987-on models with dim-dip (all circuits except lighting and Turbo ignition)

WD

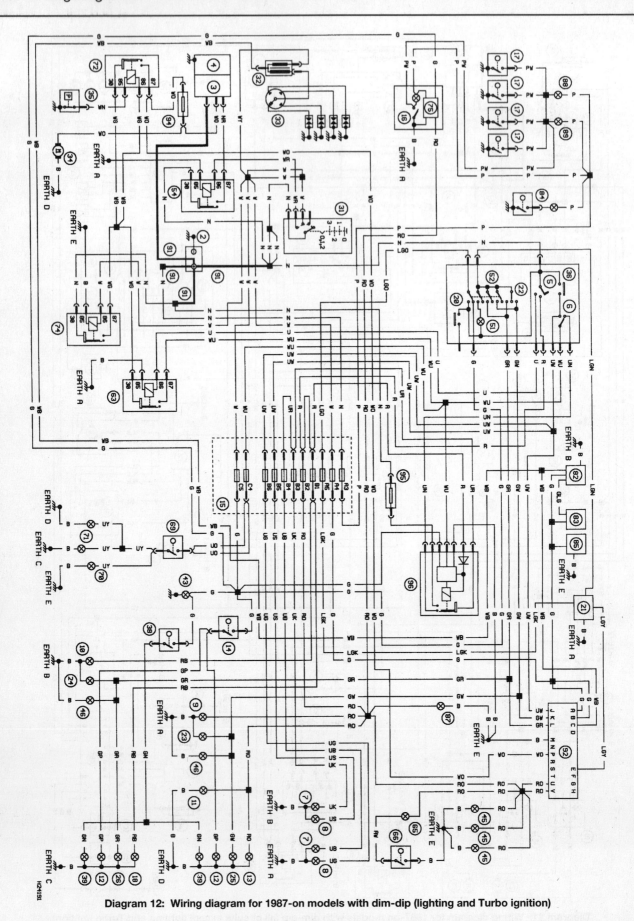

Diagram 12: Wiring diagram for 1987-on models with dim-dip (lighting and Turbo ignition)

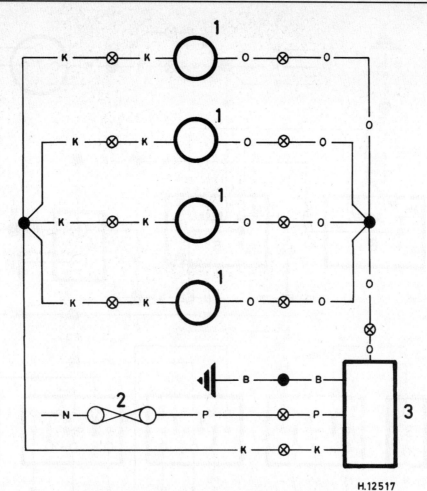

Diagram 13: Wiring diagram for central locking system

For symbols see page 12•26

1 Door lock motor
2 Fusebox
3 Door lock motor/control unit - driver's door

For colour code see page 12•26

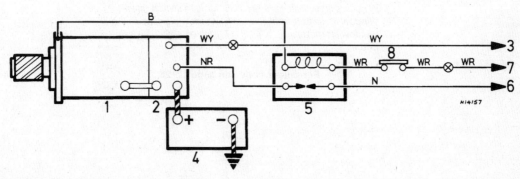

Diagram 14: Wiring diagram for pre-engaged starter fitted to models with automatic transmission. For colour code see page 12•26

1 Starter motor
2 Solenoid
3 To ignition coil
4 Battery
5 Solenoid relay
6 Feed from battery
7 From ignition switch
8 Starter inhibitor switch

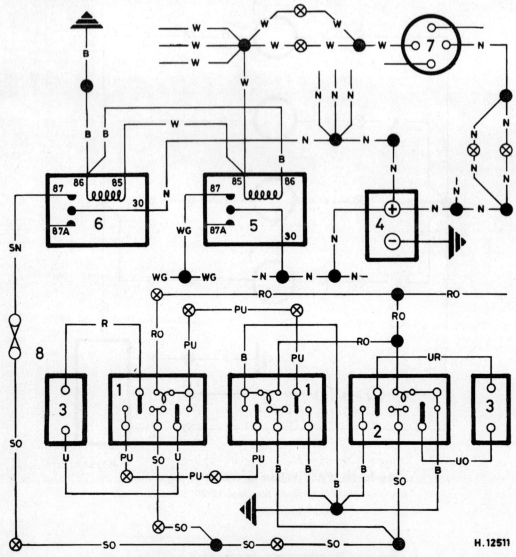

Diagram 15: Wiring diagram for electric window system
For symbols see page 12•26

1 Windows lift switch front LH
2 Window lift switch front RH
3 Window lift motor
4 Battery
5 Ignition switch relay
6 Window lift relay
7 Ignition switch
8 Fusebox

For colour code see page 12•26

Dimensions and Weights

Note: *All figures are approximate, and may vary according to model. Refer to manufacturer's data for exact figures.*

Dimensions

Turning circle (between kerbs)	33 ft 6 in (10.2 m)
Wheelbase	7 ft 5 in (2.3 m)
Overall length	11 ft 2 in (3.4 m)
Overall width (excluding mirrors)	5 ft 2 in (1.6 m)
Overall height (approx.)	4 ft 6 in (1.4 m)
Ground clearance (approx.)	4.5 in (112 mm) to 6.7 in (170 mm)
Track (all models except those below):	
Front	4 ft 3 in (1.3 m)
Rear	4 ft 3 in (1.3 m)

Weights

	lb	kg
Kerb weights (approx., with full fuel tank):	1594 to 1918	723 to 870
Maximum braked trailer weight (subject to local legislation):		
1.0 HLE and automatics	1433	650
All other 1.0 models	1874	850
All other 1.3 models	2095	950
Maximum downward load on towing hitch	100 to 120	45 to 55
Maximum vehicle loading:		
All except Turbo	882	400
Turbo	705	320
Maximum roof rack load	106	48
Van loading:		
Gross vehicle weight	2536	1150
Maximum front and rear axle loads	1323	600
Maximum vehicle loading excluding driver	683	310

Length (distance)

Inches (in)	x 25.4	= Millimetres (mm)	x 0.0394	= Inches (in)
Feet (ft)	x 0.305	= Metres (m)	x 3.281	= Feet (ft)
Miles	x 1.609	= Kilometres (km)	x 0.621	= Miles

Volume (capacity)

Cubic inches (cu in; in³)	x 16.387	= Cubic centimetres (cc; cm³)	x 0.061	= Cubic inches (cu in; in³)
Imperial pints (Imp pt)	x 0.568	= Litres (l)	x 1.76	= Imperial pints (Imp pt)
Imperial quarts (Imp qt)	x 1.137	= Litres (l)	x 0.88	= Imperial quarts (Imp qt)
Imperial quarts (Imp qt)	x 1.201	= US quarts (US qt)	x 0.833	= Imperial quarts (Imp qt)
US quarts (US qt)	x 0.946	= Litres (l)	x 1.057	= US quarts (US qt)
Imperial gallons (Imp gal)	x 4.546	= Litres (l)	x 0.22	= Imperial gallons (Imp gal)
Imperial gallons (Imp gal)	x 1.201	= US gallons (US gal)	x 0.833	= Imperial gallons (Imp gal)
US gallons (US gal)	x 3.785	= Litres (l)	x 0.264	= US gallons (US gal)

Mass (weight)

Ounces (oz)	x 28.35	= Grams (g)	x 0.035	= Ounces (oz)
Pounds (lb)	x 0.454	= Kilograms (kg)	x 2.205	= Pounds (lb)

Force

Ounces-force (ozf; oz)	x 0.278	= Newtons (N)	x 3.6	= Ounces-force (ozf; oz)
Pounds-force (lbf; lb)	x 4.448	= Newtons (N)	x 0.225	= Pounds-force (lbf; lb)
Newtons (N)	x 0.1	= Kilograms-force (kgf; kg)	x 9.81	= Newtons (N)

Pressure

Pounds-force per square inch (psi; lbf/in²; lb/in²)	x 0.070	= Kilograms-force per square centimetre (kgf/cm²; kg/cm²)	x 14.223	= Pounds-force per square inch (psi; lbf/in²; lb/in²)
Pounds-force per square inch (psi; lbf/in²; lb/in²)	x 0.068	= Atmospheres (atm)	x 14.696	= Pounds-force per square inch (psi; lbf/in²; lb/in²)
Pounds-force per square inch (psi; lbf/in²; lb/in²)	x 0.069	= Bars	x 14.5	= Pounds-force per square inch (psi; lbf/in²; lb/in²)
Pounds-force per square inch (psi; lbf/in²; lb/in²)	x 6.895	= Kilopascals (kPa)	x 0.145	= Pounds-force per square inch (psi; lbf/in²; lb/in²)
Kilopascals (kPa)	x 0.01	= Kilograms-force per square centimetre (kgf/cm²; kg/cm²)	x 98.1	= Kilopascals (kPa)
Millibar (mbar)	x 100	= Pascals (Pa)	x 0.01	= Millibar (mbar)
Millibar (mbar)	x 0.0145	= Pounds-force per square inch (psi; lbf/in²; lb/in²)	x 68.947	= Millibar (mbar)
Millibar (mbar)	x 0.75	= Millimetres of mercury (mmHg)	x 1.333	= Millibar (mbar)
Millibar (mbar)	x 0.401	= Inches of water (inH₂O)	x 2.491	= Millibar (mbar)
Millimetres of mercury (mmHg)	x 0.535	= Inches of water (inH₂O)	x 1.868	= Millimetres of mercury (mmHg)
Inches of water (inH₂O)	x 0.036	= Pounds-force per square inch (psi; lbf/in²; lb/in²)	x 27.68	= Inches of water (inH₂O)

Torque (moment of force)

Pounds-force inches (lbf in; lb in)	x 1.152	= Kilograms-force centimetre (kgf cm; kg cm)	x 0.868	= Pounds-force inches (lbf in; lb in)
Pounds-force inches (lbf in; lb in)	x 0.113	= Newton metres (Nm)	x 8.85	= Pounds-force inches (lbf in; lb in)
Pounds-force inches (lbf in; lb in)	x 0.083	= Pounds-force feet (lbf ft; lb ft)	x 12	= Pounds-force inches (lbf in; lb in)
Pounds-force feet (lbf ft; lb ft)	x 0.138	= Kilograms-force metres (kgf m; kg m)	x 7.233	= Pounds-force feet (lbf ft; lb ft)
Pounds-force feet (lbf ft; lb ft)	x 1.356	= Newton metres (Nm)	x 0.738	= Pounds-force feet (lbf ft; lb ft)
Newton metres (Nm)	x 0.102	= Kilograms-force metres (kgf m; kg m)	x 9.804	= Newton metres (Nm)

Power

Horsepower (hp)	x 745.7	= Watts (W)	x 0.0013	= Horsepower (hp)

Velocity (speed)

Miles per hour (miles/hr; mph)	x 1.609	= Kilometres per hour (km/hr; kph)	x 0.621	= Miles per hour (miles/hr; mph)

Fuel consumption*

Miles per gallon (mpg)	x 0.354	= Kilometres per litre (km/l)	x 2.825	= Miles per gallon (mpg)

Temperature

Degrees Fahrenheit = (°C x 1.8) + 32   Degrees Celsius (Degrees Centigrade; °C) = (°F - 32) x 0.56

* It is common practice to convert from miles per gallon (mpg) to litres/100 kilometres (l/100km), where mpg x l/100 km = 282

Spare parts are available from many sources, for example: Rover dealers, other garages and accessory shops, and motor factors. Our advice regarding spare parts is as follows.

Officially appointed Rover dealers - This is the best source of parts that are peculiar to your car and are otherwise generally not available (e.g. complete cylinder heads, internal gearbox components, badges, interior trim etc.). It is also the only place at which you should buy parts if your car is still under warranty; non-Rover parts may invalidate the warranty. To be sure of obtaining the correct parts it will always be necessary to give the storeman your car's engine number and chassis number. If possible, to take the old part along for positive identification. Many parts are available under a factory exchange scheme - any parts returned should always be clean! It obviously makes good sense to go to the specialists on your car for this type of part as they are best equipped to supply you.

Other garages and accessory shops - These are often very good places to buy material and components needed for the maintenance of your car (e.g. oil filters, spark plugs, etc.). They also sell general accessories, usually have convenient opening hours, charge lower prices and can often be found not far from home.

Motor factors - Good factors will stock all the more important components that wear out relatively quickly (e.g. clutch components, pistons, valves, exhaust systems, brake pipes/seals and pads, etc.). Motor factors will often provide new or reconditioned components on a part exchange basis - this can save a considerable amount of money.

Vehicle identification numbers

Modifications are a continuing and unpublicised process in vehicle manufacture quite apart from major model changes. Spare parts manuals and lists are compiled upon a numerical basis, the individual vehicle numbers being essential to correct identification of the component required.

When ordering spare parts, always give as much information as possible. Quote the car model, year of manufacture, body and engine numbers as appropriate.

The vehicle identification number is stamped on a plate on the left-hand side of the bonnet lock crossmember **(see illustration)**.

The engine number is stamped on a plate attached to the front of the cylinder block by the alternator upper mounting **(see illustration)**.

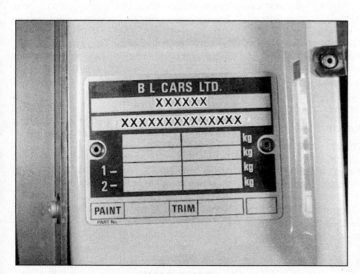

Vehicle identification plate

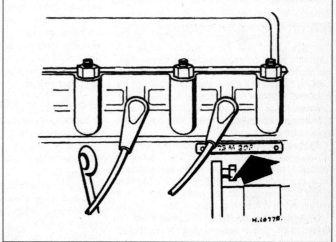

Engine number location (arrowed)

Whenever servicing, repair or overhaul work is carried out on the car or its components, it is necessary to observe the following procedures and instructions. This will assist in carrying out the operation efficiently and to a professional standard of workmanship.

Joint mating faces and gaskets

When separating components at their mating faces, never insert screwdrivers or similar implements into the joint between the faces in order to prise them apart. This can cause severe damage which results in oil leaks, coolant leaks, etc upon reassembly. Separation is usually achieved by tapping along the joint with a soft-faced hammer in order to break the seal. However, note that this method may not be suitable where dowels are used for component location.

Where a gasket is used between the mating faces of two components, ensure that it is renewed on reassembly, and fit it dry unless otherwise stated in the repair procedure. Make sure that the mating faces are clean and dry, with all traces of old gasket removed. When cleaning a joint face, use a tool which is not likely to score or damage the face, and remove any burrs or nicks with an oilstone or fine file.

Make sure that tapped holes are cleaned with a pipe cleaner, and keep them free of jointing compound, if this is being used, unless specifically instructed otherwise.

Ensure that all orifices, channels or pipes are clear, and blow through them, preferably using compressed air.

Oil seals

Oil seals can be removed by levering them out with a wide flat-bladed screwdriver or similar implement. Alternatively, a number of self-tapping screws may be screwed into the seal, and these used as a purchase for pliers or some similar device in order to pull the seal free.

Whenever an oil seal is removed from its working location, either individually or as part of an assembly, it should be renewed.

The very fine sealing lip of the seal is easily damaged, and will not seal if the surface it contacts is not completely clean and free from scratches, nicks or grooves. If the original sealing surface of the component cannot be restored, and the manufacturer has not made provision for slight relocation of the seal relative to the sealing surface, the component should be renewed.

Protect the lips of the seal from any surface which may damage them in the course of fitting. Use tape or a conical sleeve where possible. Lubricate the seal lips with oil before fitting and, on dual-lipped seals, fill the space between the lips with grease.

Unless otherwise stated, oil seals must be fitted with their sealing lips toward the lubricant to be sealed.

Use a tubular drift or block of wood of the appropriate size to install the seal and, if the seal housing is shouldered, drive the seal down to the shoulder. If the seal housing is unshouldered, the seal should be fitted with its face flush with the housing top face (unless otherwise instructed).

Screw threads and fastenings

Seized nuts, bolts and screws are quite a common occurrence where corrosion has set in, and the use of penetrating oil or releasing fluid will often overcome this problem if the offending item is soaked for a while before attempting to release it. The use of an impact driver may also provide a means of releasing such stubborn fastening devices, when used in conjunction with the appropriate screwdriver bit or socket. If none of these methods works, it may be necessary to resort to the careful application of heat, or the use of a hacksaw or nut splitter device.

Studs are usually removed by locking two nuts together on the threaded part, and then using a spanner on the lower nut to unscrew the stud. Studs or bolts which have broken off below the surface of the component in which they are mounted can sometimes be removed using a proprietary stud extractor. Always ensure that a blind tapped hole is completely free from oil, grease, water or other fluid before installing the bolt or stud. Failure to do this could cause the housing to crack due to the hydraulic action of the bolt or stud as it is screwed in.

When tightening a castellated nut to accept a split pin, tighten the nut to the specified torque, where applicable, and then tighten further to the next split pin hole. Never slacken the nut to align the split pin hole, unless stated in the repair procedure.

When checking or retightening a nut or bolt to a specified torque setting, slacken the nut or bolt by a quarter of a turn, and then retighten to the specified setting. However, this should not be attempted where angular tightening has been used.

For some screw fastenings, notably cylinder head bolts or nuts, torque wrench settings are no longer specified for the latter stages of tightening, "angle-tightening" being called up instead. Typically, a fairly low torque wrench setting will be applied to the bolts/nuts in the correct sequence, followed by one or more stages of tightening through specified angles.

Locknuts, locktabs and washers

Any fastening which will rotate against a component or housing in the course of tightening should always have a washer between it and the relevant component or housing.

Spring or split washers should always be renewed when they are used to lock a critical component such as a big-end bearing retaining bolt or nut. Locktabs which are folded over to retain a nut or bolt should always be renewed.

Self-locking nuts can be re-used in non-critical areas, providing resistance can be felt when the locking portion passes over the bolt or stud thread. However, it should be noted that self-locking stiffnuts tend to lose their effectiveness after long periods of use, and in

such cases should be renewed as a matter of course.

Split pins must always be replaced with new ones of the correct size for the hole.

When thread-locking compound is found on the threads of a fastener which is to be re-used, it should be cleaned off with a wire brush and solvent, and fresh compound applied on reassembly.

Special tools

Some repair procedures in this manual entail the use of special tools such as a press, two or three-legged pullers, spring compressors, etc. Wherever possible, suitable readily-available alternatives to the manufacturer's special tools are described, and are shown in use. In some instances, where no alternative is possible, it has been necessary to resort to the use of a manufacturer's tool, and this has been done for reasons of safety as well as the efficient completion of the repair operation. Unless you are highly-skilled and have a thorough understanding of the procedures described, never attempt to bypass the use of any special tool when the procedure described specifies its use. Not only is there a very great risk of personal injury, but expensive damage could be caused to the components involved.

Environmental considerations

When disposing of used engine oil, brake fluid, antifreeze, etc, give due consideration to any detrimental environmental effects. Do not, for instance, pour any of the above liquids down drains into the general sewage system, or onto the ground to soak away. Many local council refuse tips provide a facility for waste oil disposal, as do some garages. If none of these facilities are available, consult your local Environmental Health Department for further advice.

With the universal tightening-up of legislation regarding the emission of environmentally-harmful substances from motor vehicles, most current vehicles have tamperproof devices fitted to the main adjustment points of the fuel system. These devices are primarily designed to prevent unqualified persons from adjusting the fuel/air mixture, with the chance of a consequent increase in toxic emissions. If such devices are encountered during servicing or overhaul, they should, wherever possible, be renewed or refitted in accordance with the vehicle manufacturer's requirements or current legislation.

OIL CARE
FOLLOW THE CODE
OIL BANK LINE
0800 66 33 66

Note: It is antisocial and illegal to dump oil down the drain. To find the location of your local oil recycling bank, call this number free.

Introduction

A selection of good tools is a fundamental requirement for anyone contemplating the maintenance and repair of a motor vehicle. For the owner who does not possess any, their purchase will prove a considerable expense, offsetting some of the savings made by doing-it-yourself. However, provided that the tools purchased meet the relevant national safety standards and are of good quality, they will last for many years and prove an extremely worthwhile investment.

To help the average owner to decide which tools are needed to carry out the various tasks detailed in this manual, we have compiled three lists of tools under the following headings: *Maintenance and minor repair*, *Repair and overhaul*, and *Special*. Newcomers to practical mechanics should start off with the *Maintenance and minor repair* tool kit, and confine themselves to the simpler jobs around the vehicle. Then, as confidence and experience grow, more difficult tasks can be undertaken, with extra tools being purchased as, and when, they are needed. In this way, a *Maintenance and minor repair* tool kit can be built up into a *Repair and overhaul* tool kit over a considerable period of time, without any major cash outlays. The experienced do-it-yourselfer will have a tool kit good enough for most repair and overhaul procedures, and will add tools from the *Special* category when it is felt that the expense is justified by the amount of use to which these tools will be put.

Maintenance and minor repair tool kit

The tools given in this list should be considered as a minimum requirement if routine maintenance, servicing and minor repair operations are to be undertaken. We recommend the purchase of combination spanners (ring one end, open-ended the other); although more expensive than open-ended ones, they do give the advantages of both types of spanner.

☐ *Combination spanners:*
   Metric - 8 to 19 mm inclusive
☐ *Adjustable spanner - 35 mm jaw (approx.)*
☐ *Spark plug spanner (with rubber insert) - petrol models*
☐ *Spark plug gap adjustment tool - petrol models*
☐ *Set of feeler gauges*
☐ *Brake bleed nipple spanner*
☐ *Screwdrivers:*
   Flat blade - 100 mm long x 6 mm dia
   Cross blade - 100 mm long x 6 mm dia
   Torx - various sizes (not all vehicles)
☐ *Combination pliers*
☐ *Hacksaw (junior)*
☐ *Tyre pump*
☐ *Tyre pressure gauge*
☐ *Oil can*
☐ *Oil filter removal tool*
☐ *Fine emery cloth*
☐ *Wire brush (small)*
☐ *Funnel (medium size)*
☐ *Sump drain plug key (not all vehicles)*

Repair and overhaul tool kit

These tools are virtually essential for anyone undertaking any major repairs to a motor vehicle, and are additional to those given in the *Maintenance and minor repair* list. Included in this list is a comprehensive set of sockets. Although these are expensive, they will be found invaluable as they are so versatile - particularly if various drives are included in the set. We recommend the half-inch square-drive type, as this can be used with most proprietary torque wrenches.

The tools in this list will sometimes need to be supplemented by tools from the *Special* list:

☐ *Sockets (or box spanners) to cover range in previous list (including Torx sockets)*
☐ *Reversible ratchet drive (for use with sockets)*
☐ *Extension piece, 250 mm (for use with sockets)*
☐ *Universal joint (for use with sockets)*
☐ *Flexible handle or sliding T "breaker bar" (for use with sockets)*
☐ *Torque wrench (for use with sockets)*
☐ *Self-locking grips*
☐ *Ball pein hammer*
☐ *Soft-faced mallet (plastic or rubber)*
☐ *Screwdrivers:*
   Flat blade - long & sturdy, short (chubby), and narrow (electrician's) types
   Cross blade – long & sturdy, and short (chubby) types
☐ *Pliers:*
   Long-nosed
   Side cutters (electrician's)
   Circlip (internal and external)
☐ *Cold chisel - 25 mm*
☐ *Scriber*
☐ *Scraper*
☐ *Centre-punch*
☐ *Pin punch*
☐ *Hacksaw*
☐ *Brake hose clamp*
☐ *Brake/clutch bleeding kit*
☐ *Selection of twist drills*
☐ *Steel rule/straight-edge*
☐ *Allen keys (inc. splined/Torx type)*
☐ *Selection of files*
☐ *Wire brush*
☐ *Axle stands*
☐ *Jack (strong trolley or hydraulic type)*
☐ *Light with extension lead*
☐ *Universal electrical multi-meter*

Sockets and reversible ratchet drive

Brake bleeding kit

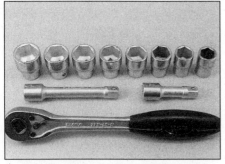

Torx key, socket and bit

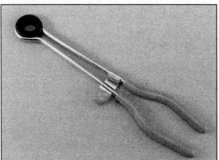

Hose clamp

Angular-tightening gauge

Special tools

The tools in this list are those which are not used regularly, are expensive to buy, or which need to be used in accordance with their manufacturers' instructions. Unless relatively difficult mechanical jobs are undertaken frequently, it will not be economic to buy many of these tools. Where this is the case, you could consider clubbing together with friends (or joining a motorists' club) to make a joint purchase, or borrowing the tools against a deposit from a local garage or tool hire specialist. It is worth noting that many of the larger DIY superstores now carry a large range of special tools for hire at modest rates.

The following list contains only those tools and instruments freely available to the public, and not those special tools produced by the vehicle manufacturer specifically for its dealer network. You will find occasional references to these manufacturers' special tools in the text of this manual. Generally, an alternative method of doing the job without the vehicle manufacturers' special tool is given. However, sometimes there is no alternative to using them. Where this is the case and the relevant tool cannot be bought or borrowed, you will have to entrust the work to a dealer.

- ☐ *Angular-tightening gauge*
- ☐ *Valve spring compressor*
- ☐ *Valve grinding tool*
- ☐ *Piston ring compressor*
- ☐ *Piston ring removal/installation tool*
- ☐ *Cylinder bore hone*
- ☐ *Balljoint separator*
- ☐ *Coil spring compressors (where applicable)*
- ☐ *Two/three-legged hub and bearing puller*
- ☐ *Impact screwdriver*
- ☐ *Micrometer and/or vernier calipers*
- ☐ *Dial gauge*
- ☐ *Stroboscopic timing light*
- ☐ *Dwell angle meter/tachometer*
- ☐ *Fault code reader*
- ☐ *Cylinder compression gauge*
- ☐ *Hand-operated vacuum pump and gauge*
- ☐ *Clutch plate alignment set*
- ☐ *Brake shoe steady spring cup removal tool*
- ☐ *Bush and bearing removal/installation set*
- ☐ *Stud extractors*
- ☐ *Tap and die set*
- ☐ *Lifting tackle*
- ☐ *Trolley jack*

Buying tools

Reputable motor accessory shops and superstores often offer excellent quality tools at discount prices, so it pays to shop around.

Remember, you don't have to buy the most expensive items on the shelf, but it is always advisable to steer clear of the very cheap tools. Beware of 'bargains' offered on market stalls or at car boot sales. There are plenty of good tools around at reasonable prices, but always aim to purchase items which meet the relevant national safety standards. If in doubt, ask the proprietor or manager of the shop for advice before making a purchase.

Care and maintenance of tools

Having purchased a reasonable tool kit, it is necessary to keep the tools in a clean and serviceable condition. After use, always wipe off any dirt, grease and metal particles using a clean, dry cloth, before putting the tools away. Never leave them lying around after they have been used. A simple tool rack on the garage or workshop wall for items such as screwdrivers and pliers is a good idea. Store all normal spanners and sockets in a metal box. Any measuring instruments, gauges, meters, etc, must be carefully stored where they cannot be damaged or become rusty.

Take a little care when tools are used. Hammer heads inevitably become marked, and screwdrivers lose the keen edge on their blades from time to time. A little timely attention with emery cloth or a file will soon restore items like this to a good finish.

Working facilities

Not to be forgotten when discussing tools is the workshop itself. If anything more than routine maintenance is to be carried out, a suitable working area becomes essential.

It is appreciated that many an owner-mechanic is forced by circumstances to remove an engine or similar item without the benefit of a garage or workshop. Having done this, any repairs should always be done under the cover of a roof.

Wherever possible, any dismantling should be done on a clean, flat workbench or table at a suitable working height.

Any workbench needs a vice; one with a jaw opening of 100 mm is suitable for most jobs. As mentioned previously, some clean dry storage space is also required for tools, as well as for any lubricants, cleaning fluids, touch-up paints etc, which become necessary.

Another item which may be required, and which has a much more general usage, is an electric drill with a chuck capacity of at least 8 mm. This, together with a good range of twist drills, is virtually essential for fitting accessories.

Last, but not least, always keep a supply of old newspapers and clean, lint-free rags available, and try to keep any working area as clean as possible.

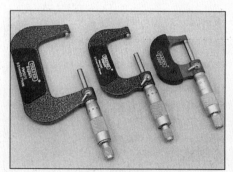

Micrometers

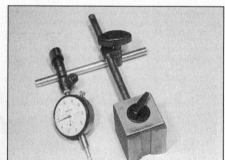

Dial test indicator ("dial gauge")

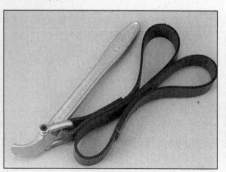

Strap wrench

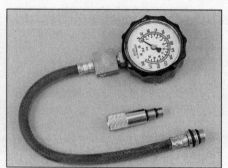

Compression tester

Fault code reader

This is a guide to getting your vehicle through the MOT test. Obviously it will not be possible to examine the vehicle to the same standard as the professional MOT tester. However, working through the following checks will enable you to identify any problem areas before submitting the vehicle for the test.

Where a testable component is in borderline condition, the tester has discretion in deciding whether to pass or fail it. The basis of such discretion is whether the tester would be happy for a close relative or friend to use the vehicle with the component in that condition. If the vehicle presented is clean and evidently well cared for, the tester may be more inclined to pass a borderline component than if the vehicle is scruffy and apparently neglected.

It has only been possible to summarise the test requirements here, based on the regulations in force at the time of printing. Test standards are becoming increasingly stringent, although there are some exemptions for older vehicles. For full details obtain a copy of the Haynes publication Pass the MOT! (available from stockists of Haynes manuals).

An assistant will be needed to help carry out some of these checks.

The checks have been sub-divided into four categories, as follows:

1 Checks carried out **FROM THE DRIVER'S SEAT**

2 Checks carried out **WITH THE VEHICLE ON THE GROUND**

3 Checks carried out **WITH THE VEHICLE RAISED AND THE WHEELS FREE TO TURN**

4 Checks carried out on **YOUR VEHICLE'S EXHAUST EMISSION SYSTEM**

1 Checks carried out **FROM THE DRIVER'S SEAT**

Handbrake

☐ Test the operation of the handbrake. Excessive travel (too many clicks) indicates incorrect brake or cable adjustment.

☐ Check that the handbrake cannot be released by tapping the lever sideways. Check the security of the lever mountings.

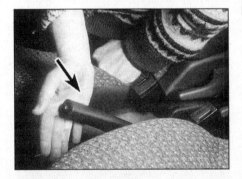

Footbrake

☐ Depress the brake pedal and check that it does not creep down to the floor, indicating a master cylinder fault. Release the pedal, wait a few seconds, then depress it again. If the pedal travels nearly to the floor before firm resistance is felt, brake adjustment or repair is necessary. If the pedal feels spongy, there is air in the hydraulic system which must be removed by bleeding.

☐ Check that the brake pedal is secure and in good condition. Check also for signs of fluid leaks on the pedal, floor or carpets, which would indicate failed seals in the brake master cylinder.

☐ Check the servo unit (when applicable) by operating the brake pedal several times, then keeping the pedal depressed and starting the engine. As the engine starts, the pedal will move down slightly. If not, the vacuum hose or the servo itself may be faulty.

Steering wheel and column

☐ Examine the steering wheel for fractures or looseness of the hub, spokes or rim.

☐ Move the steering wheel from side to side and then up and down. Check that the steering wheel is not loose on the column, indicating wear or a loose retaining nut. Continue moving the steering wheel as before, but also turn it slightly from left to right.

☐ Check that the steering wheel is not loose on the column, and that there is no abnormal

movement of the steering wheel, indicating wear in the column support bearings or couplings.

Windscreen and mirrors

☐ The windscreen must be free of cracks or other significant damage within the driver's field of view. (Small stone chips are acceptable.) Rear view mirrors must be secure, intact, and capable of being adjusted.

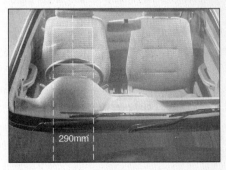

290mm

Seat belts and seats

Note: *The following checks are applicable to all seat belts, front and rear.*

☐ Examine the webbing of all the belts (including rear belts if fitted) for cuts, serious fraying or deterioration. Fasten and unfasten each belt to check the buckles. If applicable, check the retracting mechanism. Check the security of all seat belt mountings accessible from inside the vehicle.

☐ The front seats themselves must be securely attached and the backrests must lock in the upright position.

Doors

☐ Both front doors must be able to be opened and closed from outside and inside, and must latch securely when closed.

2 Checks carried out WITH THE VEHICLE ON THE GROUND

Vehicle identification

☐ Number plates must be in good condition, secure and legible, with letters and numbers correctly spaced – spacing at (**A**) should be at least twice that at (**B**).

☐ The VIN plate and/or homologation plate must be legible.

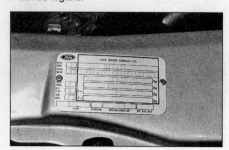

Electrical equipment

☐ Switch on the ignition and check the operation of the horn.

☐ Check the windscreen washers and wipers, examining the wiper blades; renew damaged or perished blades. Also check the operation of the stop-lights.

☐ Check the operation of the sidelights and number plate lights. The lenses and reflectors must be secure, clean and undamaged.

☐ Check the operation and alignment of the headlights. The headlight reflectors must not be tarnished and the lenses must be undamaged.

☐ Switch on the ignition and check the operation of the direction indicators (including the instrument panel tell-tale) and the hazard warning lights. Operation of the sidelights and stop-lights must not affect the indicators - if it does, the cause is usually a bad earth at the rear light cluster.

☐ Check the operation of the rear foglight(s), including the warning light on the instrument panel or in the switch.

Footbrake

☐ Examine the master cylinder, brake pipes and servo unit for leaks, loose mountings, corrosion or other damage.

☐ The fluid reservoir must be secure and the fluid level must be between the upper (**A**) and lower (**B**) markings.

Steering and suspension

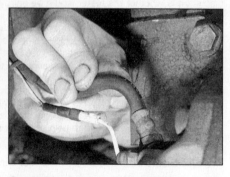

☐ Inspect both front brake flexible hoses for cracks or deterioration of the rubber. Turn the steering from lock to lock, and ensure that the hoses do not contact the wheel, tyre, or any part of the steering or suspension mechanism. With the brake pedal firmly depressed, check the hoses for bulges or leaks under pressure.

☐ Have your assistant turn the steering wheel from side to side slightly, up to the point where the steering gear just begins to transmit this movement to the roadwheels. Check for excessive free play between the steering wheel and the steering gear, indicating wear or insecurity of the steering column joints, the column-to-steering gear coupling, or the steering gear itself.

☐ Have your assistant turn the steering wheel more vigorously in each direction, so that the roadwheels just begin to turn. As this is done, examine all the steering joints, linkages, fittings and attachments. Renew any component that shows signs of wear or damage. On vehicles with power steering, check the security and condition of the steering pump, drivebelt and hoses.

☐ Check that the vehicle is standing level, and at approximately the correct ride height.

Shock absorbers

☐ Depress each corner of the vehicle in turn, then release it. The vehicle should rise and then settle in its normal position. If the vehicle continues to rise and fall, the shock absorber is defective. A shock absorber which has seized will also cause the vehicle to fail.

Exhaust system

☐ Start the engine. With your assistant holding a rag over the tailpipe, check the entire system for leaks. Repair or renew leaking sections.

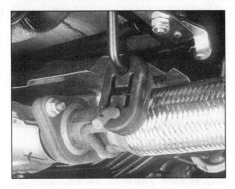

3 Checks carried out **WITH THE VEHICLE RAISED AND THE WHEELS FREE TO TURN**

Jack up the front and rear of the vehicle, and securely support it on axle stands. Position the stands clear of the suspension assemblies. Ensure that the wheels are clear of the ground and that the steering can be turned from lock to lock.

Steering mechanism

☐ Have your assistant turn the steering from lock to lock. Check that the steering turns smoothly, and that no part of the steering mechanism, including a wheel or tyre, fouls any brake hose or pipe or any part of the body structure.
☐ Examine the steering rack rubber gaiters for damage or insecurity of the retaining clips. If power steering is fitted, check for signs of damage or leakage of the fluid hoses, pipes or connections. Also check for excessive stiffness or binding of the steering, a missing split pin or locking device, or severe corrosion of the body structure within 30 cm of any steering component attachment point.

Front and rear suspension and wheel bearings

☐ Starting at the front right-hand side, grasp the roadwheel at the 3 o'clock and 9 o'clock positions and shake it vigorously. Check for free play or insecurity at the wheel bearings, suspension balljoints, or suspension mountings, pivots and attachments.
☐ Now grasp the wheel at the 12 o'clock and 6 o'clock positions and repeat the previous inspection. Spin the wheel, and check for roughness or tightness of the front wheel bearing.

☐ If excess free play is suspected at a component pivot point, this can be confirmed by using a large screwdriver or similar tool and levering between the mounting and the component attachment. This will confirm whether the wear is in the pivot bush, its retaining bolt, or in the mounting itself (the bolt holes can often become elongated).

☐ Carry out all the above checks at the other front wheel, and then at both rear wheels.

Springs and shock absorbers

☐ Examine the suspension struts (when applicable) for serious fluid leakage, corrosion, or damage to the casing. Also check the security of the mounting points.
☐ If coil springs are fitted, check that the spring ends locate in their seats, and that the spring is not corroded, cracked or broken.
☐ If leaf springs are fitted, check that all leaves are intact, that the axle is securely attached to each spring, and that there is no deterioration of the spring eye mountings, bushes, and shackles.

☐ The same general checks apply to vehicles fitted with other suspension types, such as torsion bars, hydraulic displacer units, etc. Ensure that all mountings and attachments are secure, that there are no signs of excessive wear, corrosion or damage, and (on hydraulic types) that there are no fluid leaks or damaged pipes.
☐ Inspect the shock absorbers for signs of serious fluid leakage. Check for wear of the mounting bushes or attachments, or damage to the body of the unit.

Driveshafts (fwd vehicles only)

☐ Rotate each front wheel in turn and inspect the constant velocity joint gaiters for splits or damage. Also check that each driveshaft is straight and undamaged.

Braking system

☐ If possible without dismantling, check brake pad wear and disc condition. Ensure that the friction lining material has not worn excessively, (A) and that the discs are not fractured, pitted, scored or badly worn (B).

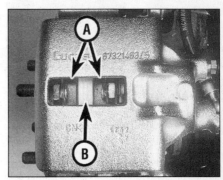

☐ Examine all the rigid brake pipes underneath the vehicle, and the flexible hose(s) at the rear. Look for corrosion, chafing or insecurity of the pipes, and for signs of bulging under pressure, chafing, splits or deterioration of the flexible hoses.
☐ Look for signs of fluid leaks at the brake calipers or on the brake backplates. Repair or renew leaking components.
☐ Slowly spin each wheel, while your assistant depresses and releases the footbrake. Ensure that each brake is operating and does not bind when the pedal is released.

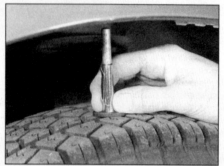

☐ Examine the handbrake mechanism, checking for frayed or broken cables, excessive corrosion, or wear or insecurity of the linkage. Check that the mechanism works on each relevant wheel, and releases fully, without binding.

☐ It is not possible to test brake efficiency without special equipment, but a road test can be carried out later to check that the vehicle pulls up in a straight line.

Fuel and exhaust systems

☐ Inspect the fuel tank (including the filler cap), fuel pipes, hoses and unions. All components must be secure and free from leaks.

☐ Examine the exhaust system over its entire length, checking for any damaged, broken or missing mountings, security of the retaining clamps and rust or corrosion.

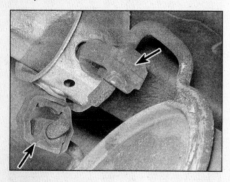

Wheels and tyres

☐ Examine the sidewalls and tread area of each tyre in turn. Check for cuts, tears, lumps, bulges, separation of the tread, and exposure of the ply or cord due to wear or damage. Check that the tyre bead is correctly seated on the wheel rim, that the valve is sound and properly seated, and that the wheel is not distorted or damaged.

☐ Check that the tyres are of the correct size for the vehicle, that they are of the same size and type on each axle, and that the pressures are correct.

☐ Check the tyre tread depth. The legal minimum at the time of writing is 1.6 mm over at least three-quarters of the tread width. Abnormal tread wear may indicate incorrect front wheel alignment.

Body corrosion

☐ Check the condition of the entire vehicle structure for signs of corrosion in load-bearing areas. (These include chassis box sections, side sills, cross-members, pillars, and all suspension, steering, braking system and seat belt mountings and anchorages.) Any corrosion which has seriously reduced the thickness of a load-bearing area is likely to cause the vehicle to fail. In this case professional repairs are likely to be needed.

☐ Damage or corrosion which causes sharp or otherwise dangerous edges to be exposed will also cause the vehicle to fail.

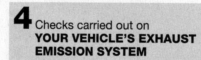

4 Checks carried out on **YOUR VEHICLE'S EXHAUST EMISSION SYSTEM**

Petrol models

☐ Have the engine at normal operating temperature, and make sure that it is in good tune (ignition system in good order, air filter element clean, etc).

☐ Before any measurements are carried out, raise the engine speed to around 2500 rpm, and hold it at this speed for 20 seconds.

Allow the engine speed to return to idle, and watch for smoke emissions from the exhaust tailpipe. If the idle speed is obviously much too high, or if dense blue or clearly-visible black smoke comes from the tailpipe for more than 5 seconds, the vehicle will fail. As a rule of thumb, blue smoke signifies oil being burnt (engine wear) while black smoke signifies unburnt fuel (dirty air cleaner element, or other carburettor or fuel system fault).

☐ An exhaust gas analyser capable of measuring carbon monoxide (CO) and hydrocarbons (HC) is now needed. If such an instrument cannot be hired or borrowed, a local garage may agree to perform the check for a small fee.

CO emissions (mixture)

☐ At the time of writing, the maximum CO level at idle is 3.5% for vehicles first used after August 1986 and 4.5% for older vehicles. From January 1996 a much tighter limit (around 0.5%) applies to catalyst-equipped vehicles first used from August 1992. If the CO level cannot be reduced far enough to pass the test (and the fuel and ignition systems are otherwise in good condition) then the carburettor is badly worn, or there is some problem in the fuel injection system or catalytic converter (as applicable).

HC emissions

☐ With the CO emissions within limits, HC emissions must be no more than 1200 ppm (parts per million). If the vehicle fails this test at idle, it can be re-tested at around 2000 rpm; if the HC level is then 1200 ppm or less, this counts as a pass.

☐ Excessive HC emissions can be caused by oil being burnt, but they are more likely to be due to unburnt fuel.

Diesel models

☐ The only emission test applicable to Diesel engines is the measuring of exhaust smoke density. The test involves accelerating the engine several times to its maximum unloaded speed.

Note: *It is of the utmost importance that the engine timing belt is in good condition before the test is carried out.*

☐ Excessive smoke can be caused by a dirty air cleaner element. Otherwise, professional advice may be needed to find the cause.

Engine

- [ ] Engine fails to rotate when attempting to start
- [ ] Starter motor turns engine slowly
- [ ] Engine rotates, but will not start
- [ ] Engine difficult to start when cold
- [ ] Engine difficult to start when hot
- [ ] Starter motor noisy or excessively-rough in engagement
- [ ] Engine starts, but stops immediately
- [ ] Engine idles erratically
- [ ] Engine misfires at idle speed
- [ ] Engine misfires throughout the driving speed range
- [ ] Engine hesitates on acceleration
- [ ] Engine stalls
- [ ] Engine lacks power
- [ ] Engine backfires
- [ ] Oil pressure warning light illuminated with engine running
- [ ] Engine runs-on after switching off
- [ ] Excessive oil consumption
- [ ] Engine noises

Cooling system

- [ ] Overheating
- [ ] Overcooling
- [ ] External coolant leakage
- [ ] Internal coolant leakage
- [ ] Corrosion

Fuel and exhaust systems

- [ ] Excessive fuel consumption
- [ ] Fuel leakage and/or fuel odour
- [ ] Excessive noise or fumes from exhaust system
- [ ] Insufficient fuel supply or weak mixture

Clutch

- [ ] Pedal travels to floor - no pressure or very little resistance
- [ ] Clutch fails to disengage (unable to select gears)
- [ ] Clutch slips (engine speed increases, with no increase in vehicle speed)
- [ ] Judder as clutch is engaged
- [ ] Noise when depressing or releasing clutch pedal

Manual gearbox

- [ ] Noisy in neutral with engine running
- [ ] Noisy in one particular gear
- [ ] Difficulty engaging gears
- [ ] Jumps out of gear
- [ ] Vibration
- [ ] Lubricant leaks

Automatic transmission

- [ ] General gear selection problems
- [ ] Transmission will not downshift (kickdown) with accelerator pedal fully depressed
- [ ] Engine will not start in any gear, or starts in gears other than Park or Neutral
- [ ] Transmission slips, shifts roughly, is noisy, or has no drive in forward or reverse gears

Driveshaft

- [ ] Clicking or knocking noise on turns (at slow speed on full-lock)
- [ ] Vibration when accelerating or decelerating

Braking system

- [ ] Vehicle pulls to one side under braking
- [ ] Noise (grinding or high-pitched squeal) when brakes applied
- [ ] Excessive brake pedal travel
- [ ] Brake pedal feels spongy when depressed
- [ ] Excessive brake pedal effort required to stop vehicle
- [ ] Judder felt through brake pedal or steering wheel when braking
- [ ] Brakes binding
- [ ] Rear wheels locking under normal braking

Suspension and steering systems

- [ ] Vehicle pulls to one side
- [ ] Wheel wobble and vibration
- [ ] Excessive pitching and/or rolling around corners, or during braking
- [ ] Wandering or general instability
- [ ] Excessively-stiff steering
- [ ] Excessive play in steering
- [ ] Low suspension ride height
- [ ] Tyre wear excessive

Electrical system

- [ ] Battery will not hold a charge for more than a few days
- [ ] Ignition/no-charge warning light remains illuminated with engine running
- [ ] Ignition/no-charge warning light fails to come on
- [ ] Lights inoperative
- [ ] Instrument readings inaccurate or erratic
- [ ] Horn inoperative, or unsatisfactory in operation
- [ ] Windscreen/tailgate wipers inoperative, or unsatisfactory in operation
- [ ] Windscreen/tailgate washers inoperative, or unsatisfactory in operation
- [ ] Electric windows inoperative, or unsatisfactory in operation
- [ ] Electric windows inoperative, or unsatisfactory in operation
- [ ] Central locking system inoperative, or unsatisfactory in operation

Introduction

The car owner who does his or her maintenance according to the recommended schedules should not have to use this section of the manual very often. Modern component reliability is such that, provided those items subject to wear or deterioration are inspected or renewed at the specified intervals, sudden failure is comparatively rare. Faults do not usually just happen as a result of sudden failure, but develop over a period of time. Major mechanical failures in particular are usually preceded by characteristic symptoms over hundreds or even thousands of miles. Those components that do occasionally fail without warning are often small and easily carried in the car.

With any fault finding, the first step is to decide where to begin investigations. Sometimes this is obvious, but on other occasions a little detective work will be necessary. The owner who makes half a dozen haphazard adjustments or replacements may be successful in curing a fault (or its symptoms), but he will be none the wiser if the fault recurs and he may well have spent more time and money than was necessary. A calm and logical approach will be found to be more satisfactory in the long run. Always take into account any warning signs or abnormalities that may have been noticed in the period preceding the fault - power loss, high or low gauge readings, unusual noises or smells, etc. - and remember that failure of components such as fuses or spark plugs may only be pointers to some underlying fault.

The pages which follow here are intended to help in cases of failure to start or breakdown on the road. Whatever the fault, certain principles apply. These are as follows:

Verify the fault. This is simply a matter of being sure that you know what the symptoms are before starting work. This is particularly important if you are investigating a fault for someone else who may not have described it very accurately.

Don't overlook the obvious. For example, if the car won't start, is there petrol in the tank? (Don't take anyone else's word on this particular point, and don't trust the fuel gauge either!). If an electrical fault is indicated, look for loose or broken wires before digging out the test gear.

Cure the disease, not the symptom. Substituting a flat battery with a fully charged one will get you off the hard shoulder, but if the underlying cause is not attended to, the new battery will go the same way. Similarly, changing oil-fouled spark plugs for a new set will get you moving again, but remember that the reason for the fouling (if it wasn't simply an incorrect grade of plug) will have to be established and corrected.

Don't take anything for granted. Particularly, don't forget that a "new" component may itself be defective (especially if it's been rattling around in the boot for months), and don't leave components out of a fault diagnosis sequence just because they are new or recently fitted. When you do finally diagnose a difficult fault, you'll probably realise that all the evidence was there from the start.

Engine

Engine fails to rotate when attempting to start

- [ ] Battery terminal connections loose or corroded (Chapter 1).
- [ ] Battery discharged or faulty (Chapter 5).
- [ ] Broken, loose or disconnected wiring in the starting circuit (Chapter 5).
- [ ] Defective starter solenoid or switch (Chapter 5).
- [ ] Ignition/starter switch faults (Chapter 5).
- [ ] Defective starter motor (Chapter 5).
- [ ] Starter pinion or flywheel/driveplate ring gear teeth loose or broken (Chapters 2A or 5).
- [ ] Engine earth strap broken or disconnected (Chapter 5).
- [ ] Major mechanical failure (seizure) or long disuse (piston rings rusted to bores), (Chapters 2A and 2B).

Starter motor turns engine slowly

- [ ] Partially-discharged battery (recharge, use jump leads, or push start) (Chapter 5).
- [ ] Battery terminals loose or corroded (Chapter 1).
- [ ] Battery earth to body defective (Chapter 5).
- [ ] Engine earth strap loose (Chapter 5).
- [ ] Starter motor (or solenoid) wiring loose (Chapter 5).
- [ ] Starter motor internal fault (Chapter 5).

Engine rotates, but will not start

- [ ] Fuel tank empty.
- [ ] Excessive choke (hot engine) or insufficient choke (cold engine).
- [ ] Battery discharged (engine rotates slowly) (Chapter 5).
- [ ] Battery terminal connections loose or corroded (Chapter 1).
- [ ] Ignition components damp or damaged (Chapters 1 and 5).
- [ ] Dirty or incorrectly gapped contact breaker points (Chapter 1).
- [ ] Dirt or water in carburettor (Chapter 4).
- [ ] Carburettor vent filter blocked (economy models only) (Chapter 4).
- [ ] Broken, loose or disconnected wiring in the ignition circuit (Chapters 1 and 5).
- [ ] Worn, faulty or incorrectly-gapped spark plugs (Chapter 1).
- [ ] Major mechanical failure (e.g. broken timing chain) (Chapter 2A).

Engine difficult to start when cold

- [ ] Battery discharged (Chapter 5).
- [ ] Battery terminal connections loose or corroded (Chapter 1).
- [ ] Worn, faulty or incorrectly-gapped spark plugs (Chapter 1).
- [ ] Other ignition system fault (Chapters 1 and 5).
- [ ] Low cylinder compressions (Chapter 2A).

Engine difficult to start when hot

- [ ] Air filter element dirty or clogged (Chapter 1).
- [ ] Low cylinder compressions (Chapter 2A).

Starter motor noisy or excessively-rough in engagement

- [ ] Starter pinion or flywheel/driveplate ring gear teeth loose or broken (Chapters 2A or 5).

- [ ] Starter motor mounting bolts loose or missing (Chapter 5).
- [ ] Starter motor internal components worn or damaged (Chapter 5).

Engine starts, but stops immediately

- [ ] Loose or faulty electrical connections in the ignition circuit (Chapters 1 and 5).
- [ ] Wet HT leads or distributor cap (after traversing water splash), (Chapters 1 and 5).
- [ ] Coil or condenser failure (check for spark) (Chapters 1 and 5).
- [ ] Vacuum leak at the throttle body or inlet manifold (Chapter 4).

Engine idles erratically

- [ ] Incorrectly adjusted idle speed (Chapter 1).
- [ ] Air filter element clogged (Chapter 1).
- [ ] Vacuum leak at the throttle body, inlet manifold or associated hoses (Chapter 4).
- [ ] Worn, faulty or incorrectly gapped spark plugs (Chapter 1).
- [ ] Carburettor adjustment incorrect (Chapter 1).
- [ ] Faulty coil or condenser (Chapter 5).
- [ ] Incorrect valve clearances (Chapter 2A).
- [ ] Worn rocker arms, timing chain, and gears (Chapter 2A).
- [ ] Faulty fuel pump (Chapter 4).
- [ ] Uneven or low cylinder compressions (Chapter 2A).
- [ ] Camshaft lobes worn (Chapter 2A).

Engine misfires at idle speed

- [ ] Worn, faulty or incorrectly gapped spark plugs (Chapter 1).
- [ ] Faulty coil or condenser (Chapter 5).
- [ ] Vacuum leak at the throttle body, inlet manifold or associated hoses (Chapter 4).
- [ ] Distributor cap cracked or tracking internally, where applicable (Chapter 1).
- [ ] Carburettor adjustment incorrect (Chapter 4).
- [ ] Dirt or water in carburettor (Chapter 4).
- [ ] Burnt out valve (Chapter 2A).
- [ ] Leaking cylinder head gasket (Chapter 2A).
- [ ] Incorrect valve clearances (Chapter 2A).
- [ ] Worn carburettor (Chapter 4).
- [ ] Uneven or low cylinder compressions (Chapter 2A).
- [ ] Disconnected, leaking, or perished crankcase ventilation hoses (Chapter 4).

Engine misfires throughout the driving speed range

- [ ] Fuel filter choked (Chapter 1).
- [ ] Fuel pump faulty, or delivery pressure low (Chapter 4).
- [ ] Fuel tank vent blocked, or fuel pipes restricted (Chapter 4).
- [ ] Vacuum leak at the throttle body, inlet manifold or associated hoses (Chapter 4).
- [ ] Worn, faulty or incorrectly gapped spark plugs (Chapter 1).
- [ ] Faulty spark plug HT leads (Chapter 1).
- [ ] Distributor cap cracked or tracking internally, where applicable (Chapter 1).

- ☐ Faulty ignition coil (Chapter 5).
- ☐ Uneven or low cylinder compressions (Chapter 2A).

Engine hesitates on acceleration

- ☐ Worn, faulty or incorrectly gapped spark plugs (Chapter 1).
- ☐ Vacuum leak at the throttle body, inlet manifold or associated hoses (Chapter 4).
- ☐ Carburettor adjustment incorrect or blocked (Chapter 4).
- ☐ Insufficient choke (cold engine).

Engine stalls

- ☐ Vacuum leak at the throttle body, inlet manifold or associated hoses (Chapter 4).
- ☐ Fuel filter choked (Chapter 1).
- ☐ Fuel pump faulty, or delivery pressure low (Chapter 4).
- ☐ Fuel tank vent blocked, or fuel pipes restricted (Chapter 4).
- ☐ Carburettor adjustment incorrect or blocked (Chapter 4).

Engine lacks power

- ☐ Fuel filter choked (Chapter 1).
- ☐ Fuel pump faulty, or delivery pressure low (Chapter 4).
- ☐ Uneven or low cylinder compressions (Chapter 2A).
- ☐ Pressure reducing valve or ECU fault (Chapter 9).
- ☐ Worn, faulty or incorrectly gapped spark plugs (Chapter 1).
- ☐ Vacuum leak at the throttle body, inlet manifold or associated hoses (Chapter 4).
- ☐ Exhaust manifold leak (Chapter 4).
- ☐ Turbocharger fault, if fitted (Chapter 4).
- ☐ Crankcase ventilation system fault (Chapter 2A).
- ☐ Carburettor adjustment incorrect or blocked (Chapter 4).
- ☐ Brakes binding (Chapters 1 and 9).
- ☐ Clutch slipping (Chapter 6).

Engine backfires

- ☐ Vacuum leak at the throttle body, inlet manifold or associated hoses (Chapter 4).
- ☐ Carburettor adjustment incorrect or blocked (Chapter 4).

Oil pressure warning light illuminated with engine running

- ☐ Low oil level, or incorrect oil grade ("Weekly Checks").
- ☐ Faulty oil pressure sensor (Chapter 2A).
- ☐ Wire to sender unit earthed (Chapter 5).
- ☐ Worn engine bearings and/or oil pump (Chapters 2A or 2B).
- ☐ Excessively high engine operating temperature (Chapter 3).
- ☐ Oil pressure relief valve defective (Chapter 2A).
- ☐ Oil pick-up strainer clogged (Chapter 2A).

Note: *Low oil pressure in a high-mileage engine at tickover is not necessarily a cause for concern. Sudden pressure loss at speed is far more significant. In any event, check the gauge or warning light sender before condemning the engine.*

Engine runs-on after switching off

- ☐ Excessive carbon build-up in engine (Chapters 2A or 2B).
- ☐ Carburettor adjustment incorrect or blocked (Chapter 4).
- ☐ Excessively high engine operating temperature (Chapter 3).

Excessive oil consumption

- ☐ Excessive oil consumption is an indication that piston rings, valve seals and/or valve guides are in need of attention. Make sure that oil leaks are not responsible before deciding that the rings and/or guides are worn.

Engine noises

Pre-ignition (pinking) or knocking during acceleration or under load

- ☐ Ignition timing incorrect/ignition system fault (Chapters 1 and 5).
- ☐ Incorrect grade of spark plug (Chapter 1).
- ☐ Incorrect grade of fuel (Chapter 1).
- ☐ Vacuum leak at throttle body, inlet manifold or associated hoses (Chapter 4).
- ☐ Distributor faulty or worn (Chapter 5).
- ☐ Carburettor adjustment incorrect or blocked (Chapter 4).
- ☐ Excessive carbon build-up in engine (Chapters 2A or 2B).

Whistling or wheezing noises

- ☐ Leaking inlet manifold or throttle body gasket (Chapter 4).
- ☐ Leaking exhaust manifold gasket (Chapter 4).
- ☐ Leaking vacuum hose (Chapters 4 and 9).
- ☐ Blowing cylinder head gasket (Chapter 2A).

Tapping or rattling noises

- ☐ Worn valve gear, timing chain, camshaft (Chapter 2A).
- ☐ Incorrect valve clearances (Chapter 2A).
- ☐ Ancillary component fault (i.e. water pump, alternator, etc.), (Chapters 3, 5, etc.).
- ☐ Broken piston ring (ticking noise), (Chapter 2B).

Knocking or thumping noises

- ☐ Worn big-end bearings (regular heavy knocking, perhaps less under load), (Chapter 2B).
- ☐ Worn main bearings (rumbling and knocking, perhaps worsening under load), (Chapter 2B).
- ☐ Piston slap (most noticeable when cold), (Chapter 2B).
- ☐ Ancillary component fault (water pump, alternator, etc.), (Chapters 3, 5, etc.).

Cooling system

Overheating

- ☐ Auxiliary drivebelt broken - or, where applicable, incorrectly adjusted (Chapter 1).
- ☐ Insufficient coolant in system ("Weekly Checks").
- ☐ Thermostat faulty.
- ☐ Radiator core blocked, or grille restricted.
- ☐ Electric cooling fan or thermostatic switch faulty.
- ☐ Pressure cap faulty.
- ☐ Ignition timing incorrect, or ignition system fault (Chapters 1 and 5).
- ☐ Inaccurate temperature gauge sender unit.
- ☐ Airlock in cooling system (Chapter 1).

Overcooling

- ☐ Thermostat faulty.
- ☐ Inaccurate temperature gauge sender unit.

External coolant leakage

- ☐ Deteriorated or damaged hoses or hose clips (Chapter 1).
- ☐ Radiator core or heater matrix leaking.
- ☐ Expansion tank leakage.
- ☐ Pressure cap faulty.
- ☐ Water pump gasket leaking.
- ☐ Boiling due to overheating.

Internal coolant leakage

- ☐ Leaking cylinder head gasket (Chapter 2A).
- ☐ Cracked cylinder head or cylinder block (Chapters 2A or 2B).

Corrosion

- ☐ Infrequent draining and flushing (Chapter 1).
- ☐ Incorrect coolant mixture or wrong coolant type ("Weekly Checks").

Fuel and exhaust systems

Excessive fuel consumption

- [ ] Air filter element dirty or clogged (Chapter 1).
- [ ] Ignition timing incorrect or ignition system fault (Chapters 1 and 5).
- [ ] Float level incorrect.
- [ ] Mixture adjustment incorrect (Chapter 1).
- [ ] Valve clearances incorrect (Chapter 2A).
- [ ] Brakes binding (Chapter 9).
- [ ] Tyres under-inflated ("*Weekly Checks*").

Fuel leakage and/or fuel odour

- [ ] Damaged fuel tank, pipes or connections (Chapters 1 and 4).

Excessive noise or fumes from exhaust system

- [ ] Leaking exhaust system or manifold joints (Chapters 1 and 4).
- [ ] Leaking, corroded or damaged silencers or pipe (Chapters 1 and 4).
- [ ] Broken mountings causing body or suspension contact (Chapter 4).

Insufficient fuel supply or weak mixture

- [ ] Sticking needle valve.
- [ ] Faulty fuel pump.
- [ ] Leaking fuel pipe unions.
- [ ] Leaking manifold gasket.
- [ ] Leaking carburettor mounting gasket.
- [ ] Mixture adjustment incorrect (Chapter 1).

Clutch

Refer to Chapter 6 for further details.

Pedal travels to floor - no pressure or very little resistance

- [ ] Leak in clutch hydraulic system, if applicable.
- [ ] Faulty hydraulic master or slave cylinder, if applicable.
- [ ] Broken clutch cable, if fitted.
- [ ] Broken clutch release bearing or fork.
- [ ] Broken diaphragm spring in clutch pressure plate.

Clutch fails to disengage (unable to select gears)

- [ ] Leak in clutch hydraulic system.
- [ ] Faulty hydraulic master or slave cylinder.
- [ ] Incorrect adjustment.
- [ ] Broken clutch cable, if fitted.
- [ ] Clutch disc sticking on gearbox input shaft splines.
- [ ] Clutch disc sticking to flywheel or pressure plate.
- [ ] Faulty pressure plate assembly.
- [ ] Clutch release mechanism worn or incorrectly assembled.

Clutch slips (engine speed increases, with no increase in vehicle speed)

- [ ] Clutch disc linings excessively worn.
- [ ] Clutch disc linings contaminated with oil or grease.
- [ ] Incorrect adjustment.
- [ ] Faulty pressure plate or weak diaphragm spring.

Judder as clutch is engaged

- [ ] Clutch disc linings contaminated with oil or grease.
- [ ] Clutch disc linings excessively worn.
- [ ] Faulty or distorted pressure plate or diaphragm spring.
- [ ] Worn or loose engine or gearbox mountings (Chapter 2A or 2B).
- [ ] Flywheel damaged (Chapter 2A).
- [ ] Clutch disc hub or gearbox input shaft splines worn.

Noise when depressing or releasing clutch pedal

- [ ] Worn clutch release bearing.
- [ ] Worn or dry clutch pedal bushes.
- [ ] Worn or faulty clutch cable, if fitted.
- [ ] Faulty pressure plate assembly.
- [ ] Pressure plate diaphragm spring broken.
- [ ] Broken clutch disc cushioning springs.

Manual gearbox

Refer to Chapter 7A, unless shown otherwise.

Noisy in neutral with engine running

- [ ] Input shaft bearings worn (noise apparent with clutch pedal released, but not when depressed).
- [ ] Clutch release bearing worn (noise apparent with clutch pedal depressed, possibly less when released), (Chapter 6).

Noisy in one particular gear

- [ ] Worn, damaged or chipped gear teeth.

Difficulty engaging gears

- [ ] Clutch fault (Chapter 6).
- [ ] Worn or damaged gear linkage.
- [ ] Incorrectly adjusted gear linkage.

- [ ] Worn synchroniser units.

Jumps out of gear

- [ ] Worn or damaged gear linkage.
- [ ] Worn synchroniser units.
- [ ] Worn selector forks.

Vibration

- [ ] Lack of oil (Chapter 1).
- [ ] Worn bearings.

Lubricant leaks

- [ ] Leaking oil seal.
- [ ] Leaking housing joint.

Automatic transmission

General gear selection problems

☐ The most likely cause of gear selection problems is a faulty or poorly adjusted gear selector mechanism. The following are common problems associated with a faulty selector mechanism.
  a) *Engine starting in gears other than Park or Neutral.*
  b) *Indicator on gear selector lever pointing to a gear other than the one actually being used.*
  c) *Vehicle moves when in Park or Neutral.*
  d) *Poor gear shift quality, or erratic gear changes.*
  Incorrect engine oil, (especially when cold).

Transmission will not downshift (kickdown) with accelerator pedal fully depressed

☐ Low engine/transmission fluid level (Chapter 1).

☐ Incorrect selector cable adjustment (Chapter 7B).

Engine will not start in any gear, or starts in gears other than Park or Neutral

☐ Incorrect starter inhibitor switch adjustment - where applicable (Chapter 7B).
☐ Incorrect selector cable adjustment (Chapter 7B).

Transmission slips, shifts roughly, is noisy, or has no drive in forward or reverse gears

☐ Before taking the vehicle to a dealer or transmission specialist, check the fluid level as described in Chapter 1. Correct the fluid level as necessary, or change the fluid and filter if needed. If the problem persists, professional help will be necessary.

Driveshafts

Refer to Chapter 8 for further details

Clicking or knocking noise on turns (at slow speed on full-lock)

☐ Lack of constant velocity joint lubricant, possibly due to damaged gaiter.

☐ Worn outer constant velocity joint.

Vibration when accelerating or decelerating

☐ Worn inner constant velocity joint.
☐ Bent or distorted driveshaft.

Braking system

Note: *If brake problem exists, make sure that the tyres are in good condition and correctly inflated, that the front wheel alignment is correct, and that the vehicle is not loaded with unequal weight. Check the condition of all pipe and hose connections.*
Refer to Chapter 9 (unless shown otherwise), for further details.

Vehicle pulls to one side under braking

☐ Worn, defective, damaged or contaminated front pads or rear brake linings on one side (Chapters 1 and 9).
☐ Seized or partially seized front brake caliper piston or rear wheel cylinder.
☐ Incorrect adjustment.
☐ A mixture of brake pad lining materials fitted between sides.
☐ Brake caliper mounting bolts loose.
☐ Worn or damaged steering or suspension components (Chapters 1 and 10).

Noise (grinding or high-pitched squeal) when brakes applied

☐ Brake pad friction lining material worn down to metal backing (Chapters 1 and 9).
☐ Excessive corrosion of brake disc - may be apparent after the vehicle has been standing for some time (Chapters 1 and 9).

Excessive brake pedal travel

☐ Faulty master cylinder.
☐ Rear brake shoes out of adjustment.
☐ Air in hydraulic system.
☐ Faulty vacuum servo unit.

Brake pedal feels spongy when depressed

☐ Air in hydraulic system.
☐ Deteriorated flexible rubber brake hoses (Chapters 1 and 9).

☐ Master cylinder mountings loose.
☐ Faulty master cylinder.

Excessive brake pedal effort required to stop vehicle

☐ Disconnected, damaged or insecure brake servo vacuum hose (Chapters 1 and 9).
☐ Brake linings contaminated.
☐ Seized brake caliper piston or wheel cylinder(s).
☐ Damaged brake line.
☐ Brake pads incorrectly fitted.
☐ New linings not yet bedded-in.
☐ Incorrect grade of brake pads fitted.
☐ Primary or secondary hydraulic circuit failure.
☐ Faulty vacuum servo unit, where fitted.

Judder felt through brake pedal or steering wheel when braking

☐ Worn drums and/or discs.
☐ Brake pad linings worn (Chapters 1 and 9).
☐ Brake caliper mounting bolts loose.
☐ Wear in suspension or steering components or mountings (Chapters 1 and 10).

Brakes binding

☐ Seized brake caliper piston(s).
☐ Incorrectly adjusted handbrake mechanism.
☐ Faulty master cylinder.

Rear wheels locking under normal braking

☐ Rear brake linings contaminated.
☐ Faulty brake pressure regulator.

Suspension and steering systems

Note: *Before diagnosing suspension or steering faults, be sure that the trouble is not due to incorrect tyre pressures, mixtures of tyre types, or binding brakes. Refer to Chapter 10, unless shown otherwise.*

Vehicle pulls to one side

- ☐ Defective tyre (*"Weekly Checks"*).
- ☐ Excessive wear in suspension or steering components (Chapters 1 and 10).
- ☐ Incorrect front wheel alignment.
- ☐ Accident damage to steering or suspension components (Chapters 1 and 10).

Wheel wobble and vibration

- ☐ Front roadwheels out of balance (vibration felt mainly through the steering wheel).
- ☐ Rear roadwheels out of balance (vibration felt throughout the vehicle).
- ☐ Roadwheels damaged or distorted.
- ☐ Faulty or damaged tyre (*"Weekly Checks"*).
- ☐ Worn steering or suspension joints, bushes or components (Chapters 1 and 10).
- ☐ Worn shock absorbers.
- ☐ Wheel bolts loose.

Excessive pitching and/or rolling around corners, or during braking

- ☐ Defective shock absorbers (Chapters 1 and 10).
- ☐ Broken or weak suspension component (Chapters 1 and 10).
- ☐ Worn or damaged anti-roll bar or mountings.

Wandering or general instability

- ☐ Incorrect front wheel alignment.
- ☐ Worn steering or suspension joints, bushes or components (Chapters 1 and 10).
- ☐ Roadwheels out of balance.
- ☐ Faulty or damaged tyre.
- ☐ Wheel bolts loose.
- ☐ Defective shock absorbers (Chapters 1 and 10).

Excessively- stiff steering

- ☐ Lack of steering gear lubricant.
- ☐ Seized track rod end balljoint or suspension balljoint (Chapters 1 and 10).
- ☐ Incorrect front wheel alignment.
- ☐ Steering rack or column bent or damaged.

Excessive play in steering

- ☐ Worn steering column universal joint(s).
- ☐ Worn steering track rod end balljoints (Chapters 1 and 10).
- ☐ Worn rack-and-pinion steering gear.
- ☐ Worn steering or suspension joints, bushes or components (Chapters 1 and 10).

Low suspension ride height

- ☐ Leaking Hydragas unit or rear interconnecting pipe.

Tyre wear excessive

Tyres worn on inside or outside edges

- ☐ Tyres under-inflated (wear on both edges) (*"Weekly Checks"*).
- ☐ Incorrect camber or castor angles (wear on one edge only).
- ☐ Worn steering or suspension joints, bushes or components (Chapters 1 and 10).
- ☐ Excessively hard cornering.
- ☐ Accident damage.

Tyre treads exhibit feathered edges

- ☐ Incorrect toe setting.

Tyres worn in centre of tread

- ☐ Tyres over-inflated (*"Weekly Checks"*).

Tyres worn on inside and outside edges

- ☐ Tyres under-inflated (*"Weekly Checks"*).
- ☐ Worn shock absorbers (Chapters 1 and 10).

Tyres worn unevenly

- ☐ Tyres/wheels out of balance (*"Weekly Checks"*).
- ☐ Excessive wheel or tyre run-out (*"Weekly Checks"*).
- ☐ Worn shock absorbers (Chapters 1 and 10).
- ☐ Faulty tyre (*"Weekly Checks"*).

Electrical system

Note: *For problems associated with the starting system, refer to the faults listed under "Engine" earlier in this Section.*

Battery will not hold a charge for more than a few days

- ☐ Battery defective internally (Chapter 5).
- ☐ Battery electrolyte level low - where applicable (*"Weekly Checks"*).
- ☐ Battery terminal connections loose or corroded (Chapter 1).
- ☐ Auxiliary drivebelt worn - or incorrectly adjusted, where applicable (Chapter 1).
- ☐ Alternator not charging at correct output (Chapter 5).
- ☐ Alternator or voltage regulator faulty (Chapter 5).
- ☐ Short-circuit causing continual battery drain (Chapters 5 and 12).

Ignition/no-charge warning light remains illuminated with engine running

- ☐ Auxiliary drivebelt broken, worn, or incorrectly adjusted (Chapter 1).
- ☐ Alternator brushes worn, sticking, or dirty (Chapter 5).
- ☐ Alternator brush springs weak or broken (Chapter 5).
- ☐ Internal fault in alternator or voltage regulator (Chapter 5).
- ☐ Broken, disconnected, or loose wiring in charging circuit (Chapter 5).

Ignition/no-charge warning light fails to come on

- ☐ Warning light bulb blown (Chapter 12).
- ☐ Broken, disconnected, or loose wiring in warning light circuit (Chapter 12).
- ☐ Alternator faulty (Chapter 5).

Lights inoperative

- [ ] Bulb blown (Chapter 12).
- [ ] Corrosion of bulb or bulbholder contacts (Chapter 12).
- [ ] Blown fuse (Chapter 12).
- [ ] Faulty relay (Chapter 12).
- [ ] Broken, loose, or disconnected wiring (Chapter 12).
- [ ] Faulty switch (Chapter 12).

Instrument readings inaccurate or erratic

Instrument readings increase with engine speed

- [ ] Faulty voltage regulator (Chapter 12).

Fuel or temperature gauges give no reading

- [ ] Faulty gauge sender unit (Chapters 3 and 4).
- [ ] Wiring open-circuit (Chapter 12).
- [ ] Faulty gauge (Chapter 12).

Fuel or temperature gauges give continuous maximum reading

- [ ] Faulty gauge sender unit (Chapters 3 and 4).
- [ ] Wiring short-circuit (Chapter 12).
- [ ] Faulty gauge (Chapter 12).

Horn inoperative, or unsatisfactory in operation

Horn operates all the time

- [ ] Horn contacts permanently bridged or horn push stuck down (Chapter 12).

Horn fails to operate

- [ ] Blown fuse (Chapter 12).
- [ ] Cable or cable connections loose, broken or disconnected (Chapter 12).
- [ ] Faulty horn (Chapter 12).

Horn emits intermittent or unsatisfactory sound

- [ ] Cable connections loose (Chapter 12).
- [ ] Horn mountings loose (Chapter 12).
- [ ] Faulty horn (Chapter 12).

Windscreen/tailgate wipers inoperative, or unsatisfactory in operation

Wipers fail to operate, or operate very slowly

- [ ] Wiper blades stuck to screen, or linkage seized or binding ("Weekly Checks" and Chapter 12).
- [ ] Blown fuse (Chapter 12).
- [ ] Cable or cable connections loose, broken or disconnected (Chapter 12).
- [ ] Faulty relay (Chapter 12).
- [ ] Faulty wiper motor (Chapter 12).

Wiper blades sweep over too large or too small an area of the glass

- [ ] Wiper arms incorrectly positioned on spindles ("Weekly Checks").
- [ ] Excessive wear of wiper linkage (Chapter 12).
- [ ] Wiper motor or linkage mountings loose or insecure (Chapter 12).

Wiper blades fail to clean the glass effectively

- [ ] Wiper blade rubbers worn or perished ("Weekly Checks").
- [ ] Wiper arm tension springs broken, or arm pivots seized (Chapter 12).
- [ ] Insufficient windscreen washer additive to adequately remove road film ("Weekly Checks").

Windscreen/tailgate washers inoperative, or unsatisfactory in operation

One or more washer jets inoperative

- [ ] Blocked washer jet.
- [ ] Disconnected, kinked or restricted fluid hose (Chapter 12).
- [ ] Insufficient fluid in washer reservoir ("Weekly Checks").

Washer pump fails to operate

- [ ] Broken or disconnected wiring or connections (Chapter 12).
- [ ] Blown fuse (Chapter 12).
- [ ] Faulty washer switch (Chapter 12).
- [ ] Faulty washer pump (Chapter 12).

Washer pump runs for some time before fluid is emitted from jets

- [ ] Faulty one-way valve in fluid supply hose (Chapter 12).

Electric windows inoperative, or unsatisfactory in operation

Window glass will only move in one direction

- [ ] Faulty switch (Chapter 12).

Window glass slow to move

- [ ] Regulator seized or damaged, or in need of lubrication (Chapter 11).
- [ ] Door internal components or trim fouling regulator (Chapter 11).

Electric windows inoperative, or unsatisfactory in operation

Window glass will only move in one direction

- [ ] Faulty switch (Chapter 12).

Window glass slow to move

- [ ] Regulator seized or damaged, or in need of lubrication (Chapter 11).
- [ ] Door internal components or trim fouling regulator (Chapter 11).
- [ ] Faulty motor (Chapter 11).

Window glass fails to move

- [ ] Blown fuse (Chapter 12).
- [ ] Faulty relay (Chapter 12).
- [ ] Broken or disconnected wiring or connections (Chapter 12).
- [ ] Faulty motor (Chapter 11).

Central locking system inoperative, or unsatisfactory in operation

Complete system failure

- [ ] Blown fuse (Chapter 12).
- [ ] Faulty relay (Chapter 12).
- [ ] Broken or disconnected wiring or connections (Chapter 12).

Latch locks but will not unlock, or unlocks but will not lock

- [ ] Faulty switch (Chapter 12).
- [ ] Broken or disconnected latch operating rods or levers (Chapter 11).
- [ ] Faulty relay (Chapter 12).

One solenoid/motor fails to operate

- [ ] Broken or disconnected wiring or connections (Chapter 12).
- [ ] Faulty solenoid/motor (Chapter 11).
- [ ] Broken, binding or disconnected latch operating rods or levers (Chapter 11).
- [ ] Fault in door latch (Chapter 11).

A

ABS (Anti-lock brake system) A system, usually electronically controlled, that senses incipient wheel lockup during braking and relieves hydraulic pressure at wheels that are about to skid.

Air bag An inflatable bag hidden in the steering wheel (driver's side) or the dash or glovebox (passenger side). In a head-on collision, the bags inflate, preventing the driver and front passenger from being thrown forward into the steering wheel or windscreen.

Air cleaner A metal or plastic housing, containing a filter element, which removes dust and dirt from the air being drawn into the engine.

Air filter element The actual filter in an air cleaner system, usually manufactured from pleated paper and requiring renewal at regular intervals.

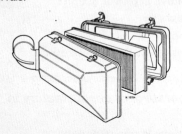

Air filter

Allen key A hexagonal wrench which fits into a recessed hexagonal hole.

Alligator clip A long-nosed spring-loaded metal clip with meshing teeth. Used to make temporary electrical connections.

Alternator A component in the electrical system which converts mechanical energy from a drivebelt into electrical energy to charge the battery and to operate the starting system, ignition system and electrical accessories.

Alternator (exploded view)

Ampere (amp) A unit of measurement for the flow of electric current. One amp is the amount of current produced by one volt acting through a resistance of one ohm.

Anaerobic sealer A substance used to prevent bolts and screws from loosening. Anaerobic means that it does not require oxygen for activation. The Loctite brand is widely used.

Antifreeze A substance (usually ethylene glycol) mixed with water, and added to a vehicle's cooling system, to prevent freezing of the coolant in winter. Antifreeze also contains chemicals to inhibit corrosion and the formation of rust and other deposits that

would tend to clog the radiator and coolant passages and reduce cooling efficiency.

Anti-seize compound A coating that reduces the risk of seizing on fasteners that are subjected to high temperatures, such as exhaust manifold bolts and nuts.

Anti-seize compound

Asbestos A natural fibrous mineral with great heat resistance, commonly used in the composition of brake friction materials. Asbestos is a health hazard and the dust created by brake systems should never be inhaled or ingested.

Axle A shaft on which a wheel revolves, or which revolves with a wheel. Also, a solid beam that connects the two wheels at one end of the vehicle. An axle which also transmits power to the wheels is known as a live axle.

Axle assembly

Axleshaft A single rotating shaft, on either side of the differential, which delivers power from the final drive assembly to the drive wheels. Also called a driveshaft or a halfshaft.

B

Ball bearing An anti-friction bearing consisting of a hardened inner and outer race with hardened steel balls between two races.

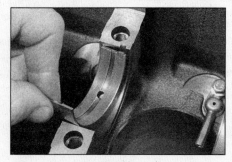

Bearing

Bearing The curved surface on a shaft or in a bore, or the part assembled into either, that permits relative motion between them with minimum wear and friction.

Big-end bearing The bearing in the end of the connecting rod that's attached to the crankshaft.

Bleed nipple A valve on a brake wheel cylinder, caliper or other hydraulic component that is opened to purge the hydraulic system of air. Also called a bleed screw.

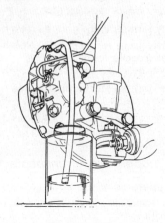

Brake bleeding

Brake bleeding Procedure for removing air from lines of a hydraulic brake system.

Brake disc The component of a disc brake that rotates with the wheels.

Brake drum The component of a drum brake that rotates with the wheels.

Brake linings The friction material which contacts the brake disc or drum to retard the vehicle's speed. The linings are bonded or riveted to the brake pads or shoes.

Brake pads The replaceable friction pads that pinch the brake disc when the brakes are applied. Brake pads consist of a friction material bonded or riveted to a rigid backing plate.

Brake shoe The crescent-shaped carrier to which the brake linings are mounted and which forces the lining against the rotating drum during braking.

Braking systems For more information on braking systems, consult the *Haynes Automotive Brake Manual*.

Breaker bar A long socket wrench handle providing greater leverage.

Bulkhead The insulated partition between the engine and the passenger compartment.

C

Caliper The non-rotating part of a disc-brake assembly that straddles the disc and carries the brake pads. The caliper also contains the hydraulic components that cause the pads to pinch the disc when the brakes are applied. A caliper is also a measuring tool that can be set to measure inside or outside dimensions of an object.

Camshaft A rotating shaft on which a series of cam lobes operate the valve mechanisms. The camshaft may be driven by gears, by sprockets and chain or by sprockets and a belt.

Canister A container in an evaporative emission control system; contains activated charcoal granules to trap vapours from the fuel system.

Canister

Carburettor A device which mixes fuel with air in the proper proportions to provide a desired power output from a spark ignition internal combustion engine.

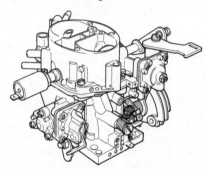

Carburettor

Castellated Resembling the parapets along the top of a castle wall. For example, a castellated balljoint stud nut.

Castellated nut

Castor In wheel alignment, the backward or forward tilt of the steering axis. Castor is positive when the steering axis is inclined rearward at the top.

Catalytic converter A silencer-like device in the exhaust system which converts certain pollutants in the exhaust gases into less harmful substances.

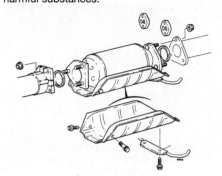

Catalytic converter

Circlip A ring-shaped clip used to prevent endwise movement of cylindrical parts and shafts. An internal circlip is installed in a groove in a housing; an external circlip fits into a groove on the outside of a cylindrical piece such as a shaft.

Clearance The amount of space between two parts. For example, between a piston and a cylinder, between a bearing and a journal, etc.

Coil spring A spiral of elastic steel found in various sizes throughout a vehicle, for example as a springing medium in the suspension and in the valve train.

Compression Reduction in volume, and increase in pressure and temperature, of a gas, caused by squeezing it into a smaller space.

Compression ratio The relationship between cylinder volume when the piston is at top dead centre and cylinder volume when the piston is at bottom dead centre.

Constant velocity (CV) joint A type of universal joint that cancels out vibrations caused by driving power being transmitted through an angle.

Core plug A disc or cup-shaped metal device inserted in a hole in a casting through which core was removed when the casting was formed. Also known as a freeze plug or expansion plug.

Crankcase The lower part of the engine block in which the crankshaft rotates.

Crankshaft The main rotating member, or shaft, running the length of the crankcase, with offset "throws" to which the connecting rods are attached.

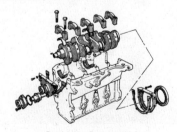

Crankshaft assembly

Crocodile clip See Alligator clip

D

Diagnostic code Code numbers obtained by accessing the diagnostic mode of an engine management computer. This code can be used to determine the area in the system where a malfunction may be located.

Disc brake A brake design incorporating a rotating disc onto which brake pads are squeezed. The resulting friction converts the energy of a moving vehicle into heat.

Double-overhead cam (DOHC) An engine that uses two overhead camshafts, usually one for the intake valves and one for the exhaust valves.

Drivebelt(s) The belt(s) used to drive accessories such as the alternator, water pump, power steering pump, air conditioning compressor, etc. off the crankshaft pulley.

Accessory drivebelts

Driveshaft Any shaft used to transmit motion. Commonly used when referring to the axleshafts on a front wheel drive vehicle.

Driveshaft

Drum brake A type of brake using a drum-shaped metal cylinder attached to the inner surface of the wheel. When the brake pedal is pressed, curved brake shoes with friction linings press against the inside of the drum to slow or stop the vehicle.

Drum brake assembly

E

EGR valve A valve used to introduce exhaust gases into the intake air stream.

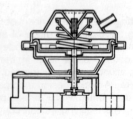

EGR valve

Electronic control unit (ECU) A computer which controls (for instance) ignition and fuel injection systems, or an anti-lock braking system. For more information refer to the *Haynes Automotive Electrical and Electronic Systems Manual*.

Electronic Fuel Injection (EFI) A computer controlled fuel system that distributes fuel through an injector located in each intake port of the engine.

Emergency brake A braking system, independent of the main hydraulic system, that can be used to slow or stop the vehicle if the primary brakes fail, or to hold the vehicle stationary even though the brake pedal isn't depressed. It usually consists of a hand lever that actuates either front or rear brakes mechanically through a series of cables and linkages. Also known as a handbrake or parking brake.

Endfloat The amount of lengthwise movement between two parts. As applied to a crankshaft, the distance that the crankshaft can move forward and back in the cylinder block.

Engine management system (EMS) A computer controlled system which manages the fuel injection and the ignition systems in an integrated fashion.

Exhaust manifold A part with several passages through which exhaust gases leave the engine combustion chambers and enter the exhaust pipe.

Exhaust manifold

F

Fan clutch A viscous (fluid) drive coupling device which permits variable engine fan speeds in relation to engine speeds.

Feeler blade A thin strip or blade of hardened steel, ground to an exact thickness, used to check or measure clearances between parts.

Feeler blade

Firing order The order in which the engine cylinders fire, or deliver their power strokes, beginning with the number one cylinder.

Flywheel A heavy spinning wheel in which energy is absorbed and stored by means of momentum. On cars, the flywheel is attached to the crankshaft to smooth out firing impulses.

Free play The amount of travel before any action takes place. The "looseness" in a linkage, or an assembly of parts, between the initial application of force and actual movement. For example, the distance the brake pedal moves before the pistons in the master cylinder are actuated.

Fuse An electrical device which protects a circuit against accidental overload. The typical fuse contains a soft piece of metal which is calibrated to melt at a predetermined current flow (expressed as amps) and break the circuit.

Fusible link A circuit protection device consisting of a conductor surrounded by heat-resistant insulation. The conductor is smaller than the wire it protects, so it acts as the weakest link in the circuit. Unlike a blown fuse, a failed fusible link must frequently be cut from the wire for replacement.

G

Gap The distance the spark must travel in jumping from the centre electrode to the side

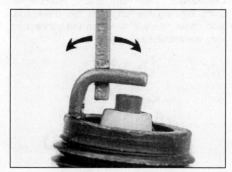

Adjusting spark plug gap

electrode in a spark plug. Also refers to the spacing between the points in a contact breaker assembly in a conventional points-type ignition, or to the distance between the reluctor or rotor and the pickup coil in an electronic ignition.

Gasket Any thin, soft material - usually cork, cardboard, asbestos or soft metal - installed between two metal surfaces to ensure a good seal. For instance, the cylinder head gasket seals the joint between the block and the cylinder head.

Gasket

Gauge An instrument panel display used to monitor engine conditions. A gauge with a movable pointer on a dial or a fixed scale is an analogue gauge. A gauge with a numerical readout is called a digital gauge.

H

Halfshaft A rotating shaft that transmits power from the final drive unit to a drive wheel, usually when referring to a live rear axle.

Harmonic balancer A device designed to reduce torsion or twisting vibration in the crankshaft. May be incorporated in the crankshaft pulley. Also known as a vibration damper.

Hone An abrasive tool for correcting small irregularities or differences in diameter in an engine cylinder, brake cylinder, etc.

Hydraulic tappet A tappet that utilises hydraulic pressure from the engine's lubrication system to maintain zero clearance (constant contact with both camshaft and valve stem). Automatically adjusts to variation in valve stem length. Hydraulic tappets also reduce valve noise.

I

Ignition timing The moment at which the spark plug fires, usually expressed in the number of crankshaft degrees before the piston reaches the top of its stroke.

Inlet manifold A tube or housing with passages through which flows the air-fuel mixture (carburettor vehicles and vehicles with throttle body injection) or air only (port fuel-injected vehicles) to the port openings in the cylinder head.

J

Jump start Starting the engine of a vehicle with a discharged or weak battery by attaching jump leads from the weak battery to a charged or helper battery.

L

Load Sensing Proportioning Valve (LSPV) A brake hydraulic system control valve that works like a proportioning valve, but also takes into consideration the amount of weight carried by the rear axle.

Locknut A nut used to lock an adjustment nut, or other threaded component, in place. For example, a locknut is employed to keep the adjusting nut on the rocker arm in position.

Lockwasher A form of washer designed to prevent an attaching nut from working loose.

M

MacPherson strut A type of front suspension system devised by Earle MacPherson at Ford of England. In its original form, a simple lateral link with the anti-roll bar creates the lower control arm. A long strut - an integral coil spring and shock absorber - is mounted between the body and the steering knuckle. Many modern so-called MacPherson strut systems use a conventional lower A-arm and don't rely on the anti-roll bar for location.

Multimeter An electrical test instrument with the capability to measure voltage, current and resistance.

N

NOx Oxides of Nitrogen. A common toxic pollutant emitted by petrol and diesel engines at higher temperatures.

O

Ohm The unit of electrical resistance. One volt applied to a resistance of one ohm will produce a current of one amp.

Ohmmeter An instrument for measuring electrical resistance.

O-ring A type of sealing ring made of a special rubber-like material; in use, the O-ring is compressed into a groove to provide the sealing action.

O-ring

Overhead cam (ohc) engine An engine with the camshaft(s) located on top of the cylinder head(s).

Overhead valve (ohv) engine An engine with the valves located in the cylinder head, but with the camshaft located in the engine block.

Oxygen sensor A device installed in the engine exhaust manifold, which senses the oxygen content in the exhaust and converts this information into an electric current. Also called a Lambda sensor.

P

Phillips screw A type of screw head having a cross instead of a slot for a corresponding type of screwdriver.

Plastigage A thin strip of plastic thread, available in different sizes, used for measuring clearances. For example, a strip of Plastigage is laid across a bearing journal. The parts are assembled and dismantled; the width of the crushed strip indicates the clearance between journal and bearing.

Plastigage

Propeller shaft The long hollow tube with universal joints at both ends that carries power from the transmission to the differential on front-engined rear wheel drive vehicles.

Proportioning valve A hydraulic control valve which limits the amount of pressure to the rear brakes during panic stops to prevent wheel lock-up.

R

Rack-and-pinion steering A steering system with a pinion gear on the end of the steering shaft that mates with a rack (think of a geared wheel opened up and laid flat). When the steering wheel is turned, the pinion turns, moving the rack to the left or right. This movement is transmitted through the track rods to the steering arms at the wheels.

Radiator A liquid-to-air heat transfer device designed to reduce the temperature of the coolant in an internal combustion engine cooling system.

Refrigerant Any substance used as a heat transfer agent in an air-conditioning system. R-12 has been the principle refrigerant for many years; recently, however, manufacturers have begun using R-134a, a non-CFC substance that is considered less harmful to

the ozone in the upper atmosphere.

Rocker arm A lever arm that rocks on a shaft or pivots on a stud. In an overhead valve engine, the rocker arm converts the upward movement of the pushrod into a downward movement to open a valve.

Rotor In a distributor, the rotating device inside the cap that connects the centre electrode and the outer terminals as it turns, distributing the high voltage from the coil secondary winding to the proper spark plug. Also, that part of an alternator which rotates inside the stator. Also, the rotating assembly of a turbocharger, including the compressor wheel, shaft and turbine wheel.

Runout The amount of wobble (in-and-out movement) of a gear or wheel as it's rotated. The amount a shaft rotates "out-of-true." The out-of-round condition of a rotating part.

S

Sealant A liquid or paste used to prevent leakage at a joint. Sometimes used in conjunction with a gasket.

Sealed beam lamp An older headlight design which integrates the reflector, lens and filaments into a hermetically-sealed one-piece unit. When a filament burns out or the lens cracks, the entire unit is simply replaced.

Serpentine drivebelt A single, long, wide accessory drivebelt that's used on some newer vehicles to drive all the accessories, instead of a series of smaller, shorter belts. Serpentine drivebelts are usually tensioned by an automatic tensioner.

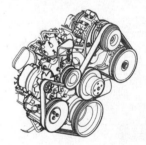
Serpentine drivebelt

Shim Thin spacer, commonly used to adjust the clearance or relative positions between two parts. For example, shims inserted into or under bucket tappets control valve clearances. Clearance is adjusted by changing the thickness of the shim.

Slide hammer A special puller that screws into or hooks onto a component such as a shaft or bearing; a heavy sliding handle on the shaft bottoms against the end of the shaft to knock the component free.

Sprocket A tooth or projection on the periphery of a wheel, shaped to engage with a chain or drivebelt. Commonly used to refer to the sprocket wheel itself.

Starter inhibitor switch On vehicles with an

automatic transmission, a switch that prevents starting if the vehicle is not in Neutral or Park.

Strut See MacPherson strut.

T

Tappet A cylindrical component which transmits motion from the cam to the valve stem, either directly or via a pushrod and rocker arm. Also called a cam follower.

Thermostat A heat-controlled valve that regulates the flow of coolant between the cylinder block and the radiator, so maintaining optimum engine operating temperature. A thermostat is also used in some air cleaners in which the temperature is regulated.

Thrust bearing The bearing in the clutch assembly that is moved in to the release levers by clutch pedal action to disengage the clutch. Also referred to as a release bearing.

Timing belt A toothed belt which drives the camshaft. Serious engine damage may result if it breaks in service.

Timing chain A chain which drives the camshaft.

Toe-in The amount the front wheels are closer together at the front than at the rear. On rear wheel drive vehicles, a slight amount of toe-in is usually specified to keep the front wheels running parallel on the road by offsetting other forces that tend to spread the wheels apart.

Toe-out The amount the front wheels are closer together at the rear than at the front. On front wheel drive vehicles, a slight amount of toe-out is usually specified.

Tools For full information on choosing and using tools, refer to the *Haynes Automotive Tools Manual*.

Tracer A stripe of a second colour applied to a wire insulator to distinguish that wire from another one with the same colour insulator.

Tune-up A process of accurate and careful adjustments and parts replacement to obtain the best possible engine performance.

Turbocharger A centrifugal device, driven by exhaust gases, that pressurises the intake air. Normally used to increase the power output from a given engine displacement, but can also be used primarily to reduce exhaust emissions (as on VW's "Umwelt" Diesel engine).

U

Universal joint or U-joint A double-pivoted connection for transmitting power from a driving to a driven shaft through an angle. A U-joint consists of two Y-shaped yokes and a cross-shaped member called the spider.

V

Valve A device through which the flow of liquid, gas, vacuum, or loose material in bulk may be started, stopped, or regulated by a movable part that opens, shuts, or partially obstructs one or more ports or passageways. A valve is also the movable part of such a device.

Valve clearance The clearance between the valve tip (the end of the valve stem) and the rocker arm or tappet. The valve clearance is measured when the valve is closed.

Vernier caliper A precision measuring instrument that measures inside and outside dimensions. Not quite as accurate as a micrometer, but more convenient.

Viscosity The thickness of a liquid or its resistance to flow.

Volt A unit for expressing electrical "pressure" in a circuit. One volt that will produce a current of one ampere through a resistance of one ohm.

W

Welding Various processes used to join metal items by heating the areas to be joined to a molten state and fusing them together. For more information refer to the *Haynes Automotive Welding Manual*.

Wiring diagram A drawing portraying the components and wires in a vehicle's electrical system, using standardised symbols. For more information refer to the *Haynes Automotive Electrical and Electronic Systems Manual*.

Note: *References throughout this index are in the form - "Chapter number" • "page number"*

Haynes Manuals – The Complete List

Title	Book No.
ALFA ROMEO	
Alfa Romeo Alfasud/Sprint (74 - 88) up to F	0292
Alfa Romeo Alfetta (73 - 87) up to E	0531
AUDI	
Audi 80 (72 - Feb 79) up to T	0207
Audi 80, 90 (79 - Oct 86) up to D & Coupe (81 - Nov 88) up to F	0605
Audi 80, 90 (Oct 86 - 90) D to H & Coupe (Nov 88 - 90) F to H	1491
Audi 100 (Oct 82 - 90) up to H & 200 (Feb 84 - Oct 89) A to G	0907
Audi 100 & A6 Petrol & Diesel (May 91 - May 97) H to P	3504
Audi A4 (95 - Feb 00) M to V	3575
AUSTIN	
Austin/MG/Rover Maestro 1.3 & 1.6 (83 - 95) up to M	0922
Austin/MG Metro (80 - May 90) up to G	0718
Austin/Rover Montego 1.3 & 1.6 (84 - 94) A to L	1066
Austin/MG/Rover Montego 2.0 (84 - 95) A to M	1067
Mini (59 - 69) up to H	0527
Mini (69 - Oct 96) up to P	0646
Austin/Rover 2.0 litre Diesel Engine (86 - 93) C to L	1857
BEDFORD	
Bedford CF (69 - 87) up to E	0163
Bedford/Vauxhall Rascal (86 - Oct 94) C to M	3015
BMW	
BMW 316, 320 & 320i (4-cyl) (75 - Feb 83) up to Y	0276
BMW 320, 320i, 323i & 325i (6-cyl) (Oct 77 - Sept 87) up to E	0815
BMW 3-Series (Apr 91 - 96) H to N	3210
BMW 3- & 5-Series (sohc) (81 - 91) up to J	1948
BMW 520i & 525e (Oct 81 - June 88) up to E	1560
BMW 525, 528 & 528i (73 - Sept 81) up to X	0632
CITROEN	
Citroën 2CV, Ami & Dyane (67 - 90) up to H	0196
Citroën AX Petrol & Diesel (87 - 97) D to P	3014
Citroën BX (83 - 94) A to L	0908
Citroën C15 Van Petrol & Diesel (89 - Oct 98) F to S	3509
Citroën CX (75 - 88) up to F	0528
Citroën Saxo Petrol & Diesel (96 - 01) N to X	3506
Citroën Visa (79 - 88) up to F	0620
Citroën Xantia Petrol & Diesel (93 - 98) K to S	3082
Citroën XM Petrol & Diesel (89 - 98) G to R	3451
Citroën Xsara (97 - 00) R to W	3751
Citroën ZX Diesel (91 - 98) J to S	1922
Citroën ZX Petrol (91 - 98) H to S	1881
Citroën 1.7 & 1.9 litre Diesel Engine (84 - 96) A to N	1379
FIAT	
Fiat 500 (57 - 73) up to M	0090
Fiat Bravo & Brava (95 - 00) N to W	3572
Fiat Cinquecento (93 - 98) K to R	3501
Fiat Panda (81 - 95) up to M	0793
Fiat Punto Petrol & Diesel (94 - Oct 99) L to V	3251
Fiat Regata (84 - 88) A to F	1167
Fiat Tipo (88 - 91) E to J	1625
Fiat Uno (83 - 95) up to M	0923
Fiat X1/9 (74 - 89) up to G	0273

Title	Book No.
FORD	
Ford Capri II (& III) 1.6 & 2.0 (74 - 87) up to E	0283
Ford Capri II (& III) 2.8 & 3.0 (74 - 87) up to E	1309
Ford Escort (Sept 80 - Sept 90) up to H	0686
Ford Escort & Orion (Sept 90 - 97) H to P	1737
Ford Escort Mk II Mexico, RS 1600 & RS 2000 (75 - 80) up to W	0735
Ford Fiesta (76 - Aug 83) up to Y	0334
Ford Fiesta (Aug 83 - Feb 89) A to F	1030
Ford Fiesta (Feb 89 - Oct 95) F to N	1595
Ford Fiesta Petrol & Diesel (Oct 95 - 97) N to R	3397
Ford Granada (Sept 77 - Feb 85) up to B	0481
Ford Granada & Scorpio (Mar 85 - 94) B to M	1245
Ford Ka (96 - 99) P to T	3570
Ford Mondeo Petrol (93 - 99) K to T	1923
Ford Mondeo Diesel (93 - 96) L to N	3465
Ford Orion (83 - Sept 90) up to H	1009
Ford Sierra 4 cyl. (82 - 93) up to K	0903
Ford Sierra V6 (82 - 91) up to J	0904
Ford Transit Petrol (Mk 2) (78 - Jan 86) up to C	0719
Ford Transit Petrol (Mk 3) (Feb 86 - 89) C to G	1468
Ford Transit Diesel (Feb 86 - 99) C to T	3019
Ford 1.6 & 1.8 litre Diesel Engine (84 - 96) A to N	1172
Ford 2.1, 2.3 & 2.5 litre Diesel Engine (77 - 90) up to H	1606
FREIGHT ROVER	
Freight Rover Sherpa (74 - 87) up to E	0463
HILLMAN	
Hillman Avenger (70 - 82) up to Y	0037
HONDA	
Honda Accord (76 - Feb 84) up to A	0351
Honda Civic (Feb 84 - Oct 87) A to E	1226
Honda Civic (Nov 91 - 96) J to N	3199
HYUNDAI	
Hyundai Pony (85 - 94) C to M	3398
JAGUAR	
Jaguar E Type (61 - 72) up to L	0140
Jaguar MkI & II, 240 & 340 (55 - 69) up to H	0098
Jaguar XJ6, XJ & Sovereign; Daimler Sovereign (68 - Oct 86) up to D	0242
Jaguar XJ6 & Sovereign (Oct 86 - Sept 94) D to M	3261
Jaguar XJ12, XJS & Sovereign; Daimler Double Six (72 - 88) up to F	0478
JEEP	
Jeep Cherokee Petrol (93 - 96) K to N	1943
LADA	
Lada 1200, 1300, 1500 & 1600 (74 - 91) up to J	0413
Lada Samara (87 - 91) D to J	1610
LAND ROVER	
Land Rover 90, 110 & Defender Diesel (83 - 95) up to N	3017
Land Rover Discovery Petrol & Diesel (89 - 98) G to S	3016
Land Rover Series IIA & III Diesel (58 - 85) up to C	0529
Land Rover Series II, IIA & III Petrol (58 - 85) up to C	0314
MAZDA	
Mazda 323 (Mar 81 - Oct 89) up to G	1608

Title	Book No.
Mazda 323 (Oct 89 - 98) G to R	3455
Mazda 626 (May 83 - Sept 87) up to E	0929
Mazda B-1600, B-1800 & B-2000 Pick-up (72 - 88) up to F	0267
MERCEDES BENZ	
Mercedes-Benz 190, 190E & 190D Petrol & Diesel (83 - 93) A to L	3450
Mercedes-Benz 200, 240, 300 Diesel (Oct 76 - 85) up to C	1114
Mercedes-Benz 250 & 280 (68 - 72) up to L	0346
Mercedes-Benz 250 & 280 (123 Series) (Oct 76 - 84) up to B	0677
Mercedes-Benz 124 Series (85 - Aug 93) C to K	3253
Mercedes-Benz C-Class Petrol & Diesel (93 - Aug 00) L to W	3511
MG	
MGA (55 - 62)*	0475
MGB (62 - 80) up to W	0111
MG Midget & AH Sprite (58 - 80) up to W	0265
MITSUBISHI	
Mitsubishi Shogun & L200 Pick-Ups (83 - 94) up to M	1944
MORRIS	
Morris Ital 1.3 (80 - 84) up to B	0705
Morris Minor 1000 (56 - 71) up to K	0024
NISSAN	
Nissan Bluebird (May 84 - Mar 86) A to C	1223
Nissan Bluebird (Mar 86 - 90) C to H	1473
Nissan Cherry (Sept 82 - 86) up to D	1031
Nissan Micra (83 - Jan 93) up to K	0931
Nissan Micra (93 - 99) K to T	3254
Nissan Primera (90 - Aug 99) H to T	1851
Nissan Stanza (82 - 86) up to D	0824
Nissan Sunny (May 82 - Oct 86) up to D	0895
Nissan Sunny (Oct 86 - Mar 91) D to H	1378
Nissan Sunny (Apr 91 - 95) H to N	3219
OPEL	
Opel Ascona & Manta (B Series) (Sept 75 - 88) up to F	0316
Opel Ascona (81 - 88) *(Not available in UK see Vauxhall Cavalier 0812)*	3215
Opel Astra (Oct 91 - Feb 98) *(Not available in UK see Vauxhall Astra 1832)*	3156
Opel Calibra (90 - 98) *(See Vauxhall/Opel Calibra Book No. 3502)*	
Opel Corsa (83 - Mar 93) *(Not available in UK see Vauxhall Nova 0909)*	3160
Opel Corsa (Mar 93 - 97) *(Not available in UK see Vauxhall Corsa 1985)*	3159
Opel Frontera Petrol & Diesel (91 - 98) *(See Vauxhall/Opel Frontera Book No. 3454)*	
Opel Kadett (Nov 79 - Oct 84) up to B	0634
Opel Kadett (Oct 84 - Oct 91) *(Not available in UK see Vauxhall Astra & Belmont 1136)*	3196
Opel Omega & Senator (86 - 94) *(Not available in UK see Vauxhall Carlton & Senator 1469)*	3157
Opel Omega (94 - 99) *(See Vauxhall/Opel Omega Book No. 3510)*	
Opel Rekord (Feb 78 - Oct 86) up to D	0543
Opel Vectra (Oct 88 - Oct 95) *(Not available in UK see Vauxhall Cavalier 1570)*	3158
Opel Vectra Petrol & Diesel (95 - 98) *(Not available in UK see Vauxhall Vectra 3396)*	3523

* Classic reprint

Title	Book No.
PEUGEOT	
Peugeot 106 Petrol & Diesel (91 - 01) J to X	1882
Peugeot 205 Petrol (83 - 97) A to P	0932
Peugeot 206 Petrol and Diesel (98 - 01) S to X	3757
Peugeot 305 (78 - 89) up to G	0538
Peugeot 306 Petrol & Diesel (93 - 99) K to T	3073
Peugeot 309 (86 - 93) C to K	1266
Peugeot 405 Petrol (88 - 97) E to P	1559
Peugeot 405 Diesel (88 - 96) E to N	3198
Peugeot 406 Petrol & Diesel (96 - 97) N to R	3394
Peugeot 505 (79 - 89) up to G	0762
Peugeot 1.7/1.8 & 1.9 litre Diesel Engine (82 - 96) up to N	0950
Peugeot 2.0, 2.1, 2.3 & 2.5 litre Diesel Engines (74 - 90) up to H	1607
PORSCHE	
Porsche 911 (65 - 85) up to C	0264
Porsche 924 & 924 Turbo (76 - 85) up to C	0397
PROTON	
Proton (89 - 97) F to P	3255
RANGE ROVER	
Range Rover V8 (70 - Oct 92) up to K	0606
RELIANT	
Reliant Robin & Kitten (73 - 83) up to A	0436
RENAULT	
Renault 5 (Feb 85 - 96) B to N	1219
Renault 9 & 11 (82 - 89) up to F	0822
Renault 18 (79 - 86) up to D	0598
Renault 19 Petrol (89 - 94) F to M	1646
Renault 19 Diesel (89 - 95) F to N	1946
Renault 21 (86 - 94) C to M	1397
Renault 25 (84 - 92) B to K	1228
Renault Clio Petrol (91 - May 98) H to R	1853
Renault Clio Diesel (91 - June 96) H to N	3031
Renault Espace Petrol & Diesel (85 - 96) C to N	3197
Renault Fuego (80 - 86) up to C	0764
Renault Laguna Petrol & Diesel (94 - 00) L to W	3252
Renault Mégane & Scénic Petrol & Diesel (96 - 98) N to R	3395
ROVER	
Rover 213 & 216 (84 - 89) A to G	1116
Rover 214 & 414 (89 - 96) G to N	1689
Rover 216 & 416 (89 - 96) G to N	1830
Rover 211, 214, 216, 218 & 220 Petrol & Diesel (Dec 95 - 98) N to R	3399
Rover 414, 416 & 420 Petrol & Diesel (May 95 - 98) M to R	3453
Rover 618, 620 & 623 (93 - 97) K to P	3257
Rover 820, 825 & 827 (86 - 95) D to N	1380
Rover 3500 (76 - 87) up to E	0365
Rover Metro, 111 & 114 (May 90 - 98) G to S	1711
SAAB	
Saab 90, 99 & 900 (79 - Oct 93) up to L	0765
Saab 900 (Oct 93 - 98) L to R	3512
Saab 9000 (4-cyl) (85 - 95) C to N	1686
SEAT	
Seat Ibiza & Cordoba Petrol & Diesel (Oct 93 - Oct 99) L to V	3571
Seat Ibiza & Malaga (85 - 92) B to K	1609

Title	Book No.
SKODA	
Skoda Estelle (77 - 89) up to G	0604
Skoda Favorit (89 - 96) F to N	1801
Skoda Felicia Petrol & Diesel (95 - 99) M to T	3505
SUBARU	
Subaru 1600 & 1800 (Nov 79 - 90) up to H	0995
SUZUKI	
Suzuki SJ Series, Samurai & Vitara (4-cyl) (82 - 97) up to P	1942
Suzuki Supercarry (86 - Oct 94) C to M	3015
TALBOT	
Talbot Alpine, Solara, Minx & Rapier (75 - 86) up to D	0337
Talbot Horizon (78 - 86) up to D	0473
Talbot Samba (82 - 86) up to D	0823
TOYOTA	
Toyota Carina E (May 92 - 97) J to P	3256
Toyota Corolla (Sept 83 - Sept 87) A to E	1024
Toyota Corolla (80 - 85) up to C	0683
Toyota Corolla (Sept 87 - Aug 92) E to K	1683
Toyota Corolla (Aug 92 - 97) K to P	3259
Toyota Hi-Ace & Hi-Lux (69 - Oct 83) up to A	0304
TRIUMPH	
Triumph Herald (59 - 71) up to K*	0010
Triumph TR2, TR3, TR3A, TR4 & TR4A (52 - 67)*	0028
Triumph TR5 & 6 (67 - 75)*	0031
Triumph Spitfire (62 - 81) up to X	0113
Triumph Stag (70 - 78) up to T	0441
VAUXHALL	
Vauxhall Astra (80 - Oct 84) up to B	0635
Vauxhall Astra & Belmont (Oct 84 - Oct 91) B to J	1136
Vauxhall Astra (Oct 91 - Feb 98) J to R	1832
Vauxhall/Opel Calibra (90 - 98) G to S	3502
Vauxhall Carlton (Oct 78 - Oct 86) up to D	0480
Vauxhall Carlton & Senator (Nov 86 - 94) D to L	1469
Vauxhall Cavalier 1600, 1900 & 2000 (75 - July 81) up to W	0315
Vauxhall Cavalier (81 - Oct 88) up to F	0812
Vauxhall Cavalier (Oct 88 - 95) F to N	1570
Vauxhall Chevette (75 - 84) up to B	0285
Vauxhall Corsa (Mar 93 - 97) K to R	1985
Vauxhall/Opel Frontera Petrol & Diesel (91 - Sept 98) J to S	3454
Vauxhall Nova (83 - 93) up to K	0909
Vauxhall/Opel Omega (94 - 99) L to T	3510
Vauxhall Vectra Petrol & Diesel (95 - 98) N to R	3396
Vauxhall/Opel 1.5, 1.6 & 1.7 litre Diesel Engine (82 - 96) up to N	1222
VOLKSWAGEN	
Volkswagen Beetle 1200 (54 - 77) up to S	0036
Volkswagen Beetle 1300 & 1500 (65 - 75) up to P	0039
Volkswagen Beetle 1302 & 1302S (70 - 72) up to L	0110
Volkswagen Beetle 1303, 1303S & GT (72 - 75) up to P	0159

Title	Book No.
Volkswagen Golf & Bora Petrol & Diesel (April 98 - 00) R to X	3727
Volkswagen Golf & Jetta Mk 1 1.1 & 1.3 (74 - 84) up to A	0716
Volkswagen Golf, Jetta & Scirocco Mk 1 1.5, 1.6 & 1.8 (74 - 84) up to A	0726
Volkswagen Golf & Jetta Mk 1 Diesel (78 - 84) up to A	0451
Volkswagen Golf & Jetta Mk 2 (Mar 84 - Feb 92) A to J	1081
Volkswagen Golf & Vento Petrol & Diesel (Feb 92 - 96) J to N	3097
Volkswagen LT vans & light trucks (76 - 87) up to E	0637
Volkswagen Passat & Santana (Sept 81 - May 88) up to E	0814
Volkswagen Passat Petrol & Diesel (May 88 - 96) E to P	3498
Volkswagen Polo & Derby (76 - Jan 82) up to X	0335
Volkswagen Polo (82 - Oct 90) up to H	0813
Volkswagen Polo (Nov 90 - Aug 94) H to L	3245
Volkswagen Polo Hatchback Petrol & Diesel (94 - 99) M to S	3500
Volkswagen Scirocco (82 - 90) up to H	1224
Volkswagen Transporter 1600 (68 - 79) up to V	0082
Volkswagen Transporter 1700, 1800 & 2000 (72 - 79) up to V	0226
Volkswagen Transporter (air-cooled) (79 - 82) up to Y	0638
Volkswagen Transporter (water-cooled) (82 - 90) up to H	3452
VOLVO	
Volvo 142, 144 & 145 (66 - 74) up to N	0129
Volvo 240 Series (74 - 93) up to K	0270
Volvo 340, 343, 345 & 360 (76 - 91) up to J	0715
Volvo 440, 460 & 480 (87 - 97) D to P	1691
Volvo 740 & 760 (82 - 91) up to J	1258
Volvo 850 (92 - 96) J to P	3260
Volvo 940 (90 - 96) H to N	3249
Volvo S40 & V40 (96 - 99) N to V	3569
Volvo S70, V70 & C70 (96 - 99) P to V	3573
AUTOMOTIVE TECHBOOKS	
Automotive Air Conditioning Systems	3740
Automotive Brake Manual	3050
Automotive Carburettor Manual	3288
Automotive Diagnostic Fault Codes Manual	3472
Automotive Diesel Engine Service Guide	3286
Automotive Electrical and Electronic Systems Manual	3049
Automotive Engine Management and Fuel Injection Systems Manual	3344
Automotive Gearbox Overhaul Manual	3473
Automotive Service Summaries Manual	3475
Automotive Timing Belts Manual – Austin/Rover	3549
Automotive Timing Belts Manual – Ford	3474
Automotive Timing Belts Manual – Peugeot/Citroën	3568
Automotive Timing Belts Manual – Vauxhall/Opel	3577
Automotive Welding Manual	3053
In-Car Entertainment Manual (3rd Edition)	3363

* Classic reprint

CL11.3/01

Preserving Our Motoring Heritage

< The Model J Duesenberg Derham Tourster. Only eight of these magnificent cars were ever built – this is the only example to be found outside the United States of America

Almost every car you've ever loved, loathed or desired is gathered under one roof at the Haynes Motor Museum. Over 300 immaculately presented cars and motorbikes represent every aspect of our motoring heritage, from elegant reminders of bygone days, such as the superb Model J Duesenberg to curiosities like the bug-eyed BMW Isetta. There are also many old friends and flames. Perhaps you remember the 1959 Ford Popular that you did your courting in? The magnificent 'Red Collection' is a spectacle of classic sports cars including AC, Alfa Romeo, Austin Healey, Ferrari, Lamborghini, Maserati, MG, Riley, Porsche and Triumph.

A Perfect Day Out

Each and every vehicle at the Haynes Motor Museum has played its part in the history and culture of Motoring. Today, they make a wonderful spectacle and a great day out for all the family. Bring the kids, bring Mum and Dad, but above all bring your camera to capture those golden memories for ever. You will also find an impressive array of motoring memorabilia, a comfortable 70 seat video cinema and one of the most extensive transport book shops in Britain. The Pit Stop Cafe serves everything from a cup of tea to wholesome, home-made meals or, if you prefer, you can enjoy the large picnic area nestled in the beautiful rural surroundings of Somerset.

> John Haynes O.B.E., Founder and Chairman of the museum at the wheel of a Haynes Light 12.

< Graham Hill's Lola Cosworth Formula 1 car next to a 1934 Riley Sports.

The Museum is situated on the A359 Yeovil to Frome road at Sparkford, just off the A303 in Somerset. It is about 40 miles south of Bristol, and 25 minutes drive from the M5 intersection at Taunton.

Open 9.30am - 5.30pm (10.00am - 4.00pm Winter) 7 days a week, *except Christmas Day, Boxing Day and New Years Day*
Special rates available for schools, coach parties and outings Charitable Trust No. 292048